Ancient Mediterranean Civilizations

A Captivating Guide to Carthage, the Minoans, Phoenicians, Mycenaeans, and Etruscans

Free Bonus from Captivating History (Available for a Limited time)

Hi History Lovers!

Now you have a chance to join our exclusive history list so you can get your first history ebook for free as well as discounts and a potential to get more history books for free! Simply visit the link below to join.

Captivatinghistory.com/ebook

Also, make sure to follow us on Facebook, Twitter and Youtube by searching for

Table of Contents

Part 1: Carthage

A Captivating Guide to the Carthaginian Empire and Its Conflicts with the Ancient Greek City-States and the Roman Republic in the Sicilian Wars and Punic Wars

Introduction

Very few of the ancient empires and nations were able to challenge the Romans, who were famous for their military might and later on became a vast empire. Even fewer were able to make them shiver just by mentioning their name. In fact, only one enemy of Rome managed to engrave such fear into their bones. That was Carthage, sometimes called the Carthaginian Empire. It was a formidable state that stretched across northern Africa, from Algeria and Tunisia to the shores of Morocco and southern Spain. In its heyday, it was a formidable force that controlled much of the western Mediterranean. As such, it was the first real obstacle to the rise of the Roman state, the only one which almost brought it down before it even became an ancient superpower. Hannibal Barca, the most famous Carthaginian leader, was at one point in front of the gates of Rome. Because of that, the Carthaginian Empire, usually personified by Hannibal himself, is typically seen and described as the great foe of Rome, one of the rare daunting opponents the Romans faced.

However, despite the truth behind such sentiments, Carthage was much more than just an enemy of Rome. It was a thriving state, with its own culture and way of life. Its people were more than just soldiers. Among them were merchants, artists, artisans, priests, farmers, and much more. They built temples and palaces, houses and markets, and they erected entire cities across their not-so-small empire. In fact, behind the visage of Carthage as the adversary of the Romans lays an entire civilization worthy of our attention. Uncovering it from the shrouded veils of the past will not only help us understand Carthage itself, as well as its conflicts with Rome, but it will also give us a better comprehension of the ancient world as a whole. This guide will try to do precisely that, paint both sides of the coin that is the Carthaginian Empire, hopefully sparking your interest to find out more about both Carthage and history in general.

Chapter 1 – A New City in the West

The story of Carthage, one of the ancient jewels of the west, begins on the other side of the Mediterranean Sea in the 2nd millennium BCE. On its eastern shores, in the region known as the Levant, which is roughly the equivalent of modern-day Syria, Lebanon, Jordan, Israel, and Palestine, lived a large group of people that we call today the Canaanites. That is a modern reading of *Kn'nm*, which is what they called themselves. However, these people, despite speaking a quite similar language, were not united into a single state. Instead, they mostly lived in small city-states, like the ancient Greeks. Among them was a smaller distinct tribe, a nation of sorts, which was called Phoenicia by the ancient Greeks. It is among them that the tale of the Carthaginians has its roots.

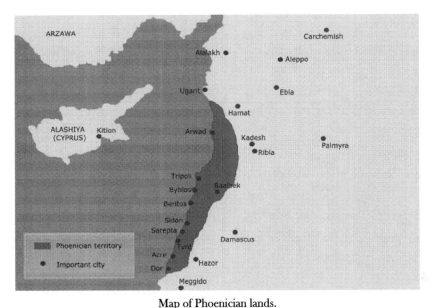

Map of Phoenician lands.
Kordas, based on Alvaro's work, CC BY 3.0
<https://creativecommons.org/licenses/by/3.0>, via Wikimedia Commons
https://commons.wikimedia.org/wiki/File:Phoenicia_map-en.svg

What separated the Phoenicians from other Canaanites was the fact that since around 1500 BCE, their primary profession was trade. In an era where the ancient Greeks were still to find how fruitful commerce could be, Phoenician merchants roamed across the eastern Mediterranean. Their location helped them to thrive in that, as they lived mostly in what is today Lebanon. In ancient times, it was an important crossroads, connecting Mesopotamia, Egypt, Asia Minor, and Greece. However, despite their riches, the Phoenicians never created an empire, and, like the other Canaanites, they never united into a single state. Yet their city-states, among which the most important were Sidon, Byblos, and Tyre, were wealthy and powerful enough to start spreading across the Mediterranean, creating colonies as far as Spain. Some of the earliest Phoenician colonies were dated to around 1100 BCE, centuries before the Greeks began their wave of colonization. However, these dates remain debated among historians. Like the Greeks, the Phoenicians weren't trying to conquer new lands and create empires as much as they wanted to expand their trade network and access to tradable goods.

By the 10ᵗʰ century BCE, Phoenician colonization picked up the pace, and dozens of new cities spawned from Tunisia to Spain. The new colonies were so prosperous that it wasn't long before they grew from trade settlements into urban centers, helped by the fact that the local indigenous population was far behind in civilizational development. The majority of them were formed by the city of Tyre, which became the leading Phoenician city-state, as it was the wealthiest and most powerful. However, its power wasn't measured with a large army, as the Phoenicians were never really interested in waging wars. Thus, when the Neo-Assyrian Empire began expanding outside Mesopotamia, the Phoenician treasure wasn't enough to keep them out of harm's way, and by the mid-9ᵗʰ century BCE, they began sending tributes to the Assyrians. This marked the slow downfall of the Phoenician cities, though they were still not fully conquered. Despite spiraling downward, Tyre was still capable of founding new cities in the late 9ᵗʰ century. Fate would have it that one of the last colonies to be established by this city-state would grow to eclipse not only its founder but also the entire Phoenician nation.

The newly established settlement was aptly named "the new city," *Qart-hadasht* in the Phoenician language, as it was in the vicinity of an earlier colony called Utica. The name was later transcribed as *Carchedon* by the Greeks. As with many other things, the Romans appropriated the Hellenized version, calling that city *Carthago*, which is very similar to the name we use today. According to mythological histories left to us by the ancient writers, the town was founded around 814 BCE by Elishat (often Hellenized into Ellisa). Later on, she became known by the name Dido, meaning beloved in Phoenician. She was the sister of the Tyre king Pygmalion, who, according to most of the myths, cheated her from the shared rule by killing her husband. The exact details of his transgression differ in various versions of the legend. Still, they all lead to Dido leaving the city, sailing to the west.

According to one of the stories, on her way to North Africa, Dido and her followers stopped at the Phoenician colonies on Cyprus. There, she saved eighty virgins from ritual prostitution and was joined by a priest of Baal, the Phoenician god equivalent to Zeus or Jupiter. With this enlarged fellowship, Dido proceeded toward what is today Tunisia.

Upon their arrival in Africa, the queen and her followers encountered both the indigenous population, known to us as Berbers and Libyans to the Romans, as well as the Phoenician colonists from Utica. The ancient writers tell us that both groups welcomed Dido without hostility. The Berbers were reportedly interested in trade and mutually beneficial dealings. Still, they wouldn't just give up their land to the newcomers. Their king welcomed them but allowed the queen and her followers to stay only on the land a single ox hide could cover. In response, Dido cut the hide into strips and enclosed the hill of Byrsa with it, which would become the citadel of Carthage. The king accepted this but imposed a yearly rent. At the same time, the Phoenicians from Utica helped their brethren through trade. The newly founded city prospered quickly due to its favorable position, which, according to myths, led to numerous suitors asking for Dido's hand. Yet she refused them all, in respect of her late husband. Most of the stories end with her throwing herself onto a funeral pyre either because she is forced to marry a local Berber king or because the Trojan hero Aeneas refuses to marry her and sails away to Italy.

Late ancient illustration of Dido's death as she sets her own funeral pyre ablaze.
https://commons.wikimedia.org/wiki/File:Meister_des_Vergilius_Vaticanus_001.jpg

However, the myth of Carthage's founding, despite its thrilling narrative, is considered to be mostly a folktale by modern historians. First of all, all the surviving versions come from Roman or Greek writers who lived centuries after the supposed event, as there are no surviving records written by the Carthaginians. That fact is true for all written accounts of Carthage's history, which is especially troublesome as both the Greeks and the Romans were at one point its adversaries. Further complicating the issue is the fact that most of those writers lived after the fall of Carthage and were mostly interested in contacts and dealings between the Carthaginians and other nations. Archeology can do little to help in this matter for two reasons. First is the fact that the site of Carthage is still inhabited, limiting the possibility of significant research. Secondly, few inscriptions and engravings written in Punic, the language of the Carthaginians, that can be found are hard to interpret. Modern knowledge has a partial understanding of the Punic language, so the exact meaning of the words is debated among scholars. Despite that, archeological findings in recent decades are crucial for our understanding of Carthage, giving us a clearer and fuller picture of its history.

That being said, historians and archeologists have found evidence that confirms parts of Dido's myth. Several objects found at the site of Carthage have confirmed the first Phoenician settlement was founded in the second half of the 9th century or very early 8th century, which is when most ancient writers date the arrival of Dido in Africa. Furthermore, a golden locket was found with inscriptions that mention King Pygmalion of Tyre. Historians are still debating if the locket and the other objects were correctly dated, though. Thus, it is quite probable that the city of Tyre indeed founded Carthage in the period mentioned. When it comes to the question of Dido herself, historians tend to believe she, like her brother, was a real person. The reason behind this is the fact that women in founding myths are rare in ancient times, as they were usually seen as somewhat lesser than men. Additionally, the legends aren't proclaiming her to be of some divine or heroic ancestry, which would've given Carthage a propaganda point in ancient times. Therefore, the Carthaginians wouldn't have gained anything from inventing such a character as their founder. Later practices of Carthaginians sending gifts to a temple in Tyre and to the local Berber population corroborate the likelihood of Dido's founding myth to be based on reality to a certain degree. However, it definitely should not be taken as entirely factual.

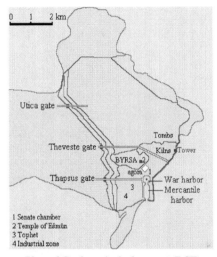

Plan of Carthage in 2nd century BCE
https://commons.wikimedia.org/wiki/File:Carthage.png

Location of Carthage
Robert Dodier, CC BY-SA 2.0 <https://creativecommons.org/licenses/by-sa/2.0>, via Wikimedia Commons
https://commons.wikimedia.org/wiki/File:Carthage_location.png

Regardless of the founding myth, whoever chose the location of the New City selected an unusually favorable position. Locally, the settlement was erected on an arrow-shaped peninsula in the Gulf of Tunis. The citadel on the Byrsa Hill overlooked the shores beneath, providing decent protection from both the sea and land. On the northern half of the peninsula laid fertile lands that were first used as a food source but later became the city suburbs as it grew. And despite not having a river near them, the Carthaginians had freshwater springs capable of servicing their needs. Moreover, Carthage was also quite well connected. The Gulf of Tunis provided calmer waters needed for a good harbor, while the city had easy access inland as well. That allowed it to trade both with the local Berber or Libyan population and with merchants across the sea. This foreign trade was what became the backbone of the Carthaginians' rise, as the city also had a favorable position in global trade. It stood on an important intersection of international trafficking routes linking the entire Mediterranean, both the east to the west and the north to the south. This shouldn't come as a surprise, though, as the New City was founded by the capable Phoenician merchants.

As such, Carthage quickly became an important factor in international trade, with archeological remains linking it with the Greeks in southern Italy and Greece, Egypt, Levant, and Spain. Its trading potential was only increased as the Phoenicians erected new cities, like, for example, in Sardinia, which only expanded the network, of which Carthage was a part of. The archeological evidence shows that it wasn't long before the New City reestablished its connections with Tyre, if they were ever even fully broken. Some historians even argue that Carthage's close ties with the Tyrian aristocracy, if there is any truth to Dido's myth, would only enhance its ties and place in the Phoenician trading system. However, the Carthaginians were not solely middlemen in these mercantile relations. It wasn't long before they began producing their own goods, most notably pottery, which was similar in style to the Greeks, and famous scarlet clothing dye from shellfish, for which the Phoenicians were already known. Archeologists also found evidence of iron foundries and other metallurgical shops from the earliest periods of the city, making metal products part of Carthage's exports as well. Recent archeological discoveries additionally indicate that at some point, the Carthaginians developed the smelting technique of adding calcium to their furnaces, which neutralizes the sulfur in iron, improving its quality. As such, their ironmaking was likely very sought after in the Mediterranean world.

The rise of the New City's production and trade, as well as its favorable position, quickly attracted a new population. Newcomers came from various nations, who were openly welcomed by the Carthaginians. However, despite the urban globalism it attained, Carthage retained its Phoenician cultural heritage, which it held in high regard. Yet the influx of inhabitants meant that the city of Carthage grew rather quickly. According to researchers, in about a century, it had a population of roughly thirty thousand. They state that it took less than two centuries for it to grow to the size of its founding city, covering an area roughly 136 to 148 acres (55 to 60 hectares). In that period, which was no later than the early 7th century BCE, the city was enclosed by an almost ten-foot (three-meter) wide wall with bastions and gates. Yet despite that early growth, Carthage remained under the influence of Tyre, though likely with quite a broad autonomy. It would seem that despite the sharp break hinted in the myth of Dido, the reality was that Carthage remained a part of the Phoenician network. This is further proven by the founding of the new Phoenician colonies on Sardinia during the 7th century BCE. They were small settlements without any considerable public buildings, whose sole purpose seemed to be growing food for the Carthaginians and acquiring metal ores for its growing metallurgical industry.

Thus, by the end of the 7th century, it was clear that Carthage was a linchpin in the Phoenician trade network. The city quickly grew from a small provincial settlement into a bustling, fully developed urban center. However, it was not quite yet the Jewel of the West, prosperous, independent, and proud.

Chapter 2 – Becoming a Mediterranean Power

The early centuries of the Carthaginian history remain mostly blurry, faded by the long-gone centuries. In that period, the New City, despite its growth, remained just that, one of many Phoenician settlements in the west. We have very few details on its development, only broad outlines. However, this changed as historical circumstances pushed it into the light, allowing us to see its past much clearer from then on.

The rise of Carthage was caused by two significant changes in the political landscape of the Mediterranean world during the late 7th and early 6th centuries BCE. In the east, Tyre continued to spiral down in power and influence. It was pressured continuously by vast Mesopotamian empires, such as the Neo-Assyrians and Neo-Babylonians, who wanted to have such an important trading city under their control. Yet those empires were never fully capable of conquering the city itself. It was largely protected by its own importance both as a merchant power and an important source of precious metals, most notably silver. That led to an extended period, roughly from 800 to 600 BCE, during which Tyre was in a somewhat vassal relationship with whatever empire was in its hinterland. It paid tribute but was not under direct control. That was, in fact, the fate of most, if not all, Phoenician cities in the Levant at the time. However, in the late 7th century BCE, the value of silver began to collapse due to oversupply. The economic crisis of the Near East meant that the mercantile influence of Tyre was dwindling, making it a much easier target for the Mesopotamians, as their empires were no longer dependent on it as a source of silver.

The added pressure on Tyre was enough for it to rebel in 586 against the Babylonians, who had supremacy over them at the time. Tyre was aided by the Egyptians, who were enemies of the Neo-Babylonian Empire, but it stood no real chance. For thirteen years, the city was besieged, but it did not fall. However, the city suffered economically as its trade was almost totally cut off. In the end, the city surrendered, accepting a humiliating peace, after which Tyre never recuperated completely. It was at this point that Carthage unquestionably gained its full independence, as its mother city was not able to influence it anymore. Yet even before this, Carthage was acting more or less on its own accord. During the latter part of the 7th century BCE, the Greeks began to expand more aggressively in Sicily and toward the Iberian Peninsula. As such, they began exerting pressure upon already existing Phoenician colonies. However, at the time, Tyre and other Phoenician cities were mostly too weak to help due to their problems with the Mesopotamians. This, in turn, pushed the Carthaginians to slowly rise as the leaders of all the Phoenician colonies in the west, as it was vital for them to protect the existing trade network upon which the New City relied for survival.

Despite that, the upsurge in Carthage's importance was not immediate. It was a slow process that took quite some time to evolve fully. In the last decades of the 7th and in the early 6th century, Carthage was acting more as an ally than a patron of the other Phoenician cities in the west. Circumstances changed in 580 BCE when the Sicilian Greeks tried to expel them from the entire island. Their motive for the attack was most likely caused by their wish to take control over trade with settlements in Sicily while further cutting off the Phoenicians from their colonies on Sardinia. The timing of the attack, coinciding with the siege of Tyre, also brings up the possibility that the Greeks were encouraged by the supposed weakness of the Phoenicians. However, there are no details regarding this in historical sources, which are sparse in general when talking about this attack. The ancient writers only mention that the attack failed, as the Phoenicians allied with the indigenous population from Sicily. The Carthaginians aren't referred to as direct participants in these early clashes. Still, after the Greek attack, they began intervening on the island. Keeping a foothold in Sicily became one of the Carthaginian cardinal policies, swaying their further development. Thus, it was the Greeks who prompted Carthage to become protectors and in the end rulers of the Phoenicians in the west.

Despite that, due to their ongoing conflicts with the Greeks and later the Romans, the ancient writers tended to categorize the Carthaginians as aggressive and imperialistic. That sentiment is, at the very least, historical propaganda, as the Carthaginians were no more hostile or hegemonic than the rest of the nations. Their activities were partly caused by the sympathy for their fellow Phoenicians, as well as their own trade interests. The idea of Carthage trying to occupy Phoenician colonies, especially in the 7th and 6th centuries, doesn't hold up when looking at the evidence. For example, Roman historian Justin claims that around that period, the Phoenician city of Gades or Gadir, modern-day Cadiz in southwest Spain, asked for Cartage's help against the indigenous population. They supposedly answered the plea but ended up acquiring Gades as a part of their empire. Archeological evidence disproves this story as there is no sign of occupation, and historians doubt it was even possible. At the time, the Carthaginians were still trying to gain influence over Sardinia and Sicily, and they were barely capable of achieving that. Thus, it was highly improbable they would be able to directly rule over a city more than 1,000 miles (1,600 kilometers) away. If Carthage did ever sent help, it was much later, and it didn't result in annexation.

On top of that, Justin claims that the Carthaginians were invited by the citizens of Gades, further tainting the possibility of Carthage's imperialism. However, this most likely made-up story hints at something else with this request. The Carthaginians were, in fact, maintaining close ties with their Phoenician brethren in Spain, keeping the trade alive. It kept a similar, if not closer, relationship with other Phoenician settlements across northwest Africa. Carthage's influence over those proliferated during the 5th century. Combined with forming new colonies on the African coast, the New City was slowly becoming a clear hegemon over that part of Africa, though its influence wasn't spread too deep inland. Their motivation for this was, as before, the necessity to keep their merchant network alive. Yet they were not content with only maintaining it. They sought to expand it as well. During the late 7th and early 6th centuries, Phoenicians, led by Carthage, began forming close trading ties with Etruscans, a nation that lived in modern-day Tuscany. It proved to be a rather fruitful relationship, as it was beneficial to both sides. Their bonds were further tightened when the Ionian Greeks, fleeing from the Persian conquest in the east, came to the northwestern Mediterranean around 540 BCE. The newcomers started pillaging the coasts, attacking both the Carthaginians and the Etruscans and disrupting their trade and colonies, which prompted the two nations to ally against them.

The main targets of the Greek pirates were the Etruscan colonies on Corsica and the Phoenician colonies on Sardinia, which were both rather weak and small. According to the written records, the outnumbered pirates were able to defeat the allied fleet but suffered such high casualties that they were forced to stop their plundering and retreat to the Greek colony of Massilia, also spelled as Massalia, modern-day Marseille in southern France.

Thus, despite the defeat, the allies managed to deal with Greek piracy. From that point onward, relations between Etruscan cities, which were never united into a single state, and the Carthaginian towns flourished, and this friendship was crowned with official trading agreements in the late 6th century. At roughly the same time, the Carthaginians also approached a rising power in middle Italy, now known as the famous city of Rome. At the time, it was relatively young and still a fairly insignificant town, but the African merchants realized it had potential, and they began trading with it. The importance of this new business partner was recognized, and according to Roman histories in 509, in the first year of the Roman Republic, the two nations signed a friendship treaty. The exact year has since been debated by modern historians, with some claiming the recorded year is likely to be true. In contrast, others are more skeptical, dating it to a later period, somewhere between the late 5th or early 4th century.

The treaty between Carthage and Rome showcases two essential aspects of their relationship. Firstly, through the regulation of trade, it illuminates the fact that, at the time, the Phoenicians were much more powerful and influential. The treaty limited and ordered how the Romans had to trade on Phoenician soil, while the latter had no restrictions on how to conduct business in Roman territory. Secondly, it outlined the extent of Carthage's dominion in the Mediterranean, as it divided the spheres of influence between the two nations. Rome was confined to Italy, while Carthage was recognized as controlling Sicily, Sardinia, and northern Africa. It is important to note that even by the late 6th century, if we accept the traditional date, Spain isn't mentioned as part of Carthage's protectorate. That indicates that it was incorporated into what was to become its empire in a later period. The treaty also implies that Carthage was able to secure both its position in Sicily and Sardinia against the Greeks. Later Roman and Greek historians claim that this consolidation of the Carthaginian power over the two islands happened in the second half of the 6th century, though their accounts are fragmented, conflicting, and at times vague. However, there is an outlining picture that could be roughly patched up from their works.

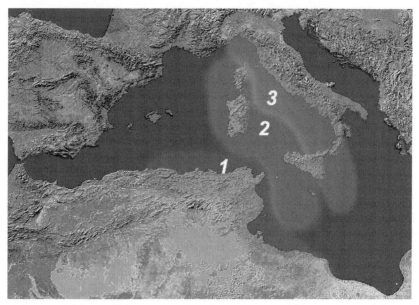

Division of Mediterranean according to the treaty of 509 - 1: Area prohibited to Rome, 2: Area tolerated in emergencies, 3: Open waters.
https://commons.wikimedia.org/wiki/File:West_Mediterranean_navigation_limit_509_BC.png

Ancient historians tell us that a Carthaginian general named Malchus, whose Phoenician name was more likely Mazeus or Mazel, was sent to Sicily to secure Carthaginian positions. His historicalness is doubtful, causing much debate among historians, but if the sources are to be trusted, Malchus lived and led the Carthaginians between about 560 and 530 BCE. He commanded several expeditions on Sicily, in which he fought both the Greeks and quite likely some of the Phoenician cities opposing Carthage's influence or rule over them. These skirmishes or wars weren't constant but intermittent and with opponents often changing sides in them. Some of the sources claim he was ultimately unsuccessful, while others tell us he managed to fortify the Carthaginian grasp over the western part of the island. The truth possibly somewhere in between, with Malchus being able to strengthen Carthaginian positions but not completely secure them. He is later attested as a leader of Carthage's troops in an alliance with the Etruscans. Despite gaining a strategic victory over the Greeks, it seems that Carthage's government saw his tactical defeat as a failure, sentencing him and his troops to exile. Some of the ancient writers convey that he and his soldiers rebelled afterward, possibly even attacking Carthage itself. In the end, it seems he was executed.

He was succeeded in the position of general by a man named Mago, who led the Carthaginian army both in Sicily and Sardinia. From the accounts, it seems he was more successful than his predecessor, possibly because the Carthaginian army was reformed at the time. It changed from the usual citizen levy to a mercenary army. This was done because Carthage had a population too small to sustain prolonged campaigns. Thus, it was seen as better for the citizens to continue their trading while the mercenary army would be paid from the taxes. In turn, Mago was later succeeded by his two sons, Hasdrubal and Hamilcar, though his exact fate is unknown. Familial ties and the fact that the Greek sources gave them titles of *basileus*, king in Greek, have led some historians to conclude that Mago may have usurped the power in Carthage. However, it seems that the Greeks mistakenly gave them the title as some ancient historians, for example, Herodotus, describes Hamilcar as a king because of his valor, not because it was his rightful title. Thus, modern historians think that Carthage remained a republic, whose structure and functions will be described in more detail in a later chapter. In that case, Mago and his Magonid house were not actual monarchs but only a political dynasty, which at the time held the highest offices in the state.

Despite not being true sovereigns, the Magonids were rather successful in defending Carthage and her interests. Around 515 BCE, the Greeks tried to settle near the Phoenician city of Lepcis, better known by its Roman name Leptis Magna, located in modern-day western Libya, at the mouth of the Wadi Lebdam in the Mediterranean. It was the easternmost city in Carthage's dominion. As such, the New City felt it was necessary to defend it against the Greeks, who were supposedly led by Spartan King Dorieous. With the help of the locals Libyans, they were defeated and chased away. Not long afterward, a border was established between Carthage's zone of influence and the Greek city of Cyrene, located in eastern Libya near present-day Shahhat. It was drawn around the modern town of Ra's Lanuf, on the coast of the Gulf of Sidra. Carthaginian influence in northern Africa was also spread to the west, to Gibraltar. On the seas, Carthage's dominion incorporated Phoenician colonies on the Balearic Islands, most notably on Ibiza. Under the leadership of the Magonids, the New City also continued to send small expeditions in an ongoing attempt to solidify control over both Sardinia and western Sicily.

That proved to be no easy task, as Hasdrubal lost his life fighting on Sardinia, most likely in 510. His younger brother Hamilcar, who became the new general, continued the fight. In that very same year, Dorieous once again tried to overstep the boundaries, settling this time in territories on Sicily, which Carthage saw as its sphere of influence. Carthage levied its army, either mercenary or from their local vassals, or even a mix of both, and by 509, the forces had forced the Spartan king out of their land. In the process, Dorieous and his followers lost their lives, putting an end to one of Carthage's problems. It is possible that some smaller expeditions were sent to Sardinia, as by that year, the already mentioned treaty with Rome states both islands as Carthage's undisputed dominion. It is important to note that this doesn't mean the indigenous population or the vassal Phoenicians never again rebelled. Smaller mutinies and revolts were possible, if not probable, but Carthage's influence was cemented henceforth. It also shows that both Mago's and Hasdrubal's contribution was significant, as Hamilcar only had to give finishing touches to it. The next roughly two decades were a peaceful period in Carthage's history, allowing for the newly attained territories to be better incorporated in the dominion.

Some historians tend to brand this as the beginning of Carthage's empire, which may be considered valid. The New City dominated much of the western Mediterranean, especially when it came to trading. However, it's important to note this empire was not structured as most others. Cities under Carthage's domination were still self-governed, with their local governments in place, but they paid their tributes and sent levies when asked. On the other hand, Carthage slowly became culturally dominant over its territories throughout the next couple of centuries. During this time, Carthage's subordinates gradually accepted the Carthaginian variation of the Phoenician language, its artistic styles and religious customs, and other aspects of its culture. It is also important to note that the Carthaginians also adopted some of the local traditions as well as foreign influences. Because of this, from the early 5th century BCE, we can talk about a Carthaginian civilization in its own right, not as a part of an old Phoenician one. Today, everything associated with it, from the language to the people, is often referred to as Punic, a Romanized variation of the Greek Phoenician. It is done so to differentiate it from its predecessor, though it should be noted that the Carthaginians never called themselves Punics (Punes) or their culture Punic.

Whether we accept that the Carthaginian sphere of influence was an empire, in its process of becoming one, or a "mere" dominion, one thing is clear. By the early 5th century, the New City managed to rise up, overcome countless hurdles, and become a leader of the western Mediterranean, which would eventually become known as the Punic world. However, its rise to power was not to end here, nor to remain unchallenged for too long.

Chapter 3 – Fighting for Control over Sicily

By the early 5th century, Carthage managed to become one of the most important actors on the historical stage. It was no longer just one of the many Phoenician cities in the west; it was the leader of the Punic world. This newly acquired status brought it more riches and power, but it also meant that it had to defend its positions against others aiming to take it. Thus, Carthage was ushered into the turbulent age of wars and conflicts.

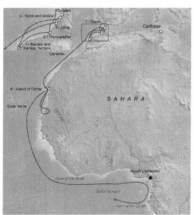

Possible route of Hanno's great voyage.
Bourrichon, CC BY-SA 3.0 <https://creativecommons.org/licenses/by-sa/3.0>, via Wikimedia Commons https://commons.wikimedia.org/wiki/File:HannoRouteMap.svg

However, before the significant conflicts with the Greeks began, there was a short period of peace and prosperity for the Carthaginians. It was in that period of the late 6th and early 5th centuries that Carthage was able to dispatch two exploratory expeditions in the Atlantic Ocean. Again, the primary sources for these are later Greek accounts, which means the exact year is unknown, prompting some historians to date it more toward the mid-5th century. However, it seems likely to assume these kinds of missions would be carried out during more peaceful times. The first voyage was led by Hanno, another high-ranking official in the republic, possibly also a member of the Magonids. He sailed with a large fleet, though the sources most likely exaggerate when mentioning 30,000 people, down the coast of Morocco and possibly farther south down the African coast. Due to vague descriptions and unfamiliar names of places and peoples mentioned in the account, modern historians are debating how far south the Carthaginians arrived. Some claim no farther than Senegal or Sierra Leone, while others state the Carthaginians went as far as Gabon or Cameroon, though the latter two seem less plausible. The goal of this expedition was twofold: one was to establish new colonies down the Atlantic coast and the other to explore new possible trading partners in the region.

The goals seem to have not been achieved. From the archeological evidence, it is clear that no long-lasting Punic settlement had been founded even on the southern Moroccan coast, while the texts don't mention any significant contacts with the locals to prompt any further trade. The longest-lasting impact of Hanno's voyage was, in fact, its account of capturing savage hairy humans that their local interpreters called "Gorillas." Later on, readers of this account assumed the Carthaginians had captured apes, prompting a 19th-century scientist to call a newly found species of apes by that name. At roughly the same time as Hanno's voyage, another Carthaginian, named Himilco, led a second expedition into the Atlantic. This group went the opposite way from Hanno, sailing up north instead. According to the later Roman sources, Himilco followed an already existing trade route used by the local Iberian population, at least to a certain point. Once again, the texts are vague, but most modern historians think that Himilco and his crew sailed all the way to the British Isles and northern France. It seems the goal of his voyage, unlike Hanno's, was only to establish trade connections. The success of the mission is questionable, but the archeological evidence suggests that Carthage's trade network at least reached the tin rich regions of modern-day Portugal.

Regardless of what the expeditions into the Atlantic achieved, the Carthaginians were keen on keeping the trade hegemony beyond Gibraltar for themselves. Some modern historians have even guessed that the vagueness, as well as the tales of sea monsters and other threats, were intentionally written to discourage others, mainly Greeks, from trying to venture that far west. This is possible, as despite having a formidable navy, the Carthaginians were not able to control or block the seas entirely. None of the ancient naval powers were able to do that due to the technological limitations of the era. On the other hand, the Greeks continued to try to thaw the Carthaginian wariness, especially on Sicily. In the early 6th century, the Greek cities on the island were going through political upheavals, with the Ionian and the Dorian Greeks starting to clash. This was only furthered by the rise of the tyrants in cities who simply sought more power for themselves. One of the Dorian tyrants named Gelo, whose capital was at one point the famous Sicilian city of Syracuse, dreamt of uniting the entire island under his rule. Allied with another Dorian despot called Theron, he actively waged wars against the Ionians during the 480s. Their opponents, the Ionians, realized that on their own, they were helpless; thus, in 483 BCE, they turned to Carthage for help.

The New City was aware that it had to intervene. If the Dorians were to unite all of the Greek territories in Sicily, the Carthaginian cities in the western regions of the island would be seriously threatened. However, for unknown reasons, their help was held back for three whole years before Hamilcar was sent with the largest expeditionary force amassed by the Carthaginians at that time. Ancient historians claim it was no less than 300,000 strong, but modern assessments usually don't go much higher than 30,000. Most of these, if not all, were mercenaries who were transported by the Carthaginian fleet. It supposedly consisted of 3,000 transport and 200 battleships. The latter number is in the range of reality, as it represents the Punic potential, but it is also likely to have been far smaller, while the number of transports is surely significantly exaggerated. Gelo's force wasn't much smaller; according to the sources, he had around 26,000 soldiers. In that regard, the two sides were quite evenly matched, but Gelo proved to be more opportunistic and cunning. Near the city of Himera, in northern Sicily, he intercepted a message Hamilcar sent to his Sicilian allies, in which Hamilcar expected them to send cavalry as reinforcements. Gelo saw an opportunity and sent his own cavalry instead to meet with the Carthaginians near their anchored ships. The rouse was successful; the Syracusans burnt most of the vessels, killed Hamilcar, and then turned toward the main Carthaginian camp, completely destroying the mercenary force.

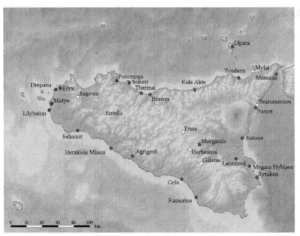

Map of colonies on Sicily (purple marks Carthaginian and red Greek cities).
Uwe Dedering, CC BY-SA 3.0 <https://creativecommons.org/licenses/by-sa/3.0>, via Wikimedia Commons https://commons.wikimedia.org/wiki/File:SicilyBC.svg

The Greek victory was absolute, but Gelo was wise enough to realize that the Carthaginians were still strong enough to defend their own cities in Sicily. Thus, he sued for peace, asking only for two thousand talents (about fifty tons of silver), and the Punes had to build two temples where the treaty would be displayed. Carthage was eager to accept. Ancient Greek historians later hinted that this Carthaginian "attack," as they saw it, was arranged with the Persian Empire, as in that very same year, Xerxes I launched his attack on the Greeks. Modern historians, on the other hand, highly doubt it. The Persians certainly knew enough about Carthage as the new masters of Tyre. They even supposedly wanted to conquer it around 525 BCE, but their attempt was thwarted by the refusal of the Phoenicians to fight their brethren. However, there is no other evidence than timing itself to connect the two wars. On the other hand, until recently, modern historians have often overexaggerated the scope of the Carthaginian defeat, attributing it as the reason for bleak times through which the Punic state went through afterward. Still, the losses at the Battle of Himera were insufficient to singlehandedly cause the contraction of Carthage's power. Most of the troops lost were mercenaries, while the fact that Gelo decided not to pursue further battles meant that Carthage had either more ships or capabilities to recover their losses quickly.

Nonetheless, in the decades after 480 BCE, Carthage went through sort of a recession. After their victories over the Persians, the Greek power continued to rise, and they managed to become masters of the eastern Mediterranean, with Athens leading the Greek hegemony. This meant that for the Carthaginians, their traditional markets in Phoenicia and Egypt were closed for them. At roughly the same time, Rome began pressuring the Etruscans, old Punic allies. This meant that Carthage lost another important trading partner. This isolation, more than the defeat at Himera, caused the slowing down of Carthaginian expansion. Yet, despite that, during that period, Carthage wasn't idle. Her focus merely changed due to the circumstances. Now the New City decided to expand its territories in North Africa. It began spreading more inland, incorporating the local population into its state, which proved to be a difficult task. The Berbers were trailing behind the Carthaginians in civilizational development, and more importantly, their culture was significantly different. Thus, even though the Punes weren't enslaving the Berbers en masse or tried to forcibly remove them from their lands, the local African population never fully merged with the Carthaginians. The Carthaginians did treat them differently from their own population, placing higher taxes and imposing levies on them. Furthermore, it seems they tried to impose their own culture on the Berbers, which was mostly unsuccessful.

The attempts to integrate the local population marks the beginning of Carthage's transformation from a dominion toward more of an empire. It was in this time that the New City began imposing its own administration upon its subordinate towns and settlements. Coupled with that was the political reform in the city itself. New democratic offices and political institutions were supposedly created to limit the power and influence of the aristocratic families, most notably the Magonids. However, despite the democratic feel of these reforms, Carthage remained an oligarchy republic with the Magonids at its head. This prompted some modern historians to conclude that the Magonids themselves were a part of the reforms. It's possible they tailored them to their own political needs at the time, maybe to relieve some pressure on the family after the defeat at Himera. In any case, Hamilcar seems to have been succeeded by his son Hanno. There isn't much evidence about him, but due to his name, some historians have linked him to be the famous explorer who sailed down to Africa. This is questionable but possible. If that is the case, the expeditions happened fifty years later, around 450 BCE, and it meant that the Magonids and Carthage recovered quicker than expected. This theory also explains that the voyages had been undertaken in an attempt to break the Punic isolation of the 5th century. However, it should be noted that both theories are based more on conjecture than on evidence. So far, no conclusive proof has been found for either of them.

A 19ᵗʰ-century artistic representation of the Battle of Himera (480 BCE).
https://commons.wikimedia.org/wiki/File:The_Battle_of_Himera_by_Giuseppe_Sciuti.jpg

Regardless of the exact dates of the expeditions, it seems that modern historians have slightly overexaggerated the extent of the Carthaginian crisis. Due to the expansion in Africa, the New City was less reliant on imported foodstuffs. New territories became its chief supplier, along with more developed Sardinian colonies. The trading ties with the Iberian Phoenician colonies expanded, bringing them closer under the influence of the Punic world. Finally, the lack of any major wars and conflicts meant that the Carthaginian treasury was growing richer. It was enough to impress the Greeks, most notably the wealthy Athenians, as Carthage reappears once again in the spotlight of the Greek writers. On top of that, the Athenians were also impressed by the military power of the Punes, with one of their generals claiming it was stronger than Athens. This accumulation of wealth and military might was due to decades of avoiding conflicts with the Greeks and the indigenous population of Sicily. It's not clear why, but it seems that for roughly seventy years, Carthage was content with her position on the island, while other states didn't encroach on her territory. For that reason, the New City remained out of the focus of the Greek writers, possibly enhancing our visage on the supposed crisis through which Carthage had been going through in the 5th century BCE.

Yet as the century neared its end, Carthage became a more prominent actor in the Greek world. The Athenians, capable traders themselves, realized the potential of partnering with the Carthaginians. Thus, relations between the two thalassocracies began to develop. In 416, Athens sent an expedition to Sicily to fight against Syracuse. It was an ambitious attempt to gain the upper hand in the Peloponnesian War against Sparta, in which Syracuse was on the side of the Spartans. According to some ancient historians, Athens also planned to conquer Carthage, which seems improbable. In contrast, others mention it asking for the help of the Punes. Wisely, the Carthaginians chose to once again stay out of the fight, leaving the two other Mediterranean forces to weaken themselves. By 413 BCE, Syracuse won with the help of the Spartans. This increased its power and dominance over the island as it began to seek revenge on the Sicilian cities that had sided with the Athenians. One of them, Segesta, in 410, asked for Carthaginian protection in exchange for its submission to the Punic dominion. After seventy years of passiveness in Sicily, Carthage decided to accept the offer and step in.

Several reasons prompted the Carthaginians, who were under the leadership of Hannibal Mago, the grandson of Hamilcar, to intervene this time. Most importantly, Syracuse's power was growing quickly, and its appetites rose with it. Secondly, the position of Segesta, on the northwestern tip of Sicily, was too close to the Punic territories. If it fell into Syracusan hands, Carthage's hold on the western parts of the island would be threatened. On the other hand, by that time, the strength of the Punic state had grown due to its expansion in northern Africa. Carthage needed a new direction to expand, with Sicily being the logical choice. Also, it is not unimportant to note that the Athenians completely lost their interests in Sicily, which gave Carthaginians carte blanche to do as they pleased on the island. This was further proved when the two sea powers signed a treaty of friendship in 406 BCE. Some of the Greek historians also mention that Hannibal set out to avenge his grandfather, but this seems more than unlikely. If he was driven by passion, he would have done it far sooner. It is more likely that this reasoning was formed due to the Greeks once again overplaying the importance of the Battle of Himera in history.

The war that ensued was fought with previously unseen ferocity. In 409, the Carthaginian expedition once again mainly consisted of the mercenary soldiers and the Carthaginian navy. Hannibal led them to two great victories over the cities of Selinus and Himera, which were both sacked and razed before the Carthaginians triumphantly returned to Africa. Despite losing their allies, Syracuse remained inactive during this campaign. However, one of its renegade generals raided Punic territories afterward. This prompted Hannibal Mago to return in 406 BCE with even more fury. He laid siege to the city of Akragas, modern Agrigento in southern Sicily, which was the most crucial Syracusan ally and one of the wealthiest Greek settlements on the island. During this battle, the plague ravaged the Carthaginian army, taking Hannibal with it. Still, his cousin and successor, Himilco II, managed to conquer and pillage the city. He then proceeded with capturing and sacking the cities of Gela and Camarina, slowly advancing toward Syracuse itself. On his way, he managed to defeat the Syracusan army, which was under the leadership of its new tyrant, Dionysius I. Despite these victories, the Carthaginians were still burdened by the plague, which led Himilco to agree to a peace treaty before landing a final blow to Syracuse.

It was agreed that the southern Greek cities from Akragas to Camarina would pay tribute to Carthage, and the independence of other towns in Sicily's center and northeast would be guaranteed, while the Punic dominion in the western parts of the island would be recognized. It was a favorable peace for the Carthaginians, leaving Syracuse isolated, at least on paper. However, the Carthaginians brought the plague back home, causing its government to focus on internal matters. This allowed Dionysius to ignore the treaty and conquer many of the eastern and central Sicilian cities. By around 398 BCE, Syracuse managed to rebuild its strength, gathering reportedly 80,000 soldiers, a probable exaggeration, and 200 ships. Figuring that the Punes were devastated by the illness, he besieged the island city of Motya, one of the most important Carthaginian cities on the western coast of Sicily. With large siege towers, the Syracusans were able to breach the walls, proceeding to fight on the roofs, which were connected with wooden planks. The city was ravaged and never recovered. The Carthaginians were furious. Himilco gathered the troops and returned to the island during the winter, a season during which, in ancient times, armies rarely fought. He forced out the small Syracusan force that was left in Motya and retook it. Nevertheless, Himilco chose not to rebuild the ruined city but decided to build a new one just south of it, which we know by the Latinized name Lilybaeum.

Modern reconstruction of the island city of Motya.
Selinous, Aldo Ferruggia, CC BY-SA 3.0 <https://creativecommons.org/licenses/by-sa/3.0>, via Wikimedia Commons
https://commons.wikimedia.org/wiki/File:Motya_from_above_artistic_reconstruction_1_0.jpg

The victory at Motya wasn't enough to appease the Carthaginians, and Himilco sailed to the northeastern tip of Sicily, capturing and pillaging the city of Messana. His troops then marched south, toward Syracuse, while the navy followed down the coast. Dionysius tried to stop the Carthaginian fleet but was defeated in the Battle of Catana in 397 BCE. By the winter of that year, Syracuse was besieged, as its defenses were too strong for the Carthaginians to attack. At that point, it seemed as if the Punic victory was at hand, as Himilco hoped the Syracusans would depose their tyrant and ask for peace. However, fortune once again turned against the Carthaginians. As the summer of 396 approached, another epidemic ravaged the Punic army, severely weakening it. Dionysius exploited this and began attacking the Carthaginian camps and navy. Himilco found himself in a position to be cut off, prompting him to retreat with his Carthaginian soldiers on the ships and escape to Africa, leaving the mercenaries and Sicilian allies on their own. Later, many Greek sources mention that he bribed Dionysius to escape, but it seems unlikely that even a greedy tyrant would choose short-term gain over a total victory. Nonetheless, Himilco's cowardly move was met with massive dissatisfaction in Carthage, as he was judged for leaving the rest of the army on its own.

Himilco accepted full blame for the defeat, and the disgrace soon drove him to suicide. More worryingly for Carthage, it seems that his abandonment of non-Carthaginian troops prompted the local Libyans to rebel, as they made up part of those forces. This was accompanied by a slave uprising as well, singling that there was much dissatisfaction in the Punic empire in Africa. During that turmoil, a man named Mago, Himilco's deputy, was chosen to be the highest official. Most historians assume he was a part of the Magonid family, possibly Himilco's nephew. However, some scholars are doubtful of that, as they claim there is no clear evidence to support that fact. Regardless of his familial ties, Mago managed to quell the uprisings before returning to Sicily. He clashed several times with the Syracusans, with mixed results. By 392 BCE, both sides were tired of the prolonged war and agreed to a peace treaty. It was similar to the previous agreement, with both sides keeping their spheres of influence, except for central Sicily, which Carthage left to Dionysius. Yet the peace was merely an interim, as no conclusive victory was gained. Dionysius began to expand the Syracusan dominion, acquiring territories in eastern Sicily and even in southern Italy. In the meantime, Carthage continued to prepare for the war it foresaw.

In 383 BCE, Dionysius crossed the line when he sought alliances with some of the cities in western Sicily, which were a part of the Carthaginian sphere of influence. The Punes immediately went to war, sending Mago to deal with him once again. The exact chronology and details of this new conflict are rather sketchy. It seems that Mago sent a detachment to southern Italy, where, allied with the Italics, they pressured Syracuse on a second front. Mago himself led the campaign in Sicily, where he suffered a crushing defeat, losing his life in the process. Carthage was ready for peace, but Dionysius gave an impossible ultimatum: The Punes had to abandon Sicily. In response, the New City instated Mago's son, presumably named Himilco, as its new general. He managed to defeat the Syracusans in a battle near modern-day Palermo around 376 BCE, prompting Dionysius to accept peace. Syracuse had to pay one thousand talents, and a demarcation line between the two powers was drawn. It went along the river Halycus, today's Platani, just west of Akragas, while in the north, Carthage gained the territory of Thermae Himeraeae, a successor city of Himera. Besides gaining considerable territory on the island, the Punes were also eager to end this conflict as soon as possible. However, the plague once again ravaged the city of Carthage, while the Libyans and Sardinians revolted at the same time.

Afterward, Himilco disappears from the sources. If he was indeed part of the Magonid family, with him, its dominance waned as they also vanished from the forefront of Carthaginian politics. By the late 370s, a man named Hanno, sometimes nicknamed as "the Great," appeared on the stage, quelling the rebellions. Unlike the Magonids in previous decades, he was opposed by Suniatus, which is a Latinized form of the Punic name Eshmuniaton. Thus, Punic politics entered a more fluid state. At the same time, Dionysius saw another opportunity to attack the supposedly weak Carthage, as it was still recuperating from the plague and uprisings. In 368, he attempted to conquer Lilybaeum, but Hanno was able to destroy the Syracusan fleet and force the aging tyrant to retreat. Dionysius I soon died, and his son and namesake, Dionysius II, accepted the peace in which the status quo was arranged. A decade of peace ensued, but it was broken when Syracuse plunged into a state of civil war. Dionysius II was ousted, and other Greek cities plunged into anarchy, with petty tyrants fighting for power. Despite that, Carthage itself stayed aloof. Hanno was too consumed with Carthaginian politics to pursue any gains in Sicily.

First off, he had to depose his main adversary. Hanno accused Suniatus of traitorous contacts with Dionysius, and by most likely using strong anti-Syracusan sentiment in the city, Hanno had him executed. Yet Hanno wasn't satisfied; despite losing their leader, opposition in Carthage was still very much alive. It seems that Hanno's arrogance and ambition lost him the support of most of the citizens. Aware of that, but still hungry for more power, around 350 BCE, Hanno planned a coup. First, he tried to murder a number of high-ranking state officials at his daughter's wedding banquet. The plot was discovered and avoided, prompting Hanno to retreat to his country estate for a last stand. Sources mention he tried to organize a slave revolt, though this is doubtful. He likely assembled his followers and some slaves on his estate while trying fruitlessly to win the support of the Libyans. Hanno was captured, mutilated, and finally crucified for his treachery, while his family seemed to be exiled, even though some sources mention them being executed as well. The opposition, without any particular leader that we know of, then turned its gaze upon Sicily once again.

By 345 BCE, Syracuse was under the control of Hicetas, who had strong ties to Carthage. He asked for help from the Punes when the old tyrant Dionysius II attempted to retake the city. Since the newly established leaders of Carthage needed military successes to solidify their rule, they were eager to help. A massive Carthaginian army was sent to Sicily, entering Syracuse in 344. However, at the same time, a smaller contingent of Greek troops from the city of Corinth, located in mainland Greece arrived, as Hicetas asked Corinth for assistance as well. This led to a somewhat confusing four-way standoff, as all sides attempted to fulfill their plans. In the end, the Corinthians, who were led by Timoleon, were the most successful. Timoleon exiled Dionysius to Corinth, Hicetas escaped, and by 343, the Carthaginians withdrew without a fight. This undecisive Punic action was met with substantial public outrage, as they had been in the city itself, prompting the leading Carthaginian general to take his own life. Timoleon proceeded to raid the Carthaginian territory, as he required resources to pay his troops, while moving to strengthen his positions in Sicily. The Punic response was rather slow, as it wasn't until 341 that a new expeditionary force was sent to the island. This time, alongside with usual mercenaries, a so-called Sacred Battalion, consisting of about three thousand elite aristocratic Carthaginians as well as another seven thousand regular citizens, were sent.

An artistic representation of a battle between the Carthaginians and the Greeks.

Despite having a numerical advantage, the Punic army was defeated by Timoleon in the Battle of the Crimissus, mostly thanks to terrible commanders. As a result, the Sacred Battalion and other Carthaginian citizens were killed or enslaved. The defeat was total, and the New City was panicking. They recalled Hanno's son Gisco from exile, giving him full control to prepare for the Greek invasion. Instead, Gisco managed to forge a peace with Timoleon, who had his hands full with the petty Greek tyrants in Sicily. The result of this disastrous war for Carthage was more than acceptable, though, given they went back to the *status quo* positions of 367 while promising to cut all ties with the petty Greek tyrants.

For a couple of decades, the Punes left Sicily on its own. First of all, the city needed to recover from its losses while also bringing some balance to its politics. The need for this was only furthered when Alexander the Great began his conquest of Persia in 334 BCE. Within two years, he managed to conquer Tyre from the Persians, and the Carthaginians accepted refugees from their mother city, mostly children and women. Next in line was Egypt, an old trading partner of Carthage. The Punes were afraid they could be next in line as they possessed a rich land, and Alexander reportedly warned them he would attack once he was finished with Persia. That left the Carthaginians to prepare for a possible invasion.

However, Alexander's premature death in 323 eased their fears, once again opening a possibility to meddle in Sicilian affairs. By that time, a general named Hamilcar, possibly with familial ties to Gisco, took over the rudder of the republic. It seems he attempted to retain peace and good relations with Syracuse, interfering in its internal affairs after Timoleon's death. At first, the Carthaginians supported the oligarchs before switching their backing to a populist tyrant named Agathocles. Hamilcar even led a military intervention in 319 to secure Agathocles's position. He hoped that a personal agreement with an established ruler of Syracuse would make peace last longer, but he was wrong.

Agathocles first removed any opposition in the city, then attempted to conquer Messana in 315. Hamilcar's envoys stopped Agathocles from that and, in the very next year, managed to put off a boiling conflict between Syracuse and its Sicilian opponents. The preserved peace was short-lived, though. The Syracusans soon seized Messana, and in 312 BCE, they attacked Akragas, where the Punic fleet stopped them. In retaliation, Agathocles invaded and plundered the Carthaginian territories in western Sicily. The failure of Hamilcar's policy was evident. Thus, he was supposedly convicted in his absence, but Hamilcar died before he could return to Carthage. His replacement was Gisco's son, confusingly also named Hamilcar.

The new general proved to be much more capable. He forged alliances with many Greek towns that opposed Agathocles and defeated him at the battle of Gela in 311. The combined Greco-Punic army then proceeded to besiege Syracuse. Instead of attempting to passively defend the city, Agathocles acted with unprecedented audacity. In the summer of 310, he slipped through the naval blockade and attacked the Carthaginians in Africa. What ensued was a period of total chaos. An unexpected attack on its hinterland caught Carthage by surprise. The Syracusans were able to conquer several important cities, including Utica and Tunes (modern-day Tunis), and defeated the Punic army on several occasions. In one of the battles, a new Sacred Battalion was lost, as well as Hanno, one of the two Carthaginian generals tasked with overseeing the fighting in Africa. The Carthaginian positions only deteriorated when the Libyan revolts began to ravage across its African empire. By 309, Hamilcar was defeated in Sicily, losing his life in the process. The Greek allies then abandoned the Carthaginian leadership and began to fight on their own, even amongst each other. The situation was so desperate for Carthage that its other African general, Bomilcar, attempted a coup in 308 BCE. He wanted to become a Carthaginian tyrant whose rule would be unrestrained by the republican institutions.

Despite the chaos of the Punic state, the Carthaginians were unwilling to succumb to despotic rule. The citizens stood against Bomilcar, who obviously lacked any broader support, capturing and executing him before he could finalize his coup. It is around that time that the war turned against Agathocles, as Syracuse came under pressure from other Greek cities on Sicily. The tyrant was forced to return to the island, yet he left his troops under the command of his son in Africa. Those forces continued to plunder, but the Carthaginians were able to contain them without the leadership of Agathocles. These men were encircled in Tunes by the Punic army, prompting Agathocles to return in 307. Yet he was defeated upon his arrival. Realizing his African adventure was over, the tyrant escaped, leaving his trapped troops with two of his sons to be captured and killed. By that time, both Syracuse and Carthage had enough of war. Carthage was still facing Berber rebellions, while Syracuse was facing its Greek foes in Sicily. By 306, the war was over. The boundary between the Syracusan and Carthaginian zones of influence was once again settled at the Halycus River, while the Punes also paid a smaller subsidy for the liberation of their nominally occupied territories.

The war, which Carthage had tried to avoid, proved to be the most devastating for the republic. The losses were high, and the gains almost nonexistent. Yet the Carthaginians were forced to fight it, if nothing else than to preserve their territories and position in Sicily. In fact, the result of the Sicilian Wars, as this series of conflicts fought between Syracuse and Carthage was later named by historians, could be summed up similarly. The Punes fought for nearly 180 years to retain their grip on the western portion of the island, but they never gained much for their ventures. In the end, they at least managed to withstand the pressure from the Greeks. Yet their biggest foes were still to challenge them.

Chapter 4 – From Allies to Enemies

While Carthage was preoccupied with its dealings with the Greeks in Sicily, another power rose to prominence in its neighborhood. Rome, once a small city in central Italy, managed through the years to conquer not only Latium but also the Etruscans and other surrounding nations and tribes. At first, the Punes had no quarrel with them as they were seen as lucrative trading partners.

The Carthaginian pragmatic merchant attitude toward the Romans was evident since their first trade agreement of 509. The Etruscans, old Punic allies, were already fighting with the rising power of the Roman state. Yet the Carthaginians stood aside, looking only to trade and profit. Roughly 160 years later, in 348 BCE, a new treaty was signed between Rome and Carthage. Like the previous one, it was a set of rules in mutual dealings between the two republics. For example, it stated that if Roman or Carthaginian merchants had to stop to resupply in the other state's territory, they shouldn't harm the locals and must leave within five days. The Romans were allowed free trade with the Carthaginians in Sicily, while they were banned from trading in Sardinia, Spain, and Africa. On the other hand, the Punes were free to trade in

Roman lands. It went beyond trade as well, as it also barred the Romans from plundering and founding colonies in those territories. Similarly, Carthage was forbidden from conquering any cities in Latium. Furthermore, it was agreed that if, for example, a Roman envoy brought captives from a nation with whom Carthage had an official treaty to a Punic city, the Carthaginians had the right to liberate them. This also applied to the Carthaginians.

However, this treaty raises several questions. Firstly, despite banning the Romans from founding cities in Africa and Sardinia, Carthage stayed silent about Sicily. Similarly, the Punes weren't forbidden from founding colonies in Latium. Yet it is clear that for both sides, such actions would be out of the question. Secondly, by the mid-4th century, Rome was much stronger and more influential than in 509. Nonetheless, the second treaty imposes further bans on Roman trading rights in the western Mediterranean. It is peculiar that a much stronger Rome would accept such harsher terms. The reasoning behind it could be different needs from the treaty. Carthage was attempting to recuperate economically from the financial losses of the rebellions in the 370s. Furthermore, it was, in general, a trading-oriented state, prompting it to focus more on the economic aspects of the agreement. On the other hand, Rome was militaristic and expansionistic, caring less about trading. Its primary concern would be to ban Carthage from meddling in its neighboring regions, allowing Rome to enlarge its own territory. Whatever may be the exact reasoning behind both sides accepting such an agreement, it could be said that it was a diplomatic achievement for the Punes. They managed to secure their positions against Rome despite the fact they were going through rather turbulent times.

The third treaty between Rome and Carthage, which was signed in 306 BCE, is the most controversial one. There is no factual proof of it other than reports of some Roman historians several decades later. Even then, it was a matter of debate among Roman scholars if it was real or made up. It was especially important to them as it supposedly banned Romans from entering Sicily and Carthaginians from entering Italy. If the treaty was genuine, the late Punic Wars would be blamed on the Romans. Thus, many Romans have disregarded it. However, modern historians tend to believe this agreement existed, as it fits the international politics at the time. The Romans had gained hegemony over most of Italy, except the southern Greek colonies. It was likely their hope to conquer those as well, thus prompting them to seek a way to limit possible Punic interference. On the other hand, the Carthaginians were exhausted by their last war with Syracuse. Securing peace in Sicily against possible Roman expansion on the island surely seemed like another diplomatic victory. Simultaneously, because of the Sicilian Wars, Carthage was in no shape to actually consider meddling in Italian affairs. Similarly, the Romans at the end of the 4th century were busy with their wars with the Samnites and what was left of the Etruscans to plan any expeditions to Sicily. From the perspectives of both republics, this treaty would have been a deal without any downsides.

After 306, Carthage enjoyed a brief period of peace. It lasted until Agathocles's death in 289 when Greek cities in Sicily once again reverted to their chaotic politics. Petty tyrants rose up, while Agathocles's Campanian mercenaries, known as the Mamertines, began ravaging the island, even seizing Messana for themselves in the process. In Syracuse, a new tyrant named Hicetas arose, and it wasn't long before he raided the Carthaginian territories. He was likely hoping for easy plunder and a victory to reinforce his position as a tyrant. Instead, in 280 BCE, he was defeated by the Punes and later overthrown by his rivals. However, this was enough for the Carthaginians to be vengeful. They gathered troops and ships and once again besieged Syracuse, which was also involved in internal strife amongst its leaders. It was at this point that the Greeks, presumably the Syracusans, asked Pyrrhus, the king of Epirus, to help them against the Carthaginians. At the time, Pyrrhus was warring against the Romans in Italy, as he had been invited by the Greek cities there to help them against the Latin expansion. He commanded a sizeable army and had shown prowess as a general. Yet he was unable to defeat the Romans, leading to a stalemate in Italy.

Pyrrhus was an adventurer thirsty for glory and conquest, so when he received a call for help from the Syracusans to fend off "the barbarians" attacking fellow Greeks, he didn't think too much about it, especially as it meant breaking off the deadlocked conflict with the Romans. However, the Carthaginians caught wind of this and negotiated another treaty with the Latins in 279. It confirmed the previous agreements but also added a non-compulsory alliance against Pyrrhus. In essence, no side was obliged to help, but it left the possibility of Carthage aiding the Romans with their navy, while the Romans would contribute land troops if need be. Despite the vague alliance between the two republics, neither side ended up requesting or offering assistance. In 278 BCE, Pyrrhus finally arrived on Sicily and initiated a lightning-fast campaign. First, he liberated Syracuse, where the Carthaginians retreated at the sight of his army. Then, aided by Sicilian allies, he proceeded to conquer several Punic cities in Sicily before laying siege to the heavily-fortified town of Lilybaeum. Taken by surprise with the speed and force of the Greeks, the Carthaginians tried to negotiate with Pyrrhus. They offered him money and ships to transport his troops back to Italy, but he declined. He was supposedly preparing to invade Africa and conquer Carthage itself.

It is unclear if these ambitions were real, but they align with his adventurous personality. However, his Sicilian allies were against such ventures. They began suspecting that Pyrrhus started dreaming of creating his own empire in the west. His position worsened as his allies began defecting due to his harsh treatment. By 276, the king of Epirus received another plea for help from the Italian Greeks, giving him yet another excuse to leave a stalemate of his creation. After he left, the Carthaginians had little trouble in retaking all their lost cities, while the Syracusans became more concerned with the raiding Mamertines. Thus, the peace was renewed with the territorial status quo. The only marginal gain of the Carthaginians was the fact that Syracuse lost its grip on some of the Greek cities in Sicily, like Akragas, which established friendlier relations with the Punes. Up north, in Italy, Pyrrhus was defeated by the Romans. He fled back to Epirus, while the Latins continued their conquest. By 270 BCE, the Latins controlled most of Italy. Despite their supposedly friendly or even allied relations, the Carthaginians became somewhat wary of the Roman expansion.

However, after achieving peace in Sicily, the Carthaginians remained as composed as before. They attempted to retain the peace and balance of power both with Syracuse and Rome. Yet after a few years, a new Syracusan ruler named Hiero decided to end Mamertine rule over Messana, besieging them in 264 BCE. Trapped, the Campanian mercenaries called both the Romans and the Punes for assistance. The Carthaginians were the first to arrive, yet after learning that Rome decided to answer their call as well, the Campanian mercenaries sent them away. It seems that due to their Italian background, they felt closer to the Latins. This caused considerable turmoil among the Carthaginians. The commander of the Punic forces sent to Messana was even crucified, supposedly for his stupidity. More importantly, it appears that the Carthaginian fears had begun to materialize, as Rome started to expand into Sicily. Almost immediately, the Punes sent a new army to the island, while their diplomats began gathering allies. In a surprising turn of events, the Carthaginians found them in Akragas and, even more unexpectedly, in Syracuse. Now allies, the two most powerful forces of Sicily laid siege to Messana. Seeing a new unified Sicilian force, the Romans had second thoughts about meddling in the island's affairs. One of the Roman consuls sent a negotiation offer, but both the Carthaginians and the Syracusans declined, effectively starting a conflict that was to become known as the First Punic War.

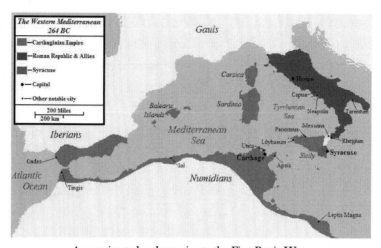

Approximate borders prior to the First Punic War.

Ever since the 3rd century BCE, there has been a debate about who was to blame for the beginning of this conflict. Even the Roman historians themselves debated the issue. If the treaties from 306 and 279 existed, and most modern historians argue they did, then the Roman decision to interfere and send troops to the Mamertines would have been a breach of an agreement. From the Carthaginian side, it is clear that a Roman presence in Sicily would be a threat, a sign of Latin expansionism on the island. Others have debated that Rome was fearful of Carthage attempting to expand its sphere of influence in southern Italy, in regions once closely tied to Syracuse. However, the initial reactions show that the Latins weren't expecting to fight the Punes, especially when considering the fact that they offered to negotiate as soon as they realized the Carthaginians were against them. It looks like the Roman plan was to fight against the growing power of Syracuse, which could have potentially threatened Roman gains in Italy. It is not unimaginable that the Romans thought that warring against the Carthaginians' traditional enemy wouldn't cause any troubles with their nominal allies. It is also worth mentioning that there weren't any signs of the Carthaginians attempting to expand into Italy, as it always seemed too far out of their reach.

However, blaming Rome for interfering in Sicily or Carthage for acting aggressively and refusing peace would only mask the real reasons for the conflict. In the end, it seems that the war started because of miscalculations, miscommunications, and, most notably, fears. And once the war began, there was no turning back. The Roman forces crossed over to Sicily with about 16,000 troops, defeating first the Syracusans then the Carthaginians. Both allies retreated to their territories, effectively ceasing to act in unison. This was exploited by the Latin army, which immediately pressed toward its primary foe, Syracuse. Their troops marched south from Messana and besieged the strongest Greek city on the island. At the time, the Carthaginians remained inactive, leaving its ally to fend for itself. It is unclear why the Punes acted so lethargic against the Romans. Some scholars have suggested that based on their previous experience, the Carthaginians predicted Syracuse would able to hold on for a long time, even under siege. With such calculations, it might have seemed to the Carthaginians that they had enough time to gather troops and adequately prepare for war. However, they were wrong. When Hiero saw that the Carthaginians weren't coming to help, he arranged peace with the Romans. By the summer of 263 BCE, Carthage lost its ally.

Syracuse was allowed to keep some of its possessions in eastern Sicily but had to pay a modest sum of one hundred talents, roughly the yearly pay for five thousand Roman legionnaires. Most importantly for the Romans, Hiero also obliged to provide supplies for the Latin forces on the island. Thus, Syracuse became a Roman ally. After this victory, half of the Roman army was sent back to Italy, showing once again that at that point, Rome was still unsure how to proceed in this unexpected war with Carthage. However, the other half of the army, led by a Roman consul, marched toward the Punic territories. There, they avoided any significant confrontations or sieges, but they managed to persuade several Carthaginian cities to defect. The most important of them was Segesta. Throughout the rest of the year, the Carthaginians remained inactive, as they lacked an army large enough to take on the remaining Roman troops. Thus, they opted for passive defense concentrated at significant fortified points. This tactic had worked for them in the past against the Greeks, but it wasn't enough to deter the Romans. A change was needed if Carthage hoped to stop defections of its allies and dependencies; thus, in 262, a large mercenary army was gathered and sent to Sicily.

The reinforcements arrived at Akragas, the largest Greek ally Carthage had, yet the Punes remained passive. However, it is unclear if that was by choice. A new Roman army, which had arrived on Sicily at almost the same time, besieged the city rather promptly, stopping any possible offensive planned by the Carthaginian general named Hannibal. Soon, another Carthaginian army, led by yet another Hanno, arrived on the island and marched toward Akragas as well. It would have been expected to see a combined attack on the Roman army; however, the Carthaginians remained inert. It was only in early 261, when famine began to plague Akragas, that the Punes tried to relieve the city. It was, incidentally, the first battle in which the sources mention the Carthaginians using war elephants. Those proved to be quite ineffective in combat since the combined Punic armies were unable to defeat the Roman legions. Hannibal and most of his troops managed to escape during the night, leaving Akragas to be sacked and a majority of its population to be enslaved. The failure of the Carthaginians could be blamed on their unwillingness to fight as if they hoped Rome would once again ask for peace. It is also unclear why the Carthaginian fleet didn't try to stop the Romans from transporting fresh troops to the island.

This lackluster leadership caused more disaster to the Carthaginians than just military defeats. Due to their victories, the Romans finally decided their ultimate goal was to push out the Carthaginians from Sicily. Thus, they continued the war with more resolve than before. However, they were unable to materialize it on the battlefield. The war entered a stalemate on the land, while the

Carthaginians began raiding the Italian coast from Sardinia. The raids achieved little, as plunder and prisoners were not bountiful, and they didn't hurt the Roman Republic much. Despite the raids, the Punes still didn't try to stop the Roman legions on their way to Sicily, allowing their enemy to continue putting its pressure on the land. Nonetheless, these raids finally prompted the Romans to build their own fleet. They likely realized that without it, they would never be able to fully dislodge the Carthaginians from the island. Roman historians tell us that they based their design on a Carthaginian quinquereme ship captured at Messana in 264. Those were large ships powered by five rows of oars, which had been used by the Greeks and the Carthaginians since the early 4th century. To staff them, they recruited people from their coastal allies. However, neither of their allies had much history of using a navy. It was clear to the Romans that their fleet would be inadequately matched against the savvy Carthaginian seaman.

To even the odds, the Romans invented a new device named the *corvus* (raven). It was essentially a bridge operated by swings and pullies with spikes on its end. The idea was to pull up next to the enemy vessel and drop the bridge onto its deck, with the spikes securing the connection. That would allow the superior Roman soldiers to board the Carthaginian ships and essentially defeat them in a "land" combat on the sea. It should be noted that many modern historians tend to dismiss the use of such a tool as fiction imagined by the Roman writers. In their opinion, the *corvus* was too complicated, as well as too big, compromising the ship's stability. Yet they do think the Romans most likely used some other simpler device, like grappling hooks, that would allow the legionnaires to board the enemy ships. Whatever the actual design of the *corvus* was, it proved to be extremely effective. In 260 BCE, two fleets, both numbering roughly 120 to 130 ships, met at the Battle of Mylae, located on the northeastern coast of Sicily. The Carthaginians were taken by surprise with the new Roman tactic, suffering a humiliating defeat. According to the sources, the Punes lost more than forty vessels, most of which were captured.

Interestingly, the Romans failed to capitalize on such a decisive victory, though Punic raids in Italy did stop. Instead, the Romans were satisfied with merely raiding the Carthaginian territories in Sardinia and Corsica. This prompted the Punic fleet to once again enter a naval duel with the Latins. They clashed in 258 near Sulci, a city in southwestern Sardinia, but the Carthaginians were once again defeated. The remainder of the fleet returned to Africa, where the leading admiral was crucified for his losses. Despite the naval victories, the Romans failed to conquer the Carthaginian colonies on those two islands. However, the Punes were unable to use them as a base for further raids on Italy. In contrast to the naval affairs, the Carthaginians had more success on land. After a slow advance of the Romans in 260, capturing some cities in central and western Sicily, the Carthaginians succeeded in achieving several victories. Led by a general named Hamilcar, who was not related to previous Hamilcars or the one yet to come, managed to defeat the Romans near Thermae Himeraeae in 259. Then he proceeded to capture the cities of Enna in central Sicily and Camarina, just west of Syracuse. However, that success was short-lived. By the next year, the Carthaginians were pushed back to their territories.

A 19th-century illustration of the Roman navy using the *corvus*.
Ellis, Edward Sylvester, 1840-1916;Horne, Charles F. (Charles Francis), 1870-1942, No restrictions, via Wikimedia Commons
https://commons.wikimedia.org/wiki/File:The_story_of_the_greatest_nations,_from_the dawn_of_history_to_the_twentieth_century_- a_comprehensive_history,_founded_upon_the_leading_authorities,_including_a_compl ete_chronology_of_the_world,_and_(14578958927).jpg

Afterward, the war stalled. The Roman advance in Sicily was slowed down by long sieges, while the Carthaginians were unable to mount a new counterattack. Even worse for the Romans was their realization that the toughest Carthaginian strongholds, like Panormus (Palermo), Drepana (Trapani), and Lilybaeum, were beyond their ability to capture. Instead, they opted to follow the example set by Agathocles, to strike the Carthaginian heartland in Africa. The front remained mostly quiet, though the Romans won another naval battle in 257. By the next year, both sides amassed their navies, as it seems the Carthaginians caught wind of the Latin plans. The Roman fleet sailed to Sicily to gather the legions and sail to Africa. However, the Punes tried to stop them in a massive naval battle near Cape Ecnomus, on the southern coast of Sicily. The Roman sources most likely exaggerate the size of the forces, citing about 330 ships and 140,000 men on each side. Yet it is clear that it was a major confrontation, more massive than previous ones. The Carthaginians, led by Hamilcar, tried to employ a new tactic to counter the *corvus*, but it failed. Once again, they suffered a crushing defeat, prompting the question of why didn't the savvy Carthaginian seamen devise a counter to the *corvus*. Whatever the reason, the Punes paid the price for their military conservativism.

The Roman army soon arrived on Cape Bon, conquering the small city of Clupea to protect their landing area. The Carthaginians were unprepared for a land campaign in Africa. Thus, the Latins met little resistance at first. However, in a rather strange and unexplained turn of events, after an initial victory, the Roman Senate recalled half of the army back, leaving one consul, Marcus Atilius Regulus, with only about 15,000 men, behind to continue the African offensive. At this point, Hamilcar was recalled back to his homeland, where he met up with two more generals to stop the Roman advance. However, even with Hamilcar's five thousand men, the Punes were outnumbered. Furthermore, due to their split leadership, their army proved to be ineffective, leading to another crushing defeat. The Carthaginian hinterland was plundered, while the Berbers began rebelling once again. Facing such a crisis, the Carthaginians asked Regulus for terms of peace. Probably overconfident and thirsty for personal glory, the consul asked for the impossible. Besides the usual indemnity and release of prisoners, he demanded that Carthage leave both Sicily and Sardinia. He possibly even added terms that banned the Punes from having a military fleet while also stipulating that they couldn't make war or peace without Rome's permission. However, most modern historians tend to see those demands as yet another exaggeration by later Roman historians. Of course, the Carthaginians refused.

Despite Carthage being in a crisis and overrun by refugees, the city elders managed to gather a new army, equal in size to the Romans. More importantly, they gave the leadership over it to a Spartan mercenary named Xanthippus. With his expertise, in the spring of 255, they defeated the Romans in a battle near Tunes. It was a crushing defeat, as only two thousand legionnaires managed to get away, retreating to Clupea, where the fleet returned them home. Regulus paid the price of his hubris, as he was one of the several hundred captured Latins. His arrogance and unwillingness to connect and ally with the Berber rebels brought disaster to the African expedition. However, even worse for the Romans, the fleet returning from Clupea was caught in a storm that sunk the majority of the ships. The sources mention that about 90,000 men drowned, though that is likely another exaggeration. Nonetheless, the Carthaginians were still losing the war. While their armies were focused on subduing the Berber uprising, the Romans managed to conquer several cities in Sicily, including Panormus. The only Carthaginian victory that was achieved was the recapture of Akragas, but the Punes realized they could not keep it. Thus, they razed the city and left. By 253 BCE, Carthaginian possessions in Sicily were pretty much reduced to the well-fortified and besieged cities of Drepana and Lilybaeum, with a small stretch of land between them.

In the meantime, the Romans renewed their fleet and began raiding the African coast. However, it was a short-lived venture, as it was once again heavily damaged by a storm. After 253, there is no mention of the *corvus* anymore, prompting historians to conclude that it was no longer used due to its weight disturbing the balance of ships in bad weather. Yet the Carthaginians were unable to use this to their advantage. Their attempt to retake Panormus failed, though they did manage to subdue the rebels. By 250, the war entered a standstill. The only pieces of Carthaginian land left were the two fortified cities, which the Romans were unable to conquer. Even when the Carthaginian fleet managed to destroy almost the entire Roman navy in two battles near Drepana in 249, the situation remained the same. The Carthaginians simply exhausted their resources to field a substantial army needed to challenge the Latin legions. By 247, the only thing Carthage could afford was a small army, which was led by a new general named Hamilcar, and it went to the area around Panormus. Using guerilla-style warfare, Hamilcar tried to distract the Romans from their sieges, disrupting their supply lines with minor and fast raids. For this, Hamilcar earned the nickname Baraq, in Latin transcription Barca, meaning in Punic either "lightning" or "blessed." Yet not even his actions managed to change the course of the war.

A Carthaginian coin of the god Melqart, with the facial features of Hamilcar Barca; on the reverse is a man riding an elephant.
https://kids.kiddle.co/Image:Dishekel_hispano-cartagin%C3%A9s-2.jpg

By then, the war became a painful stalemate. The Romans were just replacing their armies, unable to conquer the two Carthaginian cities in Sicily, and instead of rebuilding their fleet, they decided to focus on reinforcing their coast. On the other hand, the Punes were mostly passive. They defended their cities, while Hamilcar's raids never grew to anything more substantial than a nuisance for the Romans. The Carthaginian fleet avoided any larger operations, content with its occasional raids on the Italian coast. The only considerable changes in those years were the Carthaginian conquests in Africa. After the rebellions were subdued, a general named Hanno, later to become known as Hanno the Great, managed to expand the Punic hinterland deeper into the continent. He conquered areas around Sicca, modern-day El Kef in northwestern Tunisia, and Theveste, today known as Tébessa in northeastern Algeria. These were fertile lands and, more importantly, new sources of tax income needed by Carthage, not only to continue its war efforts but also to compensate for the losses in Sicily. Yet even with those new sources of revenue, Carthage was both unable and unwilling to commit to any grander action in an attempt to change its footing in the war.

The standstill remained until 242 BCE, which was when Rome built a new fleet through a citizen's loan. It was once again modeled on the most advanced captured Punic vessel and manned by highly trained seamen, although it did not have a *corvus*. The fleet sailed to Sicily, finally managing to enforce a blockade on both Drepana and Lilybaeum. It wasn't long before the defenders started to feel the effects. The Carthaginians realized something had to be done; thus, they scrambled what was left of their fleet and sailed to Sicily. In contrast to the Romans, the Punic fleet was ill-equipped. Most of their ships were old and poorly maintained, and the crews were inexperienced, as it seems the experienced seamen were unwilling to fight anymore. Further burdened by the lack of supplies, they were no match for the Latins. In 241, the Carthaginian fleet was once again destroyed in a battle near the Aegates Islands, just west of Drepana. The Romans became the unchallenged masters of both the sea and the land, while Carthage lacked the resources to try and rebuild its force. The only way out was for them to ask for peace, which they did through Hamilcar in Sicily.

The Roman terms were, of course, harsh. Carthage lost Sicily and the smaller surrounding islands, and the Carthaginians had to pay 1,000 talents upfront and another 2,200 talents over the course of 10 years. It was a hefty sum, roughly 96 metric tons of silver. No doubt that was done to prolong the recovery of the African republic. Prisoners were exchanged, and the two republics agreed not to attack each other or their respective allies. This was mostly concerning Syracuse, which remained a semi-independent ally of Rome. Finally, the treaty stated that neither side could recruit soldiers for other's land, which was more important for Rome. It wanted to preserve Italian manpower from being drained by Carthage's mercenary recruitment. However, the Latins didn't attempt to dictate what Carthage could or couldn't do elsewhere, nor did it try to ban Carthaginians from trading in Sicily or Italy. It is evident that the Romans were still eager to keep the business between them alive. Nonetheless, the war cost Carthage too much. Its treasuries were empty, her fleet destroyed, alongside its naval reputation. Carthage also lost high-income territories, and her sense of security was shattered.

After 23 years of war, the Romans managed what the Greeks couldn't for almost two centuries. They pushed the Carthaginians from their most prized possessions. This was achieved in a war that neither side particularly wanted but in which Rome showed more determination and guts. Yet, despite the losses, Carthage was still seen as a respectable power. However, her glory days were gone, and from this point onward, she began spiraling downward.

Chapter 5 – Revitalization and Demise

The First Punic War was, in every sense of the word, a disaster for Carthage. Her losses were enormous, while the gains in African expansion were rather minimal. By 241 BCE, the leading Carthaginians likely thought it couldn't get much worse, yet they were gravely mistaken.

The troubles began immediately after the war ended. About 20,000 mercenaries and Berber conscripts from Sicily returned to Africa, wanting to get paid. The Carthaginian leaders feared keeping such an unreliable foreign force near its capital, so they sent them to Sicca, along with their families. Once there, Hanno the Great tried to negotiate lowering their fees, to which the soldiers objected. Furious by such treatment and the fact that their Sicilian commander Hamilcar Barca wasn't the one dealing with them, they marched to Tunes and captured it. There, they managed to negotiate an increase in pay and secure payment for the Libyan soldiers, who weren't supposed to earn anything. However, in late 241, a coup among the mercenaries brought new leaders who were eager to wage war. They saw a defenseless enemy with bountiful plunder. The Berbers joined in, as they most likely feared retribution for siding with the mercenaries in the first place.

Thus, the so-called Mercenary War began. The mercenary army quickly rose to action, while the local Libyans promptly joined in, causing widespread rebellions across Africa. It wasn't long before they put Carthage under a blockade. Faced with such a crisis, the Carthaginian leadership reactivated Hamilcar, who had been dismissed after the First Punic War ended.

Hamilcar Barca gathered what little troops he could, broke through the mercenaries' lines, and entered the Carthaginian hinterland to reinstate control over the rebels. Using daring tactics with limited resources, Hamilcar managed to better the situation. He even persuaded the Numidian cavalry to switch sides and join him, further strengthening his army. Yet, with his focus on the Berber heartland, the rebels besieged Utica and Hippacra (modern-day Bizerte). Hanno was unable to contain them, though his presence most likely stopped them from spreading farther. Yet, by 239, both cities decided to switch sides, while the war became increasingly violent. Both sides began killing their prisoners and showed little mercy. Adding to the Carthaginian misfortune, mercenaries on Sardinia rebelled as well, managing to take over the entire island with little opposition. At that point, Hamilcar realized that the only way to defeat the mercenaries was to unite his and Hanno's army. However, by that point, Hanno and Hamilcar had become political enemies, prompting the former to refuse such an action. Hanno's reputation was already hurt by his failure, while Hamilcar once again proved to be the superior tactician and commander. As they were faced with possible insubordination, the Carthaginian authorities allowed the soldiers themselves to choose their general. They chose Hamilcar, while a more compliant commander replaced Hanno.

While the Carthaginians were preparing their counterattack, the Libyan rebels attempted to emphasize their independence by minting their own coins. These were at first used to trade with the Greeks and the Romans. The Punes attempted to stop and intercept these traders, but after the Romans protested, they stopped interfering. It proved to be an invaluable diplomatic success for Carthage, as the Latins soon banned all trade with the rebels. Also, to aid them further, they released thousands of captives from the war for free, giving a much-needed manpower boost to the Carthaginians. Hiero also sent some aid, as he realized that Syracuse needed Carthage as a counterbalance to Rome. Thus, in its dark time, two former enemies helped Carthage to survive the uprising. However, that came with a price. After the war, Rome took control of both Sardinia and Corsica. Carthage could only look on. Even though the rebellion was quelled, it wasn't in a position to do anything about it. Nonetheless, the received help signaled Carthage's reversal in the war. Hamilcar soon pressured the mercenary army enough for it to abandon its siege of Carthage, prompting it to retreat to Tunes. Despite that, he realized his army wasn't strong enough to tackle the rebels in a fortified position.

Thus, in 238 BCE, the Carthaginian army returned inland to continue its task of reasserting control over its revolting regions. A sizable rebel army foolishly followed Hamilcar on his mission. For a while, this resulted in nothing more than a series of smaller skirmishes and maneuvers, in which Hamilcar once again exhibited his ability to wage war against a numerically superior enemy. He even managed to attract some of the mercenaries back to his side. Eventually, he ambushed his pursuers, forcing them to panickily retreat into a canyon or a mountain ridge. Due to the canyon's shape, the sources name it the Saw, but historians are unsure of its exact position. Once the mercenaries retreated into it, Hamilcar shut off the exits and began starving the army. The rebels resorted to cannibalism before the Carthaginians rushed in and killed what was left of them. After annihilating a considerable chunk of the rebel forces, Hamilcar turned back to Tunes. Circumstances dictated that he and Hanno had to temporarily reconcile and work together to deal the final blow to the uprising. Working together, they managed to force the mercenaries from the city, finally crushing them all in a battle near the eastern coast of modern-day Tunisia. Most of the mercenaries died, while their leaders were gruesomely tortured before being publicly executed.

In contrast to the usual Carthaginian behavior and their treatment of the mercenaries, Carthage acted rather leniently toward the rebels. By 237 BCE, all the cities and territories were back under Carthaginian rule, with minimal if any penalization for their uprising. It seems that this new policy toward its African subordinates included a fairer rule in the ensuing years, as those cities exhibited stubborn loyalty in later conflicts with Rome. Another significant result of the Mercenary War was that Hamilcar Barca and his party became the leading force in Carthage, ousting Hanno the Great and his followers. Immediately after the war ended, Hamilcar began planning how to restore Carthage. His first step, rather logically, was to reinstate control over Sardinia, as it still wasn't annexed by Rome. However, his attempt was halted by the Latins. They claimed the actual target of the Carthaginian fleet was Italy and declared a formal war. Carthage was in no position to challenge Rome and agreed to pay 1,200 talents for peace. It was only after this crisis that the Romans officially took control over Sardinia and Corsica. These Roman actions were clearly aimed at slowing down the economic revitalization of Carthage. The annexation of Sardinia and the declaration of formal war was seen as unjust even by the ancient writers.

Despite that loss, Hamilcar wasn't thrown off balance. He switched his focus to the Iberian Peninsula and old Phoenician colonies. Some historians have argued that Carthage had control over some Phoenician cities in Iberia even before this Spanish expedition, but there is no clear evidence for that. They may have been friendly or even allies, but it is doubtful they were under direct Carthaginian rule. However, by 237 BCE, Carthage did start to expand its influence in Spain. The sources are vague about the details, but it seems Hamilcar exploited various tactics to enlarge the Punic dominion. Some cities became allies, while others were simply conquered. Though he appears to have used brutal methods to deal with stubborn resistance in some instances, in most cases, Hamilcar acted leniently toward newly acquired lands. On his expedition, he also brought his son-in-law, Hasdrubal, who acted as his second-in-command. Hamilcar's son, the famed Hannibal, also went with them. Hannibal allegedly had to swear to his father that he would never be friendly toward the Romans to be allowed to come. Together, they extended the Carthaginian rule over most of southern Spain, centered around the lower and middle valley of the River Baetis (modern Guadalquivir).

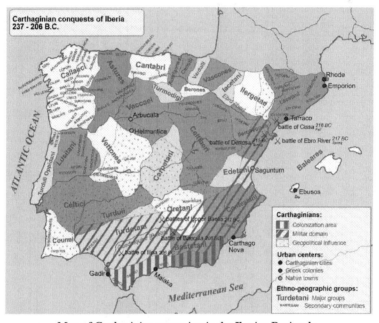

Map of Carthaginian expansion in the Iberian Peninsula.
Alcides Pinto, GFDL <http://www.gnu.org/copyleft/fdl.html>, via Wikimedia Commons
https://commons.wikimedia.org/wiki/File:Iberia_237-206BC.svg

The expansion wasn't stopped even after Hamilcar's death in a battle against an unnamed tribe in 229. He died saving Hannibal and Hasdrubal, with the latter being chosen afterward as his successor, both by the troops and the Carthaginian citizens. Hasdrubal, an acclaimed general like his father-in-law, pushed the borders of the Carthaginian dominion to the Tagus River, covering almost half of the Iberian Peninsula. The exact form of governorship across these newly acquired territories is, just like the precise details of the conquest, veiled by inconclusive sources. It is likely that local Iberian and Celtic tribes that chose to ally with the Punes had to supply them with soldiers, while those that were conquered had to pay taxes as well. The old Phoenician colonies, like Gades or Malaca (present-day Malaga), were probably only required to provide ships and crews, both for war and for transport. Of course, new Carthaginian colonies were also formed. Hamilcar founded Akra Leuke, meaning "White Cape" or "White Fort." It is unclear where it exactly stood, but modern researchers suggest it could be modern Alicante, as it would have offered an excellent link to Carthaginian Africa. More notably, Hasdrubal founded a city he named Qart-hadasht, meaning "New City." This city, today called Cartagena, was sandwiched between a safe harbor on its south and a saltwater lagoon on the north, as well as having hills behind it. It became the capital of the Carthaginian Iberian territories.

Even some of Hasdrubal's contemporaries saw it as declaring independence, especially as he began acting more like a sovereign. He also forged tighter connections with local leaders through a political marriage. He also encouraged Hannibal to take an Iberian wife. This culminated when the Spanish chiefs declared him their supreme general, *strategos autokrator*, as the Greek historians tell us. However, the evidence tells a different story. Hasdrubal, like Hamilcar before him, sent plenty of slaves, most likely captives from the conquests, as well as horses and immense wealth back to Carthage. This revitalized the Carthaginian economy and rebuilt the African provinces destroyed by the wars. It is also worth noting that the name *Qart-hadasht* was rather common for Carthaginian cities, like ones in Sardinia or eastern Tunisia. It is similar to the Greek *Neapolis*. In reality, the founding of New Carthage, as the Romans called it, proclaimed the rejuvenation of the Punic state to the Spanish people, whose loyalty Hasdrubal was working on, as well as to the Mediterranean in general. This Carthaginian renaissance was fueled not only by new tribute and taxes but also by the fact that Spain was rich with silver. Most, if not all, of the mines were owned by the state and were only leased to private contractors—a common practice across the Mediterranean and one that allowed for considerable wealth to flow into the Punic treasury.

Besides the economic advantages, Spain proved to be an important pool of manpower, a resource needed to wage a prolonged war. By the mid-220s BCE, Carthage became more of a land power, with a standing army in Iberia numbering about 60,000 infantry and 8,000 cavalrymen. In comparison, the navy had only about 130 warships, a number nearly three times smaller than at its height. The revival of Carthaginian power naturally caught the Roman eye. In around 225, an informal agreement was struck between Hasdrubal and the Latins. The Punic general promised not to advance beyond the River Iber (Ebro) in northeastern Spain. Hasdrubal only accepted the agreement because, through it, the Romans gave him tacit freedom to operate in southern Iberia as he pleased. On the other hand, it gave the Romans time to focus on their expansion into northern Italy and the Adriatic. However, circumstances began to change in 221 with Hasdrubal's assassination. His brother-in-law, who by that time had honed his military skills, became the new general and leader of Carthage. Trained from a very young age, Hannibal was a prodigious and pugnacious commander. He defeated a regional Iberian army near Toltetum, modern-day Toledo, and campaigned across central and northwestern Spain as far as the River Durius (Duero). Some of the towns and tribes he conquered himself. Others simply offered submission in awe.

Roman statue supposedly depicting Hannibal
https://commons.wikimedia.org/wiki/File:Mommsen_p265.jpg

Carthaginian coin possibly depicting young Hannibal with symbols of the god Melqart.
https://commons.wikimedia.org/wiki/File:Carthage,_quarter_shekel,_237-209_BC,_SNG_BM_Spain_102.jpg

Within twelve months, Hannibal managed to almost double the Carthaginian possessions in Spain, ruling nearly all of the Iberian lands south of the Iber. The only exception was the city of Saguntum, north of modern-day Valencia. By 220, the Romans noticed both Hannibal's prowess and Carthaginian expansion. They feared that Carthage may become too strong and that they might possibly even expand from Spain to southern Gaul, modern-day France. That region was not only home to Greek colonies that were friendly toward the Roman Republic, but it was also a backdoor to Italy. Thus, they sent an envoy to caution Hannibal not to cross the Iber as well as to not "molest" Saguntum. This angered Hannibal, as Saguntum was neither north of the Iber nor a Roman ally; it was merely a friendly city. The goal of the Romans was obviously to stall his advance. Additionally, Saguntum also acted as a good listening post for them to keep a closer eye on the matters in Spain. However, Hannibal was not about to buckle under such threats. Claiming that the Romans had no business in interfering in this matter, he sent the envoy back. He couldn't allow the Latins to exhibit enough power to meddle in Carthaginian affairs. Thus, by early 219, Hannibal besieged Saguntum, while Rome did nothing to help its supposed friends. During the entire seven-month-long siege, the Romans debated whether to act or not, with the final success of Hannibal's army swaying them over.

In the spring of 218 BCE, Roman emissaries traveled straight to Carthage, unlike before when they first went to Hannibal. After the Punic leaders refused to hand over their general, the Romans declared a formal war. The Second Punic War had begun. The war itself was avoidable, as both sides were keener on expanding elsewhere, and trade between them was flourishing. Yet the mutual mistrust and their ambitions proved to be enough to ignite another conflict. According to ancient historians, Hannibal expected it to happen. By early 218, he had his army ready. The sources tell us that Carthage had fielded about 122,000 soldiers, while Rome had roughly 71,000. However, the Roman fleet was about twice as large as the Punic one, with better-equipped ships, which was the exact opposite at the start of the First Punic War. This meant that a naval invasion of Italy was out of the question. Nevertheless, Hannibal wasn't about to wait for the Roman incursions in either Spain or Africa. Therefore, by early summer of 218, he began his march north, across the Iber toward southern Gaul. Despite his military genius, it took some time and losses to subdue the local Iberian tribes. Furthermore, upon crossing the Pyrenees, he had to send home a considerable chunk of his Spanish allies. His army dwindled to about 59,000 men, though it's worth noting that Hannibal had left much more behind in Africa and Spain.

The Carthaginian army traveled through southern Gaul away from the coast in order to avoid Greek cities allied to Rome. Most of the Gallic tribes were friendly toward the Punes, but when they arrived at the River Rhone, the hostile Volcae tried to block Hannibal's advance. He managed to defeat them with little losses. However, as they fought, Roman forces headed to Spain and landed in the city of Massilia (Marseille) on the mouth of the Rhone. The armies were far enough apart to avoid combat, though their scouts did clash in a skirmish. Hannibal chose to eschew battle and headed toward the Alps. He had to hurry before the winter made crossing them much harder. The numerically weaker Romans didn't pursue; instead, their army continued toward Spain. Yet one of its commanders traveled back to Italy to take charge of its defense. Thus, the Romans weren't very surprised when Hannibal arrived in northern Italy in November of 218. What is surprising, and still debated among historians, is the number of his troops. Hannibal's army dwindled to somewhere around 26,000 soldiers without a viable explanation. Ancient writers attributed it to the perils of crossing the Alps, as well as the skirmishes with the local Gallic tribes.

However, the evidence points to something else. By the battle of Rhone, the Punic army had dropped to about 46,000 men. Before that, there were no battles or a lack of supplies. The only possible solution was that a number of troops deserted for various reasons, for which we have no written testimony. The losses at the Rhone were minimal, while the skirmishes on the Alps were only sporadic, causing probably even fewer losses. Furthermore, crossing the Alps during the autumn isn't as deadly as it was later romanticized. There was little snow, and they had enough supplies to not cause any substantial number of deaths, though the Punic army was far from perfect condition. Modern historians tend to ascribe these losses either mainly to desertion or to the fact that Hannibal actually began his expedition with fewer troops. Regardless of the numbers, the Carthaginian army was certainly exhausted from the march, and Hannibal knew he had to gather supplies to continue south. Thus, he first clashed with a local Gallic tribe that had resisted his proposals of an alliance. He sacked their town, modern-day Turin, and slaughtered the defenders. This not only brought him supplies but also forced other local tribes into submission while impressing Gallic tribes farther east.

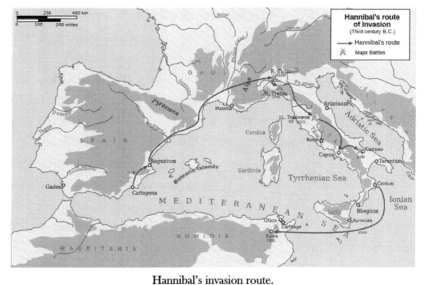

Hannibal's invasion route.
Abalg + traduction made by Pinpin, CC BY-SA 3.0
<https://creativecommons.org/licenses/by-sa/3.0>, via Wikimedia Commons
https://commons.wikimedia.org/wiki/File:Hannibal_route_of_invasion-en.svg

By December, Hannibal began his march south, while the Romans, under the command of Publius Scipio, moved north to stop him. In a battle near the juncture of the Rivers Ticinus (Ticino) and Padus (Po), the cavalry of the two forces clashed. The Romans were beaten, and Scipio was wounded. This victory finally prompted the Gallic tribes to essentially rebel and join forces with the Carthaginians. With the Gallic reinforcements, Hannibal's army grew to about 30,000 infantry and 10,000 cavalry. Simultaneously, Scipio received reinforcements, making the Roman army similar in strength. However, the Carthaginians were superior in cavalry numbers, which Hannibal used in late December when the two armies met near the Trebia River. He used his horsemen to outflank the enemy, inflicting high casualties on the Romans. Similar to the previous battle, Hannibal released the non-Roman prisoners without a fee after the battle concluded, attempting to gather more support across Italy. He began representing himself as their liberator from Roman oppression. However, winter stopped his advance. Hannibal waited until early May, when the food was more bountiful, to continue his march south with his army, now numbering around 50,000 men, many of whom were released captives. The Romans used this time to recover from their losses, levying new legions to fight the invaders.

The Roman forces were divided into two parts, one stationed in Etruria and the other on the Adriatic coast. They wanted to block Hannibal's path with one army and possibly flank him with the other. However, Hannibal managed to slip into Etruria through the marshes of the Arno River. This took a considerable toll on his troops, while the general himself lost sight in one eye due to an infection. Once Hannibal's army arrived in Etruria, it immediately began plundering, both to gather much-needed supplies but also to force the Roman army to face them without reinforcements. At first, the Romans didn't take the bait. However, when Hannibal moved eastward toward modern-day Perugia, he forced their move. Not only did Hannibal cut off one of the armies from Rome, but he was also moving toward the second army in the east. The western portion of the Roman army immediately began the chase, while the eastern one closed in. At that moment, Hannibal exhibited his strategic genius, stopping on the shores of Lake Trasimene to set up an ambush for his pursuers. Using mist as cover, the Carthaginians descended on the unsuspecting Romans, pushing them into the water. Despite being encircled and unprepared for the battle, the legionnaires did put up a fight but were eventually crushed. About 15,000 men were killed, including the consul in charge, while another 15,000 were captured.

After the battle ended, the cavalry from the eastern portion of the Roman army arrived, as they were sent as reinforcements. Hannibal easily dealt with them, killing another 2,000 Romans and capturing about the same amount. The Romans were devastated. They expected Hannibal to besiege their capital, which was roughly four days away from Lake Trasimene. It seemed like a rather logical option, further bolstered by the fact that a new Carthaginian fleet from Africa was preparing to sail to Italy. With the combined force on the sea and land, Rome could be starved into submission. However, Hannibal chose not to do so. It was a choice for which he was criticized throughout the centuries, but his reasons were sound. He aimed to move farther south, to a more pleasant climate, to give his troops much-needed rest while cutting off the Romans from their southern allies. On top of all that, he knew that the Romans might have been defeated on land, but their navy was still operational. That made the naval blockade rather risky for the Carthaginians. For a while, the Romans were unable to do anything against the invaders, allowing them to arrive in the south uncontested. There, Hannibal tried to invoke rebellions and gain new allies but failed. However, his troops did get some much-needed respite.

This allowed the Romans time to reorganize and gather fresh soldiers. However, they changed tactics. Realizing it was unlikely to beat Hannibal in an open battle, they decided to simply tail his army and harass it. They would attack foragers, scouts, and smaller detachments. The idea was to wear out the Carthaginians without allowing them to crush the main body of the Roman army. Hannibal tried to lure them into battles, but for the most part, he failed. The only notable confrontation in almost a year was when he managed to lure one half of the Roman army into an ambush before retreating when the other half came to its assistance.

Though Hannibal managed to inflict some losses, it wasn't a complete defeat of the Latin legions. Without giving Hannibal the open battle he needed, the Romans put him in a tough position. His army was getting tired, he wasn't getting reinforcements, and he couldn't achieve any notable victories to attract new allies. To worsen the Carthaginian position, the Roman army in Spain managed to achieve a significant victory over Hannibal's brother, Hasdrubal, beginning its march south of the Iber. Simultaneously, the Roman fleet raided the African coast, with the Carthaginian navy unable to stop it. By the summer of 216 BCE, the Carthaginians were in a tough position.

During that year, Roman confidence grew, while the strategy of avoiding combat with Hannibal became increasingly unpopular as a cowardly strategy both among the common population and the soldiers. This prompted the Roman Senate to authorize the consuls for that year to levy twice the usual number of legions and to finally deal with the intruder. With the allies and auxiliary troops, their combined army was about 86,000 strong, the largest Roman army up to that date. It was what Hannibal had hoped for, though, despite the discrepancy in army sizes. After some chasing around in southeastern Italy, the two armies finally met near Cannae, on the Adriatic coast of Apulia. On August 2nd, 216, the two armies clashed, allowing Hannibal to cement his legacy as a genius tactician. He knew that the Romans had more infantry, which was better equipped than most of his men, which came from the Gallic allies. However, his cavalry was better, though not noticeably numerically superior. To counter this, Hannibal arranged his infantry center in a convex line, with the additional troops on its outer end. Upon clashing with the relentless Roman legions, the Carthaginian center began to fall back in an organized manner, allowing the sides to slowly flank the advancing enemy. At the same time, his cavalry flanks managed to rout the Romans, with Hannibal's light cavalry pursuing the fleeing troops. In turn, the heavy cavalry turned back and smashed into the Roman infantry, completing the encirclement.

The Roman defeat was total. Ancient writers tell us that out of 86,000 Roman soldiers, nearly 50,000 were killed, including dozens of notable aristocrats. Another 19,000 were captured, while only 15,000 managed to escape their fates. The Roman military was crushed, totaling more than 100,000 dead since Hannibal's arrival in Italy. Once again, the Romans expected him to besiege Rome itself, yet once again, he chose not to. Modern historians often argue why he avoided attacking the heart of the Roman Republic, some claiming it was his biggest blunder and showing his lack of strategic understanding of war. Others believe that from his perspective, it made sense. Rome was too well fortified, and Hannibal lacked the equipment for a proper siege. However, it seems that Hannibal's idea of how to win a war against Rome was based on the wrong presumption that the Latins would be pressured to ask for peace at some point. Despite what later writers stated, it seems he never set out to destroy the Roman Republic, just defeat it. Hannibal sent an envoy to Rome after the Battle of Cannae to offer peace, but he was turned down. The Roman stubbornness continued afterward, despite their allies slowly defecting to the Carthaginians. Among them were not only Greek cities from southern Italy and Syracuse but also Italics, who had been granted citizenship in the Roman Republic, most notably the Samnites and Capuans.

To make matters worse for the Romans, Hannibal also formed an alliance with Philip V of Macedonia, who began attacking their territory in the Balkans. By 214 BCE, it seemed that Rome lost most, if not all, of its major allies. During all those years, Hannibal most likely expected to receive a plea for peace, yet none came. The Romans, it seems, chose to fight to the end. Even worse for Hannibal's position was the fact that the Romans returned to their previous tactics of harassment and avoidance of a head-on battle with his army, leaving him to wander across Italy seemingly without aim. As they followed him, they also began reconquering rebelled cities as well, lowering the pressure from Hannibal and replenishing their reserves. The war also expanded across the Mediterranean. Roman troops were still in Spain, where they placed pressure on Carthage, preventing Hasdrubal to reinforce his brother in Italy. Smaller detachments also fought in Sicily and Sardinia. The war expanded at sea as well, as the Carthaginians had built new fleets both in Spain and Africa. By 212, both republics had more than 100,000 active soldiers on various fronts. However, as Hannibal's sword hung above the Romans' neck, it looked like the Carthaginians still had the advantage.

Yet that soon started to change. During that year, the Romans were able to conquer Syracuse and Capua, and they threw Macedonia out of the war by allying with several Greek states. The number of Hannibal's Italian allies began to dwindle. However, in 211, his brother managed to inflict a catastrophic defeat against the Roman army in Spain, forcing them to retreat north of the Iber. Despite achieving that, Hasdrubal failed to capitalize on such a victory. Within a year, the Roman army in Spain was reinforced and placed under the command of a brilliant young general named Publius Cornelius Scipio, who was the son of the aforementioned general of the same name. He realized that the Carthaginians left New Carthage undefended, and in 209, he exploited that with a surprise attack. Conquering the center of the Carthaginian power in Spain threw Carthage off balance, and it signaled the undoing of Carthaginian control over the peninsula, with many of their allies defecting to Rome. On top of that, Scipio amassed immense wealth while slaughtering the Punic population to instill fear in his enemies. Nonetheless, the Roman conquest of Spain was slow, as they faced significant resistance. Yet their advance was relentless, finally prompting Hasdrubal in 207 to lead his troops through southern Gaul and over the Alps to link up with Hannibal in Italy. It seems that they wanted to increase the pressure on Rome so its men would refocus on Italy instead of Spain.

This strategy failed miserably. Hasdrubal was defeated and killed in northern Italy before he could even hook up with Hannibal. To add insult to injury, the Romans cut off Hasdrubal's head and sent it to his brother. Hannibal was left isolated in southern Italy, and his strength was shrinking, as the last and only reinforcement he received came in 215. Over the years, Hannibal managed to win some battles, yet they were minor victories without much influence on the course of the war. As such, the main theater of the war shifted. Scipio continued his conquest of Spain, managing to inflict two major defeats on the Punic forces before finally capturing Gades in 206. By the next year, the Carthaginians lost all of their land on the Iberian Peninsula, allowing Scipio to return to Rome and plan the invasion of Africa. Mago, Hannibal's other brother, made the last attempt to prevent that from happening. He sailed from Spain with what remained of the Punic army in 205, landing in Liguria in northern Italy. However, he was too far away to join forces with Hannibal, who was attempting to secure a port in the south, to allow him to retreat. Mago managed to cause some trouble in the north before he was finally defeated in 203, succumbing to his wounds afterward.

A 19th-century illustration of the Battle of Zama.

While the two Barcid brothers wandered in Italy, Scipio led a Roman invasion to Africa in 204, earning him the nickname "Africanus." He landed near Utica but failed to conquer it. However, he managed to defeat the Punic army and its Numidian allies twice in 203. These losses knocked the Numidians out of the war and finally forced Hannibal to return to Carthage to mount its defense. He gathered his veterans, mercenaries, and African levies to meet Scipio on the battlefield. While preparing, Hannibal attempted to negotiate peace. Still, the talks failed due to mutual mistrust, even though both Scipio and Hannibal respected each other as generals. The two of them finally clashed in 202 near Zama, almost 81 miles (130 kilometers) southwest of Tunes. It was a close battle, and at one point, it seemed that Hannibal would win. However, Scipio's cavalry managed to rout the Carthaginian cavalry and descend on the Punic rear. It was almost a reverse Battle of Cannae. Hannibal managed to get away, but by then, he realized the war was over. Upon returning to Carthage, he managed to persuade his countrymen to seek peace at any cost. In 201, the war was finally over with an overwhelming Roman victory, something that no one in 217 would have expected.

With the loss of the Second Punic War, Carthage's renaissance was over, ending as abruptly as it started. Even worse for her, the unnecessary war brought the city and its republic further down than ever before.

Chapter 6 – Succumbing to the Wounds

Losing another war against the Romans was disastrous for Carthage. After seventeen years of fighting, high expenses leaving an empty treasury, and tens of thousands lost lives, she found herself bleeding—a mere shell of a once glorious jewel of the west.

The Romans were determined not to allow the Carthaginians to rise up again. Thus, Scipio Africanus gave them terms so harsh to the point that Carthage was almost a vassal state. The Punes had to pay ten thousand talents over the next fifty years, they were banned from having a fleet of more than ten ships, and they couldn't wage war outside of Africa, while they had to seek Roman permission to do so on their own continent. In addition, the Roman Numidian allies, who had deposed of the previous ruling aristocrats who were loyal to Carthage, were given the rule over the lands of their ancestors. The issue with this clause was the fact that no clear territorial border was specified. Interestingly, Scipio didn't ask the Carthaginians to give up Hannibal, most likely since the two generals respected each other despite the vicious battles fought between them. After the terms were accepted, Scipio gathered the Carthaginian fleet in front of Carthage and ceremoniously burned it, signaling the end of Carthage's great power. Despite that, the city itself was left untouched and in control of her African territories. In fact, Scipio confirmed her existing borders before setting off back to Rome.

Nonetheless, those African territories were in a harsh state. They were raided by Scipio and by the Roman fleet. According to later sources, Hannibal supposedly employed his soldiers to plant olive trees to help the economy recovery. Despite that, if there is any truth to the story, the Barcid party lost its grip on Carthage, and Hannibal was replaced as the leading official. However, there is no mention of Hannibal receiving any penalties for losing the war, unlike many of his predecessors in the previous centuries. Sadly, the new leading faction, most likely connected with Hanno the Great or his successors, proved to be mostly incompetent and intolerant. They wanted to impose new taxes on the citizens to help with the payment of the war indemnity. On top of that, they led Carthage in discord with Numidia, which was led by King Masinissa, a Roman ally. That was enough for Hannibal to get reelected as the leading man of Carthage around 196 BCE. Almost immediately after taking control, he showed that his talents weren't limited to the battlefield. He began an inquiry of public funds, discovering embezzlement and fraud. Hannibal managed to counter those issues by stabilizing state expenditure, even recovering some of the misappropriated funds. Furthermore, he reformed the government. The officials of the highest council in Carthage were to be chosen directly by the citizens, and they were banned from serving consecutively, though their mandates remained a year long.

Hannibal's changes made a dent in the rule of the oligarchs, but more importantly, it quickly revitalized the Carthaginian economy. The Romans immediately noticed this. Under the pretext of unresolved issues with the Numidians, in 195, they sent envoys to Carthage to supposedly settle the quarrel. Hannibal was wary of their intent, realizing the Latins likely wanted to imprison him. He knew that his position in Carthage was not as strong as before, so he simply ran. Hannibal traveled to the east, serving as a general and advisor to many kings, some of whom even fought against the Romans in later years. Hannibal died around 181 BCE without ever again playing an important role in Carthaginian history. Despite that, his reforms endured, bearing fruit to Carthage in later years. It wasn't long before the Carthaginian merchants once again started doing business across the Mediterranean. The various archeological evidence shows they traded with Italy, Spain, Greece, the Balkans, and the Azores. Their network was likely even more extensive than that. Most illustrative of their quick economic recovery was the fact that, in 191, they offered Rome to pay the remaining eight thousand talents of their indemnity at once. Despite warring in the east and needing the cash, the Romans refused, opting to leave the yearly payments as a symbolic sign of their supremacy over Carthage.

The Carthaginian offer also shows that the Punes were eager to remain on the good side of the Romans. Over the years, they acted more as trusted allies than former enemies of Rome. Only a year after their defeat, they sent a gift of 200,000 bushels of grain to Rome to aid their campaign against the Macedonians. In 191, along with the offer for the full payment of the indemnity, the Carthaginians offered a large quantity of grain, about 800,000 bushels of wheat and about 500,000 of barley, as a gift. The Romans declined the gift, opting to pay for the needed supplies. This failed donation showcases two crucial facts. One was that the agriculture of Carthage's remaining domain had recovered, while the other was that the Romans remained untrusting toward the Punes. Although many of the Latins traded and maintained connections with the Carthaginians, many still saw Carthage as a possible threat. The most famous example of this was Marcus Porcius Cato, a Roman senator, historian, and orator. He often finished his speeches with the words, "Carthage must be destroyed," even if his orations did not concern the Punes. In contrast, it seems that the Carthaginians were trying their best not to antagonize the Romans and follow the letter of their peace treaty. Most notably, they never tried to rebuild their military fleet, gather a larger army, or wage war against their aggressive Numidian neighbors.

The New City itself continued to grow, expanding to cover its once garden suburbs *Megara,* modern La Marsa. The period after the Second Punic War was also marked by public projects. Temples and palaces were being built, defenses strengthened, and most notably, its famed circular harbor known as Cothon was created. The work on the port itself may have started in the last years of the war, but it became fully functional only after the conflict ended. According to sources, it could hold 220 ships that would be protected from attacks or natural calamities. Some ancient and modern historians tried to link the construction of the harbor to an attempt to revive the Carthaginian military fleet. Yet it is more likely it was created and later expanded for commercial needs. The merchant fleet grew significantly by the mid-2nd century, following the rise in trade. The influx in trade also meant an increase in population. Modern estimates of Carthage for the first half of the 2nd century BCE usually range from 200,000 to 250,000 citizens, including the Libyan population but excluding the slaves. Without a doubt, it was still one of the largest cities of its time. The entire Punic dominion numbered around two to three million people, out of whom roughly 700,000 had citizenship rights, according to contemporary research. This meant that despite the territorial losses, Carthage still had sizable manpower potential.

Modern illustration of ancient Carthage.

Despite that, the Punes, over the course of about fifty years, never tried to draw from that potential. Their chief enemy was Roman-backed Numidia, which was ruled by power-hungry Masinissa. The Roman sources are rather sketchy about details, but it seems that in the decades after the Second Punic War, on several occasions, the Numidians and the Carthaginians became involved in territorial disputes. Some were coupled with Numidian incursions, to which Carthage usually remained passive. In one instance, one of the Roman historians mentions a more significant clash between the two nations. Nonetheless, most modern historians dispute this, as the Roman reaction was too mild and tepid for it to be true. However, the Latins did usually play the role of mediators, allowing for Numidian expansion over the Carthaginian domain. Their bias was evident; around 162 BCE, they ruled that the Numidians bore more ancestral rights to the land around Leptis Magna, including the old Phoenician colony. By 151 BCE, Carthage was confined to its territories in modern northern Tunisia, as the Numidians occupied all the other African lands it once controlled. Carthage's tax income and agricultural production were halved, slowly threatening its existence. The

Punes had had enough, so they gathered their troops and finally tried to oppose the Numidian attacks.

However, it was apparent that the Carthaginian army was no longer in shape to fight, as its generals lacked much-needed capabilities, and they were defeated and massacred by Masinissa's troops. It seems that the Romans brokered some kind of a truce, as the hostilities stopped. Despite that, it was reported to the Roman Senate that the Carthaginians had broken the peace treaty by waging war without its consent. Moreover, they waged it against a Roman ally. Realizing what they had done, the Punes sent their envoys to appease the Senate and avert war, but the Roman responses were vague and cryptic. While the Latins were deliberating on whether to go to war, Utica defected to the Romans, giving them an excellent base from where to begin their campaign. Since this older sister colony was ready to desert, it also signaled that the Carthaginian grip over what was left of its territory was slipping. In 149 BCE, Rome finally declared war. Their motives have been examined throughout the centuries. Some historians claimed that they wanted to exact revenge for Hannibal's destruction, others that the Romans only wanted to plunder Carthaginian wealth. Some scholars even argued that the Latins wanted to prevent the Numidians from conquering such an important city or that some of the younger generals needed a place to prove their worth. Whatever was the real incentive, the Romans sent an army of 84,000 soldiers to Africa to deal with the Carthaginians once and for all.

Realizing they had no choice, the Punes sent another embassy to Rome, offering unconditional surrender. They were ready to leave themselves at the mercy of the Latins. Unfortunately for them, the Romans had other plans. First, they asked for three hundred hostages from the leading Carthaginian families, which the Punes complied with. Then they asked for Carthaginian military supplies. The Punes surrendered no less than 200,000 sets of armor and 2,000 artillery pieces, as well as other weapons. Finally, showing their true intentions, the Roman consuls demanded that Carthage was to be abandoned and that all the Punes had to relocate ten miles (sixteen kilometers) inland. This was unacceptable to the Carthaginians, as it basically meant their destruction. At that point, the Carthaginians exploded in rage. They massacred all the Italian residents in the city, and they, too, officially declared war. The slaves were freed, while the squares and temples were turned into impromptu workshops. The entire population was involved in the war effort, illustrated by the supposed account of women cutting off their hair to make ropes for catapults. Simultaneously, the Carthaginian general Hasdrubal, who was in the countryside most likely defending it from the Numidians, was recalled to aid in the city's defense. But before he could come, the Romans marched south from Utica and besieged the city. In the meantime, the Numidians retreated to their territory, deciding not to aggravate the bloodthirsty Romans.

The war proved to be mostly one-sided, with only impregnable walls prolonging Carthage's demise. Initially, the Latin forces suffered some minor defeats and failures—most notably, their fleet was set ablaze by burning ships, which made the naval blockade of Carthage impossible for a while. The Punic army outside the city, roughly 30,000 strong, was capable only of harassing the besiegers. Nonetheless, Carthage still had some loyal cities left, most notably Hippacra, Nepheris, and Clupea-Aspis near Cape Bon. The loyalists were unable to supply their capital with troops or relieve any pressure, but they did send food and supplies. The Romans tried to capture some of these cities, mostly failing in the process. By 147 BCE, the war entered somewhat of a stalemate. The Romans continued besieging the city, but they were unable to achieve any considerable advance. More worryingly for them, their army was slowly losing its morale and discipline. On the other hand, Carthage was slowly running out of resources and was unable to inflict any noticeable damage to the invading troops. The tides of the war changed when Scipio Aemilianus, the adopted son of

Scipio Africanus's son, was awarded command over the African campaign.

Upon his arrival, he tightened the siege, cutting off all land communication. Furthermore, the Romans managed to finally enact a complete naval blockade with the new fleet, along with a newly built embankment near the Carthaginian port. To make matters worse for the besieged Punes, Hasdrubal, who managed to get back to the city before Scipio arrived, became the despotic ruler of Carthage. He reportedly murdered anyone who criticized his rule, living in luxury while the citizens slowly starved. Desertions and deaths in Carthage were rising, while its defensive capabilities were lowering. During the winter, in late 147 BCE, Scipio finally managed to defeat the Punic army in the countryside, prompting all of Libya to capitulate, including the Punic loyalists such as Hippacra. The Carthaginian fate was sealed. In the spring of 146, the Romans mounted their final assault. They managed to break into the city, but they were met by fierce resistance by its citizens, who fought to defend every single house from the attackers. Here, the scenes from the fall of Motya were reenacted, with Roman and Carthaginian troops fighting on the rooftops connected by wooden planks. Eventually, the Punes retreated to the heart of Carthage, to the Byrsa citadel, to hold their final stand. On the seventh day of the battle, when the Romans began to crack down on Byrsa, what was left of the Carthaginians surrendered.

A 19th-century illustration of the final assault on Carthage.
https://commons.wikimedia.org/wiki/File:Assaut_final_de_Carthage_en_146_av_J.-C.jpeg

By that time, only about 50,000 Carthaginians were left alive in the city, and all of them were sold into slavery. Hasdrubal, the last ruler of Carthage, surrendered as well, but his wife and children took their own lives. He was later brought back to Rome to be paraded as the defeated general. The city itself, now emptied, was razed to the ground. Everything worthy was taken, while all the buildings and walls were entirely and systematically destroyed with fire that supposedly lasted for seventeen days. While the city was burning, Scipio Aemilianus cursed anyone who might seek to once again reside in that place, finalizing the destruction of Carthage. The famous story of sowing the Carthaginian soil with salt is 19th-century fiction, as the sources tell us that the land on which Carthage once stood was used as public fields by local farmers. The supposed curse of the victorious Scipio was short-lived. By the time of Caesar in the mid-1st century BCE, Carthage was rebuilt by the Romans, and it quickly rose to become one of the largest, richest, and most important cities of the Roman Empire, a center of the Roman province known as Africa Proconsularis.

Thus, the once great and powerful Carthage, the jewel of the west, ended its story in a shameful and bloody defeat. At least, that was the fate of the republic. However, the Punic culture continued to live on in the Roman state for a long time after the Carthaginians had lost their independence until it slowly disappeared from the historical stage and our collective memory.

Chapter 7 – The Carthaginian Society and Government

Usually, when talking about Carthage and the Punes, they are mentioned as a single entity, without delving deeper inside their social fabric. This is generally done for the sake of simplicity, like in the previous chapters, but also because not many surviving sources talk about this issue. Yet, to fully understand the history of Carthage, we have to take a closer look at how their state and society actually functioned.

As has been mentioned, Carthage was founded as a Phoenician colony. The creation myth of Dido, as well as the fact that Tyre and other Phoenician cities were monarchies, suggests that, in its early days, the New City was also ruled by some sort of king or monarch. However, there are no sources that tell us more about the ancient Carthaginian past. It seems that at some point, most likely during the 7th century, the Carthaginians chose to abandon the monarchical system, opting for a republic instead. Why and how this exactly happened is unknown, but by the time Greek and Roman sources write about the Punes, their state was a well-developed republic. Nonetheless, the remnants of the old monarchy can be seen through the fact that the Carthaginian state was an oligarchy, as the authority was concentrated in the hands of what we could define as an aristocracy. However, it is worth noting that the ruling elite, unlike in some other societies, was not a small and exclusive group that primarily relied on ancestry as its defining attribute. Genealogy was, of course, important to the Punes, as many took great pride in their ancestors who achieved greatness. Still, with enough talent and wealth, any Carthaginian citizen could actually become a part of the aristocracy. It is also likely that if one lacked in both, one could lose that status.

Of course, the primary condition for becoming a member of the aristocracy was to have Carthaginian citizenship. Once again, there is no clear evidence of how the Carthaginians legally or socially defined themselves. Some sources indicate that citizenship was limited to adult male indigenous Carthaginians who could theoretically link their families to the founders. This meant that women, children, and foreigners were excluded from this status. It is worth mentioning that the sources don't suggest there was a minimum wealth criterion, but it possibly existed. In addition, some scholars have argued that the Carthaginian system recognized a semi-citizenship status. Though there is no straightforward evidence for this, it has been suggested that, in some cases, it was possible to achieve a lesser citizen status, which granted some benefits of citizenship like lower taxes but possibly banned a person from rising through the governmental ranks or participating in elections. All in all, on paper, the Carthaginian citizens had the same rights and obligations. However, as throughout history and even today, inequalities stemming from birth, wealth, education, and opportunity were present. This meant that certain aristocratic families, like the Magonids and Barcids, were able to achieve longer-lasting supremacies over the state and society. Common Carthaginians could, at certain times, play essential roles in the leadership of Carthage, but it was usually under the patronage of some aristocratic family or party.

From the Greek sources, we know that the Carthaginian citizens gathered in associations or smaller groups. These were known as *mizrehims*, and their members usually bonded over communal meals, similar to the ancient Greeks. Those associations were formed based on various things. Some were focused on the following of a certain god, while others were linked to the professions of its members. There are also signs that soldiers who served in the same units also formed their own *mizrehims*. However, there is no evidence that being a member of an association was obligatory to the Carthaginian citizens, nor does there seem to be a reason for it to be compulsory. There are no explicit depictions of any other roles these gatherings had other than social bonding. The sources don't mention if they played any role in the functioning of the assembly of the citizens, yet it seems likely they played at least an unofficial role in politics. It is not unimaginable that the *mizrehims* were used by the political elites to sway the popular vote in the assembly. In some cases, that would be of the utmost importance in Punic politics, as the citizen's assembly was, in fact, the broadest form of popular rule in the Carthaginian governmental system.

Punic ruins in Carthage on Byrsa hill.
https://commons.wikimedia.org/wiki/File:Quartier_Punique.JPG

The assembly was known as *ham* in the Punic language, meaning "the people." Like in the Greek cities, the *ham* gathered in the city's great marketplace, which was located southeast of Byrsa in the later centuries. How the assembly exactly functioned is unknown, as once again, surviving sources don't mention it. It has been suggested that the citizens voted in groups, maybe representing specific neighborhoods or clans, but so far, this is merely speculation. Nonetheless, it seems that through the centuries, the powers and influence of the assembly grew. The first possible mention of the *ham* is from the mid-6th century BCE when Malchus supposedly restored Carthage to its laws, treating the citizenry with reasonable respect. At the time, it seems the assembly was still more of a voice of the people than a genuine part of the governmental system. Later on, it gained the right to elect magistrates and government officials. Yet by the time of the Barcids and the Second Punic War, the assembly of the citizens had the power of ratification, at least to a certain degree, on the decisions made by the upper assemblies of the state. Aristotle also conveys that the *ham* was a place of debate, not only voting, praising the democratic nature of the Carthaginian government. Of course, it should be noted that the ancient notion of democracy is far different and less liberal than our modern ideals.

Yet, like in many modern republics, Carthage also had a small high council, usually called by its Roman name, the senate. In the Punic language, its name was *adirim*, roughly translated to "the great ones," invoking a feeling that this governmental body was superior to the *ham*. This authority most likely came from the fact that the *adirim* was the oldest governmental assembly. It seems it existed since the monarchical era, at first functioning as the king's advisory council of leading men of the city. Though there is no clear evidence for it, the historians think it is rather likely that the senate was responsible for ending the monarchy and instituting the republic, thus giving the *adirim* the theoretical supremacy in the state. Its influence was only greatened by the fact that all of its 200 to 300 members were from aristocratic families, though how they were precisely chosen is unknown. The *adirim*'s authority seems to have been rather broad. From the sources, we know that it was tasked with diplomatic decisions, matters of war and peace, treaties, etc. Its members also acted as judges, while the surviving sources hint at the fact that the *adirim* also played a role in the internal affairs of the state. However, like the *ham*, the sources don't mention how the *adirim* exactly functioned, leaving yet another aspect of the Carthaginian governmental system in the dark.

Besides the *ham* and the *adirim*, the Carthaginian state was also ruled by the *suffets*. The *suffets* were an annually elected pair of chief officials. The name we use for them is a Latinized version of the Punic *shophetim* or *shuphetim*, which is usually translated as "judge." Historians have concluded, though not with substantial evidence, that the *suffets* most likely existed in the form of actual judges in the time of the monarchy. Yet when the republic was instated, the *adirim* transformed the office into one of the high magistrates. It has been suggested that in the early days of the republic, there was only one *suffet*, but this cannot be proved. If that was the case, by later periods, two became the norm. Their authority was mainly executive, though it seems that at certain times they also proposed laws or decrees to the *adirim*. The remnants of the judicial roots of the *suffets* also remained as, in some instances, they presided in civil lawsuits. Yet, like other aspects of the Carthaginian government, much about the *suffets* remains shrouded in mystery. The exact nature of the high magistrate office has only been made more convoluted by the fact that that the Greek writers usually called them kings (*basileis*), even when Aristotle talks about them as elected officials. In turn, the Romans have used their terms, such as consuls or praetors, when talking about the *suffets*, inferring at least some similarities between them.

What seems to be certain is the fact that wealth and ancestry were a requirement for the office. However, there are no details about how much capital was required or how the distinction of birth was defined. From the sources, the scholars have deemed that in the early days of the republic, it was most likely the *adirim* who chose the *suffets*, but in later periods, at least from the 4th century BCE, this power was transferred to the *ham*. This was a sign of gradual democratization of the Carthaginian government, which was praised by the Greeks and condemned by the Romans. In fact, Aristotle, writing in the 4th century, admired the Carthaginian system as one in which the ideals of a monarchy, in the form of the *suffets*, an oligarchy, in the form of the *adirim*, and a democracy, in the form of the *ham*, intertwined, balancing each other out. However, this democratization was not intentional, nor was it fueled by some idealistic altruism or liberalism. The main power behind such developments was the fact that in the earlier republic, when the *suffets* and the *adirim* clashed, the *ham* broke the tie. Over time, the opinion of the people became more important, leading to the involvement of a broader public into political decisions. By the end of the Second Punic War, the Carthaginian government was democratized enough for the *ham* to vote in every major decision made by the other two groups. It was democratized enough for Polybius, a Roman historian and contemporary of the war, to deem that the Latins won because of their superior aristocratic political system.

Apart from these three central bodies of the Carthaginian governmental system, sources give us glimpses of other lesser offices, though they mainly remain opaque and mysterious. Aristotle mentions an institution of "pentarchies" or five-man commissions that delved into judicial and other vital matters. Beyond this, we have no other mentions of them. Still, the Carthaginian state likely had a number of commissions and bureaucrats who were appointed for a longer period, serving the state apparatus. The Punic inscriptions hint at the existence of commissions for sacred places and for supervising taxes, though none numbered exactly five members. Those inscriptions also attest to the existence of treasurers or accountants, *mehashbim* in

Punic, who dealt with the enforcement of tax payments. Above them stood a head treasurer, the *rab*, meaning "chief" or "head," who was in charge of the state finances. It seems likely that the *mehashbim* were his subordinates, but unlike them, the *rab* was a position with a time limit, most likely constrained to a year. Of course, the mentioned commissions and offices were probably only a part of the Carthaginian apparatus, but so far, there has been no evidence to shed more light on its complexity. The only additional details that we have is that one person was banned from holding two offices at the same time, like simultaneously being a *suffet* and a *rab*.

As for the nature of the Carthaginian political scene, we can see from many sources that corruption and misuse of held positions were rather prevalent, at least until Hannibal reformed the state after the Second Punic War. Besides that, we know that the Carthaginians were often divided into two or more political factions, usually centered around one leader, but they weren't officialized as parties like in modern republics. They were more fluid and everchanging. The struggle between factions was sometimes so high that they put the survival of Carthage at stake, though in some cases, all differences would be set aside to assure the New City wouldn't fall. The contested political landscape was only further complicated with military offices. Martial functions in the Carthaginian republic were separated from the civil offices, unlike the Roman state. The highest of them was *rab mahanet*, translated simply as general. However, despite the official segregation, it was possible to hold military and governmental positions at the same time. It wasn't unheard of that the *suffets* were also awarded military commands. Along with the disjunctions of offices came a military tribunal, known as the Court of One Hundred and Four. Additional details about the military branch of the Carthaginian republic will be given in the subsequent chapter about the Punic army.

A 19th-century painting of Carthage.
https://commons.wikimedia.org/wiki/File:William_Turner_-_The_Decline_of_the_Carthaginian_Empire.JPG

One thing is somewhat noticeable when looking at the entire Carthaginian government and politics. It does revolve quite openly around wealth. Whether it was about having enough of it to apply for the top state offices, being rich enough to be counted as part of the ruling aristocracy, or using it for simple bribery and corruption, the Carthaginians seemed to have been quite fond of money, orientating their entire state toward earning it. This goes rather well with the notion of the Carthaginians being primarily merchants interested only in profit and nothing else. However, these are mostly modern exaggerations, as the ancient sources rarely dwelled on such topics, focusing more on warfare and politics. Despite that, the Greek and Roman sources do praise the mercantile capabilities of the Carthaginians, giving an honorary title of the wealthiest city in the world to Carthage in several texts. Thus, despite supposedly having a merchant-run oligarchical republic where trade was everything, no surviving sources touch on the topic of the Carthaginian traders except a single Roman comedy. In *Poenulus* (*The Little Carthaginian*), a Punic merchant named Hanno is traversing the Mediterranean in search of his long-lost daughters.

The plot itself is less important, but in the play, Hanno is shown trying to sell various cheap items like pipes, ladles, lard, spades, nuts, and even "African mice." Through this comic representation, we are shown that the Carthaginians would trade in anything as long as it would turn a profit.

Though an exaggeration, this description in recent years has become increasingly accepted as plausible. The archeological evidence shows that the Carthaginians traded a wide variety of goods, from raw materials to finished products. In their wares, one could find various precious metals, like silver and gold, but also tin, copper, iron, animal skins, ivory, wool, amber, and incense. They also traded in foodstuffs like olives, olive oil, wine, cereals, salted fish, spices, herbs, and garlic. The crafted goods were also as variable as the raw products, including, among others, embroidered textiles, purple-dyed cloth, food utensils, various tools, furniture, jewelry, ceramics, eating utensils, glassware, and even weapons. This made the Carthaginians among the most versatile traders of their time, especially when we take into account the fact that they sold not only high-grade products but also cheaper low-grade items. They used them to trade with less-developed tribes in Iberia and Africa or anyone else willing to buy them. With that in mind, Hanno's fictional stock is more realistic than it would seem initially. Combining the archeological and written sources, it becomes clear that the Carthaginians were indeed avid traders, making it quite intriguing that they began minting coins only in the late 5th and early 4th centuries BCE.

Considering the coinage spread throughout the Mediterranean from the 6th century, this was a relatively late development for an advanced state like Carthage. However, this can be explained by the fact that most of their dealings were done with less-developed societies in the western Mediterranean, thus leaving them to use barter and weighed pieces of precious and semi-precious metals in trade. Herodotus claims they only accepted gold, but this seems like yet another exaggeration. The fact that the first coins were minted to be used as payments for the mercenaries proves that the barter economy was still functional for the Carthaginians even in the early 4th century. It also goes to show that the Carthaginian state was not run as a trading company by merchants merely trying to achieve a profit. However, the state did try to protect its own traders, both from the pirates and foreign competition. Carthage protected the former with its military fleet, while the latter it tried to achieve with trade agreements like it had with Rome in 509. It is also worth noting that there were state-run business ventures, but it is hard to distinguish between them and private endeavors, as many of the wealthy merchants were a part of the government.

Nonetheless, not all the aristocrats were merchants, or at least not entirely. From the early 5th century BCE, when Carthage began its expansion in the African hinterlands, the class of landowners also emerged. It is important to mention that there was a clear distinction between Carthage's city-territory that consisted of its immediate hinterlands, including Tunes and the Cape Bon Peninsula, subjected Libyan lands, and the territory of its African allies. Despite that, nothing barred the Carthaginians from owning property in all three areas. By the late 3rd century, the sources mention that the city-territory was developed enough to provide the Carthaginians with their needs, while the taxes from Libya covered the expenses of the state. That meant that the immediate hinterland of the city was capable of feeding its entire population, which numbered about 650,000 at the time. This coincides with the fact that Aristotle, as well as other ancient writers, praised the Carthaginians for their agricultural expertise, depicting their bountiful fields and filled granaries. This reached a point where a manual on estate management, in effect, a complete encyclopedia of farming, which was written by a retired Carthaginian general in the 4th century, was so acclaimed that the Romans saved it for themselves after the destruction of Carthage. Unfortunately, its text survives only as excerpts in the works of later Roman authors.

In those passages, the workers are mentioned, who, in fact, constituted a significant part of the Punic society. Among them were, of course, non-citizens, foreigners, and slaves but also common Carthaginians. Many of them were unskilled laborers like dockworkers, porters, or other physical workers. However, the exact relations between employers and workers, and their wages, are still much of a mystery for modern scholars. Above them were skilled artisans, producing various goods from tools and pottery to finer jewelry and glasswork. The expert craftsmen were so sought after in Carthaginian society that it has been suggested that foreign workers were possibly given the aforementioned semi-citizenship. This also refutes the usual depictions of Punes as mere middlemen in trade. Many of the goods they sold were made by their artisans and were, in fact, much sought-after in the Mediterranean world. Apart from the craftsmen, other skilled professions existed as well, like scribes, teachers, architects, and doctors, which were all needed to keep a bustling city like Carthage working. It was common for workers of the same trade to live in a specific area in the town, forming guilds to protect and improve their business. Of course, like the landowners, not all of them were rich and respected or owned a large workshop. Most of them lived thriftily in tightly packed neighborhoods in simple homes, some even living in multi-storied buildings, which would have housed several families.

On the margins of the Carthaginian society were two noticeable groups. One such group was the foreigners, who were always present in a cosmopolitan city like Carthage. They came from all over the Mediterranean, looking for their fortune in various ways. Like in many ancient societies, they were always clearly separated from the local population. However, the citizens of Carthage's allies were possibly treated somewhat better, at least having the same legal rights and once again conceivably falling in the semi-citizen category. The other marginalized group was women. Not much is known about their position in society, as sources remain almost dead silent about them. As mentioned, they were banned from having citizenship, which is in line with other ancient republics like Rome and Athens. This suggests that they lacked the legal rights of male Carthaginians, not to mention that they were surely not allowed to delve into the world of politics. Some women are mentioned in the temple dedications but never alone. They were always mentioned with their fathers, husbands, or brothers. Also, there are no records of women owning any businesses or properties. All that combined indicates, though not proves, that the majority of, if not all, women were unable to own anything. It seems that despite having a princess, Dido, as their founding figure, the Carthaginians, like most ancient societies, treated women as second- or even third-class members of their community.

The only group that had it worse than women were, of course, the slaves. Like in other ancient societies, the Carthaginians deemed slaves as a regular part of everyday life. A number of them were prisoners of war, but one could be enslaved for an unpaid debt or traded in the markets as a commodity. If a child was born to slave parents, it would also become a slave. The life of the slaves was no doubt harsh, but there are some indications that the Carthaginians treated some of them with a bit more leniency than was usual in the ancient world. The already mentioned manual on farm management suggests that one should not be too harsh on slaves in order to inspire loyalty and better productivity as a result. In other sources, we hear of slaves actually running businesses for their masters, amassing enough wealth for temple dedications or even gaining their own freedom. Though, it should be noted that even when freed, slaves were never fully integrated into society. In turn, except for the previously mentioned two major revolts, the Carthaginian slaves proved to be quite loyal, even fighting until the end alongside their masters in 146. That being said, it shouldn't be imagined that the life of the Carthaginian slaves was much better than in other societies of that time. Not everyone followed the instructions of the farm manual, and the slaves, regardless of that, lacked basic human rights, not to mention other aspects that make life worth living.

With all that has been said in this chapter, it is clear that the Carthaginian society had some unique traits, while others fit perfectly into the mold set by other better-known ancient civilizations. Yet the most glaring fact is that much about the Carthaginians remains a mystery still to be uncovered from the fog of time.

Chapter 8 – Army of the Carthaginian Republic

Even though the Carthaginians were never really considered to be a militaristic or warmongering state, warfare proved to be a significant part of their history. They often fought wars to preserve their dominance and expand their sphere of influence. Because of that, their army, despite not being the most impressive one in the ancient world, deserves a short overview as well.

At the head of the Punic army stood the *rab mahanet* (general), who was elected as a governmental magistrate, separating civil and military duties in the governmental system. This office proved to be more flexible than others, as the length of service was not fixed. One would serve as a general until the war was over or until he was recalled and substituted by another commander. Also, the number of active *rab mahanets* could vary depending on the needs of Carthage. In smaller conflicts, it was usually one or at most two commanders appointed, but in the Second Punic War, up to seven men, mostly from the Barcid family, held ranks of generals. It is also worth noting that generals also commanded the navy; there was no separate admiral rank title. However, a deputy or a second-in-command existed in some cases, holding the title of the *rab sheni,* roughly translated to "second general." Usually, generals had full autonomy in deciding the course of action, both in military and diplomatic decisions, though in some instances, the *adirim* or the *ham* needed to ratify peace treaties or truces. Another issue that sometimes came up was when two equally ranked generals led armies in the same area, raising the question of who held the higher command. It is also important to note that generals were always held accountable for their actions, with harsh penalties hovering above their heads.

In the early days of the republic, it seems that a general's competence was judged by the senate or some of the lesser commissions. However, by the late 5th and early 4th centuries, a special military tribunal was formed. Known as the Court of One Hundred and Four, it was supposedly the highest authority in Carthage. The number of members was deemed odd by modern historians, with some claiming it was more likely around one hundred. However, it's more likely that it constituted the one hundred members of the *adirim* and the four principal magistrates that were active. Once again, the question on how the judges were precisely chosen remains a mystery apart from Aristotle informing us it was based on merit. At first, the Court of One Hundred and Four was given authority over only the generals, but over time, it began to widen, allowing for subordinate officials to be judged as well. By the late 3rd century, it seems that the court began to infringe on other bodies' functions, instituting a somewhat despotic rule over Carthage. This was cut short by Hannibal's reforms, reducing the membership in the court from a life term to a single year.

Regardless of those reforms, the intended role of the One Hundred and Four to keep the generals in line and in the service of the senate and the people remains questionable. Most of the generals and members of the court were also aristocrats and members of the *adirim*. Thus, an accused general would be tried by his political enemies and allies, leading to a high possibility of a politicized tribunal that had little to do with merit or competence.

In addition, as the court had the right to execute the failed generals, usually in a gruesome fashion like crucifixion, it was a perfect constitutional platform to get rid of possible political rivals. Additionally, such pressure also backfired on many Carthaginian generals, prompting them to remain passive and overcautious, afraid of the repercussions of failure. In some cases, the defeated generals opted to take their own lives instead of waiting for the trial in front of the One Hundred and Four. Nonetheless, despite all its shortcomings, the Court of One Hundred and Four proved to be a long-lasting and quite important feature of Carthaginian military and political life.

Illustration of a Carthaginian hoplite
https: User:Aldo Ferruggia, CC BY-SA 3.0 <https://creativecommons.org/licenses/by-sa/3.0>, via Wikimedia Commons
https://commons.wikimedia.org/wiki/File:Carthaginian_hoplite_-_Oplita_cartaginese.JPG

Carthaginian horseman.
https://commons.wikimedia.org/wiki/File:Sacred_Band_cavalryman.png

The organization and structure of the Carthaginian army also passed through several stages throughout its history. In its earliest history, it was likely shaped upon the Eastern models, most likely following the Assyrian archetype. However, by the 6th century, the Carthaginians began reshaping their army according to the Greek model, basing their military upon the heavy spearmen in phalanx formation. At the time, the majority of soldiers were citizen recruits who were conscripted by the state. However, during the 5th century, the Carthaginians slowly began turning toward mercenaries. At first, they were just additional troops, but by the 4th century, they became the primary fighting force. This was done most likely to preserve the population of Carthage, which, despite its relative size, was unable to withstand prolonged wars with higher casualties. However, it seems that in most cases, the Carthaginians tried to retain their own officers among the mercenaries to ensure their loyalty. The mercenaries were recruited from all over the Mediterranean, most commonly from their African and Iberian domains, as well as southern Gaul, Greece, and southern Italy. It seems that the Greeks were especially valued, as in some cases during the 3rd century, their captains were given commands over the entire Carthaginian army due to their expertise.

In turn, this brought another change to Carthaginian warfare. Influenced by the Greek commanders, the Carthaginians accepted the Hellenistic combined arms model, which no longer relied solely on the phalanx. The new style also utilized both light and heavy cavalry, as well as the light infantry and skirmishes. In addition, the Carthaginian army also used war chariots and elephants. This made the Punic army much more versatile and adaptable, which was more suited for the wars with Rome, as they were on a much larger scale and broader fronts than the ones with the Sicilian Greeks, which was led mostly on a single island. Honed by the long Punic Wars, by the end of the 3rd century, the Carthaginian army was no longer a mish-mashed group of mercenaries gathered for a shorter altercation. It became more of a standing army with experienced commanders at its head. However, after the loss of the Second Punic War, the Carthaginian domain shrank, as well as its monetary power, leading to the downsizing of its military. There were fewer and fewer mercenaries, and once again, Carthage had to rely more on its citizens, though, in the last fifty or so years of its existence, the Carthaginians tried to avoid major conflicts. By the end of the Third Punic War, the Carthaginian military became a citizen militia, even aided by the slaves, as they tried and failed to ward off the Roman legions.

Due to its mostly mercenary basis, the Carthaginian army was quite fluid in composition, not always consisting of the same types of troops. However, throughout most of its history, an elite formation consisting of young aristocrats existed. The Greeks called it the Sacred Battalion, though no Punic name is mentioned. It consisted of about 2,500 young nobles trained in the Greek phalanx formation and equipped with the best quality armor. Prepared from a young age, they were said to be quite disciplined— the best Carthage could field. However, their track record was not that impressive. It seems that despite their drills, professional Greek soldiers were able to outmatch them in most cases. This may come from the fact that the Sacred Battalion was only fielded in times of crisis and quite rarely outside of Africa. That meant they fought mostly in tough battles against enemies who were stronger than usual. Besides the Sacred Battalion, other Carthaginian citizens usually served as heavy cavalry and officers, most of them also from wealthier classes. Their numbers were limited, serving mostly to ensure loyalty and discipline among the mercenaries and levied troops. In later periods, when citizens once again became prominent in the infantry, they used the Hellenistic phalanx as their basis. However, it's fair to assume they were not as viable as the Sacred Battalion was.

Other soldiers that served in the infantry were mercenaries from across the Mediterranean world, most of which also formed phalanx formations. Thus, they carried long spears, round shields, metal helmets, and tunics, as well as short swords and greaves. Some of the Celtic and Iberian tribes also provided skilled swordsmen, with the former preferring the long sword and the latter the short sword. Among the Libyan tribes, some preferred double-headed axes, as well as crescent-shaped shields. Interestingly, women warriors were also mentioned among those African mercenaries. How many, if any, were present remains a question, though. Archers were also deployed, like the expert Moors and Cretans, but in far lesser number than in most other armies. Among the ranged units, the Balearic slingers were especially distinguished. They were famed for the precision of their slingshots, making them perfect for initial skirmishes and harassment of enemy lines. However, for harassing enemies, the preferred type of troops among the Carthaginian generals were the light cavalry. These soldiers were also mercenaries, usually equipped with lighter armor, javelins, and short swords. They were capable of maneuvering across the battlefield easily, making them more versatile than the heavy cavalry of the Carthaginian aristocrats, which usually could only dive straight into the enemy lines. The Numidians were considered the best light cavalry, followed by the Iberians and Moors.

Balearic slinger
https://commons.wikimedia.org/wiki/File:Balearic_Slinger.jpg

Iberian infantry
Museo de Prehistoria de Valencia, CC BY-SA 2.0
<https://creativecommons.org/licenses/by-sa/2.0>, via Wikimedia Commons
https://commons.wikimedia.org/wiki/File:Guerrer_Iber_-_MPV.jpg

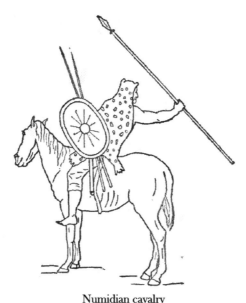

Numidian cavalry
https://commons.wikimedia.org/wiki/File:Numidian_cavalry.png

Other mounted units were used as well. War chariots were used up to the 3rd century before being abandoned as too impractical for any terrain apart from flat open fields. The chariots usually had two-man crews, with a driver and an archer or spear thrower. With scythes on the wheels, they were supposed to crash into the enemy lines, causing disarray and panic. However, they mostly failed in their role as mobile field artillery, leading to them being replaced by the famed war elephants of Carthage. The Carthaginians used now-extinct North African elephants (*Loxodonta africana pharaohensis*), which were smaller than its living African cousin. Reaching only about eight feet (2.5 meters), these animals were likely not large enough to carry a wooden tower as the Indian war elephants did. Still, they were capable of carrying one rider and one archer. However, this assumption has been widely debated as they were often depicted as having a tower on their backs, leaving scholars without any conclusive decision. Regardless of that, the main goal of the war elephant was the same as the chariots. They were to charge the enemy lines and create gaps for infantry and cavalry to exploit. Adding to the fact that they had long tusks, maybe even adorned with additional spears, the elephants were, if anything, a psychological weapon capable of inflicting fear into Carthage's enemies.

Despite being rather famous for the use of elephants, especially after Hannibal crossed the Alps with them, the war elephants in Carthaginian warfare proved to be rather ineffective. When they fought against well-trained enemies, like the Roman legions, the elephants were unable to instill fear, especially after the first surprise encounter. Even worse, they were known to get frightened or anxious and turn on the Carthaginians themselves. Additionally, like the chariots, the elephants had trouble fighting on non-flat battlefields. Thus, the war elephants proved to be more of a symbol than functional mobile field artillery. In contrast, the regular siege artillery of the Carthaginians was rather useful. Those were mostly used in the wars in Sicily, as most of the cities there were well-fortified. In this aspect, the Carthaginians once again learned from the Greeks, adopting their catapults and crossbows. Less sophisticated weapons were also used, like battering rams and siege towers, while tactics of mining and building mounds were employed to bypass enemy walls. Besides using the artillery for offensive purposes, the Carthaginians used them for defense as well. They at least equipped their own capital with artillery weapons to add an additional deterrent to possible invaders.

Another important part of Carthaginian warfare was the tactics they used. In the earlier days of employing the Greek hoplite formation, it is likely they used a similar straight-on tactic of the Greeks. A wall of hoplites would directly clash with the enemy, where their raw strength and endurance were the key elements. In such clashes, there was little maneuvering, and if some were capable of outflanking the enemy, it usually proved to be decisive. However, with the later development of the Hellenistic combined warfare, it was this maneuvering that became vital for victory. Despite that, the heavy phalanx infantry, which was lacking in maneuverability, remained at the center of the Carthaginian army.

With its high defensive capabilities, it was there to take on the brunt of the enemy attacks. The lighter infantry was on its immediate flanks, protecting them while also trying to flank the enemy. On the outer flanks stood the cavalry. Its first task was to harass the enemy lines before either clashing with enemy horsemen or trying to outflank the enemy army. The heavy cavalry was also sometimes used to break the enemy's formation. Moreover, the cavalry was occasionally used to set up ambushes and attack from behind. Yet, with the use of Hellenistic warfare, the battles became less predictable, and the tactics varied depending on the circumstances, making this description of Carthaginian tactics less of a rule and more an oversimplified generalization.

Finally, when talking about the Carthaginian army, its fleet also needs to be mentioned. According to the ancient sources, at its height, the Punic armada numbered about 350 warships. Those were large ships, powered by both sails and oars, with two steering oars on both sides of the stern. Although some historians argue if both rudders were used simultaneously, ancient sources hint at this. It possibly explains why they considered the Carthaginian ships to be the most maneuverable on the battlefield. As for the armaments, the Carthaginians principally used bronze rams mounted on the prow, below the surface, using it to puncture enemy vessels. Unlike land warfare, in the naval battles, there were usually two simple overall tactics, one in which the ships tried to ram the enemy head-on. In the other, a flanking maneuver would be attempted. Different tactics were possible but less common. In battles, the oars were the primary source of propulsion, allowing for more reliable and consistent speeds. However, it was also important not to penetrate the enemy ships too much, as it could lead to a Carthaginian ship getting stuck. It is worth noting that these tactics were not solely used by the Carthaginians, as it was a common way of fighting among the civilizations of the ancient Mediterranean.

In addition to ramming, it was also commonplace to use javelins or other missiles against foes. However, unlike the Romans, the Punes avoided boarding enemy ships. Heavier artillery was usually avoided, as it made the vessel unstable, even in later periods when the vessels were larger. Early in Carthaginian history, the primary type of ship used was a trireme, named after having three rows of oars on each side. These were no small vessels, though. They fit 180 rowers, plus additional crew members, and the ship itself was usually about 120 feet (37 meters) long and about 16 feet (5 meters) wide. The origins of the trireme, used across the Mediterranean, are disputed. Some researchers claim the Carthaginians themselves developed it, while others ascribe it to their Phoenician brethren. However, as time went by, the idea of making larger ships that were more impervious against ramming drove the Punes to be the first one to develop the quadrireme, a larger version of a trireme with four rows of oars. Eventually, a quinquereme, a ship with five rows of oars, was developed by Dionysius of Syracuse, but it was quickly adopted by the Carthaginians, becoming their primary type of battleship. It was about 147 feet (45 meters) long, 16 feet (5 meters) wide at water level, while its deck was around 10 feet (3 meters) above the surface. It required about 420 seamen to fully man it, out of whom no less than 300 were rowers.

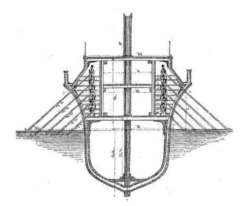

A 19th-century diagram of a quinquereme ship.
https://commons.wikimedia.org/wiki/File:Penteres.png

The crews of the Carthaginian ships were, unlike the ground forces, made up almost exclusively of the Punes themselves. Though mostly from the lower classes, the Carthaginian seamen were considered among the best in ancient times due to their extensive training. This was only helped by the fact that many of the Punes were already familiar with the sea as merchants. However, it's worth noting that in the last two hundred years of Carthaginian history, their navy had lost its edge from inactivity. The majority of the crew were rowers, who, besides rowing, were expected to take arms and fight if the ships were beached or boarded by the enemy. Additionally, there were marines and archers, trained soldiers whose sole purpose was to fight. Above all of them were three officers, one of whom was the navigator. Above them stood only the chosen admiral of the entire fleet. The fleet itself had a variety of purposes. During peacetime, it safeguarded Carthaginian merchants both from pirates and from competitors that were supposedly trespassing into Carthaginian waters. In times of war, besides fighting off the enemy navy, the fleet also served for transporting armies and supplies, raiding the enemy coast, and aiding in sieges through naval blockades. Additionally, they could disrupt the enemy supply convoys and even relieve and resupply besieged Carthaginian cities or forces.

All in all, when considering all the facts, the Carthaginian army, both its ground and naval forces, proved to be one of the better ones of ancient times. If nothing else, it was one of the rare forces that were able to knock on the doors of Rome itself. Despite that, only a handful of its components originated in Carthage but were instead imported from other places, both in manpower and in technology and tactics. That was a two-sided blade. It allowed the Carthaginians to follow the best military trends. Yet, once it stopped evolving, their army and navy quickly became obsolete. In the end, that was what happened. During their clashes with the Greeks, they were willing to learn from their enemies, adopting the hoplite formation as well as the later Hellenistic type of armies.

However, after clashing with the Romans, the Carthaginians were not quick enough to realize the advantages of the Roman style of warfare, leading to their ultimate demise.

Chapter 9 – The Punic Civilization

Often when talking about Carthage and the Punes, the focus is solely on their wars against Rome and the Greeks, maybe on their mercantilism and economy as well. Yet it is rare to delve on the topic of their culture and religion; it is almost as if that aspect of their society is less important or, even worse, nonexistent. However, the truth is that the Punes had quite a developed civilization that is worthy of our attention.

One of the most important aspects of Carthaginian culture was no doubt their religion, like in all other ancient societies. Like many others throughout history, the Punes believed in a multitude of gods. The basis of their pantheon was the Phoenician one, as the early settlers brought their old beliefs with them. However, not much is known about the exact mythology behind the gods. We do know which were the most respected deities, like, for example, Melqart and Baal and his many incarnations. Melqart was originally the god protector of Tyre, a role which he most likely had in Carthage as well. Later on, the Greeks saw Heracles (the Roman Hercules) in him, leading to a cult of Melqart-Heracles spreading across the Mediterranean. As a hero-god, many generals, including the Barcid family, worshiped Melqart keenly. Baal was the chief god, like Zeus or Jupiter, but he had many incarnations that may have been praised as separate deities. In Carthage, Baal Hammon was the chief god, as well as the god of weather and fertility of vegetation. Other important gods were Eshmun, the god of renewal and healing; Reshef, the god of fire; and Rasap, the god of war. Less significant Phoenician deities in the Punic religion were Semes, the sun goddess; Hudis, the god of the new moon; Kese, the god of the full moon; Hawot, the goddess of the dead; and Kusor, which had a female form of Kusarit, god/goddess of intelligence.

Yet not all deities were directly taken from the old Phoenician religion. For example, a major Carthaginian goddess, Tanit, which in later periods surpassed both Melqart and Baal in importance, was most likely not worshiped in Phoenicia. Her origins are disputed, as some researchers argue the Punes created her. In contrast, others trace her beginnings as an insignificant servant of the Phoenician goddess Astarte. Often coupled with Baal, Tanit was the goddess of fertility, life, and motherhood. She is also the only Carthaginian deity that had her own symbol, at least that is known today. It was a triangle with a horizontal line and a sphere above it, a stylized representation of a woman in a dress spreading her arms. Besides the Phoenician and original Punic deities, the Carthaginians also accepted gods of other neighboring nations. Among more prominent ones were the Greek Demeter and Persephone, whose worship began in 396 BCE after the Carthaginians burned their temple in Syracuse, which was seen as the cause for the ensuing disasters that followed. Another borrowed deity was the Egyptian Isis, which came through close trading relations among the two nations. Other gods were surely worshiped, though. Some may have been brought by the immigrants and settlers that came to Carthage during its long cosmopolitan history, yet their existence is unclear. The Greek and Roman sources tend to call all Punic deities with the names of their gods, making it hard to decipher the exact Punic pantheon.

A 4th-century bust of goddess Tanit

Symbol of Tanit on a stele

Likewise, there is little information on the theology and practice of religion among the Carthaginians. They had a multitude of temples, likely resembling the old Phoenician sanctuaries with two large columns, one on either side of the entrance, leading into a three-chambered interior. Inside it would be a large bronze bowl with an eternal flame instead of a representation of a particular deity. Religious life was maintained by a number of priests, known as *kohanim*, led by a head priest with the title of *rab kohanim*. He was possibly linked with preserving the cult of Melqart and performing yearly death and rebirth rituals of this god. The higher priestly titles were reserved for the aristocratic families and were considered quite significant. The *rab kohanim* was even a member of the *adirim*. Beneath him were chief priests of particular temples, who would have been aided by lesser priests. It has been suggested that female priestess also existed, but their role and importance is unknown. However, it seems that the temples were off-limits to common women. In addition to the religious functions, the priests may have had some hand in education and the upkeep of libraries. As for the belief system itself, we have little clues to go on. It was common for the aristocratic families to have patron deities, whom they worshiped in various ways, like providing patronage to a temple. Besides that, it is hinted that the Punes believed in the afterlife as they placed their eating and drinking utensils in tombs to accompany the dead.

The exact rituals performed by the priests also remain a mystery, but it has been suggested the majority of them were practiced outside of the temples, including prayers, ritual dances, burning incense, and making offerings to the gods at a specially dedicated altar. Apart from offering them various foods, drinks, and animals, it is hinted they also practiced human sacrifice. Many ancient sources mention that yearly sacrifices of children to Baal were made on a sacred site, which historians today call the *tophet*, located south of Byrsa. According to them, those were made to appease the gods. However, the archeological evidence suggests otherwise. Upon closer examination, it seems that most of the remains in the *tophet* were infants and stillborn babies, almost all of whom died of natural causes. That suggests that the *tophet* was nothing more than a children's cemetery. However, it is possible that they did perform human sacrifices in times of utmost crisis, like a Syracusan invasion or some great pestilence. Some of the Roman and Greek writers actually state such claims, writing that the sacrificed kids were of the ages between six and twelve, sometimes even older. This could be the reason why only a handful of the remains in the *tophet* were of older children. If the sacrifices were real, it's likely they weren't performed at the *tophet* and that the sacrificed children were not related to the people offering them as a tribute, despite what the sources claim. It is also worth noting that *tophets* were also found across several Punic and Phoenician colonies across the Mediterranean.

Remains of the Carthaginian tophet.
User: (WT-shared) Shoestring at wts wikivoyage, CC BY-SA 4.0
<https://creativecommons.org/licenses/by-sa/4.0>, via Wikimedia Commons
https://commons.wikimedia.org/wiki/File:Tophet,_Carthage,_Tunisia.JPG

The case of child sacrifices showcases the constant issue with Carthaginian history. Most of our accounts have been written by the Greeks and the Romans. This doesn't mean the Punes didn't write about themselves, but rather, as with many other aspects of the Carthaginian civilization, their literary works were lost. As it was mentioned previously, we know some of their authors wrote about agriculture and farming, hinting that others may have written about other aspects of the economy, possibly trade. From the travel logs of Hanno, though they are known to us only from Greek excerpts, it is clear they also wrote about sea voyages and explorations. The question about written histories or annals is still a matter of debate. Some think that historiography wasn't a developed genre in Carthage, explaining the lack of Punic history books. However, others point out that Hannibal left personal accounts of his campaigns in Hera's temple in southern Italy, while in Carthage, an inscription was found that reports on actions taken in Sicily in 406 BCE. This indicates that the Punes did write about at least their military exploits. Coupled with that is the fact that we know they took great pride in their ancestry, meaning they took an interest in family history. That together suggests that the Carthaginians were, in fact, familiar with the historiographical genre and were indeed practicing some form of it. This suggests that Punic histories existed but were not saved.

Other genres are also hinted by Greek and Roman accounts, like philosophy and poetry. However, again, we have little factual evidence about those works. The main reason is the fact that the Romans had little desire to preserve them, proved by the fact that they gave almost all of the Punic libraries to the local African kings in 146. However, through the preserved inscriptions, we know that Carthaginian literary accomplishments were written in what we today call the Punic language. As it's easy to assume, early Carthaginians spoke the Phoenician language. However, over time, they developed their own distinct dialect thanks to the influences of the local Berber population, as well as from their trading partners and immigrants. Nonetheless, they kept using the Phoenician alphabet, which is, in fact, the blueprint for both Latin and Greek alphabets. Like the Phoenicians, the Punes wrote without vowels from right to left in horizontal lines. Thanks to its likeness with other Semitic languages, researchers today can decipher most of it, though there are still many uncertainties and debates about some of the translations of the Punic inscriptions. The Punic language itself survived long after the fall of Carthage, transforming into Neo-Punic, which was spoken in parts of northern Africa until about the 6th century CE.

Unlike the literary works, Carthaginian art has been preserved at least to some degree. Yet there are some limitations to what has been found, as the majority of items were found in graves and temples. This could explain why most of them had religious motifs, though there is no evidence that profane art differed much in that aspect. Regardless of that, their visual arts show a similar path of development as the rest of their culture. The oldest influence was, of course, the old Phoenician style, with common eastern or Mesopotamian motifs, though early on, Egyptian art caught on as well. Somewhat unexpectedly, the Egyptian influence proved to be quite strong and long-lasting. Later on, the Etruscan style also began to permeate Carthaginian art; however, it was the Greeks who became a primary influence in later periods. Ironically, the Greek fad began in the 5th century, after the Punes had looted prosperous Greek cities in Syracuse. The Carthaginian artists reproduced all of these styles, and to the finest level, despite the outdated belief that they mainly imported high-quality art products. However, in some cases, it is hard to determine if an item was locally made or imported. That being said, the Carthaginian artisans and craftsmen weren't just mere copiers of others. In time, they began to merge and blend various styles and motifs to create art pieces unique to the Punic culture.

Among the most commonly found items are small figurines, usually of some goddess or in some cases of Melqart. These were often buried with the deceased or given as offerings in temples. Early types of these statuettes are quite simple; the female figurines have flat-topped heads and cylindrical bodies, while Melqart is posed sitting on a throne with a raised hand in blessing. With the arrival of Greek influences, the figurines were made with Greek clothing and robes. Yet the Punes never made nude statuettes, unlike the Greeks. It is worth noting that these clay figurines were also painted, like in other ancient cultures. Other notable themes for these small sculptures were female figures playing tambourines or flutes. In some cases, there was a blend of influences, such as the winged-depictions of Isis wearing a typical Egyptian wide collar with Greek robes. Other commonly found items are various vessels shaped like animal heads, such as ducks and cows. Most of these were made from clay. However, not all Punic art was static, as shown by figurines of dancing females, usually made in ivory, and a relief of a fully galloping armed horseman, followed by his dog. One of the more distinctively Punic motifs were slightly more abstract faces, usually grinning, which were also found on various statues that were mixed in with the other elements mentioned above.

However, this motif of a grinning face was far more common in clay masks, which the Punes used to ward off evil spirits. These masks are small and not actually made for wearing but were instead usually placed in tombs or hung on walls. With stylized features like ferocious grins and staring eyes, often painted in vivid colors, these votive masks are somewhat unique to the Carthaginians. Another type of mask commonly found is of a smiling woman's face, without any grotesque features, which was more in line with Greek influences. The motif of faces and heads was translated into jewelry as well. A common item among the Carthaginians were necklaces made out of glass beads in the shape of male heads. Those were also colorful, with staring eyes, curly hair, and beards. Besides glass, these beads, as well as other jewelry items, were made out of precious metals and pearls. Other items like earrings, pendants, bracelets, and diadems were commonly decorated with Egyptian motifs of lions, falcons, and lotus blossoms, as well as various gods and more Punic images like palms and eyes. It seems that jewelry was worn by anyone who could afford them, regardless of sex. Amulets of glass paste and semi-precious stones and scarabs were also made with Egyptian symbols and gods, and they were worn for magical protection and as a class symbol. The Greek influence was more prominent in intaglios, small engraved gems, which commonly depicted scenes from Greek mythology.

The Carthaginians also created other decorative objects like bowls, jars, and vases, and more famously painted ostrich eggs. These were ornamented with various geometric forms, palms, and lotus blossoms, commonly in red paint. Similar symbols can be found on metal jewelry boxes, as well as mirror handles, which were sometimes carved from ivory or wood. Of course, besides those, deities were also engraved. The colorful glass was also used to create smaller vessels, usually two-handled, which were commonly used for storing perfumes and ointments. This type of glassware was common across the Mediterranean, but the Carthaginian ones are characterized by dark blue glass adorned with white, yellow, green, and turquoise stripes, colors commonly seen in other Carthaginian art pieces. Among the representations of Carthaginian art are coins as well. Though not meant to be artwork, these often exhibited an impressive artistic quality. The most common motifs were a horse or a horse's head, a palm tree, and the profile of a goddess or god. The goddess was usually Tanit, less commonly Dido or Isis, while the god was typically Melqart, commonly depicted as Heracles. Other less common elements were lions, elephants, or war elephants, as well as warships prows. The latter two were struck by the Barcids in Spain. Notably, the craftsmanship and quality of design worsened with lesser denominations, which were made out of bronze. The style of these coins is clearly based on the Sicilian Greek coins, even though the motifs are distinctively Carthaginian.

A Carthaginian coin with depictions of goddess Tanit and a horse.
Classical Numismatic Group, Inc. http://www.cngcoins.com, CC BY-SA 2.5
<https://creativecommons.org/licenses/by-sa/2.5>, via Wikimedia Commons
https://commons.wikimedia.org/wiki/File:Carthage,_c.350-320_BC,_Stater.jpg

On a larger scale, there are a lot of Carthaginian stone stelae preserved in various cemeteries and *tophets*. They were placed above tombs, as markers or possibly altars, and were carved with reliefs of diverse religious natures. The most common symbols depicted were the symbols of Tanit, as well as the sun and crescent moon; there were, of course, also other religious motifs alongside these ones. In some cases, they were engraved with a commemorative inscription. In later periods, the decorations became more complex, once again mixing various styles. One example of that is a stele with a carved Greek Ionian column holding an Egyptian sphinx, with stylized Punic palms above it. By the last century, Carthaginian artists began adorning stelae with animal and human figures, hand motifs, and even in some cases with attempted portraits. At times, instead of stelae, the Punes opted for stone ossuaries or sarcophagi, which were used to preserve the deceased remains. The early ones bore clear Egyptian marks and symbols, with a two-dimensional representation of the departed. With the arrival of the Hellenistic influences, the figures became three-dimensional, combining, in some cases, Egyptian motifs and the Greek style. It's worth noting that not all of the ossuaries were of a full length of a human, and it seems that most, if not all, of them were colored. It is also likely that they were used only by wealthier classes.

Similar development and style can be seen in the Punic architecture as well. Though most of Punic Carthage was destroyed, there are remains of Punic constructions in the Carthaginian colonies, while carvings on stelae and the writing in ancient sources also shed some light on the topic. Common homes were usually built with mud bricks with flat roofs. Usually single storied, some went up to six floors high, at least according to the sources. These simple homes tend to be more evocative of Phoenicia and Egypt than the Greek-Roman world. The temples were similarly flat-roofed, clearly derived from the same eastern traditions. Older ones had geometrical and Egyptian-styled symbols on their entablatures, which were further adorned with columns on their porches. Larger temples also had courtyards for ceremonies. With the arrival of the Hellenistic influences, the columns became fluted, usually decorated with Ionian or Doric capitals, though, in some cases, the Punic palm was also used. However, it was rare to see a clear copy of Greek-styled temples, with the two-sided sloping roof and the triangular facade. The mixing of styles is, however, most evident in mausoleums found across the Punic world. One, about 69 feet (21 meters) high, has three tiers. The first tier is cubic and adorned with a relief of chariots on each vertical face. On top of this is the second square, slightly narrower and decorated with Greek columns. The third tier is also narrower but rests on a pedestal, which has horsemen on its corner. Finally, topping it all off is a low pyramid on another pedestal adorned with sea-nymphs.

The architecture, like all other aspects of the Punic civilization, exhibits their tendency to adopt and adapt the influences of other nations and cultures, using what suited their tastes to create an original and unique creation. Thus, paradoxically, the Punic culture seems to have been derivative of others, as well as being creative and original.

Conclusion

The Carthaginians are usually seen as the glorious yet defeated enemies of the Greeks and Romans, the greedy merchants that would do anything for a coin. However, this guide hopefully counters some of these prejudices that started back in ancient times. Instead of seeing the Carthaginians as a two-dimensional nemesis of two better-known civilizations, this book has tried to present them as a worthy civilization on their own. From humble beginnings, with great explorations and expansion, to their crumbling fall, the Carthaginians created their own path, their own story, and it consisted of more than just soldiers and traders. They created their own art, farmed lands, and wondered about the world around them. They built cities and traveled across the Mediterranean, transporting not only goods and resources but also other more valuable things like ideas and knowledge. They were not afraid to learn from anyone, not even their supposedly sworn enemies. Their openness went in the other direction as well, as their city gates were open for many migrants and new settlers, from wherever they may be from, leading to a cosmopolitanism seen in their entire civilization—a trait that is more reminiscent of the modern global world than ancient societies.

That kind of cosmopolitanism, in a way, makes their entire culture seem like a scrapbook of borrowed ideas and images. Yet it shows how adaptive they really were, as they were often capable of overcoming various hurdles and losses. Not afraid to learn, they accepted when others knew something they didn't. In that, the Carthaginians were capable of making their own unique creations, something undeniably Punic, yet something so hard to pinpoint precisely, as it shared so much with so many other civilizations. They were, in fact, a truly global culture. Some see this as a negative thing, as if they refused to accept the achievements of others. However, the history of Carthage teaches us that once we stop learning and adapting, we fail. After they were defeated by Rome for the second time, the Carthaginians were not quick enough to adjust and absorb the new Roman ideas, leading to their fall. Yet even though they were finally defeated, their culture continued to live on for centuries, influencing many others to come after them.

Part 2: Minoans

A Captivating Guide to an Essential Bronze Age Society in Ancient Greece Called the Minoan Civilization

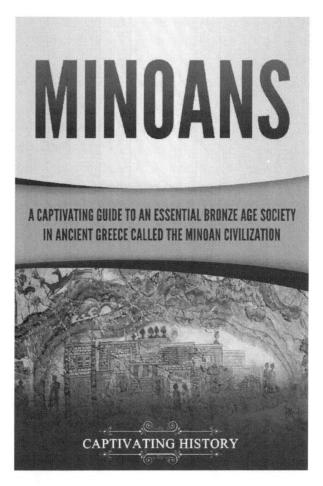

Introduction

The Minoans continue to be an intriguing subject for modern audiences because they are like a puzzle missing half of its pieces. Individuals have a rough idea of what it might look like, but there could be surprises no one even thinks of because all traces of the image are gone. For archaeologists, historians, tourists, scholars, fans of mythology, and students of the ancient world, the Minoans are this broken puzzle.

The Minoans were an ancient civilization that built their settlements on islands in the Aegean Sea. They lived almost 5,000 years ago and left behind traces of their lives but not enough for people to create a complete picture. Ever since the early 20th century, the Minoans have been a subject of interest thanks to the discoveries and excavations by Sir Arthur Evans, a British archaeologist who found the first Minoan ruins and named them after the mythological King Minos and his Minotaur. Evans was able to gain almost sole access to the lands of the Cretan government for excavation by paying for it with funds generated by his supporters in 1900. He and his crew unearthed the massive palace complex of Knossos, one of the most famous archaeological excavation sites in history.[1]

From the work of Evans and others, the puzzle of the Minoans has slowly gained more pieces. Through the study of material culture, modern audiences now know quite a bit about artistic techniques, favorite subjects, fashion, daily life, gender roles, and who the Minoans traded with. An observer can tell that the Minoans were a seafaring mercantile civilization, that they built magnificent urban centers, and that they had a form of writing. However, much remains a mystery. We, as a global culture, have almost no idea about Minoan history.

Who were their enemies?

Did they war with their neighbors?

Did they have great monarchs and nobles?

Who was the snake goddess in their sculptures?

Did they really practice human sacrifice?

Were women the true leaders of religion?

What on earth was bull-leaping?

Perhaps most importantly: Which catastrophes weakened the civilization enough that they were overrun by their militaristic neighbors on mainland Greece?

This volume is less of a history and more of an interpretation and description of archaeological findings based on the testimonies and research of hundreds of scholars in the field. Based on the information contained herein, what do you, the reader, think the Minoans were like?

---

[1] Rodney Castledon, *Minoans: Life in Bronze Age Crete*, Routledge: Philadelphia, 1993.

Chapter 1 – Where and When Did the Minoans Live?

The Minoans were one of the Aegean Bronze Age civilizations that lived on islands like Crete and other landmasses on the Aegean Sea. They were a seafaring people who built their settlements on a series of small islands near modern-day Greece, and evidence indicates they traveled across the entirety of the Mediterranean Sea to trade with nearby cultures. The Minoans lived from c. 2700 BCE-c. 1100 BCE. When it comes to years, the designation BCE stands for Before Common Era, or before the contemporary year 1 in the modern Gregorian calendar. The Minoans would have therefore lived almost 5,000 years ago.

The World of the Minoans

The Bronze Age was a period in human development where civilizations were capable of creating bronze weapons and tools. Other requirements to be considered a Bronze Age civilization were possessing some form of writing as well as urban civilization. To create bronze, the Minoans would have been able to smelt copper and alloy with other metals like tin and components like arsenic. The Minoans were actually one of the first people to master the ability to not only create bronze but also trade it with other civilizations that were unable to mine the necessary materials.

According to Homer, the Minoans supposedly built 90 settlements on the island of Crete and numerous towns on the small islands nearby. Archaeologists have found concrete evidence of Minoan civilization only on Crete and a nearby cluster of islands originally called Thera, now known as Santorini. Crete is, by far, the most significant of the two areas because the majority of surviving Minoan artifacts have been found at large sites like Knossos, which archaeologists believe was the capital of Minoan civilization.[2] Although small, there is evidence indicating the population of Knossos grew rapidly and attracted the Minoan social and cultural elite. Estimates state that the city's population was 1,300 to 2,000 in 2500 BCE, 18,000 in 2000 BCE, 20,000 to 100,000 in 1600 BCE, and 30,000 in 1360 BCE.

Numerous artifacts come from Minoan palace structures which managed to survive the Mediterranean climate, attacks by enemies, and even a tsunami that devastated parts of Crete during the Late Minoan Age. Palaces tended to be massive stone structures with multiple rooms for storage, recordkeeping, and habitation. Other important sites for information and artifacts are caves where objects from ritualistic cult worship have been uncovered, as well as hamlets that contained pottery fragments. Some of the most significant locations for Minoan information, besides Knossos, are Phaistos, Agia Triada, Vasiliki, Arkalochori, and Akrotiri.

[2] Ibid.

Some of the people the Minoans traded and interacted with were the Egyptians, the civilizations on mainland Greece, the societies of the Levant, the peoples of Anatolia, and potentially eastern European civilizations in places like contemporary Romania. Many Minoans spent their life on the sea, traveling, fishing, and trading. Unlike other ancient civilizations, the Minoans had no need for a large standing army because they were surrounded by water on all sides and there weren't many powerful navies in the region. Instead, the Minoans stayed safe by shoring up their vessels and warding off pirates.

Excavations

A big problem when studying a civilization as ancient as the Minoans is that records were scarce and what did exist has suffered thousands of years of erosion and devastation. The Minoans, in particular, were a small group that did not keep many records, and while they did have the writing system of Linear A, the existing documents are currently untranslated and unintelligible. Even worse, their homeland islands were hit by several disasters, including a massive volcanic eruption and a tsunami, as well as the conquest by their neighbors on mainland Greece, the Mycenaeans.

To obtain information about the civilization, archaeologists and other professionals excavate significant sites to find artifacts and preserved information. They then need to use logic and evidence to piece together who the Minoans might have been, how they lived, and their general social structure. Although there are currently dozens of different excavation sites throughout the Aegean and Mediterranean Seas, the most important are on Crete and Santorini, which is called Thera, the name found in ancient records from the Mycenaeans and Ancient Greeks.

From these sites, archaeologists, historians, and other scholars have managed to piece together a cohesive picture of the Minoans, although large gaps in knowledge still remain.

Chapter 2 – Known History of the Minoans before the Mycenaeans

The Minoans were an ancient civilization that stretched back thousands of years if one considers the original humans that settled on Crete. Humans have been living in and around the Mediterranean Sea for over 130,000 years, which is when scientists speculate that the first hominins arrived at places like Crete. The first modern humans are believed to have evolved around 10,000 BCE or 12,000 BCE based on archaeological evidence like stone tools, pottery, and skeletons discovered around the island. This evidence supports the idea that the Minoans and the Greeks shared common ancestors that originated in Anatolia or the Levant.

Because a Minoan civilization existed for centuries, historians and others tend to divide the years into three separate periods: The Early Minoans EM), the Middle Minoans (MM), and the Late Minoans (LM). Despite having numerous examples of material culture from each period, little is known about the civilization's actual history. As mentioned, the people did not keep detailed records and did not often engage in wars, so major events are a mystery. Even the names of kings and nobles are difficult to come by, although there is adequate evidence to suggest disparate economic classes.

So, instead of details, historians are able to craft rough approximations of what developments occurred during each period. These are what are listed here.

The Early Minoans (EM)

The first vestiges of Minoan civilization developed around the Early Bronze Age, which lasted from 3500 BCE to 2100 BCE. Numerous authors indicated this time demonstrated the potential promises of the future Minoan civilization, which managed to thrive with little warfare. Evidence indicates that the hominins first started to form urban centers around the late 3000s BCE and then gradually developed recognizable Minoan civilization. These centers tended to be along the coastline and were locations where the elites could flock to engage in commerce and prepare a rudimentary social structure. Early Minoan life was characterized by the rise of monarchies. The monarchs displaced local elites who were more akin to tribal leaders, individuals influential in their own small communities that probably experienced some form of popular election. The first Minoan palaces date to this period.

The Middle Period (MM)

Middle Minoan life continued much the same as it had for the Early Minoans. The population grew exponentially, and there is some evidence for technological and artistic developments that made it easier for traders to cross the Aegean and Mediterranean Seas. The Middle Minoan period lasted from roughly 2100 BCE to 1600 BCE. Something big happened toward the end of this period which resulted in a massive disturbance and widespread destruction on Crete. Palaces across the island were destroyed, including Phaistos, Knossos, Malia, and Kato Zakros. Archaeologists and historians believe the disruption was caused by a massive earthquake, potentially from the nearby volcanoes.

There is also some speculation that the Minoans suffered an invasion from nearby Anatolia, but little evidence of armed combat remains.

During this period, the Minoan population declined and remained low for several decades. Toward the end of the Middle Period, the population once again saw an increase. Between the 17th and 16th centuries BCE, archaeologists think the Minoans entered their golden age, or the apex of civilization. This would have been a time when the culture and economy thrived and where the Minoans were at the height of their trading capabilities with other civilizations. Examples of material culture, or objects like pottery and jewelry, were found in high numbers on the Greek mainland. This meant the Minoans were producing more goods and significant demand for them existed in other places.

The Late Minoans (LM)

Around 1600 BCE, the Minoans suffered another devastating catastrophe, this time the eruption of the volcano in Thera. Although the eruption itself was not far-reaching, the force generated by the underground explosion created a massive tsunami that struck other islands, including Crete. Much of the Minoan architecture was destroyed, and settlements struggled to rebuild. The Minoans had to reconstruct several of their palaces, which resulted in different functions.[3] They were less about beauty and more used for sheer practicality.

However, they didn't last. In 1450 BCE, there's evidence the Minoans struggled with the aftermath of another natural disaster, most likely an earthquake. Multiple palaces were destroyed, including those at the settlements of Malia and Phaistos. Although the palace of Knossos remained largely intact, the living quarters and personal chambers did not. Scientists believe the earthquake was the result of another eruption at Thera, and historians think

---

[3] John C. McEnro, *Architecture of Minoan Crete: Constructing Identity in the Aegean Bronze Age*, University of Texas Press, 2010.

the earthquake was instrumental in the downfall of the Minoans.

Why though is mostly a mystery. The safety of the palace of Knossos meant the Minoans still had their center of culture and trade, so they were able to continue to influence other regions in the Aegean and Mediterranean Seas. They were, however, severely weakened. Scholars believe this weakness led to the Minoans eventually being overrun by the Mycenaeans on mainland Greece.

The decline during the period of the Late Minoans was therefore slow yet steady until the conquest of the Mycenaeans. Sometime around the 13th century BCE, the cities and palaces throughout the Aegean started to decline and lose their influence and population. Linear A, the Minoan writing system, started to disappear. By 1200 BCE, even Knossos lost its power as an administrative center.

What Happened?

There is little-known history about the Minoans, so it's almost impossible to ascertain the civilization's story. Historians and archaeologists do not know the names of influential nobles or kings, whether there were any significant battles, or even the ups and downs of daily life. The limited history of the Minoans does point to one potential avenue though: the Mycenaeans.

As far as scholars can tell, the Minoans most likely disappeared because a series of natural disasters left their civilization weak. This weakness led the Mycenaeans, who lived nearby on mainland Greece, to invade and take over important cultural and administrative centers. The presence of the Mycenaean writing system and artifacts in Minoan cities, dating to after the time of the Minoans, indicates the Mycenaeans most likely moved in and took over.

This strange enemy of the Minoans actually was not that different. The Mycenaeans as a people shared many of their roots with the Minoans and actually engaged in similar behaviors, relying heavily on trade to make ends meet. Some of the main differences were in military and religion. The Mycenaeans needed to possess a strong military since they lived on the mainland, and the culture prized military prowess and abilities more than the Minoans. The Mycenaeans were also the precursor to ancient Greek religion, developing the predecessors of famous gods and beliefs.

Who Were the Mycenaeans?

The Mycenaean Greeks, also called the Mycenaeans, were the last group in the Aegean Sea that belonged to the Bronze Age. They rose to power around 1600 BCE and lasted until 1100 BCE, creating a civilization that lasted for about 500 years. The people developed numerous urban organizations, created beautiful works of art, and possessed a writing system that historians understand which could have been used for recordkeeping and messages. The primary centers of power for the Mycenaeans were Athens, Midea, and Mycenae. Mycenae could have been considered the capital and was located in the Argolid and hosted the most influential nobles and greatest examples of culture. Outside of mainland Greece, the Mycenaeans developed settlements in Macedonia, the Levant, and Italy.[4]

The Mycenaeans would fall during the Bronze Age Collapse, which was when the Bronze Age civilizations throughout Europe, Asia, and Africa simultaneously crumbled. The exact causes are unknown, with theories ranging from sudden natural disasters to the invasion of the Sea Peoples, a strange group referred to in several documents that no one is sure about. When the Mycenaeans fell, they took with them some of their great advancements and pushed the Aegean civilizations into the Greek Dark Age. Their successors would be the ancient Greeks, perhaps the most famous civilization known to Western audiences.

Since so much Minoan history is an empty canvas, historians haven't pieced together whether the Minoans and Mycenaeans had

---

[4] Louise Schofield, *The Mycenaeans*, J. Paul Getty Museum, 2007.

any significant conflicts before 1600 BCE. There is some evidence they knew of one another and traded though, which would mean their contact was a regular occurrence. The Mycenaean invasion of Minoan territory was likely not for any personal reason: The Mycenaean emphasis on power and conquest meant it would have been a wise decision to dominate a weaker neighbor like the Minoans.

Similarities and Differences

People tend to mix up the Minoans with the Mycenaeans because of their similarities, but there were several distinct differences between the two civilizations. In particular was each one's method of rising to power. While the Minoans built an empire based on trade and craftsmanship, the Mycenaeans fought and scrapped their way throughout the Aegean and Mediterranean. The Mycenaean economy was not mercantile; it relied on conquest to bring in valuable goods and keep their civilization functioning. Following the eruptions on Thera and a general decline, the Minoans became a prime candidate for more domination.

Chapter 3 – Society, Culture, and Daily Life

Information about the Minoans is scarce when compared to the wealth of knowledge scholars possess about other ancient Mediterranean civilizations. However, they still know quite a bit about general social structure, the economy, and what daily life might have been like for the average Minoan. Because of their small population, the Minoans tended to be more egalitarian than their larger neighbors, allowing opportunities for social advancement and even granting men and women similar rights. The average individual in Minoan society would have been relatively young due to lower ages of mortality, be married and have a family, perform some form of physical labor, and participate in the same religion as their neighbors. The specifics of their lives would look something like this.

Social Structure and Economy

Much of the information about the Minoans comes from images so the social structure can be difficult to ascertain. However, the Minoan society shared some characteristics with other ancient civilizations. In particular, there were different socioeconomic classes which indicated a person's wealth and authority over others. Kings continued to be the highest position, and there were also the priestesses, priests, and administrators. One unique aspect of the Minoan world was that women held similar positions to men and were frequently depicted in positions of authority.[5] This makes sense since priestesses held more sway than the priests. Several pictures also show seated women above men, but no existing ones show seated men above women.

The Minoan economy also seemed to be based around commerce. Since they lived on islands throughout the Mediterranean Sea, the Minoans needed to travel across the water to interact with other cultures and trade. Discovered manufactured goods indicate that the Minoans most likely had contact and trade with the Mycenaeans, Egyptians, Mesopotamians, and others. Fish and other goods from the sea were common Minoan products, as was saffron and bronze sculptures. The Minoans traded for things they could not produce themselves or didn't have access to in their island civilization, including advanced weaponry, new textiles, and even cats from Egypt.[6] Minoan civilization, because it relied so heavily on commerce, started to decline when the rival Mediterranean power, the Mycenaeans, started to take over Minoan trade routes. Historians believe that the Minoans and Mycenaeans did have peaceful relations before the sudden attacks occurred.

The Roles of Men and Women

The Minoans were unusual among the ancient cultures. A recurring trend in human civilization was that as people became more urbanized, gender equality faded. A fact few know is that humans did not always have disparate gender roles in part because of the difficulty of survival. Before centralized agriculture and animal husbandry, nomadic peoples tended to be more egalitarian

---

[5] Ellen Adams, *Cultural Identity in Minoan Crete: Social Dynamics in the Neopalatial Period,* New York: Cambridge University Press, 2017.

[6] Castleden, *Minoans.*

in how they conducted themselves. Even monogamy was not common. With the development of agriculture, it was possible for humans to focus less on survival or constant travel and more on the building of stagnant civilizations. Stagnant here means a society that did not need to migrate and travel. These more stable societies led to the rise of powerful figures like kings, administrators, generals, warlords, priests, and others. These important officials tended to be male, which led to the gradual shifting of roles and the removal of rights and important roles from women.

These shifts can be seen in many of the ancient civilizations, including ones from Africa, the Middle East, Asia, and Europe. The Minoans were a special case, though. It's possible that the small size of the Minoan civilization meant that urbanization did not result in the stripping of roles from women. Indeed, Minoan artwork and existing artifacts indicate that the men and women actually possessed similar rights and roles, though it's obviously unclear since written text is limited. Some historians even believe that the Minoans were a matriarchal society, one where women were in charge rather than men. The predominance of female leaders and priestesses are what led to this speculation. Another possibility is since the Minoans would not have had a land army but instead a navy, the men would have frequently been away for long periods of time. This meant women would need to do double duty at home while they were gone.

Minoan women appeared to have more rights, opportunities, and freedoms than their counterparts in similar cultures like the Mycenaeans and the ancient Greeks. Childrearing and raising was not their sole job. Many free women seemed to hold regular jobs or were the high priestesses and temple attendants of the Minoan religion. They could even become craftswomen and hold important positions or participate in sports like the significant bull jumping. Elegant women can be frequently seen in Minoan frescoes and art as priestesses or in agricultural roles like saffron gatherers, those who picked and cared for saffron crops. An example found in Santorini can be seen below.

Fresco of a Saffron Gatherer
https://commons.wikimedia.org/wiki/File:Saffron_gatherers_detail_Thera_Santorini.png

Men had similar roles and freedoms. Although there were a few different socioeconomic classes and limited upward mobility, these did not preclude men from being able to improve themselves and hold a variety of positions. Men might be soldiers, craftsmen, farmers, laborers, nobles, priests, or administrators. The Minoan civilization was small, so urbanization meant everyone jumbled together and had more options and possibilities available to them. Men also participated in sports like bull jumping and might have been saffron gatherers, but it's ambiguous. Men did not have a large role in childrearing and instead focused on working outside of the home.

Saffron

Archaeologists and anthropologists alike believe saffron possessed a unique position in Minoan culture. Saffron crocus is a plant commonly known as the *crocus sativus* and is characterized by its purple color and strands of crimson styles that poke from the center. Both the Minoans and modern societies pluck the styles from the saffron to create spices and dyes. Minoan art depicts saffron as being a common wild plant, but it no longer grows outside of carefully cultivated farms and gardens. In ancient times, it was also used as a medicine. The Minoans frequently depicted saffron in association with women in a sort of production line, indicating it was harvested for common use.[7]

Several scholars speculate that the first goddess of medicine in the Mediterranean world came from the Minoans living on the island of Thera. The murals and other artwork discovered on the island include drawings of a female goddess surrounded by botanically accurate depictions of the saffron plant and its unique properties compared to other flora that grew on the island.[8] It's believed that the Minoans thought that saffron was special for treating medical conditions as well as for dyes, spices, and other uses.

Food and Diet

As can be imagined, the Minoan diet consisted of a wide variety of seafood and products taken from the Mediterranean. Their island home meant large-scale agriculture was out of the question, especially since the population focused on growing crops of saffron to treat illnesses. This meant the primary source of consumable goods was the waters of the Mediterranean itself, as well as nearby

---

[7] J.S., "Saffron and the Minoans.," *Pharmacy in History* 47, no. 1 (2005): pg. 28-31. https://www.jstor.org/stable/41112251.

[8] S.C. Ferrence and G. Bendersky, "Therapy with saffron and the goddess at Thera," *Perspectives in Biology and Medicine* 47, no. 2 (Spring 2004): pg. 199-226. https://www.ncbi.nlm.nih.gov/pubmed/15259204.

groups that the Minoans could trade with for sustenance.

A known delicacy was young squid, which could be caught and served raw or cooked to remove parasites. Squid ink was also used to flavor foods or give color to dyes. Numerous varieties of fish, clams, and other fresh meat additionally came from the sea. These were combined with a broad range of agricultural crops that could be cultivated in the rocky terrain and a variety of vegetables. These vegetables were not grown like regular agricultural crops. Instead of being planted in large groups, they were confined to smaller household gardens. Some of the most popular vegetables were peas, lentils, field beans, asparagus, wild artichokes, wild mustard, okra, and endives. These vegetables tended to have bitter, sharp tastes that lent themselves well to fresh meat.

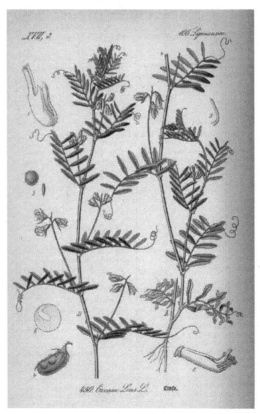

The Lentil Plant
https://commons.wikimedia.org/wiki/File:Illustration_Lens_culinaris0.jpg

The Mediterranean climate was also conducive to growing multiple varieties of grapes and olives, which the Minoans used to make wine and olive oil. Their wine tended to have a low alcoholic content because the fermentation process was used to eliminate bacteria and waterborne parasites rather than create a fun beverage. However, the Minoans did also produce wine with high alcohol content for special occasions, libations during religious ceremonies, and general consumption. Other popular drinks were barley beer, mead, and wines seasoned and flavored with herbs. The Minoans also made a mild milk drink flavored with local herbs as well. Drinking vessels found on Crete contain the faint remnants of ancient wine that appear to have been flavored with toasted oak wood to give it a sharper, smokier flavor.

Olive oil, meanwhile, was eaten with grains and vegetables and provided a major source of nutrition and calories for the general public. Olives could also be consumed from the tree. Aside from vegetables, the Minoans did grow some grains. They managed to cultivate barley, rye, and three separate types of wheat. These were typically not made into bread but could be eaten as a porridge or turned into beer.

Like most ancient peoples, the Minoans mastered animal domestication and appeared to own sheep, cattle, goats, and some pigs. These animals wouldn't have been eaten all the time; while most contemporary societies use domesticated animals as a primary source of meat, the Minoans would have needed the animals to provide usable resources like wool and milk. Goat milk was more popular than that of cows, and sheep were needed for the wool to make clothes. Pigs seem to be one of the only large mammals whose purpose was solely for food. The Minoans primarily used goat milk to make sharp-flavored but physically soft white cheeses similar to those made by the ancient Greeks. An example in contemporary times would be the modern feta.

Feta Cheese
https://commons.wikimedia.org/wiki/File:Greek_feta.jpg

In addition to domesticated animals, the Minoans consumed creatures they could hunt like rabbits and boar. There is evidence that the Minoans kept dogs and cats to help them hunt and keep their homes free of pests. The cats most likely came from Egypt and were traded in exchange for goods from the Mediterranean.

Fashion

The Minoans made unusual and complex fashion choices based heavily on the Mediterranean climate. Most garments were sewn in a similar manner to contemporary clothing, with blouses, skirts, and dresses being fitted to the body and designed to accentuate the waist on men and women. Fabric was made from lightweight materials like linen, although wool was not uncommon in rural areas. Men typically wore simple loincloths with the occasional draping robe. These loincloths were decorated and often included a pagne, or sheath, that protected the penis and drew attention to the individual's masculinity. As time went on, men's garments became more modest and often included tasseled aprons that covered the front and back of the hips and thighs. Toward the end of the Late Minoan Period, men started to wear simple tunics and robes that protected the upper body as well.[9]

---

[9] Bernice R. Jones, "Revealing Minoan Fashions," *Archaeology* 53, no. 3 (May/June

When archaeologists discovered examples of women's garments on Crete, they were astonished by the similarities between the ancient clothing and modern dress. A woman's skirt tended to be fitted and cinched around the waist before flaring out in a popular bell shape that accentuated the female figure. Decorations and embroidery were often sewn onto the skirts to add character, and designs grew more elaborate as time wore on. Some designs featured long strips of fabric sewn into the sides of the skirts to create vertical ruffles along the length of the material. Their tops were not modest. Most women wore fitted garments with large vertical openings in the front that exposed the entire breast and the ideal slim waist. There is some evidence to suggest that men and women were fitted with tight metal belts from childhood to further accentuate a slender midsection.[10]

Minoan fashion was based around having the ideal Minoan figure, which meant exposing the waist, muscular arms and chests, or large breasts and hips with a defined waist. Some historians noted that the ideal feminine shape was similar to European fashions in the 1800s CE when women wore corsets and padded their skirts to achieve a rounded, full look. One ancient Minoan painting earned the nickname "La Parisienne" because of the female character's similarities to the fashions of French women.

The Parisienne
https://commons.wikimedia.org/wiki/File:The_Parisian,_fresco,_Knossos,_Greece.jpg

---

2000): pg. 36-41. https://www.jstor.org/stable/41779314.
[10] Ibid.

This fresco highlights some other characteristics of Minoan fashion that were present in larger urban centers like Knossos. Archaeologists discovered what appeared to be beautification centers in palace complexes and objects that seemed to be used to accentuate features deemed attractive by the Minoans. Nobles would use natural mixtures and compounds to lighten their skin and paint their lips red, providing a contrast to the tanned skin of laborers and other lower-class individuals. Women would also wear elaborate knots and tie their hair back in creative designs, and both men and women wore jewelry made from gold, silver, or bronze to indicate their wealth and social status. Semi-precious stones, minerals, and other objects could be inlaid in the metal; popular choices were garnet, lapis lazuli, soapstone, ivory, and shells taken from the Mediterranean. The Minoans frequently traded with the Egyptians to obtain a material called Egyptian blue as well.

Were the Minoans Peaceful?

A running theory about the Minoans is that they were a peaceful civilization. This theory was first put forth by Arthur Evans, the archaeologist who discovered some of the greatest deposits of artifacts of the Minoans. According to Evans, the *Pax Minoica* (Minoan Peace) existed. This peace explained that there was little to no conflict in Minoan civilization until they came face to face with the Mycenaeans on mainland Greece. More contemporary scholars dispute Evans' idea as idealism, but the fact remains that there is no surviving evidence of a legitimate Minoan army, any form of domination beyond the island of Crete, or even warfare. Artwork, which depicts numerous aspects of life like saffron cultivation, has no indication that warfare existed. Violence seemed dedicated to sports and potentially ritual sacrifices.

The idea of Minoan peace is partially based on architectural evidence discovered on islands like Crete. Although archaeologists found some fortifications and watchtowers, such buildings do not indicate actual warfare. This is because most ancient fortified sites served more than one function. They could be used as storage areas, indicate important borders such as those of the palaces, or express the wealth of powerful officials. Some fortresses also served as significant gathering places or areas where people could go during harsh weather, natural disasters, and other problems. However, scholars cannot rule out warfare, especially since the Minoans did make numerous weapons that could not be used for hunting. More confusing was the presence of intimidating longboats and rapiers, which were standard weapons used for war by ancient civilizations.[11]

[11] Barry P.C. Molloy, "Martial Minoans? War as Social Process, Practice and Event in Bronze Age Crete," *The Annual of the British School at Athens* 107 (2012): pg. 87-142. https://www.jstor.org/stable/41721880.

Chapter 4 – Trade and Shipbuilding on the Mediterranean Sea

The Minoan civilization is called a thalassocracy, or a political state that relies on its navy to guarantee population safety and unite different regions of the same culture. Scholars can tell that the Minoans shored up their navy and built dozens of trading vessels designed to facilitate commerce with places all across the Mediterranean.[12] Crete was the center of their commercial industry, including the palace settlement of Knossos on the east coast of the island. Craftspeople tended to sell their finished goods like pottery and ceramics overseas. The Minoans did not produce enough agricultural products or foodstuffs to develop any major consumable trade, and records show that the citizens might have even traded their finished products for surplus crops in places like Egypt.

---

[12] Malcom H. Weiner, "Realities of Power: The Minoan Thalassocracy in Historical Perspective," *AMILLA: The Quest for Excellence*, 2013, https://www.academia.edu/30141237/_Realities_of_Power_The_Minoan_Thalassocracy_in_Historical_Perspective_AMILLA_The_Quest_for_Excellence_Studies_Presented_to_Guenter_Kopcke_in_Celebration_of_His_75th_Birthday_2013_pp_149_173

Year round, merchants would gather goods that could be traded to places like Egypt, Mesopotamia, mainland Greece, Anatolia, and even Spain. Minoan art and other objects have been found in all five locations. As a maritime civilization, it's believed the Minoans owed the majority of their success to being able to trade for goods and luxuries that would have been unavailable on Santorini and Crete.

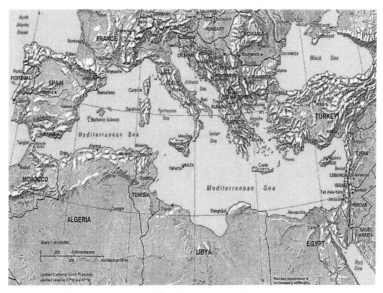

Map of the Mediterranean Sea
https://commons.wikimedia.org/wiki/File:Mediterranean_Relief,_1028_x_1024.jpg

The Minoans had little need for an army because of their location. The majority of people lived in relatively undefended coastal cities protected by large fleets of seafaring vessels. Minoan ships featured modifications and weapons to protect traders and settlements from pirates, but archaeologists note that these additions to the ships are almost always unused and untouched. This fact helps support Arthur Evans' idea about the "Minoan Peace," or the theory that the Minoans as a culture did not need to engage in warfare with their neighbors and experienced little fighting or aggression.

Two of the goods the Minoans were known for were tin and saffron. Tin was a necessary material for the making of bronze weapons and armor during the Bronze Age. Minoan miners gathered the metal from Cyprus, where it could be alloyed with copper to make rough bronze for shipping to other civilizations. Saffron, meanwhile, grew rampant in places like Akrotiri on Santorini. The plant was highly sought after in the ancient world for its taste, color, and supposed medicinal properties. Some records indicate that the Minoans might have even completed the process of using saffron as a dye for fabrics before shipment, although there is not enough evidence to support the presence of large-scale textile production. Luxury resources like gold and silver taken from small Mediterranean islands also formed valuable goods that the Minoans could trade.

Minoan Fleet

All commerce in the thalassocracy needed to be protected by the Minoan fleet. Unlike the ships of other seafaring civilizations, the Minoan fleet was not designed to engage in heavy warfare or conquest. Each vessel's primary purpose appeared to be trade with extra weapons added to defend goods from pirates. Before the Mycenaeans, the Minoans did not fight their neighbors and thus had little use for a dedicated navy.

Minoan Fleet Fresco
https://commons.wikimedia.org/wiki/File:Minoan_fresco,_showing_a_fleet_and_settleme
nt_Akrotiri.jpg

Frescoes, like the one above, provide an excellent example of what the standard Minoan ship looked like. Shipbuilders created longboats using wood and bronze tools. These longboats were roughly thirty-five meters (114.8 ft.) long and six meters wide (19.7 ft.). Each ship was capable of carrying 50 metric tons worth of goods and could be manned by fifty people rowing the oars that stuck out on either side of the vessel. There was extra room for individuals like the captain and his specialty crew who were capable of repairing the ship in case of emergency.

The Minoans possessed a clear process for the creation of a ship capable of traversing the Mediterranean. Trees were a finite resource on their islands, so the Minoans saved larger ones for the building of boats. Entire cypress trunks were favored because the shipbuilders could shave off excess bark and material using massive bronze saws that measured roughly 6 ft. in length and 1 ft. wide. The process consisted of a few deceptively simple but physically challenging steps.

Professionals would identify a tree with good characteristics and chop it down using bronze axes.

The branches would then be removed, and the tree would be transported by rudimentary wagons to a shipbuilding center on one of the coasts.

The cypress bark would be stripped from the tree using basic wooden or bronze scrapers.

Clean logs would then be marked by the master shipbuilder so he and his workers (shipbuilding was primarily a male profession due to the strength required) could identify where cuts needed to be made.

Once the marks were made, the shipbuilding team started to cut, slice, and saw away extra wood. The finished product would be one solid boat with few to no attached pieces. This created sturdy construction and prevented leaks.

The upward curves on the bow and stern (the front and rear of the boat, respectively) were pushed into shape by making the wood malleable by heat and steam.

Extra bands of cypress were then added to the completed shell of the ship using the process of edge-jointing. Mortises, or rectangular notches, were cut into the boat, and then notches and the slabs of wood were joined together. Resins were used to prevent slippage and seal any major cracks or gaps that could let water into the boat. The mortises would become fully sealed when the ship was pushed into the seawater upon completion.

The process of adding extra cypress bands was used all around the ship to give the vessel needed height and protection from the waters of the Mediterranean. Once the banding was completed, the shipbuilder would add rowing benches and decking for the sailors.

Completed ships were then covered in white woven linen and decorated with pictures of blue dolphins and other creatures of the sea.

The Striped Dolphin – The Minoans' Favorite Animal
https://commons.wikimedia.org/wiki/File:Stenella_coeruleoalba.jpg

Those nine steps created the basic ship the Minoans would have used for trading. Oars for rowing were made from oak, which was more solid and heavier than the cypress used for the boat's frame. Some shipbuilders would add masts and sails to the completed vessels, so the seafarers did not need to rely solely on manpower to travel across the Mediterranean. Masts were made with oak and tended to be a whopping 52.5 ft. tall. Sails were made of wool and treated with oil to be waterproof.[13]

Such simple vessels were not meant to carry complicated weapons. Frescoes indicate that the defensive measures against pirates were probably fundamental additions like long spears that would be held by sailors along the sides of the ship. This would have stopped pirates or other invaders from boarding and taking trade goods. Most crewmembers also carried basic weapons like knives that could double as tools and eating utensils.

Ultimately, the Minoans' role as a maritime civilization can be seen in the simplicity and beauty of their ships. The vessels did not include massive defensive constructs or weapons and featured a basic open-air design that favored the sunny climate of the Mediterranean. Manpower was needed to move the ships across the sea, and the sailors provided the only line of defense against enemies. However, they did not appear to engage in combat often. This idea is supported not only by the simple design but also the immense amount of time spent painting and decorating completed vessels. Ships were works of art to the Minoans, often sporting their favorite dolphin and bird motifs. These designs made the vessels attractive, alerted potential commercial partners to the wealth of the Minoans, and made the ships conspicuous on the waters. As some scholars say, if the Minoans were worried about attack, would they have made their trading vessels so distinct and undefended?

---

[13] Cemal Pulak and George F. Bass, "Bronze Age Shipwreck Excavation at Uluburun," Institute of Nautical Archaeology.

Chapter 5 – Language and Linear A

Multiple writing systems dating from the time of the Minoans have been found in Crete and Santorini, although most of them are undeciphered. The first known written script for the Minoans was something called the Cretan hieroglyphs. Scholars are unsure if these hieroglyphs were actually used by the Minoans, and their entire origin is debated. However, they were used before Linear A and can be found in the regions where the Minoans lived, having appeared sometime during the 19th century BCE. The Cretan hieroglyphs were also used at the same time as Linear A and disappeared around the 17th century BCE when they appeared to fall out of favor.

A Jaspar Seal with Cretan Hieroglyphics (c. 1800s BCE)
https://commons.wikimedia.org/wiki/File:Pini-plombe-orig-II2_316d_3.2.jpg

After the Cretan hieroglyphs came the two most well-known writing systems, Linear A and Linear B. Linear A came before Linear B and is considered its parent, or the writing system on which Linear B was based. Linear B was not used by the Minoans. Linear A dates from 2500 BCE and 1450 BCE and is almost unintelligible to contemporary scholars due to the incompleteness of preserved documents and the language used in the script. However, Linear A is frequently called Minoan, and multiple professionals believe the language is the written form of the Minoan spoken word. Although there are some similarities to ancient Greek, there are not enough.

An Example of Linear A
https://commons.wikimedia.org/wiki/File:Linear_A_cup.png

Scholars attempted to translate the values of Linear B into Linear A to create an example of the language, but the result was unintelligible. This translation process took the values of the symbols in Linear B and then applied them to their known counterpart in Linear A. This procedure would be similar to someone taking the sound associated with the letter "R" and applying it to the Cyrillic equivalent, which is "P." However, the result did not make sense, indicating that the Minoan language might not have been related to any known languages. There is a current belief that the Minoans actually did not use their written alphabet to record their language and instead used it for accounting.

Another form of writing discovered in the region of the Minoans is a script found on an artifact called the Phaistos Disc. The Phaistos Disc was found at the ruins of the palace complex of Phaistos on the southern coast of Crete. Luigi Pernier, an Italian archaeologist, found the disc in the basement. It measures 5.9 in. in diameter and was found in an area full of items like bovine bones. Scholars believe that the rooms were used for general storage and appeared to collapse upon themselves following the Therian eruption.

The Phaistos Disc contains images of a pictorial script that hasn't been found in any other location. Archaeologists now believe it to be of Cretan origin and is currently indecipherable. Examples of the symbols can be seen transcribed in the image below.

a   *b*

The Writing on the Phaistos Disc
https://commons.wikimedia.org/wiki/File:Table_Ph1.png

In short, modern scholars can't tell what the Minoan language actually sounded like, but there is some evidence for what it looked like. Similar to other ancient civilizations, the Minoans did not have much use for a written script. Almost everyone was illiterate and would have no need to read or write. The only people who did would have been court scribes, traders, and some members of the religious class. This is why the majority of documents carrying Linear A script are accounting records.

Chapter 6 – The Potential Predecessors of Greek Religion

Archaeologists, historians, and other scholars believe that the Minoans developed the elements that would evolve into the future ancient Greek religion. Some of the religious objects discovered at sites like Crete include paintings, statuettes, and seal rings that point to a specific cultic practice revolving around influential gods, goddesses, and a class of priests and priestesses. As mentioned earlier, the Minoans were unique among ancient cultures in that their religion emphasized and elevated women in its practice. Surviving artifacts and imagery indicate that priestesses held the most essential roles in worship and had more power than their male counterparts. Evidence further points toward the chief Minoan deity being a woman rather than a man. This is the famous snake goddess.

The Snake Goddess

Based on evidence, archaeologists and anthropologists believe the most significant deity in the Minoan religion was a goddess associated with snakes. Sometimes artists would also depict her with bulls, lions, or doves, significant animals in religions throughout the ancient world. This figure appeared to have some form of medical significance as women would leave offerings of saffron, their all-purpose plant, at her altars. In images, the goddess can sometimes be seen with a smaller, younger man whom archaeologists believe was either her consort or son. Although there were no formal public temples, the goddess would be worshiped and attended to by priestesses.

Archaeologists suspect that the deity would be co-opted in ancient Greek religion and depicted as Ariadne, the daughter of the famous King Minos from whom the Minoans take their name. In tablets taken from Knossos, the goddess is sometimes referred to as the "mistress of the labyrinth." These documents are written in Linear B, the language of the Mycenaean Greeks, rather than Linear A. This could indicate that civilizations like the Mycenaeans and the ancient Greeks adapted the preexisting Minoan religion into their own pantheons.[14]

The Two Snake Goddess Figurines Found in 1903
https://commons.wikimedia.org/wiki/File:TempleRepositories.jpg

The original snake goddess figurine was discovered by Arthur Evans in 1903 and depicted an obviously female individual with a

---

[14] Castledon, *Minoans.*

snake in either hand. Snakes did not have a negative connotation for the Minoans and seemed to indicate domesticity, the household, motherhood, and potentially healing and mastery over nature and animals. Evans originally postulated that the larger of the discovered figurines was a goddess while the smaller was a priestess. These particular statuettes have only been found in household shrines and other domesticate places, which is why archaeologists suspect the goddess was associated with the home. However, mentions to an overarching, powerful snake goddess could also be found in shrines throughout the Minoan landscape, leaving the situation vague.

The Sacral Knot

The sacral knot was a discovery by Evans at Knossos. This knot had a loop on top and two fringed ends that hung below. It appeared multiple times in Minoan figurines, mainly on the two snake goddess statuettes. The knot sat between their breasts and could be seen throughout Minoan religious artifacts in a variety of materials. Evans speculated that the sacral knot was an important religious symbol similar to the double-edged axe, which also occurred everywhere where the Minoans settled.

The Double-Bitted or Double-Edged Axe

The double-bitted axe was a common symbol that appeared in almost every religious site discovered in Minoan territory. Its appearance is self-explanatory: the axe had a blade on either side of the handle and was ceremonial. The axe can be found in the religious symbolism of numerous cultures across the Mediterranean in the ancient world. Contrary to its representation in other cultures though, the double-bitted axe in Minoan religion only ever appeared with female figures and did not represent a weapon or military conquest. Some scholars believe the axe was representative of the origin of the known world because of its shape, and others associate it with the significant female goddess mentioned earlier.

The Arkalochori Axe (c. 2000 BCE)
C messier, CC0, via Wikimedia Commons
https://commons.wikimedia.org/wiki/File:Arkalochori_Axe_215.jpg

The double-bitted axe did not only appear as a symbol. Some artifacts have been found, including the Arkalochori Axe dating back to the second millennium BCE. The bronze votive axe was excavated by the Greek archaeologist Spyridon Marinatos in 1934. Inscribed along the edges are fifteen symbols that some suspect is Linear A, but the material is too degraded to clearly make out the forms. Archaeologists think the axe was used during religious ceremonies and, again, was not a weapon. The axe can currently be found at the Heraklion Archaeological Museum.

The Practice of Worship: A Cultic Structure

Religious artifacts are some of the most enduring objects for the Minoans. Some of the numerous items found include metal and clay votive figures, figurines of animals and humans, special double axes, and miniatures of objects that the Minoans would have used in their daily lives. Archaeologists and anthropologists have also found over 300 separate shrines and caves filled with sacred items that might have been the centers of a prominent religious cult. This version of a cult does not have the same negative connotations of modern-day cults. When used in the discussion of ancient history, the word "cult" simply refers to a small group that worshiped a particular deity or figure, or a form of religious worship that was not officially organized or mainstream.

Temples, as contemporary audiences know them, were not a concept among the Minoans, and there were no clear sites of buildings used for formal, organized worship. It's speculated that the Minoans instead selected and educated priestesses, and sometimes priests, who then conducted ceremonies and rituals for supportive groups at open-air sites. These sites would have been the temples of the Minoans. Palace complexes did not have designated religious spaces, and no surviving Minoan frescoes show any deities. The only indicators tend to be the consistent statuettes, which depict the same woman bearing two snakes, one in each hand.

Interestingly, there was one unique cultic figure that baffled archaeologists when first discovered. This was something called the Minoan Genius. It is best described as a strange creature that blends the characteristics of a lion and a hippo. Scholars have noted that there are numerous similarities between the Minoan Genius and some of the fantastic animals depicted in ancient Egyptian art, and they think the animal demonstrates a connection between the two cultures. In the Minoan religion, the Genius seemed to be a protector of children as well as an important figure during fertility rituals. They were also frequently shown with ewers, or water pitchers, and seemed to play a significant role in the giving of libations during religious ceremonies.

Two Minoan Genii
https://commons.wikimedia.org/wiki/File:Minoan_genius.png

Bull-Leaping

Bull-leaping clearly held some significance among the Minoans as it was a popular subject for frescoes, pottery, and even scenes inscribed upon pieces of jewelry. In bull-leaping, an enterprising athlete had to leap over a charging bull by seizing the horns, propelling themselves up, and landing on the animal's back. Artwork indicates that men and women both participated in such events and that winners were lauded.

Knossos – Bull-Leaping Fresco
Heraklion Archaeological Museum, CC0, via Wikimedia Commons
https://commons.wikimedia.org/wiki/File:Bull_leaping_minoan_fresco_archmus_Herakli on_(cropped).jpg

Whether the activity possessed any sort of ritualistic, religious, or cultic belief is debated. Bull-leaping was clearly a popular subject and seemed to possess some rituals of its own, but the images don't tend to be found in temples. Some scholars of the ancient world draw connections between the depicted bulls and the Sacred Bull, a popular feature in ancient religions. This Sacred Bull was considered a symbol of awe and power and tended to be associated with the chief or supreme deity of the religion. For the Minoans, an argument can be made for a connection between the bull and the snake goddess mentioned earlier.

Others go on to argue that the bulls had no significance and that the artwork isn't even depicting bull-leaping. They claim that the scenes are actually somewhat humorous: they are stills of young men and women attempting to ride a bull for the first time and failing miserably.[15]

The Existence of Human Sacrifice

Did the Minoans participate in human sacrifice?

Maybe.

There are three chief sites where archaeologists believe they have found evidence to support the idea of ritualistic human sacrifice: Anemospilia, a complex at Fournou Korifi, and a building in Knossos known as the North House. Findings at each location are inclusive and might not actually be from sacrifice, but the sites are suspicious enough to give scholars pause. In order of the plausibility of found evidence, the least likely to be an incident of human sacrifice is the scene found at Anemospilia.

Anemospilia
https://commons.wikimedia.org/wiki/File:Anemospilia.jpg

Anemospilia presents an interesting situation for archaeologists. The site is a temple destroyed by the earthquake during the Middle Minoan period. Inside were the remains of a cult statue as well as four human skeletons: two men, one woman, and one unidentifiable. One of the male skeletons was trussed into a

---

[15] Nanno Marinatos, "Minoan Religion," Columbia: University of South Carolina, 1993.

contorted, contracted position on a raised platform that would have been painful to force oneself into. A bronze blade was discovered inside his pile of bones. The fifteen-inch knife featured depictions of a boar, a sacred animal, on either side. Discoloration on one side of the bones indicated the man most likely died of blood loss before the earthquake hit. Two skeletons were found in varying stages of surprise around the strange victim. Archaeologists believe they were startled when the earthquake hit, and their crushed bones mean the temple collapsed during the ritual.

The skeleton of indeterminate gender was discovered in one of the halls of the temple with over a hundred pottery fragments around them. Discoloration again indicated the jar they were carrying was full of blood. The archaeologists who excavated the scene never gave an official report on their findings, and the only major published document is an old article from *National Geographic* published in 1981.

Although professionals speculate, many believe Anemospilia was not a scene of human sacrifice. Some claim the man who bled out might have been dying from a wound received at sea and that the blade had been placed upon his body as a symbol of honor. Others go along with this idea and think the entire situation was a funerary rite gone wrong. Finally, quite a few people think the entire scene was caused by the earthquake and that it's likely the supposed sacrifice victim bled out from injuries caused by falling debris. The knife resembles a spearhead, which could have easily fallen from a shelf and pierced the eighteen-year-old's ribcage.

The next site is a sanctuary complex at Fournou Korifi. Here, fragments from a human skull were recovered from a chamber containing a variety of cooking equipment and a hearth. The archaeologists believe the skull was the remains of some form of human sacrifice, but the situation is—to put it simply—iffy. When working with ancient remains, the strangest things can turn up. In this situation, it's likely that the skull came from an individual who died in their kitchen or cooking area. The only caveat to this theory is that the rest of the skeleton was not found in the area. This gives rise to the idea that the human head was transported to the cooking area for potentially nefarious reasons.

Finally, there's Knossos. If there was going to be evidence of Minoan human sacrifice, ignoring the logistics of trying to find material culture from a civilization from millennia ago, it would be in Knossos. The administrative, cultural, and religious capital of the Minoans, Knossos included numerous mass burial sites where archaeologists discovered almost definitive evidence of child sacrifice. Findings indicate the victims were most likely cannibalized by their killers.[16]

The evidence of ritualistic human sacrifice comes from the stripping of the flesh from bones in a manner similar to sacrificed animals. All of the children in the burial site appeared to be healthy, so the chances of them being sick or left to die are unlikely. The archaeologists who excavated the site along with other professionals think the sacrifice might have been part of a cultic ritual wherein children were slaughtered, cooked, and then eaten as a way to renew and improve fertility in the coming year. Sometimes to have a child, one must apparently kill one.[17]

No one knows how subjects for sacrifice were chosen. Dating the skeletons reveals that almost all of the victims were below eighteen years of age with preference given to young, healthy individuals. Flesh and blood were taken from the victims, and as mentioned before, there is some evidence of cannibalism. That the Minoans might have engaged in such behavior is not surprising since many ritualistic cults from the Stone, Bronze, and even early Iron Ages included such practices. Without a doubt, humans all around the world have sacrificed and eaten one another to appease nature or the gods.

---

[16] Castledon, *Minoans.*

[17] Peter Warren, "Knossos: New Excavations and Discoveries," *Archaeology* (July /August 1984): p. 48-55.

But what does this say about Minoan religion?

On the one hand, evidence of sacrifice demonstrates the power of cultic beliefs as well as a presence of preordained rituals that needed to be complete. Historians do not know why, but they can tell that what religious practices the Minoans did have were important to them and required special sites, priestesses, priests, and specialized implements like the bronze boar knife.

Burial and Mortuary Practices

Burial remains constitute many of the artifacts from the Bronze Age because ancient peoples tended to follow strict, ritualistic behaviors during funerals and did their best to preserve the bodies of their beloved. For the Minoans, many of the remains come from the time of the Middle Minoans and from the island of Crete. Remains were kept in either house tombs or beehive tombs and followed the technique of inhumation. A site at Ayia Photia bears evidence of being a chamber reserved specifically for dead children. The Minoans did not appear to cremate their deceased but did bury more than one person in a single gravesite. Archaeologists speculate that bodies buried in the same plot were either related or members of a public tomb. Wealthy or notable families possessed crypts while poorer individuals made do with public cemeteries or their own land.

In general, families attempted to leave their deceased grave goods and furniture. No one knows whether the Minoans believed the dead could take the objects into the afterlife or whether there was a ritual for placing the objects. A current theory, based on the inordinate number of cups and rhytons—cups shaped like animals—found in tombs, is that some sort of toasting ritual was a part of preparing the deceased for the burial. Other common grave goods were tools and weapons, jewelry, pottery, and special storage jars. The objects might have been related to an individual's profession or personal preferences—for example, a farmer might be buried with his or her hoe, while a wealthy noble might be laid to rest with their favorite pendant.

Trends shifted during the time of the Late Minoans. Instead of group burial plots, the Minoans favored single burials where the body was placed in a clay storage vessel or laid to rest in a clay or wooden sarcophagus. These were not stored in a built tomb. The vessel or sarcophagus would be painted and covered with scenes similar to those on frescoes, and the body itself was folded to fit into the small container. Despite the popularity of this new method, many of the deceased continued to be buried in rock-cut tombs or old family burial places.

Lasting Influence on the Mycenaeans and the Greeks

Scholars remain divided on just how much influence the Minoans might have had on the Mycenaeans and Greeks when it comes to religion. Few concrete facts about Minoan religious culture remain, and the failure of modern professionals to translate or understand Linear A means many are in the dark about deity names, domains, and even meanings. However, there is evidence that the Mycenaeans and the Greeks were familiar with Minoan tales and legends, as they utilized some common elements and incorporated Cretan names and ideas into their own mythos. The Minoans also demonstrated influence by providing the framework for several important Greek myths, including that of the Minotaur. Despite trepidation in the field, some scholars still come forward and state that the Greek goddess Athena was derived from the Minoan snake deity seen earlier. Whatever the case may be, Minoan religion remains a mystery and will continue to be so without any breakthroughs in Linear A interpretation and translation or new site excavations.

Chapter 7 – Art

Although the Minoans left few written records, their artwork stood the test of time and continues to be excavated from sites on Crete, Santorini, and the surrounding islands. Artwork, pottery, and other examples of material culture are beneficial to scholars because they demonstrate what the Minoans found important, their standards of beauty, how people were thought to look, and can even reveal societal norms and distinctions. These crafts additionally provide an insight into how technologically advanced the Minoans were, as certain techniques required skill and an understanding of the fundamental properties of metal and chemicals or compounds found in the materials. Finally, their artwork also indicates how much the Minoans traded with other civilizations and how they influenced future Aegean cultures, as the Mycenaeans and ancient Greeks copied many of the Minoan styles even centuries later.[18]

When discussing Minoan art, it's important to note that scholars only count pieces that can be dated between 2600 BCE and 1100 BCE. Anything before or after has the possibility of belonging to a separate civilization. The largest collection is currently at the Heraklion Archaeological Museum near Knossos on Crete. Pieces

---

[18] Reynold Higgins, *Minoan and Mycenaean Art*, London: Thames and Hudson, 1997.

are categorized as belonging to the Early, Middle, or Late Minoans due to some technical differences that appear.[19] Unfortunately, textiles and other degradable materials like wood have already decomposed, so the best examples of Minoan art come from the more durable products that the wealthy would have possessed as well as pottery. Pottery is ubiquitous, as almost every individual in every civilization around the world needed a jug at some point—even now. For these reasons, the best examples of Minoan art are frescoes, pottery, metalwork, and jewelry.

Frescoes

A fresco is an image painted on a wall or ceiling as decoration. It can be done through numerous techniques and with a variety of materials, but frescoes are one of the oldest and most enduring art forms of human civilization. The Minoans left behind numerous examples, although one issue with their preservation is that they are inherently fragile, as sections can erode, the paint will fade away, and many of the discovered frescoes appear to have been moved from their original locations by enterprising individuals. Despite this, the frescoes demonstrate some important aspects of Minoan life, culture, and values through their choice of subjects and artistic tendencies.

The Fisherman Fresco
https://commons.wikimedia.org/wiki/File:Fresco_of_a_fisherman,_Akrotiri,_Greece.jpg

---

[19] Ibid.

Archaeologists and specialists in art believe the work done by the Minoans is an example of buon fresco. In this technique, the artist uses color pigments to paint on wet lime plaster. There is no binding agent, which means the plaster absorbs the paint and protects the image from fading. Professionals can detect this technique by looking at string impressions left behind in the plaster as well as the depth of the paint layers. The thickness demonstrates how the Minoans would have applied the wet paint directly without relying on extra materials.[20]

In general, Minoan frescoes possessed a three-dimensional effect and used numerous bright colors. The most popular were blue, white, red, and black, although yellow and green sometimes appeared. Shading did not seem to exist. Based on existing frescoes, professionals think the Minoans copied some of the artwork of the Egyptians by making female skin white, male skin red, and assigning different primary colors to precious metals. For example, silver was depicted as blue while bronze was red.

The Minoans depicted numerous scenes in their frescoes, many of which possessed cultural significance. Some of the most common were images of the bull leapers as well as festivals, rituals, and potentially religious ceremonies. Priestesses often appeared, as did dancers. Natural subjects and animals dotted frescoes throughout Minoan settlements with identifiable flowers like lilies and crocuses. Animals were shown in their natural habitats and included the mundane, like goats, and the mythological, like the griffin. Reeds and depictions of sea creatures like the flying fish could be found, especially in palaces. Dolphins seem to be a favorite in Minoan culture.

[20] M. A. S. Cameron, R. E. Jones and S. E. Philippakis, "Scientific Analyses of Minoan Fresco Samples from Knossos," *The Annual of the British School at Athens* 72 (1977): pgs. 121-184.

The Flying Fish Fresco
https://commons.wikimedia.org/wiki/File:Phylakopi_flying_fish.jpg

Minoan fresco techniques and subject matter lasted long after the end of their civilization. In particular, the Mycenaeans copied the Minoan fresco technique and included many of their subjects, although their artists also emphasized the importance of military and material culture. Some archaeologists also connect later Egyptian frescoes with the Minoans because they contain many of the same techniques, in particular, the work in Tell el Dab'a.[21]

Frescoes are some of the most significant artifacts for scholars because they demonstrate what was important to the Minoans. Professionals long thought the Minoans were peaceful, and part of their evidence was the clear lack of weaponry or militaristic scenes in surviving frescoes. It seemed the Minoans were content in depicting their everyday lives, beautiful men and women, and the

---

[21] Sara Cole, "The Wall Paintings of Tell el-Dab'a: Potential Aegean Connections," Pursuit - The Journal of Undergraduate Research at the University of Tennessee 1, no. 10 (2010).

glory of the nature around them. The incorporation of geometric patterns as well as artistic techniques from Egypt showed how much the Minoans traded and how these interactions affected their own culture. While frescoes reveal much, they share their position as the most significant surviving form of art with pottery, a ubiquitous skill that produced both mundane and elaborate pieces.

Pottery

Contemporary scholars know a ridiculous amount about Minoan pottery because so much of it has been found at sites throughout the Aegean Sea. Pottery is an important tool for dating the Minoan civilization because professionals can tell the age of the materials by examining the techniques used and the wear and tear on the surface. Artistic styles and choices of design reveal information about the different time periods in which the pottery was made, and the presence of samples throughout the Mediterranean in locations like Egypt, Syria, and Cyprus demonstrates how far the Minoans traded.[22]

The pottery discovered in and around Crete include pots, rhytons, ceramic figures, and some small statues. Pottery sarcophagi became popular during the late Middle and Late Minoan periods and can be found full of cremated ashes, although cremation was not common. The majority of the world's Minoan pottery collection is currently at the Heraklion Archaeological Museum on Crete. Archaeologists remain unsure how pottery was produced, but it's suspected that pieces were done individually or in small quantities at specific workshops where there was sufficient clay. Both men and women were potters and worked year-round to produce sought-after goods. Some workshops catered specifically to the palaces, while others produced objects for the general public.

---

[22] Philip B. Betancourt, *The History of Minoan Pottery*, Princeton: Princeton University Press, 1985.

Late Minoan Bull's Head Rhyton
https://commons.wikimedia.org/wiki/File:Bull%27s_head_vase.JPG

Early Minoan pottery continued traditions from the Final Neolithic period. Objects that date back to this period tend to feature local variations that indicate there was no set pattern or technique among the Minoans at this stage. This pottery can be divided into several different types: Pyrgos Ware, Incised Ware, Agios Onouphrios, Vasiliki Ware, Fine Gray Ware, Lebena Ware, and Koumasa Ware. These classifications refer to the general form the pottery took as well as its finish, color, and potential crafting technique.

Pyrgos Ware, also known as Burnished Ware, tended to be chalices created by making a cup and attaching it to a funnel-shaped stand. Archaeologists suspect this type was used for rituals at the Pyrgos site where the chalices were excavated. The site appeared to be a rock shelter with religious significance. Pyrgos Ware would be black, brown, or gray and have a linear pattern inscribed around the piece. Incised Ware, called Scored Ware, were burnished jugs and lumpy, bulbous jars covered in incised line patterns. These can be found in northern and northeastern Crete, and scholars think the pattern might have been imported from another civilization.

Agios Onouphrios is a collection of pottery with painted parallel lines around the pieces. This type of pottery was colored with a red clay slip that could be oxidized in a kiln. This style was found in northern and southern Crete. Lebena Ware was found in the same places and was a similar style of pottery with white patterns painted on red clay. Both styles date to 2600 BCE–1900 BCE.[23]

Vasiliki Ware features a mottled glaze, some efforts at controlling color, and elongated spouts. Potters would make the mottling effect by manipulating the heat through uneven firing to create dark colors. They might have placed hot coals against the clay as well to change certain spots. Vasiliki Ware can be found in eastern Crete.

Early Minoan Vasiliki Vase, c. 2400 BCE – 2200 BCE
Heraklion Archaeological Museum, CC0, via Wikimedia Commons
https://commons.wikimedia.org/wiki/File:Vasiliki_ware_tea_pot_archmus_Heraklion.jpg

---

[23] Ibid.

Finally, the Early Minoans produced Koumasa and Fine Gray Wares. Koumasa Ware is similar to Agios Onouphrios and tends to feature red and black designs on a light clay vessel. These tend to be cups, bowls, jugs, and other drinking containers. Fine Gray Ware is similar but tends to be cylindrical with a polished surface. Potters would incise shapes onto these pots to create designs.

The Middle Minoan period saw the rise of an urbanized palace culture that required versatile vessels that could be used for storage and daily use. Pottery creation became standardized in workshops, and more elite wares were produced, creating a difference between the vessels used by nobles and those used by commoners. The pottery wheel made it to the Minoans from the Levant, and craftsmen and craftswomen became more adept at used iron-red slips of clay to add colors to vessels in insulated kilns. Out of this period came the Pithoi, which were massive storage vessels capable of holding 1,100 lbs. of liquid. Over 400 were found in the ruins of the palace of Knossos. Around this time, artisans painted fewer natural scenes and instead favored motives of geometric shapes, spirals, and elaborate whorls.

With new techniques and cultural changes came new styles of pottery. These were the Incised, the Barbotine, the Eggshell, and the Kamares. The Incised resembled the incised designs of the Early Minoans with some slight changes in subject matter. Barbotine was bulbous, with raised bumps, knobs, cones, ridges, and waves applied by adding more clay to a product to give it texture and definition. In some pieces, these designs mimicked the barnacle growth seen on boats. Eggshell Ware gets its name because the pottery is composed of paper-thin clay.

A large collection of Kamares Ware was discovered in the cave sanctuary of Kamares on Mount Ida in 1890. In the collection were some of the first polychrome vessels and evidence of pottery made on the new wheel imported from the east. These vessels tended to have light backgrounds and were covered in reds, browns, and sometimes whites to create coils, floral designs, and other shapes. Symmetry was key, but the artists tended to be creative.

A Collection of Middle Minoan Cups from Phaistos
Heraklion Archaeological Museum, CC0, via Wikimedia Commons
https://commons.wikimedia.org/wiki/File:Decorated_cups_Phaistos_archmus_Heraklion.jpg

Toward the end of the Middle Minoan period, artists turned away from their geometric designs and instead focused once more on animal and nature motifs. These could include vegetation, flowers, lilies, palms, and other local flora. Surprisingly, despite the rise of the nature designs, green was not used on pottery, perhaps because of its difficulty to mix with the materials available.

Finally, there was the pottery of the Late Minoans. Around this time, the Minoans started to influence the styles of other peoples in the Aegean Sea and exported their work as far as Egypt. The floral style from the late Middle Minoan continued, with painted red and black leaves and flowers on white backgrounds being the most popular scene. Archaeologists can tell which pieces came from which workshop because the pottery exhibits hallmarks of particular artists. Names, however, remain unknown.

Later, potters started using the Marine Style. Here, entire scenes were made of sea creatures with backgrounds of seaweed, sponges, and rocks. Octopi were some of the most iconic, and the entire style avoided structure to make the animals look like they were floating on the pot. The Marine Style is considered the last true Minoan style because the eruption of Thera followed shortly after and destroyed many of the workshops and production centers.[24]

Marine Style Minoan Pottery Jug, 1575 BCE–1500 BCE
Charles Edwin Wilbour Fund, No restrictions, via Wikimedia Commons
https://commons.wikimedia.org/wiki/File:Minoan_Decorated_Jug,_ca._1575-1500_B.C.E._37.13E.jpg

This image demonstrates how important it was to Minoan artists to cover the canvas of their work with elaborate and intricate designs. This jug, produced in the 16th century BCE, features a beautiful depiction of sea life as well as simple yet opulent geometric patterns around the mouth and handle. It's likely this

---

[24] Ibid.

particular jug was meant for decoration rather than utilitarian purposes, but the artwork remains revealing nonetheless. This particular piece is an example of the Late Minoan Marine Style.

Metalwork

Still another form of artwork was metalworking, or the creation of ornaments, jewelry, and even cups from metals like gold and copper. Both materials needed to be imported, and they demonstrated the status of their owners. A common technique for metalworking was gold granulation, which allowed artists to create elaborate pieces like the famous gold bee pendant—a necklace that looks like a bee complete with wings. In order to make such items, the craftsmen and craftswomen needed to understand the basic properties of the metal and be able to manipulate fire to precise temperatures to bond gold without burning it. Such skills developed over the three Minoan periods, as the Minoans first learned to shape bronze and started to incorporate more metals as their trade networks expanded.

Archaeologists have located metal vessels on Crete that date roughly to the middle of the Early Minoan period, or c. 2500 BCE. Some of the newest metalwork comes from c. 1450, which indicates the Minoans were still producing their iconic crafts up until the fall of their civilization. The earliest examples of metalwork were made from precious metals like gold, but more recent products were made of arsenical or tin bronze. Historians suggest the adaption was the result of more individuals being able to afford metalwork as well as a greater supply of materials since precious metal objects were still being made. However, most belonged to upper-class families. Cups formed the majority of precious metal metalwork, while a more diverse array of objects could be made of bronze. These included pans, bowls, cups, lamps, basins, cauldrons, and rhytons.

The Minoans exported their metal goods to the various civilizations with whom they traded. Quite a few cups and vessels with Minoan characteristics have been found on mainland Greece. It's thought that the Minoans sold their metalwork to the Mycenaeans or gifted them elaborate pieces. Objects not traded were used at home for cooking, food storage, and perhaps toasting rituals related to the Minoan cult. Bronze and gold metalwork are frequently found in graves.

The Minoans made their metal vessels mainly through lost-wax casting or the raising of sheet metal. Stone hammers and wooden tools were used to raise hot metal into the desired shape, and extra pieces like legs and handles needed to be cast separately and then riveted onto the body of a piece. Metalsmiths knew how to inlay additional precious metals, gilded vessels, and add numerous decorations like marine life, bulls, flowers, and geometric shapes.

Jewelry

The Minoans made and wore jewelry inspired by nature, with the most popular designs including flowers, animals, and bees. Their techniques and choices were influenced by the civilizations and cultures they traded with, including the Babylonians and Egyptians. Numerous deposits of these luxury goods were discovered by archaeologists on multiple islands because of the durability of the metal. One of the largest collections of jewelry was a part of the Aegina Treasure, a hoard of precious gold found on the island of Aegina. All of the jewelry included gold, either as the primary material or as an accent to beads. The collection featured four rings for fingers, three diadems, a chest pendant or brooch, two pairs of earrings, at least five additional and non-wearable rings, a golden cup, a solid gold bracelet, and numerous decorative strips.[25]

Since their islands included deposits of natural metals and resources like silver and bronze, the Minoans were able to mine

---

[25] R. Higgins, *The Aegina Treasure - An Archaeological Mystery*, London: 1979.

materials and then refine the practices of smelting and metalwork.[26] Because of the delicate nature of jewelry making, most craftsmen and craftswomen completed individual pieces by hand. The main exceptions were when someone wanted to create rings or individual beads for necklaces. Due to the minuscule nature of these pieces, the Minoans relied on a technique called lost-wax casting.

The golden ibex below was found in Santorini and, while perhaps not Minoan, used the same process to be created as the Minoans would use to make metal structures like beads. In lost-wax casting, a wax mold would be created with a hollowed design in the interior. The mold would be sealed, and molten material would be poured through an opening near the top. The metal would harden and take shape in the mold, resulting in elaborate objects and designs that could be remade over and over.[27]

Gold Ibex Statue c. 17ᵗʰ Century BCE (Santorini)
https://commons.wikimedia.org/wiki/File:TheraLateCyccladicIbex06655.jpg

---

[26] Although the Minoans were able to extract some gold from the ground, the majority of their supply came from trade with North Africa, where the metal was more common.

[27] J.V. Noble, "The Wax of the Lost Wax Process". *American Journal of Archaeology*, 79, no. 4 (1975).

So, what did the Minoans like to use in their jewelry?

Precious metals tended to form the base of all pieces. Wealthier individuals could afford jewelry made entirely of gold or silver, while bronze and gold-plated bronze pieces were more cost-effective and worn by the common people. The Minoans were able to trade for or mine a variety of semi-precious stones and minerals that offered bright colors and contrasts. Favorites appeared to be lapis lazuli (blue), carnelian (orange), garnet (deep red), and obsidian (black). Sometimes jewelers would also use jasper, a stone which was available in a variety of hues, including the rare green. Amethysts came from Egypt and experienced a burst of popularity among the Minoans, partly because they were somewhat inexpensive to trade. According to several scholars, the decline in the value of the amethyst occurred once the Egyptian nobility stopped favoring the semi-precious stone. In short, the vibrant purple material fell out of fashion.[28]

Amethyst
https://commons.wikimedia.org/wiki/File:Insides_of_a_Amethyst_Geode.jpg

---

[28] Jacke Phillips, "Egyptian Amethyst in the Bronze Age Aegean," *Journal of Ancient Egypt Interconnections* 1, no. 2 (2009).

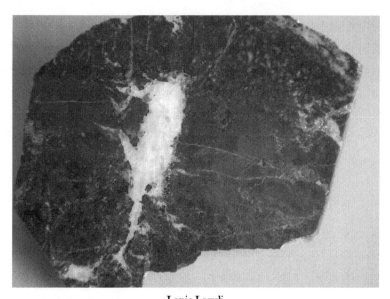

Lapis Lazuli

Other choices were more creative items and materials like shells, which could be gathered along the coasts of Thera and Crete. Steatite, or soapstone, was a hard mineral with a creamy, semi-translucent appearance that stood out against metal gathered from local islands. The Minoans traded for ivory from Africa as well. Blue materials continued to experience some of the highest demand due to the color's rarity in the natural world, as well as the Minoan's enjoyment of sea and water-based décor and motifs. Traders would sail to Egypt to bring back a substance called blue frit, or Egyptian blue, which was a synthetic material that was not quite Egyptian faience and not glass.

Egyptian faience, in general, proved to be fashionable. Egyptian faience was a particular substance developed by the Egyptians out of quartz and sand. The result was a glassy, moldable material that could be shaped, hardened, and dried. Finishes would be applied to the exterior so the end product would change to a new color once exposed to the heat of the drying process. These finishes included varying amounts of copper oxide, magnesium, calcium, potassium, and sodium. Again, the most popular choice of color for Egyptian faience was blue, although the Minoans also imported the material in green, red, black, and white. Some chemical analysis also indicates that the Minoans might have known how to make their own faience, potentially by mimicking methods learned from Egyptian craftsmen.[29] Again, the favored color was a bright blue that wasn't light but also not too rich. The best example of the color actually comes from an Egyptian artifact (and a personal favorite of this author), "William" the hippo.

"William," the Ancient Egyptian Faience Hippopotamus
Metropolitan Museum of Art, CC0, via Wikimedia Commons
https://commons.wikimedia.org/wiki/File:Standing_Hippopotamus_MET_DP248993.jpg

Despite being the rarest commodity, gold was favored because it symbolized the wearer's status and wealth. Only those of high economic status could afford even a single piece of gold jewelry. Gold is also a soft metal, making it easy to work with but also

---

[29] M.S. Tite; Y. Maniatis; D. Kavoussanaki; M. Panagiotakic; J. Shortland; S.F. Kirk, "Colour in Minoan faience," *Journal of Archaeological Science* 36, no. 2 (2009): pgs. 370-378.

simple to scratch. Metalworkers would need the experience necessary not to ruin their supplies, and their craftsmanship showed in their finished products. Due to its softness, gold appeared in numerous forms in jewelry. It could be beaten, embossed, engraved, and even punched with stamps to make a consistent design. It could also be transformed into more delicate materials like filigree or gold leaf. Some jewelry even shows the old technique of granulation, where minuscule gold spheres could be attached to a main piece of jewelry by applying and heating a mixture of copper salt and glue to the desired connection. This gold work was not for the faint of heart.

The Minoans produced almost every type of jewelry imaginable, including necklaces, bracelets, diadems, hairpins, chains, brooches, armlets, and even pectoral pieces. However, rings bore some of the greatest cultural significance because they could be used as seals on administrative documents. These rings bore distinct carvings that would form a design when pressed into hot wax. Many seal rings were solid gold, although some also included shells and hard materials that wouldn't be affected by the wax. Some could be opened and closed to expose the seal. The standard design was a convex oval attached at a right angle to the hoop of the ring.

"The Ring of Minos," c. 1500 – 1400 BCE

Signet or seal rings bore all types of patterns and full miniature scenes of events with cultural significance, including bull-leaping and hunting. Landscapes and animals were frequently depicted, including insects and arachnids like butterflies and spiders.[30] Like much Minoan jewelry and art, the artists preferred to fill the entire surface with engravings so different elements fought for space. This makes the total image difficult to see in several cases but is also a testament to the craftsmanship of the workers. At present, archaeologists have discovered over two hundred separate rings or lasting impressions, demonstrating the prevalence and importance of the seal ring.

An enduring legacy of the Minoans was their jewelry. Their techniques and styles continued to be used by other Aegean communities long after their civilization disappeared. Their successors, the Mycenaeans and the ancient Greeks, continued to use gold, included subjects like wildlife and flowers, and emphasized the importance of seals and luxury items as status symbols.

---

[30] Examples and a further study of the rings' cultural significance can be found in: "Tree Tugging and Omphalos Hugging on Minoan Gold Rings." In: Archaeologies of Cult: Essays on Ritual and Cult in Crete in Honor of Geraldine C. Gesell (Hesperia Suppl. 42), edited by Anna Lucia D'Agata and Aleydis van der Moortel, pp. 43-49. Princeton: American School of Classical Studies at Athens 2009.

Chapter 8 – Architecture

The Minoans possessed a form of architecture that was simple yet stylish. The majority of buildings used flat tiled roofs and stood between two and three stories high, including homes in cities. The lower walls would be made of compressed stone and rubble with little mortar, while mudbrick was used on the upper levels. Mudbrick is a building material composed of air-dried bricks made of a mixture of sand, loam, water, mud, and binding materials like plant husks. They were easy to make and have existed in some form since 7000 BCE. The Minoans fired their mudbrick, which made each individual brick more durable. Building interiors featured floors of flagstone, plaster, or wood. Some poorer homes might have used tamped earth, but there is little remaining proof.

Important buildings like palaces and villas were built from sturdier, more difficult to obtain materials like limestone, sandstone, and gypsum. There was no single pattern for construction, as buildings in different locations relied on either heavy, megalithic blocks of material or ashlar masonry. Ashlar stones were carefully cut to be even, small, and stable. Palaces and regular buildings alike used ceiling timbers to keep the roof in place.

Because the island settlements were small, the Minoans could have paved their roads using spare stones. This facilitated the movement of ox-drawn carts between farms, the coast, and the cities.

Plumbing

People sometimes forget that while modern plumbing is a luxury ancient humans lacked, civilizations still built intricate systems designed to handle waste management. Especially around the Mediterranean Sea and farther east toward the Levant, societies constructed sewer systems and avoided the disgusting conditions of the medieval Europeans, whom many modern audiences tend to think of when trying to imagine historical plumbing.

For the Minoans, the most important aspect of plumbing was the development of large, extensive waterways that could provide fresh water and also carry away waste and undesirable stormwater that might be contaminated with filth.[31] The Minoans were advanced and created their own aqueducts, cisterns, and isolated wells to ensure that fresh water, a precious resource in the middle of the sea, did not go to waste or become mixed with human waste. To facilitate plumbing, construction workers included the building of architecture into their designs. For example, the Minoan penchant for flat roofs and sloping entrances into open courtyards helped individuals gather the water from the rain and place it in cisterns.[32] Large structures like palaces also tended to have pipes that ran through and around the building, chasing water into designated storage areas.

[31] J.B, Rose and A.N, Angelakis, *Evolution of Sanitation and Wastewater Technologies through the Centuries*. London: IWA Publishing, 2014, pg. 2.

[32] Rose and Angelakis, *Evolution of Sanitation*, pg. 5.

Knossos' Palace Sewers Featuring a Stone Pipe
https://commons.wikimedia.org/wiki/File:Knossos_sewers_PA067399.JPG

Even more mind-blowing is that the Minoans developed some of the first water treatment devices. The most common was a porous clay pipe that water could flow through repeatedly. The water would slip through the pores in the clay, leaving behind dirt and debris too large to make it through the microscopic holes. As one can imagine, though, most examples of intricate plumbing came from the cities, and there is speculation that Minoans in rural areas were forced to live without. However, rural families still possessed the common sense to store rain and freshwater in separate cisterns or even pots to keep it clean and away from human and animal waste.

Palaces and Columns

Palaces were large building complexes designed to serve administrative and defensive purposes. Records and trading accounts could be stored in archives and kept safe from the environment, and people could also seek shelter behind the walls during attacks and natural disasters like the tsunami that hit Crete. The majority of palaces have been discovered by archaeologists on Crete, primarily in the city of Knossos. Each excavated palace possesses unique characteristics, but all Minoan palaces share some basic features like giant columns, courtyards, designated storage areas, multiple floors, and sturdy interior and exterior staircases. Because the palaces needed to survive multiple generations and preserve goods and records, they were constructed from heavy stone for maximum durability.

Archaeologists date the first palaces to the end of the Early Minoan period around the third millennium BCE. The oldest existing structures can be found at Malia and provide some basic information about the Minoan construction plan.[33] Due to the variations in foundation age for sections of the same structure, scholars believe the Minoans originally built smaller palaces and then added new developments over time to suit the needs of the community. Although there are some differences in the styles of the Early, Middle, and Late Minoan time periods, architecture and design did not change much over the centuries. Newer palaces from the Middle Minoans shared common traits with Early Minoan construction styles, including space for western courts and detailed western facades that included extra reinforcement and decoration. Some believe such treatment indicates that the cardinal direction west held some cultural significance.

Stone Ruins of the Palace of Knossos
Annatsach, CC BY-SA 4.0 <https://creativecommons.org/licenses/by-sa/4.0>, via Wikimedia Commons https://commons.wikimedia.org/wiki/File:Ruins_of_the_Minoan_Palace_in_Knossos.jpg

---

[33] Donald Preziosi and Louise A. Hitchcock, *Aegean Art and Architecture*, Oxford History of Art series, Oxford University Press, 1999.

Palaces were built to match preexisting geographical features and topography for maximum stability and flow. The buildings also aligned with significant landmarks like Mount Ida and Mount Juktas on a distinctive north-south axis, indicating the mountains possessed a form of ritual significance.[34] An example of this type of behavior from more modern societies would be the tendency of Christian churches to face east toward the sun due to the importance of the sunrise. This trend seemed to become less important in palaces constructed during the late Middle Minoan period, although the west facades were still given special treatment through the use of sandstone ashlar masonry.

Despite numerous similarities, palace architecture did slowly change due to the implementation of more efficient building techniques and a population increase that made construction easier. For this reason, scholars tend to divide architecture into the First Palace Period and the Second Palace Period. During the First Palace Period, the interior construction of a palace followed a basic square room by square room design where individuals would enter and walk directly from one room to another without intermediary structures like corridors. By the Second Palace Period, this simplistic design fell out of favor and was replaced with the tendency to build more elaborate internal divisions, hallways, and "gap" areas between main rooms.

Much of the current information about Minoan palace structure comes from the largest and most complete Minoan ruin in existence: the palace of Knossos.[35] This palace measures roughly 492 ft. across and has an area of 215,278 sq. ft. Some speculate the upper floors of the structure possessed over one thousand separate chambers varying in size and separated by corridors. The palace was so extensive during its time that many associate it with the

---

[34] Ibid.

[35] Anna Lucia D'Agata, "The Many Lives of a Ruin: History and Metahistory of the Palace of Minos at Knossos," *British School at Athens Studies* 18 (2010).

Greek myth of the bull of Minos, or the Minotaur, from which the Minoans get their modern name thanks to Arthur Evans.

An Existing Segment of the Palace of Knossos
Theofanis Ampatzidis, CC BY-SA 4.0 <https://creativecommons.org/licenses/by-sa/4.0>, via Wikimedia Commons https://commons.wikimedia.org/wiki/File:Knossos_palace.jpg

The palace of Knossos features perhaps the greatest Minoan contribution to the architecture of the Mediterranean, which is the red columns seen in the photo above. These columns were inverted, which means the top is wider than the base. This style was the opposite of that used by the Greeks, who favored broader bases that accentuated the height of the structure. The Minoans additionally made their columns of wood rather than stone, although the column was mounted on a basic rock base for stability. The top of the columns tended to be rounded or pillowed, again drawing attention upward and putting emphasis on the ceiling.[36]

The architecture of the palace of Knossos is more complex than that of other existing sites, with the entire structure built around a central court and consisting of extensive porticos, stairways, chambers, storage areas, and a potential beautification room where

---

[36] F. Bourbon, *Lost Civilizations*, New York: Barnes and Noble, Inc., 1998.

men and women alike would go for makeup—some scholars even consider it to be the equivalent of a modern-day salon! Chambers on different levels might be connected by ramps, hidden staircases, or built into previously existing geographic features like hillsides, giving the entire palace an elaborate but haphazard appearance. Despite this, the palace of Knossos is beautiful, featuring some of the most detailed and colorful frescoes painted by the Minoans. These frescoes were not just reserved for the throne room, as they were even found in storage areas.

Palace Dolphin Fresco
Jebulon, CC0, via Wikimedia Commons
https://commons.wikimedia.org/wiki/File:Queen%27s_Megaron_with_dolphins_Knossos_Palace.jpg

Once again, the most common subjects of artwork were the ever-present dolphin, fish, flowers, saffron, and bull-leapers. Some areas, such as the throne room, feature more unusual creatures, including a lounging red animal with a decorative appearance. Red and blue were the most popular colors.

Chapter 9 – Theories about the Collapse of Civilization

By all accounts, the Minoans had a thriving civilization and appeared to have a hold on the sea surrounding their islands. These advantages did not save them, though, from eventually crumbling and losing their culture to their nearby neighbors like the Mycenaeans. Evidence gathered from islands like Crete indicate something enormous happened that pushed the Minoans out of their favorable situation, making them easy prey for more militaristic neighbors. At present, there is one major theory about why the Minoan civilization collapsed: the results of the Thera eruption.

The Minoan Eruption Theory

The Minoan home of Santorini existed in a dangerous location. As one can see in the accompanying image, the Santorini island group consisted of several small landmasses, including Santorini (Thera) itself, Therasia, and the Kameni Islands. At the center of this group was a caldera that still exists in contemporary times. A caldera is a cauldron-like hollow in a volcanic region that forms when a magma chamber or reservoir erupts. This sudden evacuation displaces the ground, resulting in a collapse that creates a sinkhole of soft earth and molten material. Over time, the caldera can slowly refill with magma from surrounding volcanic bodies and become ready for eruption once more.

The Santorini Caldera
https://commons.wikimedia.org/wiki/File:Santorini_Caldera_Landsat.jpg

Today, the Santorini caldera measures 7.5 x 4.3 miles and has cliffs of 980 ft. on three sides. Overlapping shield volcanos form the basis of the caldera and often create new, smaller calderas from their eruptions. The two islands in the center, Nea Kameni and Palea Kameni, are made of volcanic rock and ash from previous eruptions.

The Greek archaeologist Spyridon Marinatos developed the Minoan eruption theory between 1935 and 1939. According to this theory, there was a massive eruption on Thera between 1550 and 1500 BCE. It was one of the largest volcanic explosions in known history and ejected between 14 and 24 cubic miles of material. On the modern scale of the Volcanic Explosivity Index, the eruption ranked a 7.[37]

The Santorini eruption generated so much flow that it devastated the nearby Minoan settlement of Akrotiri and covered it in a thick layer of pumice. Santorini was roughly 62 miles from Crete, where the main Minoan settlements sat. According to Marinatos, the eruption was so devastating that it severely affected the development and stability of the Minoan culture. In theories from the first half of the 20th century, scholars proposed that so much volcanic ash came from the explosion on Thera that the plant life on the eastern half of Crete was completely choked and unable to grow. This starved the local population and prevented new growth and the further development of culture and military.

After closer examinations with modern instruments, scientists discovered that no more than 5 millimeters of ash covered any section of Crete, indicating that plant growth would not have been affected by volcanic material. Instead, there was evidence of something just as deadly. The explosion on Thera generated so much force that a massive tsunami hit the coast of Crete and destroyed the settlements along the eastern half of the island.[38] The town of Knossos lost most of its wealth and significance, and the regional importance of the settlement declined.

However, the decline was not immediate. Numerous remains have been found in the 16th century Minoan Thera ash layer that indicate the collapse was not immediate. People continued to live, create art, reproduce, and trade with surrounding civilizations, but

---

[37] Sigurdsson H, Carey, S, Alexandri M, Vougioukalakis G, Croff K, Roman C, Sakellariou D, Anagnostou C, Rousakis G, Ioakim C, Gogou A, Ballas D, Misaridis T, & Nomikou P, "Marine Investigations of Greece's Santorini Volcanic Field," *Eos* 87, no. 34 (2006).

[38] Floyd W. McCoy and Grant Heiken, "Tsunami Generated by the Late Bronze Age Eruption of Thera (Santorini), Greece," *Pure and Applied Geophysics*, 157, no. 157 (2000).

the eruption caused significant problems. Because the Minoans relied on their position as a sea power, the disruption of the tsunami threw a wrench into their operation. Evidence indicates many of their seafaring vessels would have been destroyed, and the storehouses and goods in Knossos and other settlements on the east coast of Crete would be gone as well. This meant trade and general defense declined significantly.

Whether or not the destruction was enough to immediately initiate the collapse of the civilization is the subject of hot debate. The settlements on Crete show that Mycenaean weaponry was buried at the sites soon after the initial eruption, and the Mycenaeans still took several decades to depose the Minoans. What is certain is that the eruption resulted in a severe economic and resource crisis that made the Minoans vulnerable to attack. According to the scholar Sinclair Hood, the Minoans probably succumbed to an invading force following the eruption.[39] He and several others believe that, due to the unevenness of the damage and destruction on Crete, the Mycenaeans were the real destroyers of the Minoan civilization on Crete. This is further evidenced by the fact that the palace at Knossos was mostly preserved and used by the Mycenaeans later on. There was also severe deforestation in the area, meaning the Minoans managed to exceed the region's environmental capacity.[40] It's likely the Minoans were already on the verge of collapse before the eruption due to the stripping of resources.

The Atlantis Interpretation

The Atlantis interpretation of the Minoan fate takes much of its inspiration from the Thera eruption that devastated Santorini and potentially Crete. Because this eruption generated enough force to

---

[39] Sinclair Hood, *The Minoans: Crete in the Bronze Age*, London: Thames & Hudson, 1971.

[40] J.D.S. Pendlebury and Arthur Evans, *Handbook to the Palace of Minos and Knossos with Its Dependencies*, Kessinger Publishing, 2003.

create a massive tsunami, some believe that the fate of the Minoans not only inspired the modern tale of Atlantis but actually happened. In many ways, the idea that the Minoan civilization became Atlantis is a conspiracy theory since there is no hard evidence for a secret underwater city. However, archaeologists and historians do believe the events that led to the Minoan collapse were responsible for the development of the Atlantean narrative.

Greek writers like Plato wrote extensively about a city that was enveloped by the sea and sank into the water but are vague about the details. Some documents indicate it happened under the "Pillars of Hercules," mountains on the Gulf of Laconia, the southernmost gulf of ancient Greece (although other sources point to the pillars being near Malta, Sicily, or the Straits of Gibraltar). The settlement that was the inspiration for Atlantis was destroyed, but the rhetoric is vague about whether it actually disappeared entirely into the water or not. Most scholars think the language is just a form of creative license and that the Thera eruption, combined with the Late Bronze Age Collapse and the fall of the Minoans, was what the Greeks referred to when talking about Atlantis.[41]

L. Bakst, Terror Antiquus, 1908
https://commons.wikimedia.org/wiki/File:Terror_Antiquus_by_L.Bakst_(1908).jpg

---

[41] Spyridon Marinatos, *Some Words about the Legend at Atlantis* (2nd ed.), Athens: C. Papachrysanthou, 1972.

Whether one subscribes to the conspiracy theory or sticks more to scholarly interpretations, it's clear that the Thera eruption was perhaps the most significant event to happen to the Minoans. While ultimately the Mycenaeans brought about their end, they faced a major decline after the eruption, losing parts of their culture and important settlements due to a random natural disaster rather than any personal failing or wrongdoing.

Conclusion – Where Are They Now?

When discussing ancient civilizations, there almost always is one question prevalent in contemporary minds: What happened to them? While this query can be related to mysterious disappearances, there is also another fundamental reason for the question: Often, individuals want to know if the ancient civilization could be their predecessors or ancestors. Modern professionals in the fields of archaeogenetics have spent the last decade working to discover where the Minoans went through the examination of genetic material pulled from ancient skeletons. These professionals can compare the information taken from mtDNA to determine whether the Minoans were absorbed into the Mycenaean civilization and eventually the Greeks, if they moved to a new location and reproduced with an existing group of peoples (thus changing the general traits recorded in DNA), or if they instead were wiped out through a combination of warfare and natural disasters.

While the studies of archaeogeneticists can answer burning personal questions, they can also provide a clue to other professionals about the movement of different groups of people.[42] The field of genetics, when applied to history, has demonstrated that most groups of humans are the descendants of a few specific individuals who carried separate genetic traits. This information is important in determining how different ethnic groups developed with specific genes and adaptations. While the mtDNA taken from the Minoans doesn't say much about distinct traits, it does allow archaeologists to answer the question: Where are they now?

In 2013, a group of archaeogeneticists took mtDNA from a sample of ancient Minoan skeletons that were found sealed in a cave in the Lasithi Plateau. What happened to the individuals is unknown, but the preserved bones date back between 3,700 and 4,400 years.[43] The team compared the Minoan mtDNA to samples taken from native residents of Greece, Egypt, general North Africa, Anatolia, and a broad spectrum of places across western and northern Europe. The results of the study indicated that the Minoans shared similar genetics with modern Cretans and Neolithic Europeans to the north and west. There were few to no similarities with Egyptian or Libyan populations, which means the Minoans did not move south into Africa after their civilization collapsed. This evidence does support the idea that the Minoans were absorbed into populations to the north and that their successors most likely did not leave the island of Crete. According to the study's co-author, George Stamatoyannopoulos from the University of Washington, "We now know that the founders of the first advanced European civilization were European. They were very similar to Neolithic Europeans and very similar to present day-Cretans."[44]

---

[42] A. Bouwman and F. Rühli, "Archaeogenetics in Evolutionary Medicine," *Journal of Molecular Medicine* 94 (2016): pgs. 971-977. doi: 10.1007/s00109-016-1438-8

[43] Hughey, Jeffrey. "A European Population in Minoan Bronze Age Crete." *Nature Communications* 4 (2013): pg. 1861. 10.1038/ncomms2871.

[44] Tia Ghose, "Mysterious Minoans Were European, DNA Finds," *LiveScience*, 2013.

In 2017, another archaeogenetics study was completed on a separate group of Minoan remains. This work concluded that the Minoans were genetically related to the Mycenaean Greeks and had similar but not identical traits. The DNA was then compared to modern Greek populations. Based on the results, scholars could conclude that the Minoans, Mycenaeans, and ancient Greeks were all related and that the same genetic strains continued into contemporary times. In short, the Minoans live on in the modern Greek population and others who hail from the Mediterranean on the European side.[45]

It can be difficult for people to understand why ancient civilizations are important to the modern world, especially when discussing a group as small as the Minoans. However, the Minoans paved the way for peoples like the Mycenaeans, who would then influence the culture of the ancient Greeks, who continue to be one of the most enduring European peoples in the world. From a social aspect, learning about the Minoans can demonstrate that the ancient world was not a solid mass. Reading about the oldest civilizations can often make people believe that humans developed in one way—heavy agriculture, strict gender roles, feudal societies, and massive armies. The Minoans defied these standards by offering a civilization based on commerce with almost equal rights for men and women, room for social advancement, and a navy that spent most of its time trading.

Without the Minoans, modern life wouldn't be the same at all.

---

[45] Brigit Katz, "DNA Analysis Sheds Light on the Mysterious Origins of the Ancient Greeks," *Smithsonian*.

Part 3: The Phoenicians

A Captivating Guide to the History of Phoenicia and the Impact Made by One of the Greatest Trading Civilizations of the Ancient World

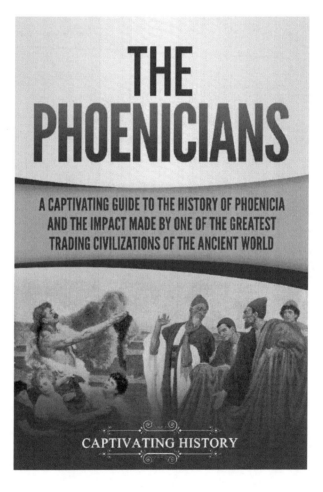

Introduction – Who Were the Phoenicians?

The Phoenicians remain one of the most enigmatic ancient civilizations, with historians and scholars prone to speculation and educated guesses. Although many Greek, Roman, and Egyptian writers reference the Phoenicians in trade records, military battles, and artistic transactions, few records were left by the original Phoenicians themselves, leaving modern scholars to fill in the blanks through educated guesses and material culture.

The ancient perception about this civilization was mixed. For every writer like Pomponius Mela who lavished praise upon the Phoenicians, there was another who derided the people as nothing more than cheats and hucksters who kept other states' trade stymied through stranglehold networks and ridiculous deals. Mela described them as such: "The Phoenicians were a clever race, who prospered in war and peace. They excelled in writing and literature, and in other arts, in seamanship, and in ruling an empire."[46]

---

[46] Pomponius Mela 1.12.

To dissect Mela's quote, the Phoenicians were great writers, yet they left almost no documents. They may have been excellent sailors and naval commanders, yet they built no territorial empire. They were stellar artists, yet their work contains few original elements. They may have been clever builders, yet their monuments crumbled. And the Phoenicians were a single civilization, yet they were split into city-states.

How could a civilization exist with so many contradictions, and how can modern historians utilize evidence that no longer seems to exist to uncover the truth?

Who were the enigmatic Phoenicians, why did their civilization crumble, and why should a modern audience care?

Read on to find out.

Chapter 1 – Origins

The origin of the Phoenician civilization had long been a mystery to those who were not members of it because of the secrecy with which the famous traders conducted themselves. Herodotus, a famous Greek historian, once wrote around 440 BCE that the Phoenicians were a people who left the shores of the Erythraean Sea and chose to settle around the Mediterranean.[47] From there, they plied their wares amongst the indigenous populations, creating one of the greatest trading civilizations in history.

Herodotus and many other Greeks thus believed the Phoenicians originated near the Erythraean Sea, which was a designation for the northwest Indian Ocean around the Gulf of Aden. This would have meant the Phoenicians came from Yemen or Somalia, although Herodotus later claimed Bahrain.[48] Another Greek historian, Strabo, would reiterate the belief that the Phoenicians hailed from Bahrain. However, archaeologists have discovered little evidence of any sort of large-scale human occupation of the region around the time the migration should have taken place: 2200 BCE to 1600 BCE. Instead, most of the

---

[47] Dates are referred to using the standard historic system of Before Common Era (BCE) and Common Era (CE).

[48] In contemporary times, Bahrain is an island nation in the Persian Gulf.

city-states were based around contemporary Lebanon, which is above modern Israel on the eastern coast of the Mediterranean Sea.

The people of the city of Tyre in South Lebanon maintain attachments to the Phoenicians, frequently noting the similarities between the names "Tylos," an ancient name of Bahrain, and "Tyre." They also point to similarities between the Persian Gulf and the culture of the Phoenicians. These claims actually have some scientific backing, as genetic studies have led some scientists to conclude that there is strong evidence that the Phoenicians were ethnically from Lebanon. The best of this evidence can be found in detailed genetic studies designed to examine the DNA fragments that exist in ancient skeletons.

Genetic Studies

Scientists have come a long way in the field of genetics, and they often work together with experts in the humanities to solve long unanswered questions about ancient peoples. Using DNA pulled directly from skeletons, geneticists and others can determine information about civilizations like the Phoenicians such as their heredity, nutrition, diet, and health. In 2008, a study published by Pierre Zalloua and his team of scientists revealed a possible connection between the Phoenicians and contemporary male populations in Lebanon and other regions in the Levant.

There were also distinct similarities between ancient Phoenician DNA and the samples taken from native individuals of southern Turkey, Malta, Sicily, Morocco, Spain, Sardinia, Ibiza, and Tunisia. These results resulted in the team concluding that the Phoenicians most likely hailed from Lebanon because they possessed a distinct genetic signature called haplogroup J2. The presence of similarities in other regions was deemed indicative of Phoenician expansion across the Mediterranean Sea following the rise of its civilization.[49]

In 2013, Zalloua led another study, this time testing more geographical communities to determine whether or not certain groups possessed a higher rate of what was termed the "Phoenician signature," or a distinct DNA sequence and genes that appeared to originate in the Phoenician civilization. Some communities did, in fact, have a higher rate of the Phoenician signature appearing in indigenous populations, which led Zalloua and his colleagues to conclude that Lebanon, the originating location of the Phoenicians, already possessed a diverse population consisting of "well-differentiated communities with their own genetic peculiarities" upon which religious and cultural divisions were then painted over.[50] In short, the Phoenicians did not represent a homogenous population of Lebanon but rather a particular ethnic group that rose to prominence and eventually unified the region, allowing the Phoenician signature to spread to new regions.

Other studies over the last two decades produced similar results but also identified the potential closest surviving relatives of the ancient Phoenicians by identifying genetic similarities. The closest contemporary ethnic group to the Phoenicians is the Levantine Semites, a category that includes a broad spectrum of Lebanese, Jewish, Palestinian, and Syrian individuals. There is also notable genetic similarity—sometimes as much as ninety percent—between the modern Lebanese population and the Bronze Age Sidonians.[51] [52] The Sidonians were Phoenicians from the city-state of Sidon,

---

[49]Pierre A. Zalloua, Daniel E. Platt, Mirvat El Sibai, Jade Khalife, et al. "Identifying Genetic Traces of Historical Expansions: Phoenician Footprints in the Mediterranean."

[50] Stieglitz, Robert (1990). "The Geopolitics of the Phoenician Littoral in the Early Iron Age". Bulletin of the American Schools of Oriental Research. 129 (9).

[51] Lucotte, Gérard; Mercier, Géraldine (2003). "Y-chromosome DNA haplotypes in Jews: comparisons with Lebanese and Palestinians." Genetic Testing. 7 (1): 67–71. doi:10.1089/109065703321560976

[52] Haber, Marc; Doumet-Serhal, Claude; Scheib, Christiana; Xue, Yali; Danecek, Petr; Mezzavilla, Massimo; Youhanna, Sonia; Martiniano, Rui; Prado-Martinez, Javier (2017-

which was north of Tyre. They were famous glass producers.

However, finding out such information, while it reveals fascinating details about genetics and the movement of people, says little about the Phoenicians as a culture. To find this information and to understand the origins of the once-great trading civilization, one has to look at who the Phoenicians were as a society. And what they were was Canaanites.

A Cultural Ancestor

Wherever the Phoenicians may have come from, they were ultimately an offshoot of the Canaanites. Although most associate the Canaanites with the state of Canaan, the term actually refers to a series of indigenous peoples and populations that lived in an area in the ancient Near East called the Levant. The Levant is an approximate historical, geographical term used to refer to a large segment of the Eastern Mediterranean. It primarily includes what modern audiences call Lebanon, Syria, Jordan, Israel, and Palestine.

The Canaanites were Semitic-speaking peoples with a unique culture derived from ancient Mesopotamian traditions and religious practices. There were many different groups that could be considered Canaanites while still maintaining their own ethnical and cultural differences. One archaeologist, Jonathan N. Tubb, said it best when he stated the "Ammonites, Moabites, Israelites, and Phoenicians undoubtedly achieved their own cultural identities, and yet ethnically they were all Canaanites."[53] To be a Canaanite was not to be part of a monolith; it meant forging one's unique identity while sharing some cultural similarities with the other Semitic-speaking groups of the Levant.

08-03). "Continuity and Admixture in the Last Five Millennia of Levantine History from Ancient Canaanite and Present-Day Lebanese Genome Sequences. "*The American Journal of Human Genetics.* 101 (2): 274–282. doi: 10.1016/j.ajhg.2017.06.013

[53] Tubb, Johnathan N. (1998). *Canaanites. British Museum People of the Past.*

As a unit, the Canaanites were forced to carve a unique niche for themselves in the ancient world because they lived in an arid region surrounded by powerful enemies like the Egyptians, Assyrians, Babylonians, Akkadians, and even Minoans from Crete. Creating a homeland was difficult, and a stable military was hard to feed and shelter while on the move. Eventually, the Canaanites discovered they operated well as intermediaries between other civilizations and became traders, shuffling goods from one place to another and profiting handsomely.

One can see where the Phoenicians developed their unique flavor by watching how the Canaanites as a whole flocked to the coast and began to educate themselves about their neighbors and what powerful rulers desired. Over time, the Phoenicians would distinguish themselves from the Canaanites in a manner similar to the Israelites. The people, while originally Canaanites, developed their own distinct culture and identity, forming a new civilization in the process.

Maintaining power would always be a struggle. The Canaanites were plagued by climate changes and issues like drought and famine that made trade and feeding a population difficult. For thousands of years, the people were on the move, attempting to find a place where they could support themselves. They were around during the infamous Bronze Age Collapse, which was when many of the powerful civilizations of the Bronze Age—the period in human history where cultures discovered how to make bronze weapons and tools—suddenly hit a dark era. During the Bronze Age Collapse, civilizations starved and warred with one another potentially due to climate change and the arrival of a foreign enemy known only as the Sea Peoples.

But what did it mean for the Phoenicians to be Canaanites?

As Canaanites, the Phoenicians inherited a rich culture rooted in the traditions of Mesopotamia. The civilization spoke a Semitic language, or a variation of the Afroasiatic language family originating in the Middle East shared by many other civilizations. A contemporary example of a Semitic language would be Arabic, which originated in the same region and evolved over time from old Semitic tongues to what it is today. This gave the Phoenicians some cultural similarities with their neighbors while ensuring they stood apart from trading partners like the Greeks and Egyptians.

The Phoenicians would also inherit the Mesopotamian religion, which was polytheistic and rooted in tribalism and multiple cultures. They believed in a supreme god who had managed to produce lesser deities, and they often performed religious rites and rituals meant to boost agriculture, wealth, and health. They had a priesthood and a mythology that they shared with their other Canaanite neighbors, including the Israelites. Each region tended to worship a different god above all others, adding new complexities to the mix.

Finally, the Phoenicians inherited Canaanite social norms. This meant they tended to dress modestly, had extreme gender roles for men and women, built their homes using traditional methods, and molded their society around city-states filled with powerful nobles. Although the Canaanites have a bad reputation among many followers of Abrahamic religions because of their depiction in holy books, they were actually a complicated culture centered on trying to survive in a harsh world. The Phoenicians would carry this legacy as they carved for themselves a powerful reputation in the ancient world as the best and most cunning traders history has ever seen.

Chapter 2 – The World of the Phoenicians

In order to understand the massive trade network and interstate relationships cultivated by this unique civilization, readers need to understand just what constituted the world at this time. Although many ancient peoples knew of something greater than themselves, it is likely that none could comprehend the sheer enormity of the planet. Instead, their world consisted of the Mediterranean Sea, parts of Southern Europe, Northern Africa, and Western Asia. The Phoenicians went to key locations on each of these continents and established cities from which to trade, forming a small yet expansive state.

The Phoenicians started their civilization in a fertile and developed region known as the Levant. The Levant was one of the original cradles of civilization and included most of what contemporaries now consider the Middle East. The Phoenicians were based right along the Mediterranean coast, but they also had territory that expanded throughout modern Lebanon. This land was excellent for farming and included great cedar forests that supplied lumber for homes and ships.

The central Phoenician territory existed in an enviable position and thus came under attack regularly from neighboring states. The territory encompassed several notable passageways used for trading between Asia and Africa. Conquerors, kings, and warlords all wanted to control the region because it would mean untold wealth and numerous political advantages when attempting to subjugate rivals.

Although Phoenicia became well known for its navy, its people still needed to be protected from ground-based attacks. Over time, a strong military and sturdy city fortifications were developed in each individual settlement. The armies of the city-states would often work together but were still separate entities under the control of a variety of local generals. Even though the military never reached the heights of more powerful Mediterranean civilizations, the Phoenicians did have an advantage, as they were a nascent civilization that didn't emerge until the end of the Bronze Age, allowing them to transition their culture and society easier than other established civilizations into the Iron Age.

The Iron Age of the ancient Near East began around 1300 BCE, and it refers to the period of time when humans learned how to create and use iron to make implements, tools, and weapons. The Phoenicians first emerged as a distinct culture once the other civilizations in the Levant experienced a societal collapse that eliminated the majority of state power and left territories that were basically free pickings for anyone who could handle the numerous raiders and the mysterious Sea Peoples that had decimated more powerful civilizations.

Having emerged just before the Iron Age, the Phoenicians inherited much of the technology and social developments of their predecessors, including the Canaanites. They were able to use these elements in combination with the relative weakness of formerly powerful enemies like Egypt to carve an advantageous position along the coast, from which they could control commerce from heavily fortified city-states.

However, the Phoenicians would be unable to form their monopoly on trade until after the Bronze Age Collapse and thus dealt with numerous other powerful civilizations in the region that posed imminent threats to the safety and success of Phoenician civilization. These were the juggernauts of the ancient Levant, powerful groups that were advantageous and yet dangerous for the Phoenicians because of their proximity. The most important were the Assyrians, Greeks, Egyptians, Babylonians, and Persians, who would appear at different times throughout the lifespan of the Phoenician civilization.

Influential City-States

Because the Phoenicians were so spread out, they possessed numerous city-states that formed essential parts of their intricate maritime trade networks. All told, archaeologists have discovered around eighty separate city-states scattered through a diverse region. The most significant city-states were in the region of Lebanon, where the Phoenicians originated. Other influential settlements could be found in Algeria, Cyprus, Italy, Libya, Malta, Spain, Tunisia, Turkey, and Morocco. Historians also think the Phoenicians controlled certain ports in Portugal and Greece, including Lisbon.

Tyre

Tyre was an island city-state based off of the coast of Lebanon. It was constructed by rulers who used dirt, sand, and rocks from the nearby beaches to fill the space between two reefs, creating a spot on which the city could be built. Over time, rulers continued to enlarge and expand the territory, creating what should have been one of the most defensible locations in the Mediterranean. Unfortunately, the arrogance of the Tyrian monarchy led to the city being sacked by Alexander the Great in the 4th century BCE, resulting in most of the city being lost.

Tyre was influential as a port for commerce and trade, but it relied heavily on the mainland to keep it supplied with building materials, food, and fresh water. Ships traveled from the island to the coast to gather natural resources, and the city controlled nearby arable land for farming and livestock. Within the walls of Tyre, the locals gathered rainwater in cisterns and engaged in a variety of influential crafts, including dye-making, pottery production, and jewelry manufacturing.

Byblos

Byblos was a seaport and a significant city at the base of the Lebanese mountains that specialized in the creation and export of papyrus scrolls. The location was originally settled in the Neolithic period and was one of the oldest and most enduring Phoenician cities. It was conquered and turned into a vassal state by invaders multiple times throughout its history, but it served as the central jewel in the Phoenician crown of commerce for many centuries during the Phoenician golden age. There was plenty of access to fresh water and copper, making this a resource-rich urban center full of craftsmen and women who benefited from the labor of nearby farmers and shepherds.

Sidon

Sidon was another city-state located in modern-day Lebanon that served as an influential seaport for commerce and trade. It had been occupied since the Neolithic period and stood out from other urban centers by having access to lush cedar wood forests, hinterlands, and fertile agricultural territory. Dye-making was a popular activity because the city was near a cove where divers could locate murex snails, which were necessary for making a luxurious and unique purple dye. In contemporary times, Sidon is well known in archaeological circles for having some of the most preserved tombs and burial grounds, providing much-needed insight into the rituals of the Phoenicians and their view on the afterlife.

Carthage

Carthage is one of the city-states many have heard about because of its famous rivalry with Rome, but it began as a colony of Tyre in North Africa (in modern-day Tunisia) that eventually rose to become a powerful city-state. Carthage was heavily militaristic, supplying the Phoenicians with weapons and formidable war elephants. However, the people also made pottery, developed their own writing style and language, and produced massive amounts of text that would be burned when Rome sacked the city.

Besides these four major players, there were dozens of additional cities and colonies that formed the massive Phoenician trade network. Most of the evidence about their comings and goings comes from archaeological excavations, which are able to locate the skeletons of temples and other significant buildings, as well as distinctly Phoenician artifacts. These other locations include:

Beirut

Tripoli

Sarepta

Baalbek

Hippo

Icosium

Marion

Tharros

Leptis Magna

Callista

Utica

Lisbon

Sexi

Some of these names will no doubt sound familiar to contemporary readers. These territories were spread out over a broad area and encompassed locations like North Africa, Cyprus, Sicily, the Iberian Peninsula, modern-day Turkey, modern-day Algeria, and modern-day Lebanon.

Chapter 3 – Political and Legal Structures

The first step in understanding the complexities of a civilization with little-known history is to take a look at what scholars do know. What they do have an understanding of is how the Phoenicians conducted their daily lives and operated their city-states. One of the underlying fundamentals of civilization is the political state, an entity that many ancient historians believe separated humans from their hunter-gatherer roots and helped develop a society based on agriculture.

The Phoenician civilization did not consist of a single state but rather several significant powers that organized themselves into hotspots of influence and trade. These would be known as the city-states, or political entities that controlled a major city and much of the surrounding territory around it. Another similar example of this type of civilization would be the ancient Greeks, who operated from individual settlements that controlled nearby agricultural lands.

The Political Structure: Social Classes Abound

The political structure of the Phoenician civilization varied by location and adopted the customs of neighbors and trading partners alike. Throughout much of the culture's history, Phoenicia was split between several independent city-states that shared a similar culture but kept political power divided between a series of hereditary monarchies. The most famous of these city-states were notable trading ports like Tyre, Sidon, and Byblos. Phoenicia never became a single political entity, and the kings would exercise almost complete control until the destruction of the civilization.

Before annihilation, though, political power was split due to the presence of multiple social classes and influential families. While the monarchs were the head of each city-state, they relied upon an administration to carry out the actual governance of the territory. In most cases, the administrators of the government were members of a class of priests as well as significant noble households. The nobles could provide resources like food and soldiers, meaning it was important for the monarchs to remain on their good sides. While almost all noble families were born into their position, some individuals managed to join this elite rank by making a fortune in international trade.

Because the city-states were independent of one another but shared a similar culture, they cooperated to foster a powerful empire built on trade. Many historians compare the Phoenicians to the ancient Greeks, who lived in city-states like Athens and Sparta, shared a culture, and occasionally got along to defend against external enemies. While the Phoenicians would sometimes unite their armies, the city-states emphasized cooperation not so much for defense but instead to build an economic powerhouse in the Levant and the nearby Mediterranean Sea.

Separate city-states would be the most powerful at different times in history. The city-state with the most resources thus had more political influence and power compared to the others. This meant the political structure of Phoenicia was liable to change based on which region was the wealthiest or possessed the most soldiers. For example, Sidon was the most powerful city-state between the 12th and 11th centuries BCE and, therefore, was able to bully or coerce the nearby city-states of Tyre and Byblos into doing what it wanted. In the 10th century BCE, Tyre became the most powerful. Although the Phoenician city-states avoided making formal alliances, they were not above making informal agreements structured around force and the ever-present trade.

When it came to foreign policy, the city-states were on their own. Phoenicia had no single recognized ruler or council, so places like Sidon and Tyre could choose to help whichever allies they wanted. If the monarch of one wished to assist the Greeks, for example, he could. If he did not, there was no political power pressuring him into joining a war effort. This could be seen throughout the history of Phoenicia. The best example is during the famous war between Greece and Persia when each city-state in Phoenicia gradually chose to help Xerxes by sending ships to bolster the Persian emperor's navy. This was not a cohesive decision but one born out of convenience and a desire for power. After all, Persia controlled several of the Phoenician territories by this point in history, and the remaining independent city-states did not want to incur the ire and wrath of Xerxes.

Hereditary Monarchies

Members of the hereditary monarchies are the most well-known Phoenician political figures. Although they did not commemorate their achievements through sculptures or artwork like the pharaohs of Egypt or the kings of Greece, Phoenician rulers did leave their names on tomb inscriptions. Archaeologists have been able to date coffins and temples, and historians have discovered numerous references to the Phoenician kings in surviving primary sources.

According to tomb inscriptions, the hereditary monarchs managed to wield absolute power until the 7th century BCE when discontented members of Phoenician society decided they would like a better slice of the political power pie. At the same time, it is obvious that the monarchs could not tax their populations much due to the small size of the civilization. Instead, kings needed to trade and fund expeditions to acquire rare goods and make money by taxing merchants.

When talking about the monarchs, it's important to note that women, while they could become queens, did not rule on their own. They were not as important as the male heirs and rarely had their names inscribed in the annals of history. The right to rule was passed down from father to son. If there were no male heirs, the husband of the closest female heir would become the new king. Historians have created a somewhat comprehensive list of the different monarchs of city-states like Sidon and Tyre. Savvy readers will realize that not a single name belongs to a woman and that many rulers incorporated "baal" in their names. In early Phoenician history, Ba'al was the chief deity and viewed as the supreme lord of the cosmos. Referencing him in royal naming practices was seen as a form of legitimizing the monarchy.

In Byblos, the line of succession looked like this:

c. 1000 BCE Ahiram

980 BCE Ittobaal

940 BCE Abibaal

920 BCE Yehimilk

900 BCE Elibaal

880 BCE Shipitbaal

The annals of Tyre and other complementary sources produce the following list of reigning kings for Tyre:

969-936 BCE Hiram I

935-919 BCE Baal-Eser I

918-910 BCE Abdastrato

909-898 BCE Methustratos

897-889 BCE Astharymos

888 BCE Phelles

887-856 BCE Ithobaal I

855-830 BCE Baal-Eser II

829-821 BCE Mattan II

820-774 BCE Pygmalion

750-740 BCE Ithobaal II

739-730 BCE Hiram II

730-729 BCE Mattan II

729-694 BCE Elulaios

680-640 BCE Baal I

591-573 BCE Ithobaal III

Baal II

Mattan III

Hiram III

The monarchs possessed reasonably long reigns for ancient history, with most having power for two to three decades. Only one inscription from Sidon is a woman, Unmiashtart, who became a regent for her son in the 5th century BCE. The only other influential female political figure comes from a quasi-mythological source and is Dido, the famous sister of Pygmalion. She was said to have left Tyre along with like-minded nobles and helped establish the city of Carthage on the northern coast of Africa.

The Priesthood

The priesthood was considered a separate class from the nobility, although most of the members came from the royal line, as well as leading merchant families. Priests were responsible for the maintenance of significant temples as well as the performance of rituals intended to maintain Phoenician society and please the gods. In multiple cases, records indicate that priests could also become royals or were closely entwined with the family. One famous example is Ozbaal, who became the king of Byblos but who was the son of a priest of Baalat named Paltibaal.

Priests worked closely with the monarchs of the city-states because, in Phoenician culture, the office of king carried religious rights and obligations. The king was seen as a representative of the gods and worked to ensure they were seen as just and righteous, as well as powerful. Occasionally, a king might claim to actually be a god incarnate on earth, although this maneuver was opposed by the priests. To become a priest, a man needed to be born in a noble family and undergo years of training. Priests had access to places commoners and even other nobles could not go, particularly the inner sanctums of many of the temples.

Senior Officials

If a man wanted power in Phoenician society, he could become a senior official to the king. Like priests, senior officials could only be nobles and needed to be elders. The king of city-states like Tyre would consult with elders for advice about the best course of political action. According to an ancient Greek historian named Arrian, the Phoenician senior officials would be called upon to make important decisions when the king was indisposed. Other historians from nearby trading partners also mentioned the council and believed it held the most power in the city-states. Membership no doubt only belonged to senior nobles and influential merchants, and it is unknown whether the king had to bow to their will. There is some evidence, though, that the council could force the king to adhere to their decisions in times of crisis.

Besides the council, the other two positions of importance were the governor and the commander of the army. Each city-state would have one each, and their roles focused on administration, tax collection, and coordinating the defense of the city. The governor also needed to supervise the courts and ensure justice was served. Unfortunately, many details about these jobs are lacking because the texts taken from El Amarna, Cyprus, and Ugarit are fragmented.

Alternative Forms of Government

At some point, Tyre bucked the original monarchy and embraced a system of government in the 6th century BCE, where everything was controlled by a pair of judges called the *suffetes*. These judges were chosen from the most powerful noble families and appeared to exert almost dictator-like control over justice and the governance of the territory. This system would be adopted by Carthage later on.

Besides the *suffetes*, the kings of the Phoenician cities would also have to rule alongside an Assyrian governor when the Assyrians dominated the region in the 7th century BCE. Even official correspondence could not be opened without the governor present, and the king became more of a figurehead in a vassal state. This system would continue when the Babylonians arrived and Nebuchadnezzar II decided a minister needed to rule alongside the king of Tyre, a system continued by the Persians later on.

However, such systems tended to occur under imperialism and the vassalage of more powerful civilizations and were confined to captured city-states. Tyre perhaps experienced the most changes in government because it was captured again and again due to its desirable position on the coast of modern-day Lebanon.

Law and Order

Scholars possess little information about the administration of law and order by the Phoenicians. It is clear that they had a system of courts with judges and justices that were responsible for meting out punishments and solving disputes between citizens. Laws were also applied differently to the varying social classes, as the murder of a commoner by a noble was not punished as harshly as a regular man would be if he hurt or killed someone of the upper classes. Likewise, women possessed far fewer rights than their male counterparts, and slaves had almost no protections for themselves.

Because the Phoenicians were Canaanites culturally, they shared some similarities to the justice systems practiced by the Canaanites,

Israelites, and others from the Levant. Unfortunately, there are no known documents because the Phoenicians typically wrote on papyrus, which rapidly degraded over time. However, historians can still piece together crucial elements of the legal system by examining clay tablets or references to the system in the documents of nearby civilizations. In general, the Phoenicians did not appear to differ much from other Levantine societies, preferring a biased and harsh legal system.

As with many other cultures that developed in the Levant, there was a somewhat codified system of laws and general practices that controlled behavior within the civilization. In general, the upper classes had the most rights in society, and laws were not always applied equally. People with money could typically escape punishment by paying fines instead of experiencing punishments, and it was not uncommon for a man to be able to deflect punishment to his wife, children, or slaves instead of on himself. For example, a man was able to send his family members and slaves to work in his stead if he had incurred a significant debt to another individual.

Laws were carried out by the state, and most legal matters were the responsibility of key administrators and rulers within the city-states. Being a lawyer did eventually become a profession but not at the outset. Instead, free men could represent themselves, while everyone else had to hope someone would plead their case for them. This made it difficult for women, underage youths, slaves, and indentured servants to receive justice.

Punishments tended to be severe, and they often focused on the concept of equal punishment for a crime. For example, if someone killed another's slave, their own slave would be executed. There were numerous major crimes that were illegal, including murder and theft. Rape tended to be a gray area. Men who raped were told to marry their victims and pay a sum of money to the father of the woman instead of facing any other punishment.

Prisons and jails did exist, but the Phoenicians used such institutions more as holding spaces before trials than as places for people to serve out sentences. It was much easier to impose a fine, punishment, or execution than it was to keep somebody alive for years. Unfortunately, out of the limited information modern audiences have on the Phoenicians, this is the majority of what is known about their legal system. It is clear that each city-state and colony would have its own bylaws, and there were also religious laws that needed to be fulfilled. All of this would affect the culture of Phoenician daily life in a variety of ways.

Chapter 4 – Daily Life

Although the courts were significant for merchants and the upper classes, they were not the only factors that determined the way of life for the majority. There were dozens of other social and cultural institutions responsible for controlling how the average individual was expected to conduct themselves and behave around others. The most significant, besides class, was gender. Men and women were assigned different roles that they were expected to adhere to at all times.

Gender Roles

As was typical among the cultures of the Levant, men were seen as the dominant gender and thus controlled law, politics, and the family. While upper-class men could be merchants, judges, senior officials, and participate in politics, the majority of the male population were poor farmers or occasionally craftsmen, laborers, carpenters, and other professions that required physical labor. Payment was often received as food, although money could change hands in the cities.

Only nobles were given full rights to participate in courts and assert their independence, but Phoenician men still had more rights than women. While they could not vote, they could legally own property, enter into contracts, and travel and trade on their own. They were responsible for the life and death of their wives and children, and they could even exert control over widowed mothers. There are some cases of Phoenician men selling their wives and children as labor to pay off debts, and men could have affairs without being punished unless they slept with another man's wife.

Women possessed few rights and were considered the property of their fathers and then their husbands. While many held jobs as laborers, weavers, and embroiderers, they were also expected to maintain households and bear and raise children. Contrary to popular belief, ancient Phoenician women, like many others in the Levant, engaged in backbreaking physical labor as farmers, construction workers, and miners, in addition to their domestic duties.

However, unlike men, they could never attain a position of power above a male counterpart. For example, a woman might be a laborer who helped build a house, but she could never be the foreman. Women also could not own property or enter into contracts, and they could not live by themselves even when widowed. They were expected to join the house of their nearest male relative, whether it be a son, brother, brother-in-law, or father. Upper-class women definitely had more rights than poor women but were still restricted and confined in their roles. Some learned to read and could exercise political influence, but they were still expected to be subservient to male relatives.

In Phoenician culture, there is an obvious Canaanite influence. Men were required to learn a trade between the ages of eleven and thirteen years old, while women remained at home and needed to care for their siblings and train under their mothers to become good wives and housekeepers. This meant understanding how to comb wool fibers and weave them into the fabric, sew, repair household items, cook, clean, bake, and also brew alcoholic beverages. Men, meanwhile, devoted their youth to becoming skilled in farming, shepherding, construction, or a similar profession that would support a family. Many learned additional skills like how to repair the tools of their trade, bartering in public markets, or basic accounting, like addition and subtraction.

Lower-class men and women would not have known how to read or write, and complex accounting was reserved for the nobility. Instead, most individuals would know basic mathematics, like simple addition. This did not mean the Phoenicians were dumb but rather that they lacked access to education. Upper-class men and women usually possessed some form of literacy, and complex counting and arithmetic were essential to learn for those who wanted to become a merchant and enter the great trading enterprises that characterized the economy. Unfortunately, most people would be simple laborers rather than wealthy participants in the industry.

As with most societies from the Levant, the Phoenicians also expected different sexual behaviors from the genders. Casual sex was frowned upon in Phoenician society, but men were still able to sleep with prostitutes, especially if the men were members of the upper classes. Women, on the other hand, needed to be virgins upon marriage and could only have sex with their husbands. While reproduction was the goal, some documents indicate that the Phoenicians also believed in sex for intimacy as a sign of a happy marriage. It is unclear whether the Phoenicians practiced polygamy like other Levantine civilizations.

Most marriages occurred when the man was around eighteen years old and the woman was closer to fifteen or sixteen. Although there were age gaps between couples and some women were married as young as twelve or thirteen, these were rare and were almost always noble marriages. In these cases, the wedding was arranged when the participants were children and would not be consummated until the bride and groom were closer to sixteen or seventeen years old. This was because the Phoenicians were aware that young women were unable to safely have children until they had grown older and developed wider hips.

Diet

The Phoenicians did not possess too much terrestrial territory but did acquire numerous foods from their trading partners in the Mediterranean Sea. The typical Phoenician diet thus tended to combine the natural foods of the Levant with some more unusual choices taken from around the sea. Some options included olives, wine, bread made from local grains, dried fish, garlic for flavor, lamb, goat, cheese, and even watermelon and grapes. Figs and dates were also local and could be used as a fresh treat to help even up the monotony of grains and assorted vegetables.

The Common Fig
https://commons.wikimedia.org/wiki/File:Ficus_carica_L,_1771.jpg

The Phoenicians did not have enough land to cultivate large farms because of their coastal cities, so they tended to rely on traded goods as well as the seafood they could take from the Mediterranean. Their fresh-caught fish would have included tuna and mackerel, and there is some evidence to suggest the Phoenicians ate crustaceans and mussels as well. Spears and boats would have been ideal for fishing, and nets could be woven of rough fibers. Hunting did occur, and the Phoenicians ate local produce from cows, boars, and even horses. After all, they had little need of these land animals when almost all their trading was done by boat on the vast expanse of the Mediterranean.

While cities might have had professional bakers and brewers, a lot of resources were made at home by women. The baking of bread was a daily chore that took several hours of hard labor, during which women needed to grind up grains like rye into a powder before mixing them with yeast and water. Bread was typically made flat along the edges of large clay pots and eaten with a variety of locally grown and gathered herbs and vegetables. They usually couldn't cook huge batches of bread at once because of the lack of preservatives, meaning any extra would have moldered quickly.

Housing and Architecture

Phoenician architecture was reminiscent of that of their Canaanite ancestors. It was typified by large temples that possessed double-columned facades front and center. Visitors could ascend to the temples by climbing a short staircase and then entering enclosed sacred spaces. These spaces tended to be closed off to all but the most significant members of society, including the priests and royalty. Once inside, the spaces were characterized by cube-like shrines with open fronts. Besides the temples, it was common to encounter dams and artificial harbors, which were necessary to keep the seafaring civilization functioning properly.

Away from the harbors and temples, the settlements were surrounded by large fortification walls that were built high and thick. The most common materials used in the building of these walls were limestone pulled from quarries in the Levant and mudbrick made from nearby resources. Square towers and large gates dotted the surface, allowing individuals who brought goods and food from the countryside to enter and trade. Although the Phoenicians did possess quite a bit of agricultural land, the majority of the population lived in cities and were typically employed in businesses related to commerce.

Domestic buildings and housing tended to be quite modest, especially among the lower classes. Mudbrick was again the most common building material, especially since builders and families could make it on their own and then put it together. Most houses would be composed of a single story with one, two, or three rooms where the family and their livestock would live together. It was easier to create a roof out of rushes than any other material, although wealthier individuals could afford a timber model. The nobility had more choices and tended to live in two- or three-story homes. While merchants might have used a mudbrick or limestone model, most nobility and royals could have had an entirely stone home. Temples were additionally made of limestone and were frequently home to their priests and priestesses.

Beyond these basics, historians and archaeologists struggle to piece together greater trends about Phoenician architecture because much of the civilization's buildings were destroyed or sieged and taken by other empires. Much of the original designs, therefore, did not remain behind, leaving scholars to fill in the blanks and attempt to make statements about the overall character of the buildings. However, Phoenician architects seemed to prefer austerity, if clay tablets left by visiting Greek and Roman authors are any indication. Their buildings were plain compared to those of their neighbors but leaned toward having an opulent elegance that sparingly used decorative elements in favor of clean lines.

After doing some research on the local geography and the practicality of acquiring stone (it was not practical at all), archaeologists think that many buildings were constructed using wood from nearby abundant cedar forests, which would have supplied a durable material. The problem with this choice is that much of the material did not remain for posterity since wood degrades far faster than stone and cannot survive the vestiges of time. So, instead of having much knowledge about smaller, more common buildings, historians instead have a better understanding of what large public temples and gathering spaces would have looked like.

Urban housing, though, can be seen depicted in the paintings and murals of other societies like the ancient Greeks, who recorded most Phoenician homes as having two columns by the entryway and sometimes encompassing multiple floors. Domestic dwellings had ovens and basalt stones used by women to grind grain for beer and bread, and the corners were rounded for a more pleasing finish. Smaller buildings had grates that allowed access to public sewer systems to stop the flow of waste from making individuals sick. Mudbrick was used as the primary building material, although wealthier folk could afford stone and rare woods like olive, oak, and strawberry. There is almost no evidence of town planning in the overall design of cities because the Phoenicians were restrained by the confines of their territory, according to records.

One cannot discuss architecture without examining how a society cared for its dead. Phoenician tombs are remarkably intact and long-lasting, especially compared to housing and more temporary structures. The *tophet* played a central role in these tombs, as it was a sacrificial altar for animals—and potentially humans—where living beings would be killed and then burned to honor the gods and the deceased. The ashes were scraped from the flat surface of the *tophet* and placed in urns, which sometimes contained the ashes of people as well. These urns were sealed with stones and placed in the *tophet*, which could hold anywhere from five to twenty urns. These *tophets* were often built within shaft tombs, which were several meters deep and accessible through a vertical corridor. The majority of the population would be burned and placed in these shaft tombs, while richer families could afford personal tombs built into hillsides, which were accessible by stairs.

When it comes to shrines and temples, there appeared to be two styles. One was of a religious center placed in a natural clearing, typically near mountains, rivers, deep in the forests, or by stones that held significance to a particular deity. Such shrines might be decorated with boughs and flowers and had elements like the *tophet* but did not possess many permanent structures. Temples, on the other hand, were lavish and made from stone and sometimes marble. Columns were essential and featured styles borrowed from civilizations like the Assyrians, Egyptians, and Greeks.

Each temple had a sacred interior sanctum where only priests could go, as well as a storage area for religious relics. Libations could be made in the temple or by the entrance, and many featured thrones and symbolically carved wall reliefs for the deities they represented. The Phoenicians, unlike the Egyptians, Assyrians, and Greeks, seem to have prohibited the creation of large sculptural likenesses of their gods. Most gods and goddesses had individual temples rather than a single central location for worship, and all of the city-states had an accessible temple for the chief deity of that place.

Chapter 5 – Beauty and Apparel

Because the Phoenicians cultivated trade and social relationships, the merchants became perhaps the most influential portion of the population. Instead of forming companies like modern traders, these merchants tended to keep the business in the family and would form long-lasting partnerships with other families in desirable locations like Egypt. Men and women in this class were not required to participate in military service or dirty work like farming and thus cultivated a culture of beauty and style, commissioning the creation of elaborate tunics, necklaces, and hats. Other wealthy nobles adopted this style, and clothing and accessories became the best way to tell just how important and influential people were.

Male Clothing

Social class determined the style of male Phoenician clothing, although there were general overarching trends. For common individuals, men could be expected to wear a close-fitting tunic that stretched from the waist to just above the knee. Linen or cotton was the preferred material because it was light and helped working men withstand the heat along the Mediterranean Sea.

Ornamentation or embroidery was lacking because of the cost of the thread, and jewelry was not common. Most men would wear a round or conical headdress with a topknot that gave the top a spherical appearance. All individuals wore sandals.

Upper-class men wore similar clothing but with more finery and detail. Their tunic, called a *shenti*, often featured sewn patterns and embroidery to denote a man's rank. The front parted to reveal an underlying piece of fabric to give more detail to the waist. Adorned lappets also decorated the front, and girdles were popular. Over the underlying *shenti* could be worn another close-fitting tunic that clung to the shoulders and upper arms. While some archaeologists in the past have described it as being similar to a modern jersey, it looks closer to a woman's bolero jacket that ends underneath the bust line.

When not following the style of a *shenti* and shoulder jacket, a wealthy or important man could wear an interior robe that reached the feet. Over it would be an outer blouse or shirt that descended to just above the knees. If they didn't wear this blouse, they could instead have a mantle thrown over their left shoulder, which would follow the man like a cape as he moved. Most men would, once again, have a conical hat with a topknot, although these headdresses were far more elaborate than those of lower-class men.

Priests were a separate class but still shared many similar elements to their secular peers. Their headdresses, for example, had topknots but also narrow crowns covered in the representations of bull heads. Their main tunic was a long robe that stretched from the base of the neck to the feet. Over the robe was a mantle that covered the right arm and shoulder and went down to the right knee. Detailed ornamentation decorated each piece of clothing, and embroidery was common around the collar and hem of the robe.

Hair, especially facial hair, was of the utmost importance to a Phoenician man because it denoted cleanliness and their position in society. Most men kept their hair underneath a cap and did not brush it often. When the cap was taken off, the hair tended to be a curly mess, although men liked to style it so that one or two rows of curls dangled from underneath the rim of the headdress. Many historians compare Phoenician beards to those of the Assyrians because men of both cultures tended to style it either as three to five rows of tight curls or as one long curly mass. Mustaches were not common and appeared to be shaved off in favor of long beards.

Ornaments for Men

The most common male accessory was the collar, which was worn around the neck and tended to be made of three rows of precious metals. These resembled Egyptian collars and were worn primarily by elites who could afford hammered gold. The collar extended from the throat down to the breast and was frequently complemented with armlets, bracelets, and rings for the fingers. Armlets tended to be the plainest of ornamentation, often being a piece of twisted metal that looped once or twice around the upper arm. Bracelets were similar but could occasionally include precious stones and agates. Rings were popular among all classes, but the best were made of silver or gold, had an inset stone, and often were used as seals for closing documents.

One well-known example of male jewelry comes from the rule of Etyander, a king of Paphos. Archaeologists discovered his armlets, which were made of small, single twists of gold that barely touched at the ends. They were bare except for a single inscription: "Eteadoro to Papo basileos," which in English means, "The property of Etyander, King of Paphos." While plain, everyone still knew that the jewelry conveyed power and respect.

Scholars do not know whether men often wore necklaces. Most artwork depicts women wearing the traditional three or four strands, but men are less frequently seen with such jewelry. Many educated historians believe men did wear necklaces based on the data currently possessed about European, Asian, and African fashions of the time. Jewelry was often used culturally to depict social status, with the wealthiest individuals often draping themselves in fine pieces made of gold and jewels. So, while there is little evidence about men possessing necklaces, it is very likely that they did.

Female Clothing

Although female goddesses were often depicted nude, Phoenician women were carefully garbed head to foot for modesty. While men had tight tunics, female robes were meant to be loose and worn in deliberately placed folds. The only points of interest were typically around the bust and waist, where it was acceptable to have some shape before the fabric became billowy and created heavy folds of drapery. Girdles were used to give the material definition and were tied in the front. Petticoats were common and typically went underneath the robes. Women wore leather sandals to protect their feet from sand, rocks, and other hazards.

Hair was an unusual case for women. Although women from some regions wore caps to hide their locks for modesty, others wore theirs loose in waves that parted at the center of the head. Hair tended to be shoulder length and could be kept in check with a single woven or leather band. Others used loose hoods, which also protected one's face from the sun. Typically, wealthier women were more likely to have styled hair with bands, while lower-class individuals covered their heads to help prevent sunburns. Because of the natural heat in the city-states, Phoenician women avoided growing their hair longer than their shoulders.

Ornaments for Women

Phoenician women wore many more ornaments and accessories than their male counterparts. Jewelry and ornamentation demonstrated familial wealth and social status, and thus, merchants, royals, and the daughters and wives of noble families were the most decorated. Excavations made in Phoenician territories reveal hundreds of rings, necklaces, bracelets, armlets, earrings, regular finger rings, brooches, lockets, buckles, and even buttons made of precious materials and jewels. Even some toiletries were made of these components, especially mirrors.

Necklaces

Necklaces are an interesting ornament among the Phoenicians and were considered a necessary part of their attire. However, archaeologists believe many of the artifacts uncovered belonged to the nobility because of their presence in tombs and royal graves, so it is unlikely the average Phoenician wore opulent strands. Instead, a commoner most likely possessed necklaces with colored clay beads that had multiple strands layered to beautiful effect.

Women are believed to have worn three to four layers of necklaces at once layered over each other. The first layer wrapped around the neck, similar to a choker, and rested right below the chin. The second necklace would be slightly more ornate and ended where the chest began, usually right around the collarbone. The third and fourth strands were much longer and tended to feature ornate ornaments made of glass, gold, crystal, and other precious stones. Many pendants were shaped after natural elements like pomegranates, acorns, and lotus flowers. Geometric shapes were also possible, especially cones and vases.

Beads adorned all of these layers. These beads could be made of clay for the lower classes, while upper-class individuals typically had large beads made of gold or glass. Precious stones were occasionally used to make beads, but these were rare. A short necklace might have between fifty to sixty beads, while a long strand could have over one hundred. Beads were often interspersed with bugles made of carnelian or onyx, and jewelry that came from Egypt often had oval beads made of blue or bluish-green glass. These beads typify a material called "Egyptian blue," which was made using a specific chemical process during firing and became a staple of trade between the Egyptians and Phoenicians.

Several necklaces that survived the decay of time come from the ladies of Cyprus. The first has a row of 103 gold beads in a pattern of alternating spheres and ovals. The oval beads are connected to gold pendants made to look like lotus blossoms, while the central pendant is a woman's head and bust in the Egyptian style. The attention to detail is clear in the workmanship, and the necklace itself is heavy. Another Cyprus piece has 64 beads. Twenty-two of the beads are larger than the rest and are affixed to eighteen pendants with delicate gold flowers.

Although tastes vary, an elegant example of Phoenician craftsmanship is a necklace made with a woven solid gold cord that was hammered and shaped to be soft and elastic. At either end of the necklace are caps to protect the cord. One side features a wrought lion's head with a ring in its mouth, while the other end has a hook to form a complete clasp. Archaeologists have been fascinated by this piece for years due to its quality, with one writing, "In this arrangement, in the curves of the thin wire, which folds back upon itself again and again, there is an air of ease, an apparent negligence, which is the very perfection of technical skill."

Other Jewelry

Women cultivated a fashion focused on opulent designs and extra ornamentation that depicted one's social class and frivolous wealth, and bracelets were a popular choice because of their visibility. Phoenician upper-class women often wore many varieties, with gold being the most common. Some bracelets were bands of solid gold without ornamentation. These could weigh anywhere between 200 and 300 grams (between a little over 7 and 10.5 ounces), which made then ornate and heavy around the wrist. Others were open designs meant to be worn around the upper arm. These did not meet at the ends but did often have designs along the ends like the heads of lions or bulls. If there were decorations, they tended to be elaborate carvings and decorations in floral patterns or depictions of the Phoenician alphabet.

Earrings were donned by men and women alike and could be as some of the most creative pieces, ranging from simple and sterile to curious and downright fanciful. Some were connected with chains to make elegant suspended patterns, others featured large medallions, and still others were shaped to resemble human heads. In general, the Phoenicians favored earrings that had a ring inserted in the ear, followed by long central chains that connected to one another and suspended long amulets or decorations representative of something significant. These were frequently the symbols of deities, small vases, or animals.

One visitor to the Museum of New York took the time to view a collection brought from Cyprus and described in lush detail the lavish nature of Phoenician earrings:

An entirely different type is that furnished by an ear-ring in the Museum of New York brought from Cyprus, where the loop of the ornament rises from a sort of horse-shoe, patterned with bosses and spirals, and surrounded by a rough edging of knobs, standing at a little distance one from another. Other forms found also in Cyprus are the ear-ring with the long pendant, which has been called "an elongated pear," ornamented towards the lower end with small blossoms of flowers, and terminating in a minute ball, which recalls the "drops" that are still used by the jewellers of our day; the loop which supports a *crux ansata*; that which has attached to it a small square box, or measure containing a heap of grain, thought to represent wheat; and those which support fruit of various kinds. An ear-ring of much delicacy consists of a twisted ring, curved into a hook at one extremity, and at the other ending in the head of a goat, with a ring attached to it, through which the hook passes. Another, rather curious than elegant, consists of a double twist, ornamented with lozenges, and terminating in triangular points finely granulated.[54]

[54] George Rawlinson, *The Great Empires of the Ancient East: Egypt, Phoenicia, Parthia, Chaldea, Assyria, Media, Babylon, Persia, Sasanian Empire, Israel, and Judah.*

Earrings were thus one of the most complicated yet desired accessories by far, although women also took great care when it came to their toiletries, buckles, and brooches. Phoenician ladies needed to fasten their dresses with buckles, but they favored simple metals over decoration for the sake of convenience. Wealthy women instead spent their fortunes on circular mirrors with metal backs, crystal vases, gold funnels, and even gold perfume bottles. Although these were not seen by the public, they were items that signified wealth and power that were enjoyed in the privacy of homes.

Oxfordshire, 1906.

Chapter 6 – An Unwritten Early History

The Phoenicians left little behind, but they did leave clues in the earth for modern archaeologists and scholars to discover. For much of the 18th and 19th centuries, people relied on religious texts and historical documents from the Greeks, Romans, Egyptians, and Assyrians to catch a glimpse of this massive seafaring civilization. This poses several major problems. First, they are all inherently biased as they were developed by rival civilizations who benefited from making the Phoenicians look good or bad depending on their current trade agreements. Second, contemporary historians cannot use religious texts as factual sources, especially since they have been translated and rewritten numerous times over the last 2,000 years.

This trend of using such unreliable sources has changed in recent decades as ongoing archaeological excavations in Lebanon, Tunisia, the Iberian Peninsula, and the rest of the Mediterranean have resulted in significant material evidence to explain various elements of the Phoenician civilization. Artifacts are considered material culture, and with material culture, scholars can study a time period, civilization, or society by looking at the kinds of goods they manufactured and used in their regular lives.

A major downfall of this approach is that the most common items a civilization uses frequently disintegrate and are lost to time because they were made from cheap materials or due to the fact that nobody saved them because of their plainness. However, one benefit of studying ancient civilizations through material culture is how groups like the Phoenicians buried items with their dead. These grave goods could be jewelry and symbols of wealth, but they were more often things used by people, like combs, mirrors, dishes, and similar objects.

Through archaeological expeditions conducted under the auspices of institutions like the National Museum of Beirut, the American University of Beirut, and the British Museum, modern scholars now have access to this material culture and have started to construct a history of the Phoenicians, albeit one that is rough and lacks details about certain city-states or elements of daily life. For context, the world knows more about World War II, which lasted for seven years, than it does about the Phoenicians, who were around for over one thousand years.

Early history is the most difficult to piece together for a plethora of reasons. First and foremost is the development of technology. Older civilizations wrote on clay or mud tablets that could be erased and rewritten upon. If someone wanted to preserve a tablet, they could harden it over a fire. These tablets did not decay from exposure to the sun or air, and thus, they could survive. As a fun fact, one massive library of clay tablets, which was burned in order to destroy it, actually survived the blaze with hundreds of tablets intact that modern audiences can still view.

Unfortunately, the Phoenicians did not use clay tablets. By the time they arrived on the scene, society had already developed papyrus. Wanting to keep an edge on their competitors, enjoying access to the raw materials needed to make it, and liking the lightness of the paper, the Phoenicians thus turned to papyrus to keep records. The major problem with this is that papyrus degrades rapidly, especially when exposed to air, water, and the sun. So, there are few written records left by the Phoenicians.

Another issue in trying to put together an early history is that the Phoenicians emerged toward the end of the Bronze Age, around a time known as the Bronze Age Collapse. They had barely distinguished themselves from their ancestors, the Canaanites, when the Near Eastern society suddenly collapsed. The Bronze Age Collapse could have been triggered by a variety of phenomena—scholars still debate to this day on how it actually occurred—including environmental issues like droughts, famine, overextended resource usage, and the arrival of a mysterious force called the Sea Peoples. These Sea Peoples are referenced in documents across several situations and appear to have been a seafaring people that arrived on the eastern coast of the Mediterranean and went to work butchering and slaughtering other peoples.

An Egyptian Image Representing the Sea Peoples
https://commons.wikimedia.org/wiki/File:Seev%C3%B6lker.jpg

As one can imagine, this unrest led to the loss of many records. Civilizations were derailed, and societies were forced to regroup and reform. The Phoenicians moved to a region of the Levant that was relatively untouched and continued to build their own society, taking advantage of the chaos to claim some viable land and an advantageous spot on the sea. Without so much unrest, would it have been possible for the Phoenicians to get an edge over nearby powers like the Canaanites, Hittites, and Egyptians? Probably not.

Phoenician history can be divided into several different periods that explain what the overall theme or trend was in their civilization. These include:

The Late Bronze Age (1550 to 1200 BCE)

Iron Age I (1200 to 900 BCE)

Iron Age II (900 to 586 BCE)

Babylonian Period (586 to 539 BCE)

Persian Period (539 to 332 BCE)

Hellenistic Period (332 to 63 BCE)

Roman Period (63 BCE to 324 CE)

These periods demonstrate when the Phoenicians first emerged as a distinct culture, when they started to become an independent power, their golden age, their subjugation under the Assyrians, becoming vassals of the Babylonians, then serving the Persians, the conquest of Alexander the Great, and their eventual fall to Greek and Roman influence and power. Throughout this time, the society and culture of the Phoenicians underwent numerous changes, especially in terms of technology, trading power, artistry, and political structure. However, only a few of these developments are left for posterity.

The Late Bronze Age

The Phoenician story begins when they were just starting to distinguish themselves from their predecessors and cousins, the Canaanites. Around this time, the native peoples of the Levant started to gravitate toward large coastal cities that offered opportunities for wealth, security, regular work, and culture. Some of the largest were Byblos and Tyre, which would go on to become two of the most successful Phoenician city-states. Individuals in these urban centers carved a niche for themselves by becoming intermediaries in the trade between Egypt and the nearby Syrian states, helping to form the tradition of the Phoenicians as traders.

However, it can be difficult to distinguish when Canaanites started to become Phoenicians. Could someone be a Canaanite and a Phoenician? Could someone be a Phoenician yet still be a Canaanite? The definite answer is sort of. Being Phoenician required having Canaanite heritage, living in the Near Eastern region, and participating in a new twist on religion and language. Someone could be a Canaanite and a Phoenician, but it would be difficult for a Phoenician to not be a Canaanite.

Before c. 1230 BCE, the Canaanites were in their own golden age, which is a term that refers to when culture, trade, and society flourish. This came to a grinding halt during the Bronze Age Collapse when a mysterious force decimated the city of Ugarit, leaving the region abandoned. At the same time, the nearby Israelites invaded and attempted to take arable farmland, while the mysterious Sea Peoples from the west arrived and started laying waste to anyone who stood in the way of total conquest. The Philistines moved in, claiming southern Canaanite cities as their territory.

To add fuel to the fire, the Near East experienced a surge of unfavorable environmental factors, including a prolonged drought. The ensuing famine led many to abandon cities in search of natural resources like wild vegetation and fresh water. The political structure of the central city died out, leaving the Canaanites to become more nomadic. The ensuing chaos called for a complete reordering of society, and when the dust fell, a new power known as Phoenicia emerged from the Canaanite survivors, becoming an independent region on the coast.

Iron Age I

Unfortunately, few sources remain to inform modern scholars about life in Phoenicia during the 12th century BCE, although some evidence indicates the cities of Byblos and Sidon were able to rapidly recover from the economic devastation of the Bronze Age Collapse. These cities would become central to the power of the

Phoenician civilization since they were economic juggernauts and had access to desirable land and water trade routes. At the same time, Sidon started to distinguish itself as a military powerhouse, and Arwad arrived on the scene as well, sporting an impressive number of chariots.

The first textual source to discuss the Iron Age Phoenicians is an account of Assyrian King Tiglath-Pileser I's campaign against the Phoenicians sometime between 1114 and 1076 BCE. Tiglath-Pileser I desired the abundant cedar forests controlled by the Phoenicians and launched ground-based military sieges against Byblos and Sidon. The king records how he managed to exact tribute from the leaders of these cities. Tyre was around at this point, but it was deemed too insignificant to add to the record.

The next main source about the Phoenicians was created by Wen-Amon, a senior Egyptian official from Thebes who worked at the temple of Amon-Ra. He traveled along the coast to procure cedar wood for the construction of a new holy barge, and he mentions that Byblos and Sidon were considered some of the most impressive coastal cities and powers of the time. Tyre is mentioned but was again thought of as insignificant in the power structure of the Mediterranean world. Wen-Amon's account hails from 1075 to 1060 BCE, indicating the sieges of Tiglath-Pileser I might not have been as effective as he had claimed.

Of particular importance was that Byblos and Sidon were in such an advantageous position that when Wen-Amon arrived and demanded cedar wood, the Phoenicians were able to negotiate instead of handing over tribute. The prince of Byblos, Zakar-Baal, told the official that Egypt needed to pay first before they would receive the wood. Because Byblos had previously been subservient to the Egyptian empire, the ability to request money before goods were given was impressive. This demonstrates how Egyptian power was in decline while the Phoenicians were on the rise.

Piecing together the exact history of the ensuing 11th century BCE is difficult, as there are fewer personal accounts and inscriptions and more vague references in the broad histories of civilizations like Egypt. Religious texts, like the biblical books of Joshua, Judges, and Samuel, start to use the term "Sidonian" at this point in time to indicate someone who could be Phoenician. There are a few reasons why this could have been, but the fact that Sidon was built near arable agricultural land did give the urban center an advantage. Tyre, after all, was trapped on an island.

Sidon's rise to power proved to change the overall Phoenician political structure. While the Phoenicians originally sided with Egypt as their default trading partner, Sidon had no interest in doing so. Instead, Sidon directed its attention to the nearby Syrian power, which was growing and proved to be a closer and more reliable trading partner. This was bad news for Tyre, who relied on Egyptian purchases of goods like cedar wood to afford to keep the people of the island city fed and commercially successful.

Iron Age II

Unfortunately for Sidon, its power did not last into the 10th century BCE. Tyre's golden age began when Hiram I (c. 969 to 936 BCE) ascended the throne. He shifted the balance of power toward Tyre by systematically exploiting nearby pan-Mediterranean trade routes. Hiram I worked to achieve a maritime monopoly and succeeded by employing a fleet capable of traveling up and down the Levantine coast to transport imports and exports and also beat off rivals through naval power.

Toward the mid-10th century BCE, a new city-state emerged as the most powerful: Tyre. Although previously ignored because it struggled to chisel its way into commerce, something changed that allowed Tyre to subsume the position of Byblos and Sidon. Tyre became urbanized and followed the new developments in the making of pottery, which necessitated craftsmen and women to settle down and work in the cities to produce this profitable item.

Tyre also adopted new commercial partners, deciding to make deals with nearby Israel. These two states underwent joint trading ventures to acquire gold and fed off of one another's strengths. In particular, Tyre gave Israel more access to the coast, while Israel allowed Tyre to have some control over overland trade routes that went deeper into Asia. Tyre could now manage the flow of goods from Syria down to Egypt, enacting taxes and only allowing traders on their own terms. It also gave the city-state access to spices and precious metals like silver and gold, which arrived from Arabia.

Hiram I's alliances could not last for long, though. King Solomon's Kingdom of Israel divided into Judah and Israel because of rival political claimants, and the Phoenician king needed to find a more stable and reliable trading partner rather than trying to get the two Israelite states to work together. Tyre thus had to reevaluate its political decisions and started to ease away from Israel and Judah, choosing to cooperate with nearby Phoenician city-states and turning south to North Africa.

Tyre underwent a brief lull in its success but managed to enter a second golden age through the coronation of Ithobaal I (ruled 887 to 856 BCE). Ithobaal's interests lay with territorial conquest. In over a decade, he managed to acquire and control so much territory that he declared himself the "King of the Sidonians," a title that would be adopted by his successors in Tyre for centuries to come. The title also appeared in the Greek Homeric poems and in the religious books of the Old Testament.

Ithobaal I combined Tyre with the territory of nearby Sidon, creating the first hints of a single Phoenician state. He labeled Tyre as the capital and went on to establish perhaps the first Phoenician colonies: Auza in Libya and Botrys, north of Byblos. These colonies were designed to add additional precious natural resources to the Tyrian commercial networks, including copper and other metals. Ithobaal would go on to create a colony on Cyprus as well.

However, Tyre's success once again came under fire, this time by the Assyrians. The Assyrian Empire was a nearby Asian juggernaut. The Phoenicians long existed on the fringes of this civilization, avoiding the numerous Assyrian military excursions by paying tribute. In fact, Tyre often took advantage of Assyrian conquests by claiming territory that was disrupted by warfare and chaos. Tyre's success changed, however, when the Assyrians crowned Shalmaneser III (ruled 859 to 824 BCE) as king.

Chapter 7 – Vassal to the Empires

While it is simple to divide the early years of the Phoenicians by technological age, the latter years are best understood by figuring out which great empire the city-states had become subservient to. Although the Phoenicians were an economic powerhouse, they exerted little military might. Clustered on the coast and with a small natural population, the city-states were repeatedly forced to submit to the much larger and more powerful empires that swept across the Levant and that boasted massive tracts of land in Asia, Africa, and Europe. The first of these empires was the Assyrians.

Vassalage to the Assyrian Empire

King Shalmaneser III rose to power in 858 BCE and ascended to the throne with plans of conquest. As soon as he gathered his military forces, he began an aggressive campaign throughout northern Syria and southern Anatolia. One of his primary targets were the Phoenician city-states along the coast of the Mediterranean Sea, which he subjugated over a period of three years. The Phoenicians were now forced to pay an inordinate amount of tribute to the Assyrians in payments that consisted of money and physical goods and resources.

At this point in time, the Phoenicians could be considered vassals of the more powerful Assyrian Empire. In political terms, a vassal is a country that is subordinate to another and engages in a relationship wherein one pays tribute to another to avoid being invaded or attacked. However, being a vassal of the Assyrians was not an unpleasant situation for the Phoenicians, who managed to garner a favorable position among the numerous vassals in the Middle East.

Unlike some of the other states in the region, the Phoenicians were treated well by Shalmaneser III, who remembered that city-states like Tyre cooperated with his father and did not plot to rebel. The geopolitical importance of the Phoenicians was further beneficial for Assyria, who needed the city-states to conduct diplomacy around the Mediterranean and continue to serve as a source of income for the ever-expanding empire. In this way, Phoenicia was able to bargain for its city-states' sanctity with its economic resources and trading authority. The Assyrians also feared the Phoenicians might fall into the hands of their rivals, the Egyptians.

Even after Shalmaneser III died in 824, the Phoenician city-states were still able to maintain a state of semi-independence. Shalmaneser III's successors did not want to interfere in the internal affairs of Phoenicia, which allowed the city-states to maintain a limited level of independence.

Unfortunately, this luck would run out around 744 BCE. At this point, Tiglath-Pileser III rose to the Assyrian throne and immediately began numerous far-reaching campaigns into the Levant. As part of the campaigns, the recently crowned ruler sought to put an end to the various independent states in the region and make their territory part of the expanding Assyrian Empire. This meant that the Phoenician city-states, particularly Tyre, became targets.

After several years of battles, the entirety of the Levant submitted to Assyrian authority in 738 BCE. The cities on the northern Phoenician coast were annexed into the empire, while southern city-states like Tyre and Byblos managed to remain as tributaries. However, they were no longer allowed to operate under a system of relative political and economic independence and had to run their decisions by Tiglath-Pileser and his administrators.

However, Tyre was not pleased with the situation. Just a year after the annexation, the king of Tyre chose to ally himself with an anti-Assyrian coalition in the Levant. Tiglath-Pileser responded by mustering his forces and sweeping down the Phoenician coast, crushing the opposition. Seeing the way the wind was blowing, Tyre immediately surrendered and offered tribute. Tiglath-Pileser accepted and left, demonstrating that the continued economic success of the Phoenician city was more important to him than crushing the city for its insolence.

Although not destroyed, Tyre still suffered. Assyria installed inspectors and market officials in the harbors of Tyre, eliminating economic and political independence. The subsequent kings were also required to pay 150 talents of gold a year to Assyria, a sum the equivalent of $150,000,000—if not more. Tyre paid the tribute for several years and then rebelled again, this time allying with nearby Sidon. The war lasted for two to three years, at which point the Phoenician city-states were captured and subjugated yet again.

The Assyrian monarch Sennacherib invaded the outlying territories of Tyre in 701 BCE, forcing the king to flee to Cyprus. The alliance between Tyre and Sidon was crushed, and Tyre lost control of nearby Sidon, as well as the majority of its population to Assyria. Thousands of residents were deported to the capital of Nineveh, and the coastal harbors were blockaded. Future blockades were established by generations of following Assyrian kings like Esarhaddon (681-669 BCE) and Ashurbanipal (669-631 BCE). By 640 BCE, all of mainland Tyre became an Assyrian province.

However, Assyrian dominance in the Levant would not last. On the rise was a new threat: the Babylonians. The Assyrian Empire became the victim of the Babylonian expansionist policy, and the Assyrians blindly allied themselves with their old enemy, the Egyptians, to try to retain control of the Levant and all of the Phoenician city-states. Unfortunately, the combined forces of Assyria and Egypt were not enough to stave off the Babylonians, who defeated both empires at Carchemish in 605 BCE.

Dominance by the Babylonians

The Babylonians were one of the most ancient peoples in known history, having developed around the city of Babylon in the 19th century BCE. The state of Babylon underwent numerous changes and waves of power throughout its lifetime, at one point being a great empire before being reduced to a small state controlled by the Assyrians. Although the Babylonians were subjugated by and paid tribute to the Assyrians from 911 to circa 612 BCE, their moment would come again. When the famous Assyrian ruler Ashurbanipal died and left a power vacuum, the Babylonians saw their chance and freed themselves from the shackles of vassalage, rebelling and forming the Neo-Babylonian Empire.

It was the Neo-Babylonian Empire that laid claim to Phoenician territory next. In the very first year of his long reign, Neo-Babylonian King Nebuchadnezzar II (605-562 BCE) began military campaigns throughout Syria with the intention of capturing and subjugating influential Assyrian territories. When he arrived on the Phoenician coast, the majority of the city-states understood which way the wind was blowing. Most immediately renounced their allegiance to the Assyrians and instead sent tribute to the Babylonians.

Tyre, however, once again rebelled. The city-state's fierce resistance resulted in a thirteen-year siege from 586 BCE until 573 BCE when the city council was forced to acknowledge defeat and surrender. The actions of the leaders had disastrous results for the citizens of Tyre. Tyre was reduced in power, and the king at the time, Ithobaal III, was sent to Babylon in captivity. A puppet ruler was installed before being replaced by a government full of Babylonian judges who ruled using their own justice system.

The once-powerful Tyre was now reduced in status among the Phoenician city-states and no longer boasted a strong military, navy, or economic success. Sidon immediately stepped into Tyre's place, essentially usurping the city's commercial contacts and natural resources. Sidon became the most prosperous Phoenician city and held this position for many years until Alexander the Great arrived and kicked it down.

Under Babylonian rule, life in Phoenicia was difficult. Commercial ventures diminished greatly, and much of the wealth of the cities instead went to line the coffers of the Neo-Babylonian monarchy. The Babylonian annexation of strategic regions, like southern Palestine, cut the Phoenicians off from their strategic trade routes, and Nebuchadnezzar II stole the cedar trade. Phoenicians were considered second-class citizens and were often subjected to Babylonian law and "encouraged" to follow Babylonian religious practices.

Things would not improve for the Phoenicians until after Nebuchadnezzar II's death. The new monarchs were not as effective as their predecessor and became distracted by the rise of yet another empire on the horizon: the Persians. King Nabonidus reinstated all of the original Phoenician royal lines in an attempt to garner the loyalty of the city-states, but it was not enough. Cyrus the Great was coming, and he would not be stopped.

The Achaemenid Empire

An Etching of Cyrus the Great

The above image of Cyrus the Great was created by copying a stone statue of the famous Persian leader from one of his numerous building projects. Cyrus ruled from 559 BCE until 530 BCE and managed to conquer Sippar and the city of Babylon later in his military conquests. This disrupted Babylonian power in the Levant, allowing the Phoenicians to exert some more influence at home. Cyrus actually treated the Phoenicians quite favorably, seemingly recognizing that their naval power and commercial contacts could be beneficial to his envisioned empire.

Under the Persians, the Phoenicians found a new purpose. They became the naval backbone of Cyrus the Great on the Mediterranean Sea and entered a prosperous period that lasted throughout the majority of the Achaemenid period. All four of the major Phoenician city-states (Tyre, Sidon, Byblos, and Arwad) were able to reinstate their monarchies and dynastic rule. They expanded physically and economically, claiming territory in the Levant as it came under the control of the Achaemenid Persians.

Initially, the Phoenician city-states were clustered into a single satrapy, or administrative district, which was under Persian control. The satrapy was called Athura, or Assyria. When Darius I took control from 522 BCE to 486 BCE, he subdivided the district into separate provinces to better control the flow of wealth and politics.

Control under the Persians could be considered perhaps one of the last golden ages for the Phoenician city-states. They found a tremendous niche serving as commercial backers and rulers of a massive portion of the Persian navy. Some Greek accounts even attest that the Phoenicians were the formidable navy commanders of Xerxes, who would traverse the Mediterranean and wage war with the ancient Greek city-states.

Unfortunately, prosperity never lasts in history. The final years of the 5th century BCE brought growing unrest for the Persians, who did not have strong rulers or an efficient administration. The territory began to fragment, and rebellions sprang up. Mainland Greece, Egypt, and western Asia Minor were some of the first locations to shirk Persian rule, and the Phoenicians grew antsy watching their influential trading partners leave. Sensing the growing weakness of the Persian state, the Phoenicians decided to leave.

At this point, people can probably guess which city-state rebelled first. The monarchs of Tyre saw an opportunity to leave and joined an anti-Persian alliance that included Egypt, Cyprus, and Athens. The alliance attacked Persia with all of its might but was decisively defeated in a naval battle in 381 BCE. In time, other city-states also rebelled against the Persians, including the powerful Sidon. Unfortunately for Sidon, the new Persian ruler, Artaxerxes III, was much more formidable than his predecessors. He led a massive army to quell the revolt in Sidon. By 344 BCE, all of the Phoenician city-states were back in Persian hands.

However, there was yet another conqueror on the horizon.

The Arrival of the Macedonians

While still under the control of the Persians, Phoenicia would be faced by another conqueror interested in the acquisition of their territories and the luxury goods they controlled. This would be the Macedonian Greeks, who were led by the famous Alexander the Great, a king who was no older than his early twenties by the time he marched upon Tyre in 332 BCE. Due to its position, Alexander was unable to attack the city directly from the sea, and it was too heavily walled along the land to be captured quickly. Instead, Alexander started a siege and ordered his men and captured slaves to build a causeway that was one kilometer long (a little over half a mile) to the island where Tyre was situated.

Alexander the Great
https://commons.wikimedia.org/wiki/File:Alexander_the_Great_mosaic.jpg

This causeway was built on a small natural land bridge that was less than two meters deep (a little over six and a half feet), making it the only realistic opportunity the Macedonians possessed to attack the city.[55] There was little the Phoenicians could do to delay destruction besides trying to stone or shoot the construction workers as they neared Tyre's walls. Eventually, it was completed, and the Macedonian artillery closed in upon the city. Some of the remains still exist in the region since the entire walkway was built of stone.

Because the water near the city was deeper than the rest, Alexander the Great could not bring his causeway straight to the walls. Instead, Alexander was forced to build two towers nearby that measured around 50 meters (160 feet) tall. The construction of the towers was delayed repeatedly by attacks from Tyre as well as the Tyrian navy, but the moving artillery platforms were soon completed. Catapults were built on top to attack the Tyrian wall defenders, while ballistas were added below to hurl rocks at the navy's ships and the lower portions of the walls. These towers and platforms were made of wood, which was easier to carry than stone, and they were covered with treated rawhide so the Phoenicians could not destroy them with flaming arrows.

The Tyrians were determined not to be beaten by the towers. Although the Macedonian platforms were the largest of their kind by that point in history, the Phoenicians used an old ship for transporting horses and devised a plan. They filled it with a variety of combustible substances, including sulfur, pitch, and dried branches. They then attached hanging cauldrons full of oil along the masts so they would fall when the masts burned down. They weighed down the back of the ship so the front tipped upward and then sent it directly at the towers before lighting it on fire.

---

[55] Stephen English, *The Sieges of Alexander the Great* (Wiltshire: Pen & Sword Books Ltd., 2010).

The boat crashed into the towers, and the flames spread fast, burning up along the massive platforms. The cauldrons of oil fell with spectacular splashes, sending fire in every direction. The Macedonians were disoriented, and the siege equipment rapidly burned down. Afterward, members of the Tyrian navy swarmed the manmade pier and destroyed everything that came within their grasp, including the remaining equipment and the Macedonian soldiers and slaves who tried to douse the fires.

Alexander was daunted and delayed, but he was not finished. He desired Tyre. After careful consideration, he became convinced that the only way to capture the Phoenician city was through the use of an accomplished navy. Unfortunately for the Phoenicians, he had one because of his previous conquests of other Phoenician city-states that had been controlled by the Persians, including Arwad, Byblos, and Sidon. Through the acquisition of Persian vessels, Alexander had a fleet of eighty strong ships. These were then joined by 120 war galleys sent by Cyprus, whose king wished to join Alexander, potentially as a way to avoid being dominated himself. Ionia in Greece sent another 23, leaving Alexander with an impressive fleet of 223 ships ready for combat. The Tyrian navy possessed no hope of victory.

Alexander sailed upon Tyre and blockaded the ports through which supplies reached the city. Slower vessels were refitted with battering rams, but they had to be removed because Tyre had placed massive underwater blocks of stone to block rams many years before. The rams were anchored near the walls instead, but the Tyrians sent out divers to cut them off. Alexander then replaced the ropes with chains. The Tyrians tried to launch another counterattack, but they were unsuccessful. The Macedonian rams broke through the walls while its navy decimated the Phoenician ships, ending the siege in an absolute bloodbath and massacre.

Once Alexander captured Tyre, he was draconian. He killed 6,000 fighting men and crucified 2,000 of its leading citizens on the beach. He then allowed the king to remain in power, but he murdered much of the royal family and anyone who opposed the Macedonians. The city was sacked, the citizens were beaten in the streets, and women were captured and raped by the soldiers. Over 30,000 Tyrians were taken as slaves for the Macedonian army. After such a brutal display of power, many of the other Phoenician city-states acquiesced to Macedonian rule without a fight, fearful of what might happen if they resisted.

When Alexander the Great perished in 323 BCE, Phoenicia became divided between several of the following empires created by Alexander's successors, although the majority was controlled by the Ptolemaic dynasty of Egypt. Between 286 and 197 BCE, the Ptolemies reduced the influence of Phoenicia over the trading routes of the Eastern Mediterranean and installed high priests of Astarte as vassal rulers throughout the region. This caused tremendous cultural backlash and a significant economic downturn in Phoenicia, which struggled to thrive and continue its culture with the influence of Persia, Greece, and Egypt.

Chapter 8 – Trade and the Economy

The Phoenicians were among the greatest traders of the ancient world, capable of controlling massive networks of goods across the Mediterranean Sea, east into Asia, and down into Africa. Most of their prosperity could be attributed to the skills of their merchants, who ruled over the seas with an iron fist and superior technology. They established numerous commercial outposts designed to be reachable by ships that needed to dock between journeys to replenish their supplies and sell goods to a variety of civilizations. The most strategic was Carthage in Northwest Africa, which was southeast of Sardinia and necessary for the transport of silver and tin from Iberia and Northern Europe. However, the Phoenicians were not always a commercial juggernaut, especially when needing to contend with more powerful neighbors.

Before the Bronze Age Collapse cleared the way for them to become powerful, the Phoenicians mainly traded with the Greeks. At this point in time, the Greeks had established a desirable civilization with numerous city-states and ports dotting the small islands throughout the Mediterranean. The Phoenicians traded wood, slaves, glass, and a powdered dye called Tyrian purple. Artisans made Tyrian purple from the crushed shells of a specific snail that lived in the seas, and it was used by elite officials to color their garments and showcase their status with a single glance. Purple was the rarest color in the ancient world, and it was almost impossible to make, earning the shade a desirable location in the color wheel.

Over time, the Greeks trusted the Phoenicians more. They released some of their hold as trading and colonizing spread across the Mediterranean Sea until the sea split into two halves, with the Phoenicians dominating the south and the Greeks controlling the north. Eventually, this situation would turn on its head, with the Greeks maintaining the east while the Phoenicians settled in the west following the Sicilian Wars.

After the Bronze Age Collapse laid waste to many of the nearby civilizations, the Phoenicians emerged as a major naval and trading power around 1200 BCE. This time, they controlled the immensely desirable Tyrian purple dye, having discovered it could be derived from the hypobranchial gland of the murex sea snail. With this knowledge and a seemingly limitless supply of snails from the coasts they controlled, the Phoenicians were able to establish a massive trade center in Sarepta, a city in modern-day Lebanon. They relied upon the murex snail so much that the Phoenicians eventually caused its local extinction out of greed for the beautiful luxury it provided. Before doing so, the Phoenicians made the snail and its dye the center of their trading empire and even managed to establish a second production center in the city of Mogador, whose ruins lay in contemporary Morocco. Besides dye, glass was another influential export of the Phoenicians because of the difficulty in making glass plates, jars, and beads.

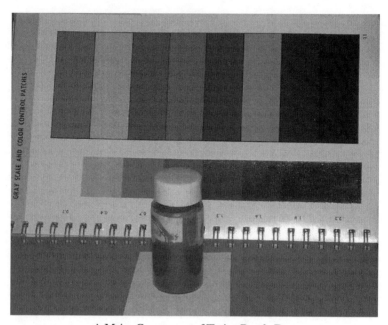
A Major Component of Tyrian Purple Dye
https://commons.wikimedia.org/wiki/File:Tyrian_purple_on_grayscale.jpg

The Phoenicians did not just content themselves with providing non-consumable luxury goods. They were also excellent at filling in gaps in the inventories of other civilizations, especially nearby Egypt. Following the Bronze Age Collapse, the Egyptians struggled to regain their footing in the ancient world, a situation not helped by years of tumultuous dynastic rule. One thing the Egyptians especially lacked when it came to luxuries was wine.

Grapevines could not grow in Egypt, but the Phoenicians possessed ample coastal landscapes to grow massive vineyards capable of producing rich wine. Barrels tended to be shipped to South Lebanon and Sarepta, where the wine would then be stored in handmade pots and sold to Egypt in exchange for Nubian gold. Historians possess a wealth of knowledge about these transactions thanks to vividly documented shipwrecks that were discovered in 1997 about thirty miles west of Ascalon, known as Ashkelon today. By all accounts, the Egyptians were one of the largest consumers of imported wine and provided much of the gold that went into making Phoenician jewelry for men and women.

At the same time, the Phoenicians had discovered that the Egyptians also lacked lumber since their land was primarily desert and flood plains around the Nile River. So, sailors and merchants started to bring massive cedar logs from the mountains of Lebanon down to Egypt and exchanged them for even more gold, linen, papyrus, and even cowhide. One well-documented transaction occurred sometime between 1075 BCE and 1060 BCE. An Egyptian envoy called Wen-Amon arrived in Phoenicia and bought seven humongous cedar logs for the inordinate sum of "4 crocks and 1 kak-men of gold; 5 silver jugs; 10 garments of royal linen; 10 kherd of good linen from Upper Egypt; 500 rolls of finished papyrus; 500 cows' hides; 500 ropes; 20 bags of lentils, and 30 baskets of fish."[56] Wen-Amon carried the goods back to Egypt by boat and was thought to have secured a great deal for his seven logs, which could be turned around and sold for an even higher sum at home.

However, the path to becoming the most powerful merchants on the Mediterranean would take time. Before they became renowned traders, archaeological evidence indicates that the early Phoenician economy relied heavily on agriculture and animal husbandry. The original Phoenicians inherited this knowledge from their predecessors in the Levant and were thus able to use the temperate climate of their position on the Mediterranean Sea to produce vast staple crops of wheat and barley. These foodstuffs could be used to support a massive and often widespread population, but the extras were also valuable trade goods that could be transferred to partners in Egypt or farther to the east.

The flourishing agricultural economies of the Phoenicians relied on profitable crops like wheat, but they would eventually branch out thanks to technological developments like systems of irrigation and durable plows pulled by oxen rather than human muscle. By

---

[56] Markoe, Glenn E. (2000). *Peoples of the Past: Phoenicians.* Berkeley, CA: University of California Press, p. 103.

1200 BCE, artifacts indicate agriculture allowed Phoenicia to become so prosperous that members of the population could engage in other pursuits, leading to burgeoning maritime economies on the banks of the Mediterranean. These economies would eventually translate to settlements and colonies throughout the Mediterranean as Phoenician maritime prowess allowed the civilization to outsail its competition and lay claim to advantageous locations.

The sea became the integral component of the entire Phoenician economy, with two primary trade goods emerging from its briny depths: A variety of palatable fish and the snails necessary to make the rare purple dye. The shipbuilding industry further flourished and was a necessary component of the economy that was bolstered by the water. To gain the wood necessary for shipbuilding, the Phoenicians logged the nearby forests for their massive cedar trees and dragged the trunks to the coast for shaping. When possible, the Phoenicians avoided buying wood from other civilizations.

Unfortunately, as is the case for most situations concerning the Phoenicians, archaeologists and historians struggle with a lack of direct evidence of trading customs and practices. Most of what is known about trading partners and goods come from the records of friendly civilizations whose tablets explain what the Phoenicians brought with them, who they preferred to conduct business with, and what prices their goods would fetch in local and foreign markets. One benefit of these tablets is that they provide excellent economic information since merchants rarely lied about their transactions, but it comes with the unfortunate lack of a Phoenician perspective on trade.

What historians do understand is that the Phoenicians relied upon soft power, or the political power of their commerce and culture to influence other civilizations and avoid warfare when possible. While their navy was powerful, Phoenicia avoided conflict because their culture, in general, focused on the acquisition of wealth to prosper. By the 12th century BCE, the Phoenicians possessed a mixed economy that had incorporated agricultural, industrial, and commercial sectors with excellent results.

Out of these three sectors, the two most important were agriculture and commerce. Besides being well known for their trade and luxury goods, the Phoenicians manufactured an impressive amount of wine that was coveted throughout the Mediterranean because of its excellent flavor and quality. If any sommeliers existed in ancient times, they no doubt would have been able to identify a Phoenician cabernet from a mile away.

For the purposes of discussing their economy, it is best to divide subjects by whether they functioned primarily as agriculture or commerce. While there was some industry, it mostly focused on shipbuilding.

The Agricultural Sector

The Phoenicians relied on agriculture to feed a growing population that consumed more than it produced when it came to food. Cereal crops and viticulture (wine-growing) were the most significant, but Phoenicia also had its own vegetables and domesticated animals reserved for local use. Up first in this discussion are the cereal grains, which refers to plants like barley and wheat that could be used to make "cereals," or a type of gruel.

Agriculture and husbandry formed the majority of the Phoenician economy, even though so many associate the civilization with trading. Most of the cereal crops grown went to the peasants who cultivated them and who needed the calories to survive. There is evidence that most Phoenician farmers used the crops to pay their taxes. These grains would be transported to a noble's stronghold, where the food would then be kept for personal use or sold to merchants. Since the economy was a mixture of rural and urban, many wealthier landowners paid laborers with food in addition to some money. Similar to the ancient Babylonians, there is evidence to indicate that the amount of food a laborer received was proportionate to gender, age, and overall size. So, a young man received almost twice as much as an elderly woman.

Agricultural cultivation was not a simple process. Because the Phoenicians were on the seacoast, frequent freshwater shortages combined with the salinity of the soil meant farmers needed to be knowledgeable about irrigation to create water reserves. The major city-states grew around arable hinterlands that formed miniature breadbaskets, and they took advantage of irrigation systems to develop rudimentary public sewer systems to keep the cities relatively healthy and clean. The technology of irrigation was also used to develop cisterns and create a network that supplied fresh water to the cities for merchants and laborers. Archaeological investigations revealed that the Phoenicians "cultivated the lower slopes of the Lebanese mountains," which increased the amount of available crop space and eased the entire process of irrigation overall.[57]

Despite extensive cultivation, Phoenicia had a grain deficit. The population grew steadily from the Iron Age onward, and the rocky, arid terrain made it difficult to maintain large fields of cereal grains. So, the Phoenicians had a tendency to grow barley whenever possible, even if it meant tending to small patches of crops. Barley would be gathered and stored in silos to preserve the grains, and it was preferred to growing wheat because it was better at resisting the salinity of the air. To supplement their food, almost everyone grew their own fruits and vegetables to round out their diet and reduce the deficit.

While cereal grain agriculture was essential for survival, the Phoenicians reinforced their agricultural sector by engaging in extensive viticulture. Viticulture is a branch of horticulture that focuses on growing grapes for wine. Unlike cereal grains, which required tons of fresh water and open space that the terrain lacked,

---

[57] Woolmer, *Ancient Phoenicia*, p. 71.

Phoenicia was actually perfectly suited for the growing of grapes. It was sunny, rocky, and remained warm throughout the year, allowing vines to grow and supply the Phoenicians with an impressive amount of wine that they could then trade for more grain to battle the deficit. Not surprisingly, the fresh grapes themselves were also desired and could be bought and sold for high prices on the market.

A similar product was the olive. Olives were a staple of the Mediterranean diet, and the Phoenicians could cultivate strong olive trees and press the fruits into oil that would be preserved, sold, or used for religious rituals. Like grapes, fresh olives were also prized and bought by civilizations like the Egyptians, who wanted to eat them fresh. Authors like Mark Woolmer, a PhD professor of ancient history, claim olives not only demonstrated political stability, but they were also important because they grew well and matured at different times than cereal grains, meaning manpower was available to harvest both.

Wine and olive oil thus enjoyed a coveted position in the Phoenician economy and became tools of trade throughout the ancient world. In 1999, archaeologists discovered two sunken merchant vessels that, when explored, revealed a series of amphorae sealed with pinewood discs. The holds were full of these vessels and appeared to have been ships dedicated to the transport of wine and oil. Not all of it was traded, of course, as members of the local population also enjoyed the fruits of their labors—literally. One of the only known Phoenician philosophers, a man named Zeno, was believed to be so fond of wine that he died from an alcoholic dose from consuming too much in a single sitting.[58]

Besides crops, Phoenicia also engaged in animal husbandry, particularly livestock. However, they also domesticated other animals to suit their purposes. Cattle were the most popular

---

[58] Some historians speculate that texts could also be referring to liver failure after lifelong consumption, but the rhetoric is unclear.

animals because of its tasty beef and ability to produce milk, but donkeys come in a close second. While cattle were eaten, the donkeys were necessary to transport goods across the rocky terrain of modern-day Lebanon. Sheep were great to possess for wool, and goats were essential for milk. Surprisingly, sheep and goats were perhaps the first animals domesticated, and they appeared to be called "small cattle" in the Phoenician language. They were kept in large flocks rather than on small farms. Most flocks were controlled by the state, regional temples, or wealthy landowners who had the means to allow for grazing.

Pastoralism was the name of the game, although most shepherds were hired hands. Because sheep and goat theft were serious crimes, any animals killed while under the watch of a hired hand needed to be presented to the owner as proof that they didn't steal it. The wool went to make clothing, and goat's milk made delicious cheese and yogurt for consumption.

Besides the shepherds, flocks were protected by domesticated dogs. The dog was the primary Phoenician domestic animal and played a serious role in animal protection from local wildlife. Historians have traced two breeds to the Phoenicians: a large greyhound and a breed that no longer exists but was as tall and strong as a modern Mastiff or Great Dane. There is some evidence that domesticated dogs could be used as war animals and were most likely not traded with other civilizations. The same could not be said for ducks, chickens, and geese, which were popular fowl.

Finally, the Phoenicians stood out for their beekeeping. Honey served as the primary source of sugar for the population, and the ability to tend to bees was a prized skill. Hive beekeeping possesses a history that stretches over thousands of years, so it should be no surprise that honey was popular at this time. In addition to this amber foodstuff, beekeepers also cultivated and used beeswax, which created a watertight sealant and could be used for medicinal purposes. Now that was a sweet deal.

The Phoenicians were merchants first and foremost, and they engaged in interregional trade on an unprecedented scale. However, despite being extensive traders, a trait that stands out about their practices was how they did not implement the minting of national coinage until the middle of the 5th century BCE. Historians trace this failure to adopt coinage to Phoenicia's history of colonization, especially when the civilization became the vassal of the Persians. It was easier to trade with a wide variety of partners while using a system of barter and exchange, and the Persians themselves used an exchange system that did not require coin money.

Eventually, coinage seeped into Phoenicia following the influx of Greek traders that arrived in the Phoenician city-states following the Persian Wars. Greece was one of the first civilizations to mint its own currency, and city-states like Sidon and Tyre followed suit to keep up with the commercial practice. The result was Phoenicia adopting coin money but also having a system where each city-state demonstrated its autonomy by producing its own coinage.[59]

The Phoenician currency drew upon themes and ideas present in their Greek counterparts, including the depiction of the current ruler or a favored deity on the front and some sort of national symbol on the back. The coin from the city-state of Carthage above has the face of the god Melqart, their preferred deity, as well as a war elephant, a staple of the North African province. Locations like Sidon, Byblos, and Arwad followed suit, choosing to depict a galley (a type of ship) on their currency.

Because the coins were developed while the Phoenicians struggled under Persian rule, gold was not used. This is because the default coin was the gold Persian shekel, and the rare metal

---

[59] Interesting Fact: Many coins do not belong to institutions like museums and are regularly bought and sold online as intriguing artifacts or prized possessions for coin collectors. Although the money is no longer in circulation, the coins remain valuable today.

went to the minting of those. Instead, the Phoenicians made a number of silver coins and then eventually incorporated bronze for smaller denominations that could be used by the average citizen. Like any other currency, it took several years for Phoenician money to become widespread.

As merchants, the Phoenician traders remained abreast of the various intricacies of the commercial sector. While they continued to trade the agricultural goods produced in the hinterlands, they also strove to work as moneylenders and needed to navigate a unique position in society. All merchants operated under the auspiciousness of the local monarchy or nobility, and they were expected to engage in a system of gift-giving, exchange, and regular trade. This system was difficult to navigate and necessitated that the merchants adopt a diplomatic role in how they conducted business.

Diplomacy and commerce became intertwined around the 14th century BCE when traders "not only took part in public administration but [were] entrusted by the state with organizing commercial agencies and with buying and selling in the capacity of envoy to the king."[60] This was a holdover from the ancient period, where members of the royal house tended to do all of the trading for the region. By the 8th century BCE, the merchants were able to break away from the old system and develop their own mercantile caste or class, which allowed private families and individuals to accrue wealth for their own purposes.

These merchants enjoyed social status and prestige that set them apart from regular nobles and the common folk. A Phoenician trader was a qualified professional and specialist; they were well educated and often became a part of the extended royal family through marriage and politics. Their skills were in high demand, and most could read, write, and do calculations to maintain their vast networks. Moneylending boomed, and by the seventh and sixth centuries BCE, historians see patterns that indicate the

---

[60] Woolmer, *Ancient Phoenicia*, p. 76.

merchants started to form their own "houses" or networks that are reminiscent of the medieval guilds of specialists and craftsmen. Even the royal family started to trade to earn more private wealth and not to help the city-state. Public and private interests were meshed together, creating a strong economy.

When all is said and done, the agricultural and commercial sectors of the Phoenician economy would not have thrived without the Mediterranean Sea. From their position on the coast, the Phoenicians were posed to exert an immense amount of influence if they could get their goods across the briny deep. To do so, they needed the best ships available that could transport items but also resist and defeat pirates: They needed a merchant navy.

Sailing with a Merchant Navy

In modern culture, the Phoenicians are the most well known for their formidable navy. Shipbuilding was done primarily in Byblos, and the completed vessels could be transported to other locations via waterways. Trading could be done on galleys, where fifty pairs of muscular sailors would row when the wind and waves could not be relied upon. The front bow could be used to ram pirates and triremes when needed, and sailors would fire arrows at oncoming vessels.

Because the Phoenicians wrote on papyrus and lack an abundance of preserved records, modern historians and archaeologists have used shipwrecks to reconstruct the templates of the vessels as well as the more common cargo. The Phoenicians were highly prized for their goods and managed to avoid the majority of military excursions, but they were often susceptible to piracy. Many people were interested in their gold and silver ingots, olive oil, wine, purple dyes, and cedar lumber.

According to archaeologists, there were three different types of ships. Each one was shallow-keeled to be able to traverse the docks and bays of the city-states. The warships were biremes, which had two long rows of oars. The front included a ram, which could be accessed across the wide deck. The second type of ship was also a bireme but had a wide hull capable of storing cargo. The sides of the deck were also high and reinforced so cargo could be stored on top as well. These trading ships often traveled in groups of between twenty and fifty at a time and would be surrounded by warships.

Finally, there was a much smaller trading vessel that could be used for short trips. This one possessed a single bank of oars and often had a horse's head at the bow for decoration and potential religious protection. These boats were not used often; archaeologists think it might have been used for fishing or minor excursions along the coast.

Because of their role as ancient mariners, the Phoenicians lacked navigational devices like the compass. Instead, they relied upon their knowledge of natural features on the coastline and the stars. Historians believe the most important constellation was Ursa Minor. The North Star was essential for navigation and keeping track of the cardinal directions. Up until recently, because of their reliance on the coastline to mark their routes, most historians believe the Phoenicians stuck to the shallows and only sailed during the daytime, weighing anchor at night and waiting for the morning before moving again. Recently, this view has been challenged. In fact, it could have actually been more dangerous for the Phoenicians to stick closer to the coastlines. The sailors would be subjected to more hazards like rocks and shallows there, which could damage their vessels and result in shipwrecks.

The average Phoenician ship was capable of moving at a speed of six miles per hour. In order to get from the Levant to a colony on the Iberian Peninsula, it would take travelers almost ninety days, which would be almost the entire sailing season. The crew would have to wait until the next year to make the voyage back.

Besides this information, it is difficult for historians to distinguish other concrete facts. The routes favored by the Phoenicians are a subject of hot debate, with scholars at one another's throats to determine which ones are true. While there are surviving shipwrecks, the natural currents of the sea would have displaced them by many miles. However, it is known that brave navigators accomplished some unusual feats, including an attempt to sail around the African continent and making it to the Indian Ocean to find new goods to trade.

Chapter 9 – Language and Alphabet

Although the Phoenicians were Canaanites, they developed their own unique language that morphed over time from the traditional Semitic Canaanite to something called Phoenician, or *Put* in ancient Egyptian documents. This language would be a part of the Canaanite subgroup of the Northwest Semitic languages because of its similar grammatical structure and roots to traditional Canaanite, but it managed to distinguish itself by being codified, ascribed a clear alphabet, and was somewhat standardized by the upper echelons of society. Other members of the same language family are Hebrew, Edomite, Moabite, and Ammonite. All developed in societies that began as Canaanites and then formed their own separate cultures.

Because the Phoenicians possessed an extensive network of city-states, the language was spoken around the coastal Mediterranean region. Some of the areas where it could have been heard include the region of Greater Syria and Anatolia, which encompasses modern-day countries like Lebanon, Israel/Palestine, Syria, Turkey, and Cyprus. It could also be heard in colonized areas like present-day Morocco, Algeria, Libya, Tunisia, Sicily, Sardinia, Corsica, Malta, the Balearic Islands, and most of southern Spain.

While it functioned as a common language, meaning lower-class people would speak it daily, it was also taught and learned as a prestige language among the Greeks and Egyptians for more effective trade between civilizations.

Although they were preceded by other Canaanite societies, the Phoenicians were the first state-level society that used the Semitic alphabet on a widespread level to teach and understand the language. The accompanying alphabet is also the oldest verified consonantal alphabet in the world, meaning it is the first alphabet with characters that represent consonants that has evidence to support its age. Most archaeologists consider the language to be "Proto-Canaanite" until 1050 BCE when remaining artifacts start to bear a more distinct language. Scholars think the Phoenician phonetic alphabet might actually be a partial ancestor to almost every current contemporary alphabet in existence, with exceptions made for distance.

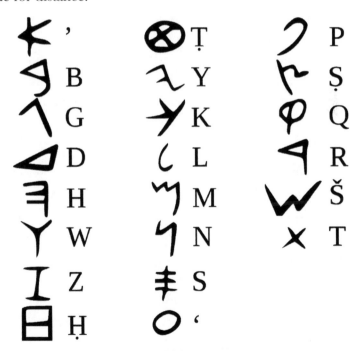

The Early Phoenician Alphabet
https://commons.wikimedia.org/wiki/File:Phoenician_alphabet.svg

Phoenician holds a unique place from a linguistic perspective simply because scholars struggle to determine just how different it was from Canaanite, which is not well understood. Texts and artifacts do not indicate whether Phoenician possessed slight differences, was superficial in its development, or if it was a truly complex and unique language. Whatever the case may be, their alphabet would be adopted around the Mediterranean because of its importance to trade. An example of this in more contemporary times is how many countries and cultures learned to speak English to conduct business with the East India Company and other modern businesses on a regular basis.

The Phoenician alphabet rapidly spread to the Greeks, who used it as a template to create their Greek alphabet. The Greek alphabet, in turn, spread to the Etruscans and Romans, with the latter creating the Latin alphabet. Several cultures in Northern Africa also adopted it, including the peoples in the region of Morocco. At some point, the future Carthaginian civilization would colonize much of the Western Mediterranean and spread Phoenician as well, where it would become the distinct Punic language. Punic died out well after Phoenician since it survived until the 5th century CE. The Romans would colonize former Carthaginian areas, spreading Latin instead.

The Alphabet

After decades of using the Proto-Canaanite script, the Phoenicians eventually developed their own alphabet to record their language. This script is called an abjad, meaning it focuses on the use of consonants rather than syllables when it comes to written characters. Many historians believe Phoenician was essential because it formed the basis of the later Greek alphabet, which, in turn, influenced the Latin alphabet. As mentioned earlier, the Carthaginians also continued to use the alphabet after the Phoenicians themselves disappeared, resulting in the unique Punic form of the script.

The Punic writing was slightly different from the original Phoenician one. While the Phoenicians wrote in large block letters, the Carthaginians developed a more cursive shape to their letters. Around the 3rd century BCE, the Punic alphabet featured the presence of vowels, which had been largely ignored by the Phoenicians. Final vowels also got more attention, and they sometimes have characters like an aleph or an ayin marking them. The letter aleph is a character derived from the appearance of an ox's head, while an ayin is a symbol in some alphabets that meant the person needed to pronounce a character with a pharyngeal fricative. In other words, both symbols changed traditional pronunciations and placed emphasis on the final vowel.

The Punic alphabet formed perhaps the most lasting imprint of the original Phoenician, and it continued to grow and evolve for centuries. Around the time of the Second Punic War, the script became even more cursive in appearance. This would evolve into Neo-Punic, which was more conservative than the original Punic. By conservative, this meant it had fewer details, which was fitting since it emerged after the destruction of Carthage by Rome around 146 BCE. Neo-Punic was more organized and standardized than regular Punic and the original Phoenician alphabet because it had specific "consonantal letters" to distinguish between vowel sounds. This was different because the original Phoenician did not mark vowels, while Punic had a couple of ways to write a single vowel sound, which could be confusing for individuals who tried to read the script, even with context.

With all of this in mind, what made Phoenician distinct? It was certainly different from other abjads at the time, like Aramaic, Arabic, and Biblical Hebrew. In the written form, long vowels were not expressed and were not recorded even if they came from diphthongs. This meant anyone reading a Phoenician document would need to know how words were pronounced and which consonants were involved; otherwise, the writing would be unintelligible. It wasn't until Phoenician evolved into Punic that scribes and writers started to use symbols to mark final and long vowels, giving modern scholars a fighting chance when it comes to deciphering the language. Linguists and historians know the most about Phoenician vowels from these Punic inscriptions, which were frequently translated into Greek and other languages.

Surviving Examples

Phoenician, combined with Punic, has approximately 10,000 surviving inscriptions around the Mediterranean that can be examined by historical linguists to piece together the language. These inscriptions can be supplemented with the glossaries of books written in other ancient languages like Greek, Latin, and Arabic, which explain a couple of the words and offer rough translations. Although the Phoenicians appeared to be prolific writers because of the nature of their trading civilization, few sources have survived, meaning it is difficult for contemporary audiences to fully understand the Phoenician language and alphabet.

When it was time to write, the Phoenicians did not choose to use mud or clay tablets and avoided inscriptions in stone unless they were meant for a coffin or tomb. Instead, the traders and scribes used papyrus or parchment sheets that would have degraded quickly, making it almost impossible for examples to survive. This means there are no histories or trading records since all of the papyrus and leather rotted or molded away in the damp conditions surrounding the Phoenician city-states by the sea. This jewel of a civilization quite literally degraded in the earth even though the Phoenicians were responsible for spreading literacy and the ability to write among numerous social classes and members of the population. The only physical sources available, besides those in tombs, are a couple of letters and notes on broken pottery, three fragments of papyri, and some monumental inscriptions carved in stone.

Such a lack of information is daunting and disappointing, considering the Phoenicians and Carthaginians seemed to write entire books, as alluded to by Roman authors like Sallust. Only a few volumes survived thanks to the rare translation into Latin or the preservation of a couple of snippets in Roman plays— for some examples, see Mago's treatise or Plautus' plays. Phoenician remained such a mystery that it was not until the Cippi of Melqart was discovered in Malta in 1694 CE that a French scholar, Jean-Jacques Barthelemy, was able to decipher and reconstruct the Punic alphabet around 1764. The Cippi of Melqart was a bilingual inscription in ancient Greek and Punic.

Guyot de Marne's Drawing of the Cippi of Melqart, c. 1760
https://en.wikipedia.org/wiki/File:Guyot_de_Marne_-_Cippus_of_Melqart.png#file

Besides the Cippi of Melqart, there are few significant surviving inscriptions of Phoenician. Some of the most well-known and influential examples are the Ahiram sarcophagus, the Nora Stone, the Pyrgi Tablets, and the Temple of Eshmun.

The Ahiram sarcophagus is the sarcophagus of a Phoenician king of Byblos who ruled c. 1000 BCE. The stone resting place was uncovered in 1923 by excavator Pierre Montet in tomb V of the royal necropolis of Byblos. The sarcophagus bears magnificent bas-reliefs and has 38 words written on it in an old Phoenician dialect from the region of Byblos. It currently resides in Lebanon and provides an excellent source of the original Phoenician alphabet and some of the common imagery and artwork from the time. The translation of the 38 words appears to say the following (according to the most recent work done by ancient linguists):

A coffin made it [Pil]sibaal, son of Ahirom, king of Byblos, for Ahirom, his father, lo, thus he put him in seclusion. Now, if a king among kings and a governor among governors and a commander of an army should come up against Byblos; and when he then uncovers this coffin – (then:) may strip off the sceptre of his judiciary, may be overturned the throne of his kingdom, and peace and quiet may flee from Byblos. And as for him, one should cancel his registration concerning the libation tube of the memorial sacrifice.[61]

The Sarcophagus of Ahiram
https://commons.wikimedia.org/wiki/File:Ahiram_sarcophag_from_Biblos_XIII-XBC.jpg

---

[61] Reinhard G. Lehmann: Die Inschrift(en) des Ahirom-Sarkophags und die Schachtinschrift des Grabes V in Jbeil (Byblos), 2005, p. 38

The Nora Stone, also called the Nora Inscription, is a stone stele discovered on the southern coast of Sardinia in 1773 CE. The stele comes from the late 9th or early 8th century BCE and is one of the oldest inscriptions found around Sardinia. The inscriptions have been difficult to translate, but scholars believe they convey the message that a general won an influential battle in the region and erected the stele as a monument to his victory. Others give the writing a more religious connotation.

The Pyrgi Tablets are a couple of bilingual tablets that present inscriptions in Etruscan and Phoenician. These have been dated to 500 BCE and were discovered in 1964 CE. Linguists were actually able to decipher more Etruscan from the slightly better-known Phoenician from these tablets. They were found during the excavation of a sanctuary of ancient Pyrgi on the Tyrrhenian coast of Italy, explaining the presence of Etruscan. The writing appears to be a dedication to the Phoenician goddess 'Ashtaret.

Finally, there is the important Temple of Eshmun. This temple was dedicated to the deity Eshmun, who was a Phoenician god of healing. The temple is located in the northeast of Sidon in Lebanon, and it appeared to be occupied between the 7th century BCE and the 8th century CE. After the Phoenicians, other cultures, like the native Sidonians and Arabs, occupied the temple. This temple serves as a great example of Phoenician architecture, but it also features several influential inscriptions that have allowed scholars to decipher a little of the Phoenician language and alphabet. Most of the inscriptions were found during the 20th century CE and include examples like the following:

As far as people have been able to tell, this particular inscription is funerary writing from the 4th century BCE for King Bodashtart of Sidon.

Chapter 10 – Religion

Historians do not possess many primary sources for the Phoenician religion and must instead rely on the biased and often negative reports given by neighboring civilizations like the Jewish and the later Christians in Israel, Babylon, and Egypt. Around this point in time, a religious schism emerged between those who practiced polytheistic religions, or religions that have multiple deities, and populations that embraced monotheism, or the belief in a single god. The early Jewish and Christians, particularly in Israel and nearby areas, wrote negatively about rival civilizations, and their works have been well preserved due to the continuing popularity of the Abrahamic religions in modern society.

Direct information about Phoenician religion only comes from the inscriptions left on sarcophagi and in tombs, but this often isn't enough to counter the accusations of base and monstrous behaviors such as ritual human sacrifice, which was common in almost every religion of the Bronze Age and early Iron Age. Inscriptions reveal the Phoenicians were deeply polytheistic and inherited the Mesopotamian pantheon from their Canaanite ancestors, which stressed the single creator god of Ba'al and a massive pantheon of other deities.

Bronze Figurine of Ba'al, c. 14ᵗʰ-12ᵗʰ century BCE
https://commons.wikimedia.org/wiki/File:Baal_Ugarit_Louvre_AO17330.jpg

However, it is difficult to describe a Phoenician pantheon, as religion was divided between the city-states. Each one adopted or stressed a different patron deity who was thought to watch over the region. This figure, whether they created the universe or not, received the most libations and prayers and was seen as the most significant or influential deity in the Phoenician pantheon, as well as the religion as a whole, within a set region. So, while one city might worship Ba'al more than the others, another might think Astarte was the most significant.

While Ba'al had tantamount importance before c. 1200 BCE, this all changed with a religious upheaval that saw the Phoenicians embracing lesser-known goddesses like Astarte and creating new deities like Melqart, Eshmun, and Reshef. Besides these gods and goddesses, the Phoenicians were also considerably influenced by the pantheons of the Egyptians, Hurrians, Mesopotamians, and others, so the total number of deities worshiped by the Phoenicians came from a hodgepodge of multiple cultures.

The Practices of the Cult

When contemporary audiences hear the phrase "cult," they often think of a secretive, evil religion or leaders like Jim Jones, who orchestrated mass suicides among fanatic followers. For ancient religions, the term cult refers to the practices of the followers of a particular deity. For example, there was the cult of Melqart and the cult of Ba'al. These practices varied between locations but also shared some significant central similarities, especially in relation to the calendar.

The Phoenician cultic calendar was inspired by the agricultural one, with sacrifices correlating with planting, harvesting, and other significant events. For example, libations were often poured when the first fruits appeared and when dairy products became available after the new year. The fertility of the earth was connected with the fertility of humans, and the movements of the sun and the moon affected the calendar as well, with sacrifices performed for solstices, eclipses, and even new or full moons. The moon, in particular, held special importance for the Phoenicians because they believed the moon died during each cycle and was then resurrected.

Cult rituals and rites took place near nature, with religious officials venturing out to mountains, near rivers, in forests, or beyond the city walls to sacred sites. Many practices mirrored religious legends, including reenacting the burning and resurrection of Melqart. However, the accusations of regular sacrifices draw the most ire from neighboring civilizations and even modern audiences. Although human sacrifice is up for debate, the faithful did kill lambs, sheep, and similar animals on a regular basis. These were often left with vegetables and other foodstuffs.

When it comes to human sacrifice, the bodies of stillborn infants were discovered in sacred sites, along with some human bones. Historians fall into two camps about the infants. They were either venerated in some way by the culture and were offered to the deities because they were born dead, or they might have been born healthy before being smothered or strangled as a sacrifice. Surviving inscriptions that do reference these practices seem to indicate that human sacrifice did occur, but it was often of adults and only performed during times of great trouble, such as a famine.

Besides animals, food, and the occasional human, the faithful tended to give the gods and goddesses votives or similar items made for a religious purpose and dedicated to the deities. Some examples include small bronze statues, bowls, dishes, jars of wine and olive oil, and sometimes ivory or stone sculptures. These could be given in individual ceremonies but were often showered *en masse* upon a deity during a feast or festival. Artifacts depict religious officials and female adherents or dancers bringing votives to sacred sites, and texts mention that there were feasts, dances, and other rituals performed on holy days. Women could be religious officials to an extent, but they were limited in their freedoms.

In the cities, ritual feasts held special importance and occurred at a *marzeh*, or "place of reunion." Each place developed as a location where friends and kin could gather and celebrate while honoring deceased ancestors. Over time, powerful *marzeh* started to influence the political and commercial lives of locations like Tyre, demonstrating how religion often blended into politics and the overall social structure.

Finally, divination and belomancy played a role in the outcomes of political decisions and personal lives. Diviners were specially trained religious officials who would search for signs or symbols in nature and interpret them to learn the outcome of future events. Belomancy was a sub-category of this practice that focused on examining the flight of arrows. Omens and portents could be found anywhere, including dreams and the entrails of animals. The result was a complex world of rituals, superstition, and political relationships that characterized the Phoenicians for over one thousand years.

Astarte

Astarte was a marginalized goddess in the Near Eastern pantheon that was brought to new importance by the Phoenicians, who worshiped her heavily in Tyre, Sidon, and Byblos. She was associated with fertility, sexuality, and war, and she possessed numerous animal motifs, including the lion, sphinx, and dove. She was further depicted with the stars and the moon, with the crescent moon being her most common symbol. She was the virgin daughter of a sky god and was perhaps the most commonly depicted female deity throughout the Phoenician territories. A marble statue of her is depicted below.

Melqart

Melqart was the chief deity of Tyre and was believed to be the progenitor of the Tyrian royal family. His worship spread from

Lebanon to Spain, and he was associated with Heracles by the Greeks and Hercules with the Romans. The majority of the archaeological evidence about him comes from temples located in North Africa and the Iberian Peninsula, but it tends to be limited to statuary and inscriptions on sarcophagi.

Melqart was associated with the sea, commerce, nobility, royalty, and colonization. He was the central focus of a festival of resurrection during a month that encompassed modern-day February and March, during which an effigy of him was burnt and then resurrected. This gives him associations with fire as well, and he was further believed to be the founder of the murex purple dye for which the Phoenicians became well known.

Special temples were dedicated to Melqart, and a sacred precinct functioned as the treasury of the city. Women, foreigners, and pigs—of all things—were not allowed to enter the precinct, even during rituals and festivals. All three groups were seen as unworthy or unclean in some fashion. Human sacrifices appear to have been given to him during times of strife and stress. Over time, as Phoenician influence waned and the Greeks and Romans started to become more powerful, Melqart became associated with Hercules (Heracles for the Greeks) and the twelve labors. Historians debate whether this has connotations to wrestling or if the twelve labors symbolized how the Phoenicians ventured all around the Mediterranean Sea.

Eshmun

Eshmun was the god of healing and the chief deity of Sidon. Unlike several other gods, he was worshiped in multiple city-states because of his benign pantheon. Little is known of him except that he had multiple dedicated temples and inscriptions that depict him wielding a staff with two snakes that could have been the inspiration for several influential contemporary symbols. He is associated with the Greek god Apollo, although some compare him to Apollo's son, Asclepius.

The Afterlife

For the Phoenicians, death appeared to be a genuine supernatural being that represented the chaos of the universe. After having lost a dispute with the other deities, Death, known as the god Mot to the Phoenicians, was punished and had its power limited to only control humans. Although Death was not worshiped like other gods and goddesses, the Phoenicians possessed a complex relationship with Death, especially in funerary rites. Periods of mourning and lamentation were required during a funeral to guarantee safe passage to the afterlife, and people covered themselves in ashes, tore out their hair, wailed, and beat themselves. Pottery and figurines were broken, and a tomb was only sealed with libations and prayers, potentially to Death itself.

When it comes to the afterlife, few sources survive that depict the exact Phoenician beliefs. The religion did not seem to draw much of a distinction between the body and the soul, and historians have been unable to determine whether the Phoenicians believed any life awaited them after death. Bodies were prepped before being left in tombs, often by being wrapped and doused with perfumed oil. Inscriptions over tombs hold warnings about visitors disturbing the eternal sleep of occupants, leading some to believe that the Phoenicians believed people, and their souls by extension, would sleep forever after death.

Chapter 11 – Warfare

The Levantine peoples often warred not only with each other but also with the nearby civilizations in North Africa and across the Mediterranean Sea, including the early ancient Greeks. These wars occurred for a variety of reasons, but the most common justifications were for the attainment of commercial wealth, the control of trade routes, a desire for local natural resources like timber or iron, and boundary disputes. Although the Phoenicians loved the sea, they were no exception to the rule and appeared to have a ground military force as well, though few records survive of battles or encounters. Like the Mesopotamian civilizations, the Phoenician city-states considered war to be a form of divine punishment or retribution.

As far as historians can tell, these city-states were unable to muster large armies because of a lack of extensive territorial resources. While Phoenicia included many city-states across the Mediterranean, they did not have sufficient ground to raise and maintain an army, and they did run on a grain deficit, which made feeding soldiers difficult. Instead of keeping a standing army then, it is likely the Phoenicians would muster a civilian force in times of need and supplement the native troops with mercenaries purchased from nearby Anatolia.

The Army

Without a form of regular training, there was no standardization for the Phoenician soldier. Records indicate men conscripted to fight brought along the dangerous tools of their trade rather than receiving training in more significant weapons like the sword or bow. For example, a hunter who was press-ganged into defending a location like Tyre would arrive and fight using his own ax, bow, or sling. Only if a man didn't have access to implements such as these—for instance, if he was a farmer—would the city government provide borrowed weapons like spears, swords, bows, maces, and small or large shields.

By the 7th century BCE, there is adequate archaeological evidence indicating the full implementation of iron weapons. Spearheads and short swords have been found in poor graves rather than just those of the rich or nobility, and masses of weaponry were discovered in locations like Sardinia. The Phoenicians appeared to make some of their own weapons, but they most likely imported the majority from centers like Anatolia, especially when they purchased the assistance of mercenaries and marauders.

A Phoenician sword varied in length but was most often between 82 and 130 centimeters (between a little over 32 and 51 inches) with a straight blade. The blade was thick and triangular in the center but had tapered edges that ended in clean, sharp ends that could be used for hacking and slashing. The tip was blunt, so piercing was not possible. This indicates a fighting style that did not incorporate thrusting, potentially because enemies most likely wore some version of iron plate mail that could not be pierced easily.

An unfortunate reality for a Phoenician soldier was that he would be well equipped for an offensive campaign but lacked defense. Besides swords, there is evidence of spears and maces being well made with fine iron and sharp tips, but little to no armor has been found. The Phoenicians themselves also rarely depicted their soldiers wearing armor, helmets, boots, gauntlets, or other basic necessities of protecting one's person from harm. This resulted in the deaths of many conscripted citizens. It is theorized that the Anatolian mercenaries were better equipped and were more likely to survive an encounter.

Like other ancient Near Eastern civilizations, the Phoenicians made heavy use of the oriental bow, and by the 1200s BCE, there is significant evidence the composite bow was adopted. Huge numbers of archers and slingers supplemented the infantry, often firing from a distance and attempting to eliminate their enemy counterparts. These older composite bows could be fired with a maximum distance of around 150 to 200 meters. Anything farther required intense strength and skill, and the archers would be unable to track individual targets. The oriental bow design was crucial for rapid-fire, as it could be drawn using several fingers and the archer could hold multiple arrows in hand for quick reloading and fast shots. Because the bow was drawn over the knee, their shots were powerful and covered a great range.

In terms of cavalry, the Phoenicians seem to have implemented the Near Eastern chariot. The Carthaginians, in particular, used over 2,000 models during the Punic Wars. These chariots were made of heavy terracotta and required four horses to function. Teams of three men would ride atop, with one driving, one firing a ranged weapon, and another equipped with a sword for close combat. Sharp blades on the wheel hubs were used to cut through the legs of enemy soldiers who got too close, and a couple of models had similar blades along the back as well. They were formidable weapons and required intensive training, meaning nobles or career soldiers were more likely to use one.

Besides chariots, the Carthaginians also used war elephants. Carthage's propensity for elephants is so well known that it is the first thing people often remember of the city-state, with many recalling how one general, Hannibal Barca, crossed the treacherous Alps with a large elephant force. Even famous TV shows like *The Simpsons* reference the conflict that ensued after Hannibal's forces crossed, and artists from previous centuries were captivated by the idea of transporting the magnificent animals across the sea and into the mountains.

Hannibal Barca Crossing the Rhône, by Henri Motte, 1878
https://commons.wikimedia.org/wiki/File:Hannibal_traverse_le_Rh%C3%B4ne_Henri_Motte_1878.jpg

The war elephants were a highly effective force. On the one hand, they formed a source of intimidation against enemy troops, who needed to contend with these large beasts that made thundering trumpet noises, had massive tusks, and could crush a man with their feet. Atop the elephants was another threat, as archers would be walled inside small shelters on the animal's back. These riders had bows and slings, often with ammo tipped in poison, and attempted to kill anyone who got near the elephant's legs.

Bringing elephants onto the battlefield was a dangerous pursuit. Although powerful, a wounded elephant would often turn on its handlers and needed to be killed, at which point the riders were at the mercy of nearby enemy soldiers. However, they intimidated enemy leaders fiercely, including Alexander the Great. When he first encountered the Indian war elephant during his conquest of Mesopotamia in the 4th century BCE, he was so startled that he made a sacrifice to the "God of Fear" (Phobos) the night before the Battle of Gaugamela.

Fortifications, Walls, and Other City Defenses

Because their civilization consisted of powerful city-states, the Phoenicians spent a great deal of time and money fortifying them from sieges and direct assaults. The necessity for walls was strengthened by the fact that each city also consisted of heavy commercial centers with cash, goods, and valuables kept stocked by the merchants in their homes and warehouses. Phoenicia and its territories were always under the threat of attack, and the location of the central city-states didn't help.

While other civilizations like Egypt had the advantage of being south of the majority of the Levant, or Greece who was across the Mediterranean Sea, most Phoenicians lived right in the center of the overland routes that connected the Mediterranean world to the fertile lands of Western Asia. As such, numerous warlords strove to take the territory to control routes of trade and transportation, including Alexander the Great in the 330s BCE.

When they first appeared, walls and other fortifications did not surround the entire city and were instead used to prevent livestock from becoming the prey of wild animals and unscrupulous poachers. Some also served as protection from flash floods, which were capable of wiping away an entire residential sector with immense crushing water. Over time, mudbrick walls gave way to genuine stone variants and became a symbol of wealth and power.

The standard wall consisted of foundations that were partly brick and partly clay. Parapets were made of brick, while stone was used to defend key points. Gates were built into the walls to allow the regular movement of people, and ramparts were necessary to support a large number of archers. When possible, the Phoenicians preferred to retreat to their cities and fire at enemies from afar, which reduced casualties and benefited the population. During the Late Iron Age, the Phoenicians implemented new construction technologies like gypsum cement for fortifications and the implementation of defensive ditches for horses to fall in.

While walls were effective against sieges, they also did lead to overconfidence, and the Phoenicians only enjoyed a brief period of peace before they became the vassals of larger, more powerful civilizations. In particular, the case of Tyre against Alexander the Great demonstrates how putting too much confidence in fortifications can result in an entire city being sieged, burned, and then ransacked. Whether or not this is the best example, though, comes down to whether or not one believes Alexander the Great is a shining example of a regular conqueror.

In the Navy

Although the Phoenicians did engage in ground warfare, they truly shone on the water. The civilization started its pattern of sea exploration on a series of clumsy rafts but eventually built up to hulled vessels based on Assyrian models and the penteconter, a galley that was rowed with fifty pairs of oars. After these developments came an expansion in overseas commerce and the eventual development of the warship, which was independent of the standard merchant vessels but could function as one if needed.

The Phoenician warship advanced significantly from the 8th century to the 5th century BCE. They were propelled by two lines of rowers and featured rams tipped with metallic heads that could be used to crush enemy ships and cause serious hull damage. Archers would line the deck and shoot at enemies as the warship came in proximity to other galleys, and it was necessary to try and break the opponent's oars so they could not row or maneuver normally.

Unlike modern vessels, ancient warships emphasized maneuverability and speed. Phoenician warships featured hollow hulls that ensured each vessel was swift and light, although this did mean hits from an enemy ram could be deadly. Like commercial ships, the standard warship was constructed with hard resin woods, like cypress, oak, and cedar, to better withstand impact. Nonessential interior components could be made of softwood, and the shell was built first. Everything received a waterproof coating, and some warships might have been treated to resist fire as well.

During the Battle of Salamis in 480 BCE, historical records indicate that 300 Phoenician warships were involved in the conflict. These ships carried a total of 30,000 sailors, meaning a single vessel could hold 100 individuals. Many of these men would have spent their time rowing, while others manned sails or shot at enemies.

In about 700 BCE, the Greeks adopted the trireme from the Phoenicians. The trireme had three banks of oars that ensured faster movement, even though the vessel was heavier than the bireme, or a ship with two rows. Relative to the Greek trireme, the Phoenician trireme had a raised deck, used a longer ram, and included amulets or figureheads of protection designed to keep the sailors safe through the supervision of the gods. Near the amulets were apotropaic eyes, which were intended to be a countercharm against misfortune but also as a symbol that would allow the ship to "see" as it sailed.[62]

Relief of a Phoenician Warship, c. 700 BCE
No machine-readable author provided. World Imaging assumed (based on copyright claims)., CC BY-SA 3.0 <http://creativecommons.org/licenses/by-sa/3.0/>, via Wikimedia Commons https://commons.wikimedia.org/wiki/File:AssyrianWarship.jpg

---

[62] Apotropaic magic is a form that is intended to prevent harm and turn away evil influences. The most common form seen in modern Western cultures is the evil eye, designed to stop misfortune from befalling the wearer.

The Phoenician trireme was considered to be the most advanced and powerful ship in the ancient Mediterranean world, with civilizations like the Greeks and Egyptians writing at length about the superiority of Phoenicia's warships and sailors. Because the city-states relied so much on naval warfare, it should not be surprising that they carved a name for themselves on the seas. However, one major reason why the Phoenician ships survived as long as they did was their regular maintenance.

The Phoenicians possessed a unique view of their ships, often considering them living entities that were under the protection of the Cabiri. The Cabiri were chthonic deities who could be appeased through blood sacrifices and who would protect the sailors and others aboard the vessel once they were satisfied.[63] The exact nature of how much the Phoenicians actually sacrificed to these gods is a subject of debate, though. Greek and Roman historians alluded to the practice, but like accusations leveled against the Canaanites, this information needs to be taken with a grain of salt.

One Roman historian, Valerius Maximus, says that the launch of the Carthaginian warships involved a brutal ceremony where prisoners were captured, tied in the water, and then crushed by the hull of a warship so their skulls would shatter and blood would splatter against the wood. The captives' blood was intended to ensure victory and the safe passage of the sailors and soldiers. As Carthage was one of the Phoenician city-states, ancient historians attribute this brutality to the civilization as a whole. However, modern historians believe this is an exaggeration designed to slander an enemy.

---

[63] The chthonic deities were subterranean or underworld gods that required blood sacrifices. Deities across multiple religions qualify as chthonic.

Chapter 12 – Artistry in Multiple Mediums

Phoenician art encompasses numerous mediums that evolved over a thousand years, resulting in creative pieces that combined cultural symbols with technological developments. Contemporary audiences are familiar with pieces from the Egyptians, Greeks, and Romans, but in the ancient Mediterranean world, it was the Phoenicians who were considered some of the most skilled artists. Craftsmen and women were lauded for their capabilities, especially when it came to dyes, textiles, and ivory. The monopoly the Phoenicians possessed on the luxurious purple dye meant that Phoenician artists were able to give their work a distinctive color, and their ability to move quickly across the sea meant goods could be transported simply and easily.

Historians and writers like Homer adored the Phoenicians and wrote passages such as:

...a mixing bowl of silver, richly wrought; six measures it held, and in beauty it was far the goodliest in all the earth, seeing that Sidonians, well skilled in deft handiwork, had wrought it cunningly, and men of the Phoenicians brought it over the murky deep, and landed it in harbor...[64]

However, modern artistic communities are less than pleased with the work of the Phoenicians. The chief criticisms of the Phoenicians are that their pieces were ultimately derivative, with motifs, symbols, and imagery heavily borrowed from other cultures and civilizations and then mixed into a hodgepodge stew served to the rest of the Mediterranean. Of glaring significance is that many of the borrowed symbols were misused and placed in situations where they didn't make any sense; instead, they were just used because the appearance was aesthetically pleasing. Some historians argue against this criticism, claiming the combination of multiple elements ultimately shows Phoenician skill and creativity.

Ultimately, whether or not Phoenician art is special or worthy of study remains up to individual preferences. It is difficult to identify characteristics that could be considered defining of the Phoenician collection overall, but Woolmer states it best when he notes, "...the primary characteristic of Phoenician art is its eclecticism."[65] It loved to adopt the styles of Egypt, Assyria, Anatolia, and Syria and translated preexisting symbolism into new mediums. The Phoenicians did so to such a great extent that ancient art historians decided to divide Phoenician artwork into categories based on which civilization the pieces seemed to emulate the most. At present, four exist:

Assyrianizing: This is a style when the Phoenicians copied elements of Assyrian and Hittite culture, usually using imagery like sphinxes, lions, Assyrian seals, and Assyrian fashion. Characteristics of Mesopotamian religion were present as well.

Cypro-Phoenician: This is a set of artworks found only in Cyprus that used solely Assyrian elements instead of combining with Egyptian culture, which became common during the broader

---

[64] Iliad 23.740

[65] Woolmer, *Ancient Phoenicia*, p. 112.

Mediterranean expansion.

Egyptianizing: Much of Phoenician art is considered to be Egyptianized, or to have copied common Egyptian imagery like sun discs, wingless sphinxes, and Egyptian fashion. It became so popular that Cyprus distinguished itself by clinging to Assyrian culture rather than adopting Egyptian elements.

Syrianizing: The Phoenicians copied Syrian art styles, depicting people in Syrian dress and profile while still retaining Egyptian elements. The main difference between Syrianized Phoenician artwork and regular Syrian work was that the Syrians drew people facing forward with more distinct facial features.

This mixing of styles and symbolism has been known to historians and archaeologists for centuries, with one commenter writing in the New York Times in 1879:

He entered into other men's labors and made most of his heritage. The Sphinx of Egypt became Asiatic, and its new form was transplanted to Nineveh on the one side and to Greece on the other. The rosettes and other patterns of the Babylonian cylinders were introduced into the handiwork of Phoenicia, and so passed on to the West, while the hero of the ancient Chaldean epic became first the Tyrian Melkarth, and then the Herakles of Hellas.[66]

Most of the information historians possess about Phoenician artwork comes from grave goods, or items that were buried with their owners. These goods were given as signs of an individual's respect toward the deceased or to represent the wealth of the buried, and they could consist of a broad range of objects like bowls, plates, jewelry, small statuettes, scarabs of protection, mirrors, ivory boxes, razors, and terracotta masks. Historians believe funerary art constituted a massive portion of artisan work,

---

[66] "Phoenician Art" (PDF). *The New York Times*. 1879-01-05. Retrieved August 22nd, 2019.

although many items were made for aesthetic reasons as well.

When examining Phoenician art, scholars must handle the realities of many buildings and papyrus documents being lost to time. While the murals and drawings of other cultures can be examined, the Phoenicians must be analyzed from the position of material objects. The most prevalent types were terracotta masks, metal goods, ivory and stone sculptures, and textiles. While artisans also worked heavily with glass and faience, the Phoenicians preferred to ship glass as a raw material but did keep some to produce jewelry and small votives.

Terracotta

Terracotta objects are clay ceramics with a distinct reddish-brown hue. Unlike other art that was heavily influenced by neighboring civilizations, the terracotta produced by the Phoenicians was intended for domestic use and therefore contained more elements of traditional folk art. Lines were cruder, more exaggerated, and rough. The most commonplace creation was a mask that could be worn for religious purposes. These masks varied, but most possessed dramatic expressions, twisted smiles, and elongated features.

Evidence exists that suggests the masks were painted with vibrant colors after being marked to indicate where the paints would go. Masks were worn by individuals of all ages, including children. Those entering their teenage years and thus coming into adulthood had ceremonious ones to be worn during initiation rituals, rites, and dances. Although early masks were handmade, newer models show signs of being mass-produced from templates.

Besides masks, the Phoenicians also created statuettes of favored gods and goddesses. In one colony, archaeologists discovered hundreds of figurines of a favored goddess that had been crafted using a mold, indicating these statuettes were popular outside of central cities. The masks, on the other hand, were limited to the Lebanon and Middle Eastern regions and are not often found on other shores of the Mediterranean.

Terracotta objects are divided into three categories: those that were handmade, those spun on a wheel, and those that were made with a mold. In general, handmade offerings are rougher, cruder, and tend to be located in the graves of the poor. These items also are far more likely to be basic goods like pots, cups, and plates than statuettes. Goods made on a wheel are more uniform, while those made in a mold tended to be small votive offerings given to the deities during religious ceremonies. The most common figure discovered is of a woman holding or supporting her breasts, perhaps depicting Astarte. The second is a pregnant woman with her hand on her stomach, symbolizing fertility.

Metalworking

The Phoenicians developed an exceptional reputation for their metalworking capabilities, with metal bowls appearing throughout the Mediterranean region. These bowls featured intricate designs, such as winged sphinxes, and synthesized numerous cultural styles and symbols. Archaeologists date Phoenician metalworking over a span of 800 years, although the best examples emerged between 900 and 700 BCE. Bowls all possessed a circular central medallion with other scenes and designs placed beyond concentric circles that surrounded the center.

Phoenician metal bowls were shallow and primarily depicted Egyptian and Assyrian imagery, with some models even showing an Egyptian pharaoh smiting nearby civilizations. Other common elements were duels, religious scenes, nature, animals, and mythological creatures—the sphinx was, again, a favorite. Copper alloy was the favored metal, but some were made of silver and gold, with personal names inscribed along the inside, potentially revealing the owners of these fine items.

The Phoenicians inherited the knowledge of bronze metalworking from their ancestors in the Levant, and they rapidly adopted ironworking and the skills to work with precious metals.

The majority of the bowls produced appear to have a religious purpose, perhaps for making libations due to their shallow nature. Archaeologists theorize that more common dishes would have been made of terracotta or similar hardened clay. An interesting characteristic of many of the bowls, though, is that while they display Egyptian characteristics and symbols, these symbols don't actually make any sense. They were not intended for an Egyptian audience but were most likely shipped as tourist items to cities and civilizations in Europe and Asia.

Other bronze items that were popular were razors and figurines. Bronze razors were common in the western territories such as Carthage and commonly figured in burial goods. It is likely that the razor was buried with the owner as a deeply personal item as it would have been used on a regular basis. Razors were considered a male item, while mirrors and combs made of bronze were more feminine. Figurines served as votive offerings for religious ceremonies and typically depicted goddesses in Egyptian dress with their hand outstretched as a gesture of welcome or offering.[67]

Ivory and Stone Sculptures

The Phoenicians were one of the first cultures from the Levant to acquire ivory in sufficient numbers to produce artwork. Ivory formed an integral part of the artwork in the ancient world, and the Phoenicians rapidly increased the demand for it by crafting exquisite sculptures and images that were sold throughout the Near East and Africa. The ivory came from city-states and colonies in North Africa, where there was an adequate elephant population to supply the material. Phoenician ivory objects have been discovered throughout the Levantine coast and in Iraq, Italy, Greece, and on numerous Mediterranean islands.

Ivory sculptures and artifacts can be divided between the large and the small. The majority of discovered large objects hail from

---

[67] There continues to be a debate about whether or not these figurines are male or female, with the majority of archaeologists believing the statues are feminine in nature.

900 to 800 BCE and mainly include furniture panels for tables, beds, chairs, footstools, and even thrones. These panels were designed to form decorative motifs when properly installed and appeared in items with gold filigree, colorful glass paste, and even precious and semiprecious gems.

Smaller objects are by far more numerous. Ivory was a popular material for toiletries such as combs and mirrors. Another frequently found item is the ivory box, which was small enough to potentially hold someone's jewelry and ornaments. Some historians believe these smaller pieces were made from the leftovers produced by the creation of larger objects. This assumption is based on the fact that elephant tusks were transported from northern Syria and were easier to work and shape when left in one piece. The long furniture panels show evidence of being carved from one piece as well.

Stone sculpture did not enjoy the success that many other mediums had. Although stone was accessible in the coastal city-states and colonies, artisans did not focus on this substance. The only times stone appeared were in wall reliefs and sarcophagi, large pieces that took advantage of preexisting stones that required little shaping. Instead, artisans worked through carving and did not develop many standalone stone sculptures or statues. Manufacturers produced stone caskets with masculine or feminine outlines on the top to indicate the occupant, and headstones were also developed with this material.

The Stone Sarcophagus of King Ahiram of Byblos, c. 1000s BCE
https://commons.wikimedia.org/wiki/File:Ahiram_sarcophag_from_Biblos_XIII-XBC.jpg

Although few textiles survived the test of time, the Phoenicians had a reputation for creating some of the finest and most richly dyed fabrics using local cotton, wool, and flax. These were well woven and used the signature murex purple dye that the civilization was renowned for. Textiles were transported by ship throughout the Mediterranean and even made an appearance in modern Abrahamic religious texts. Unfortunately, not a shred of that fabric is preserved today.

Conclusion – The Legacy of the Phoenicians

Although the sands of time took much of the history of the Phoenicians, this civilization's legacy lives on through the effects of its culture, education, and extensive trade networks. One of the most significant was the trend of alphabets being used throughout the Mediterranean to improve the literacy of not only hierarchical priests but also merchants, traders, and influential craftsmen and women. They also reopened the trade routes of the Eastern Mediterranean that had fallen during the Bronze Age Collapse, thus connecting the Greeks, Romans, Anatolians, and the Carthaginians to the Egyptian and Mesopotamian civilizations. Such an act would eventually lead to the "Orientalizing" of Greek art, or the implementation of more Eastern elements in murals and sculptures.

When it comes to politics, the Phoenicians were one of the first developers of an oligarchic social structure with roots in democracy. This was exemplified by the ability of the city-states to have influential merchants and traders who were not necessarily royals or nobles but who were still able to exert their will on traditionally hierarchical structures. Some historians believe the Phoenicians would inspire the Greek Athenian revolution and the development of a Greek constitutional government. Continuing the influence on Greece, many historians believe that Zeno of Citium, the founder of the famous school of philosophy known as Stoicism, was Phoenician.

Of course, there were other avenues of significance, especially related to the development of military and naval technology and the advancements that were copied by or passed down to the Greeks, Romans, and Etruscans. Although the Phoenicians won few great military victories, they demonstrated the power of currency by dominating their neighbors with financial strangleholds. It could be said that they proved how the pen might be mightier than the sword, but the coin outweighs them all.

While these may seem insignificant to the average individual living in contemporary society, the Phoenicians helped establish elements of both Western and Eastern cultures by reestablishing contact between civilizations following the Bronze Age Collapse. If contact had been allowed to fade, modern humans would have lost thousands of years of international trade and culture sharing, meaning the rich Mediterranean history of symbolism and exchange might not have ever occurred or would have happened in a different way entirely. How many people enjoy advancements like Judaism and Christianity in the West, and elements of modern warfare like ranged weapons in the East? What about purple clothes? Mathematics? Democratic civilization?

Without the Phoenicians to bridge the gap between the East and West, who knows when civilizations would have united once more to share culture and scientific developments. While the Mediterranean may have warred, trade fostered deep connections and ensured advancements could be shared throughout the Asian, European, and African continents.

Part 4: The Mycenaeans

A Captivating Guide to the First Advanced Civilization in Ancient Greece

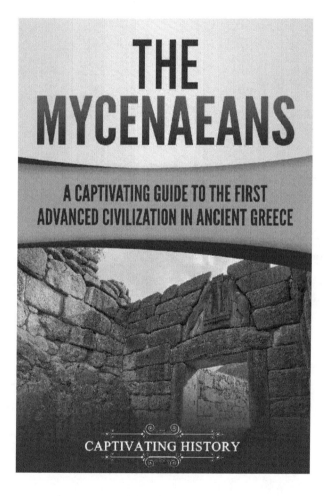

Introduction – Who Were the Mycenaeans?

What student of the Western world hasn't studied the ancient Greeks, a civilization so influential to contemporary civilization that countries around the globe continue to implement their political ideas and opulent architecture to the present day? Almost everyone has heard the stories of Athens, of Sparta, of Zeus and Hera and Poseidon. But who has heard of the Mycenaeans, the predecessors and creators of the foundations that made the ancient Greeks so great?

Anyone who has heard of the ancient Greeks is a little familiar with the Mycenaeans. Officially termed the Mycenaean Greeks, the Mycenaeans were a native civilization that lived on the Peloponnese, or the mainland portion of the Greek peninsula. They lived from approximately 1600 BCE to 1100 BCE. In historical terms, the abbreviation "BCE" stands for "before common era" and refers to the years before the modern Gregorian equivalent of year 1. So, to understand how long ago the Mycenaeans lived, someone needs to take the current year—for example, 2019—and then add the year listed before BCE. Since the Mycenaean civilization is officially measured as starting in 1600 BCE, then an individual can calculate that the Mycenaeans lived—

2019 + 1600—3,619 years ago.

Greece – The Home of the Mycenaeans
https://commons.wikimedia.org/wiki/File:EFS_highres_STS034_STS034-86-96.jpg

The Mycenaeans were the first advanced civilization to develop on mainland Greece and were responsible for much of the urban organization and cultural development seen in the early ancient Greeks. The Mycenaeans created sprawling palatial states, unique and sophisticated works of art, and possessed a writing system that could be used to make records. For these reasons, they are considered a prime example of a thriving Bronze Age civilization.

The Bronze Age is a scholarly term used to classify civilizations that developed metallurgy far enough to be able to produce bronze weapons, armor, and tools on a regular basis. This technology gave civilizations like the Mycenaean Greeks a significant advantage above those who lacked such skills since the tough metal improved combat prowess and the ability to harvest crops. Through their use of bronze, the Mycenaeans were able to create a powerful military and establish numerous centers of power, including the prominent Mycenae, Pylos, Thebes, Athens (yes, that Athens), Midea, and

Orchomenos.[68] Some settlements outside of mainland Greece were on islands in the Aegean Sea as well as in the Levant and Italy.

The Mycenaeans were responsible for numerous innovations and technological advancements for the region, including architecture and military structure. They developed their own syllabic script called Linear B and also possessed the first ever written records of the Greek language. Perhaps more surprising for modern audiences, the Mycenaeans worshipped several of the deities famous in Greek religion long before the development of the Olympic pantheon. Although the Mycenaeans would eventually fall during something called the Late Bronze Age Collapse, their civilization would survive by adapting and eventually morphing into the ancient Greeks known so well in Western civilizations.

---

[68] Charles Freeman, *Egypt, Greece and Rome: Civilizations of the Ancient Mediterranean* (3rd ed.). Oxford: Oxford University Press, 2014.

Chapter 1 – Political and Military Organization

As the first Greek civilization, the Mycenaeans laid the foundation for future political development. Like their successors the ancient Greeks, the Mycenaeans developed a complex administrative system that relied on disparate settlements that shared a culture working together. These settlements were major urban centers like Mycenae, Pylos, Athens, and Thebes. Although there were a central king and dynasty centered in Mycenae, the other palatial states possessed strong governors who had their own militaries and economic interests. It was difficult to keep everything running smoothly, and yet the civilization managed to succeed for five centuries through careful organization of the all-important palatial states.

The Palatial States

The earliest mentions of the palatial states come from famous Greek epics and mythology such as the *Iliad*, which mentions the presence of independent states that operate under a similar culture. German archaeologist Heinrich Schliemann, among numerous others, confirmed the presence of these organized palace-operating polities in the 20th century. Each Mycenaean palatial state possessed a palace from which governing and administration was done. The powerful political figures that inhabited the palace controlled the surrounding territories and often exerted influence over important industries like the making of textiles and weapons. Each palatial state was divided into subregions with their own provincial centers that were run by governors. These smaller provinces were further divided into districts called *da-mo*.[69]

Palatial states featured their own military fortifications that formed a broad defensive system for Mycenaean territory. Although there was no single ruling dynasty, records indicate that Mycenae controlled up to three times as much territory as the other states and appeared to be the most powerful. This power allowed it to control adjacent settlements like Nauplion and Tiryns and is how the Mycenaeans earned their name. Archaeological records from Greece lack any evidence to support a unified Mycenaean state, but documents from the Hittites and Egyptians reference a state existing under a figure known as the "Great King."[70] At present, scholars believe the evidence suggests that there was a coalition of the palatial states similar to what the later ancient Greeks would use. The most likely centers of power would therefore have been Mycenae or Thebes, the largest and wealthiest of the states.

Society and Political Culture

Mycenaean society, potentially because it was connected to numerous others throughout the Mediterranean, resembled other Bronze Age civilizations in its social structure. As far as historians can tell, there was a clear hierarchy between two separate groups of free men—and the emphasis is on men—and one slave class. The best way to understand Mycenaean society is as a three-tiered cake with many different delicious fillings in the layers. Each layer is

[69] Jorrit M. Kelder, *The Kingdom of Mycenae: A Great Kingdom in the Late Bronze Age Aegean*, Bethesda: CDL Press, 2010.

[70] Kelder, *The Kingdom of Mycenae*, p. 46.

distinct, and there were numerous "flavors" of social categorization in them. The main three classes were the royal or palace entourage, the commoners or *damos* (later and more commonly known as *demos*), and the slaves.

The entourage consisted of wealthy officials who came from influential and powerful families. They could be considered nobility and typically held significant administrative or military positions. They could have been tax collectors, advisors, generals, potential policymakers, and other royal agents. Historians believe these individuals inhabited the large homes and estates near the palace, though many of these homes' inhabitants were most likely little better than the rest of the population since they were servants. Their counterparts were members of the *demos*, which constituted the majority of the population. The *demos* were technically free individuals who performed backbreaking labor and held positions like farmers and craftsmen. Some might have been merchants, but the *demos* tended to be poor and of little consequence. Lower on the social ladder were the slaves, which were called the *do-e-ro* or the *do-e-ra* (masculine and feminine forms). Slaves mainly worked for the palace or for priests at religious sites.

However, these social classes possessed even more dimensions beyond the basic three. In the top class, the absolute most powerful individual was the *wanax*, or ruler.[71] The *wanax* was always a man who possessed a king-like role and the responsibilities that accompanied it. He would make laws, determine how much tax the subjects would pay, and be responsible for declarations of war and general leadership. Historians believe the *wanax* also needed to perform some religious ceremonies since the position was connected to religion. For the Mycenaeans, the king was significant as a connection between the gods and the average humans. The royal family was chosen to rule by the deities and were seen as

---

[71] Sigrid Deger-Jalkotzy and Irene S. Lemos, *Ancient Greece: From the Mycenaean Palaces to the Age of Homer*, Edinburgh: University of Edinburgh Press, 2006.

having an elevated position in society and the afterlife as well. Another important member of the top tier was the *telestai*. Researchers believe the *telestai* would have been religious leaders, similar to priests, who conducted ceremonies and worship for the general public. They most likely were landowners as well.

Other members of the top group were the military leaders. The foremost leader was the *lawagetas,* the second-highest ranked individual in the entire civilization.[72] Historians are unsure of his—as it was always a male—exact role. The *lawagetas* might have been the top general, but he also could have been a figurehead; for instance, some scholars believe the *lawagetas* was actually the eldest prince given an influential position in preparation for his role as the future *wanax*. Below the *lawagetas* were the *hequetai*. The *hequetai* were a warrior and nobility class that could have rode into battle as the cavalry or chariot operators. Their ability to ride, use, and own horses placed them above the regular foot soldiers. Members of the *hequetai* were most likely landowners like the rest of the top tier. There would also be a local *kawete* in each of the sixteen provinces that functioned as a mayor.[73]

At the bottom of the top tier, almost in the middle, were the artisans. Artisans were specialty craftsmen capable of making high-quality items such as pottery, armor, and weapons. They tended to work in the palace or at other upper-class estates and made superior items compared to their counterparts who made common goods like horseshoes. Administrators provided the artisans with materials and typically commissioned products needed for the military or the greater good of the public. These could include more spears and shields but could also be the creation of more pots to store surplus olive oil and grain in the palace.

The varying positions of the *demos* and the slaves are less known. Craftsmen were clearly placed above farmers and general

---

[72] Ibid.

[73] Ibid.

laborers but how much is unclear. Slaves were, by all accounts, treated as second-class humans, but those that worked in the palace possessed their own hierarchies. For example, a slave who worked directly for the *wanax* would be above someone in the kitchen.

The Military

Unlike the neighboring Minoans, the Mycenaeans possessed a developed and complex military structure evident by the numerous weapons unearthed throughout Greece. Combat and the ideal warrior were popular subjects in frescoes and pottery, while examples of military infrastructure and battles could be found in Mycenaean documents written in Linear B. Compared to other peoples in the northern Mediterranean region, the Mycenaeans were elaborate and dedicated to a militaristic infrastructure that dominated their civilization. Numerous historians believe the Mycenaean system would influence the following ancient Greeks, who adopted numerous traditions like the warrior elite and warrior kingdoms—for the best example, interested individuals can look at the Greek city-state of Sparta.

The Mycenaeans were one of several warrior kingdoms that existed in the Late Bronze Age on the Peloponnese. The Mycenaeans were the residents of Mycenae, a kingdom that was rapidly expanding toward the Aegean Sea by way of the Anatolian coast. Through their military prowess, the Mycenaeans managed to conquer locations like Cyprus through a combination of sophisticated tactics and heavy infantry. Their preferred weaponry during the main expansion in the 15th century BCE was the classic spear and large, rectangular shields designed to protect the majority of the holder's body. By the 13th century, technological changes forced the Mycenaeans to become more flexible, and soldiers started to use smaller, lighter weapons like swords more often. Shields also changed, turning into the well-known "figure-of-eight" design. Toward the fall of the Mycenaeans, the military possessed numerous characteristics of the Greek hoplites.

It's important to note that the materials used for weapons and shields changed over time. In the earlier centuries, the Mycenaeans made their weapons and tower shields almost entirely of solid bronze. Although a soft metal, bronze was strong enough to block the blows of spears and swords, and the design gave ample coverage to fighters. As combat became faster and armies used lighter weapons, the Mycenaeans started to make their signature figure-of-eight shields from multiple layers of bull's hide and leather strips. These shields were still strong but were much easier to carry.

The military of the Bronze Age Mycenaeans resembled that of numerous other civilizations at this point in time. Heavy infantry was the name of the game. Warriors and soldiers were armored and bore impressive weaponry that tended to be heavy, long, and difficult to swing. Pikes and spears were used to keep combat away from the body, and tower shields were also used. A tower shield could be almost as tall as the man bearing it, which gave rise to tactics that favored close-knit groups of soldiers holding the shields in tight formations to form walls.

The Mycenaeans may or may not have used war chariots—historians and archaeologists continue to debate due to a lack of evidence. Although some frescoes and records show that horse-mounted warriors could be seen on the Mycenaean battlefield, it's unclear whether they represented chariots or if the men represented archers or officers. The most information scholars can glean is that from the 16th to 14th centuries BCE, the Mycenaeans used chariots in some limited form to fight, but that they fell out of favor and were instead used to transport goods and supplies by the 13th century BCE.[74]

---

[74] Nic Fields, *Bronze Age War Chariots*, Oxford: Osprey Publishing Company, 2006.

Pylos Chariot Fresco, c. 1350 BCE
https://commons.wikimedia.org/wiki/File:Two_Mycenaean_chariot_warriors_on_a_fresc o_from_Pylos_about_1350_BC.jpg

Frescoes indicate that the Mycenaean chariot was driven by two horses and could hold more than one individual. These chariots differed from those used by other Bronze Age civilizations at the time because they were lighter and had an open cab, which is the section where the driver would stand. The cab would have left drivers and riders open to attack, giving rise to the idea that the chariots were best served for transportation to and from locations rather than as a fighting vehicle. However, archaeologists have uncovered evidence showing that the lighter chariots, which are common to find in locations like Knossos and Pylos, came after a heavier chariot that would have been better suited for battle. This is why scholars continue to debate just what purpose the vehicles might have had. It's entirely possible the Mycenaeans actually produced two separate designs to suit different purposes.

If the chariots and regular foot soldiers failed to keep back invaders, the Mycenaeans could fall back on their fortifications. These were made of thick stone and typically built upon elevated terrain for a tactical advantage against foreign armies. Some known centers were also developed on coastal plains, particularly the famous Gla.[75] Gla was in Boeotia and made of limestone. It sat on a lake that is currently drained but would have garnered several defensive benefits from being situated in such a location, as well as a supply of fresh water for troops during sieges. The fort was roughly 20 hectares (49 acres) in size and housed several buildings.

Gla is one of the best sites to study for clues about Mycenaean fortifications because the location appears to have been built solely for the military. The remains of the internal structures indicate that the buildings were meant to be temporary and created quickly, while the thickness of the walls was intended to withstand a siege. The presence of distinct fired pan and cover tiles leads archaeologists to believe that Gla once had a pitched roof similar to those used by the Mycenaeans' successors, the ancient Greeks.

Gla and other Mycenaean fortresses were created in the Cyclopean style. The walls were made of large boulders that were unworked, meaning no changes had been made to the stones when they were cut from quarries. The majority of these boulders were roughly 26 ft. thick and weighed several tons. Cut stone masonry does appear, but it was only used around gateways and doorways.[76]

Mycenaean warriors wore armor made of bronze plates or scales. A complete set would have a cuirass, shoulder pads, and coverage on the arms. The set was designed to be flexible, sturdy, and comfortable enough for men to wear for extended periods of time. A complete set called the Dendra panoply was discovered at Dendra in Greece. The entire set weighs roughly 40 lbs. and was crafted between 1450 and 1400 BCE. There are striking similarities between the armor of Mycenaean warriors and that of the ancient Greek hoplites, indicating that much of the technology and design used during classical Greek antiquity were already

---

[75] Nic Fields, *Mycenaean Citadels c. 1350-1200 BC* (3rd ed.), Oxford: Osprey Publishing Company, 2004.

[76] Ibid.

implemented by the Mycenaeans.[77]

Body armor, however, can't cover everything, and the Mycenaeans needed to defend their skulls from the dangerous swords and spears wielded by their enemies. The most common form of Mycenaean head protection was something called the boar's tusk helmet. These were conical headdresses reinforced with rows upon rows of boar tusks to create a sturdy layer of protection. The interior of the helmet was a felt-lined leather flap for comfort, and the boar tusks would be sewn to the leather. Some warriors also wore bronze helmets with broad cheek guards and crests, or horned helmets made by layering and sewing together strips of leather.

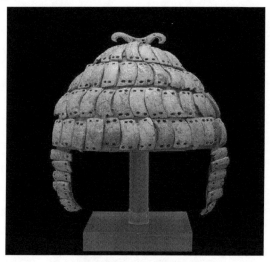

A Boar's Tusk Helmet
National Archaeological Museum of Athens, CC0, via Wikimedia Commons
https://commons.wikimedia.org/wiki/File:Boars%27s_tusk_helmet_NAMA6568_Athens_Greece1.jpg

As mentioned previously, the ancient Greeks drew much of their cultural, political, and military structure from the Mycenaeans. Historians believe that the Greek epics of poets like Homer were describing the tribulations and victories of the

---

[77] Donald Kagan and Gregory F. Viggiano, *Men of Bronze: Hoplite Warfare in Ancient Greece*, Princeton: Princeton University Press, 2013.

Mycenaean army and its warrior elite. The fortifications, weapons, armor, and tactics used by the Mycenaeans were thus the possessions of the warrior heroes that Greeks believed preceded them. However, this also means that the perception of the Mycenaean army is colored by literary interpretation, as the epics depict the Mycenaean warriors as fickle, quarrelsome, prideful, and obsessed with their own personal honor.[78] Whether or not this is true is up for debate, but between the artifacts and the epics, it's clear to modern scholars that the Mycenaean army was a force to be reckoned with even if it was not the most innovative Bronze Age combatant.

[78] Rodney Castleden, *The Mycenaeans*. London and New York: Routledge, 2005.

Chapter 2 – Culture and Daily Life

Contemporary audiences might best understand Mycenaean daily life through its similarities with the much more famous ancient Greeks. Mycenae, the home of the Mycenaeans, possessed a regional structure and a clear social hierarchy that determined a person's position in the civilization. There was a rudimentary monarchy, influential administrators and nobles, a powerful military, and a large class of farmers and laborers who formed the basis of the population. The Mycenaeans additionally practiced slavery and were known to have enslaved peoples of other ethnic groups as well as other peoples on the Peloponnese.

In terms of the daily life of the average person, archaeologists run into some roadblocks in determining the full extent of a typical individual's experiences. After all, the majority of the population could not read or write and would not have been important or wealthy enough to commission artwork of themselves or their activities. However, artifacts and other resources provide some clues.

Gender Roles

In Mycenaean civilization, the males held the most influential positions in society. They were the political leaders and administrators, priests, generals, hunters, fishermen, warriors, and sailors. They were the gender that dominated the public sphere, the aspects of society that dealt with the world at large rather than the home. Free men were considered the heads of the household and frequently held the power of life and death over their wives and children. The majority of them could inherit property, enter into legal contracts, choose who they married, and enjoy sexual freedom. Those who could not usually were under the control of their fathers, who would have had the ultimate authority as the oldest male in the house. The family name and position were inherited along patriarchal lines, meaning children belonged to the family of their father. The analysis of ancient skeletons also shows that men ate better diets filled with more protein and nutrition than their female counterparts, indicating preference was given in the distribution of resources based on gender.

Despite this situation, the majority of men in Mycenaean civilization worked difficult jobs, usually as simple farmers and laborers. Although they enjoyed greater freedoms than women, most had no political rights and no say in the administration due to the presence of the warrior elite.

In the early periods of Mycenean society, Mycenaean women were different from their counterparts in other civilizations and seemed to possess more rights, privileges, and responsibilities than others. According to ancient texts and frescoes, wealthy women were capable of owning property, serving important religious functions, conducting religious ceremonies, and working as artisans and specialty craftswomen. Although their primary role appeared to be as mothers and maintainers of the domestic sphere, some additional options seemed available to Mycenaean women.

However, this does not mean they were the equals of men. Archaeologists have discovered distinct disparities between the treatment of men and women in frescoes, in the types of grave goods they were buried with, and in how they were referenced in documents. In particular, women appeared to lack the opportunities for social advancement possessed by their male counterparts and could not hold influential positions like the *wanax*, the *lawagetas*, or the *hequetai*. Burial goods indicate women were barred from activities enjoyed by the men, including public drinking, feasting, fighting, and the ability to attend popular social events.[79]

Mycenaean women appear to have been relegated to a second-class existence and were considered the property or responsibility of their male relatives by the Late Bronze Age, being sapped of the privileges they enjoyed earlier. Although numerous women held physically demanding jobs outside of the home, such as rudimentary construction laborers and crop harvesters, they were also expected to be responsible for domestic chores and child-rearing. Women in Mycenaean frescoes typically appear as wives and mothers engaged in domestic pursuits, and they are often seen with young children, cementing their societal role in Mycenaean civilization.

[79] Lynne E. Schepartz, Sharon R. Stocker, Jack L. Davis, Anastasia Papathanasiou, Sari Miller-Antonio, Joanne M. A. Murphy, Michael Richards, and Evangelia Malapani, "Mycenaean Hierarchy and Gender Roles: Diet and Health Inequalities in Late Bronze Age Pylos, Greece," in *Bones of Complexity: Bioarchaeological Case Studies of Social Organization and Skeletal Biology* edited by Haagen D. Klaus, Amanda R. Harvey, and Mark N. Cohen, Gainesville: University of Florida Press, 2017.

Incomplete Fresco of a Mycenaean Woman, c. 13ᵗʰ Century BCE
https://commons.wikimedia.org/wiki/File:La_Dame_de_Myc%C3%A8nes,_fresco.jpg

Sexual double standards appear to have been applied to Mycenaean men and women. Men enjoyed far greater sexual freedoms while women were expected to be virgins until marriage. Adultery was a punishable offense, but laws were applied more to women than men. In terms of marriage, women were considered members of their father's household until they married, and after the wedding, they were a part of their husband's house. Although there was greater equality among the genders in the Mycenaean civilization than in others, women were still relegated to the role of property. A disparity also existed in the age of marriage; depending on the location, girls would be engaged and wed as young as thirteen or fourteen while most men would marry between the ages of eighteen and twenty.

Linear B

Linear B was the syllabic script used by the Mycenaeans to record their language.[80] The majority of the population could not read or write, so the majority of documents were created by trained scribes and administrators to keep track of trade and the quantities of supplies kept in the palaces. Linear B developed before the official Greek script but came after Linear A, which was the syllabic

---

[80] Geoffrey Horrocks, *Greek: A History of the Language and Its Speakers* (2ⁿᵈ ed.), Oxford: Wiley-Blackwell, 2010.

script discovered in sites formerly inhabited by the Minoans. Archaeologists have been unable to decipher Linear A but noticed it bore numerous similarities to Linear B.

Κατάστιχο ανδρικών ονομάτων
List of male names

Linear B Tablet
Heraklion Archaeological Museum, CC0, via Wikimedia Commons
https://commons.wikimedia.org/wiki/File:Linear_B_Phaistos_archmus_Heraklion.jpg

The earliest known instances of Linear B's use by the Mycenaeans are around 1450 BCE, meaning it developed several centuries into the civilization's existence. Linear B consisted of 87 syllabic signs and 100 ideographic signs. A syllabic sign represented a spoken syllable or sound—these would be similar to the modern alphabets used by most languages around the world in contemporary times. Ideographic signs were not spoken but were written, and it represented an object or concept. They were never used in sentences with syllabic representations.

Diet

The Mycenaean diet shared numerous similarities with traditional ancient Greek cuisine because the civilizations lived in the same place and underwent few agricultural developments over the centuries. A staple crop was olives, which could be eaten upon ripening or gathered and pressed into olive oil. Olive oil flavored vegetables and meats could be mixed in drinks, used as a dipping sauce for bread, or formed an essential part of religious ceremonies. Most people consumed olive oil on a regular basis.

Other significant crops were the regular fruits and vegetables capable of thriving in the rocky terrain of the Peloponnese. Most Mycenaeans could not consume meat regularly, and crops like legumes played a significant role in ensuring regular people met their caloric goals and staved off starvation. Nuts were a common source of protein, with families eating beechnuts, chestnuts, and the acorns from oak trees. Popular vegetables were onions, garlic, and chickpeas. Fruits like figs and pomegranates could be consumed for something sweet or were dried, preserved, or used to sweeten and flavor wines.

Grapes grew rampant and could be used to make wine. Wine appeared to be used for a variety of purposes, including as a standard beverage, beverages for parties, and an essential part of religious ceremonies. Herbs were used to give it different flavors, and grapes that weren't fermented could be dried and eaten as raisins.

The consumption of meat was based on social class. Mycenaeans of all ranks could eat seafood, but most of the lower classes ate animals they could raise themselves, like chickens. Wealthier people would have access to creatures like pigs, while goats were used for milk as well as meat. Sheep were raised for wool and were not eaten until they died. People in the countryside were able to hunt for food and thus consumed a variety of fowl and creatures like rabbits.

Cereals formed the basis of the Mycenaean diet. The most common grains were wheat and barley, which could be soaked in water or milk, or ground and baked into bread. Bread was typically eaten alongside olive oil and vegetables. While the rest of the diet may vary based on social class, time of the year, and general food availability, every Mycenaean consumed cereal grains on a daily basis.

Barley
https://commons.wikimedia.org/wiki/File:Illustration_Hordeum_vulgare1.jpg

Perhaps the strangest part of the Mycenaean diet was the consumption of a shake or drink called *kykeon* in ancient Greek. Numerous references to this beverage come from the Homeric epics, where heroes like Odysseus drank it as a beverage and meal. *Kykeon* was essentially barley gruel thinned with water and seasoned with herbs. Sometimes, the Mycenaeans would also add grated goat cheese for extra flavor and protein. *Kykeon* was popular among all of the social classes but seemed especially common among Mycenaean peasants. A contemporary equivalent would potentially be the protein shake used as a meal substitute among modern athletes and health aficionados.

The production of food and other consumables was divided by gender. While men and women would both be responsible for growing crops, the refinement of grains and baking of bread was typically woman's work, as was the creation and preparation of household meals. Men tended to be responsible for other duties such as the commercial fermentation of wine and pressing of olives to make olive oil. Again, women would create smaller batches for the household if a supply of grapes or olives was available. Butchering appeared to have been split almost equally between men and women depending on the scale of the labor; in general, women butchered animals eaten at home while professional butchers were male. Fishermen and hunters were typically male as well due to the strength requirements needed for both professions.

Archaeologists and other professionals have conducted studies and tests on known Mycenaean skeletons and determined that different social classes and even genders possessed varying diets. Based on tooth decay and the evidence of chips and pitting, they can tell that women and the lower classes did not eat as well as men and the upper echelons of society.

Clothing

Regular free men wore loincloths or short skirts made of wool or linen to work. These were long pieces of cloth that would be pulled between the legs, wrapped around the hipbones, and then tied in front. A more formal outfit would be a short skirt with a loincloth underneath and a short-sleeved belted tunic. Wealthier men could afford longer kilts with a checkered braid and potentially a fringe around the hems. Men also tended to wear black oxhide caps to keep the sun off their heads.[81] Jewelry was worn by aristocrats and elites, and they often consisted of gold necklaces, bracelets, and rings, all of which had gems embedded inside. Men's fashion tended to be simpler than women's and consisted of longer pieces of fabrics than the material used for ladies. However, men also wore the armor covered under the military section.

Mycenaean women's clothing was influenced heavily by Minoan fashion. Based on the contents of graves, archaeologists believe female fashion didn't change for over three hundred years beginning in 1550 BCE and continuing until c. 1250 BCE. Women wore long, flounced dresses with tight boleros around the torso. The bolero was cut low enough to expose the breasts but featured support underneath to push the chest up and achieve the ideal curved silhouette. Bodices were short-sleeved due to the Mediterranean climate and consisted of at least eight separate pieces of fabric. The seams were decorated and strengthened with specially woven braids created by teams of skilled women. Similar braids would be used to form headbands.

Skirts wrapped around the hips and were held in place with ties and knots. A cord belt around the waist was the simplest and most common way to hold the fabric. Some women also wore decorative weights to hold down the hems of their skirts. The base of the skirt was a simple trapezium to which different bands of colored fabrics were sewn to form an overlapping pattern. A trapezium skirt is shaped like a trapezoid, seen below. Sometimes women would wash bands, pleat them, sew the pleats together, and allow the fabric to dry. Once dry, the stitches would be pulled out and create permanent waves and pleats that would be pleasing to the eye and

---

[81] Rodney Castleden, *Mycenaeans*, p. 70.

have extra flounce.[82]

Artwork and artifacts indicate that women had shaved heads until they hit puberty, at which point they could start to grow locks. Hairstyles depended on social classes, and women with longer hair tended to be older. Many women wore their hair in plaits or braids down their backs. Jewelry was rare for the common class but appeared to be worn daily by the elites. Most jewelry was gold and embedded with stones like carnelian. Records are tenuous though, as most information comes from burial goods, which would have been the finest objects a person owned.

Both men and women either went barefoot or wore leather sandals. There continues to exist some debate about whether or not aristocrats or the elites wore metal greaves since frescoes often depict shoes as white. Other scholars think the white was meant to represent leather or perhaps cloth-bound wood, as these materials would have been more common. Elites most likely did not go barefoot like the poorer classes though.

[82] Rodney Castleden, *Mycenaeans*, p. 72-73.

Chapter 3 – Economy and Trade

Evidence indicates that the Mycenaean economy was pre-monetary. In this system, people didn't use currency, and the focus was instead on the redistribution of resources by the administration. Commodities like goods and human labor could be traded and handed out as payment for other goods and services depending on the quality of work and the quality of the products. Linear B tablets found preserved in locations like Pylos and Knossos demonstrate that the palace, the throne of the administration, was the most important redistributor and that administrators closely examined the development of industries and the commodities being grown, made, or imported. The best example of this monitoring comes from one of the Knossos tablets. The scribe who wrote upon one of these artifacts kept careful track of the number of sheep in Crete, totaling some 80,000 to 100,000 animals, how much wool was expected from the shepherds come shearing season, and how the wool would be redistributed among artisans, workers, and even the general public.[83]

---

[83] Stephanie Lynn Budin, *The Ancient Greeks: An Introduction*, New York: Oxford University Press, 2009.

The Great Wool-Maker: A Staple of the Mycenaean Economy

However, palatial control over resources like wool was not ubiquitous. The palaces and their administrations focused on industries that were near the central structure or that were produced by artisans who lived and worked in the palace itself. In particular, luxury goods like bronze and even perfume were closely monitored for several reasons. One, the resources involved were valuable and denoted status. Two, excess production could be used to trade with other civilizations or even between palaces in regional transactions. Ceramics, which were considered the work of slaves or the poor, was mostly unsupervised unless one of the elites ordered a custom piece.[84] It was the work of the poor because it was a common practice and also dirty. It was seen as requiring less skill than something rarer like metalsmithing, and the materials were coarser and easier to obtain. In general, the Mycenaean palaces also monitored the production of food and could be counted upon to store excess supplies and redistribute them as

---

[84] Budin, *The Ancient Greeks,* p. 96.

payment for labor or in times of famine. This system bears a resemblance to other Bronze Age societies, such as the Minoans, and was the most common form of pre-monetary economy management.

Because the palatial centers were the heart of the economy, they focused their resource management on projects designed to keep the civilization functioning. In particular, the administrations in settlements like Mycenae would fund elaborate projects in fields like agriculture and industry to ensure the population had enough food and the civilization developed enough manufactured goods for war and trade. Sometimes, the palatial centers would combine their efforts to plan projects that benefited more than one settlement. The greatest examples tended to do with plumbing and irrigation, such as the drainage system established in the Kopais basin on Boeotia or the draining of a massive swamp in the Nemea Valley.[85] Such works made cities more hygienic and created valuable land for farming and the raising of livestock.

Other significant sections of the economy belonged to large-scale manufacturing and shipbuilding, both of which were needed to facilitate trade. The Mycenaeans built large Bronze Age vessels designed to transport commodities, but they also functioned as naval ships in battles against pirates and enemies on the Mediterranean Sea. These vessels needed to carry dozens of men, supplies to feed them, and the valuables for commerce. To accommodate them, Mycenaean settlements on the coast constructed massive harbors such as the one at Pylos, which was capable of holding numerous vessels at any given time.

The harbors and the accompanying shipbuilding industry facilitated the development of sophisticated manufacturing centers along harbors and in settlements capable of transporting finished goods to the coast. Workshop complexes capable of holding hundreds of workers and their equipment were uncovered by

---

[85] Kelder, *The Kingdom of Mycenae*, p. 116.

archaeologists in places like Euonymeia, which is near Athens. The site was uncovered while doing work on the Alimos Metro Station and uncovered numerous objects like pottery wheels and kilns. The site at Euonymeia contained multiple hydraulic installations capable of producing important elements of shipbuilding like sails and rope, including wells and water conduits required to process flax and make it workable. These centers could also create textiles and tableware which would be commissioned by members of the elite class or sold to other civilizations.[86]

The pre-monetary economy of the Mycenaeans required an elaborate system of checks and balances, as well as detailed records. Goods produced internally needed to be allotted to the population while still generating prosperity for the administration and elites. To do this, the Mycenaeans turned to trade.

Trade

Trade formed a crucial part of the Mycenaean economy. The Peloponnese did not host an abundance of raw materials, which made it difficult for the civilization to produce luxury goods, bronze weaponry, and other finished products on its own. To get around this issue, the Mycenaeans would import raw materials from other settlements and civilizations and based their economy around the manufacture of finished goods that could then be traded back to other regions.

Some known imports were luxuries like ivory and glass as well as the raw metals needed to produce bronze—tin and copper. To acquire these products, the Mycenaeans sold their own domestic resources: olive oil, grapes fermented into wine, wool from the abundance of sheep, and clay pottery styled into vessels for storage

[86] William Gilstrap; Day, Peter; Kaza, Konstantina; Kardamaki, Elina, *Pottery Production at the Late Mycenaean Site of Alimos, Attica.* Materials and Industries in the Mycenaean World: Current Approaches to the Study of Materials and Industries in Prehistoric Greece, University of Nottingham, 9–10 May 2013, Nottingham, p. 13–14.

and decoration.[87] Between 1600 BCE and 1400 BCE, the palatial centers stopped being the only exporters of these goods as more and more independent merchants started to appear on the scene. These merchants came from the free classes and appeared to be a mix of the elites and wealthy artisans.

Archaeological evidence supports the idea that the Mycenaean Greeks managed to trade extensively with civilizations in Anatolia and the Levant. Their strong commercial ties led to interactions with most of the other Bronze Age peoples from this time period, including the Egyptians, Assyrians, Canaanites, and Kassites.[88] Examining the map below, one can see that it makes sense for the Mycenaeans to have been able to establish commercial and cultural ties with these civilizations. Anatolia was in modern-day Turkey while the Levant covered most of the Middle East. Since the Mycenaeans were seafaring people who managed to wrest control of the Aegean Sea, they would naturally come into contact with the other great Bronze Age peoples.

The Mediterranean Sea – The Trade World of the Mycenaeans
https://commons.wikimedia.org/wiki/File:Mediterranean_Relief,_1028_x_1024.jpg

[87] Eric H. Cline, *The Oxford Handbook of the Bronze Age Aegean*, Oxford: Oxford University Press, 2012.

[88] Eric H. Cline "Rethinking Mycenaean International Trade with Egypt and the Near East" in Galaty, M.; Parkinson, W. *Rethinking Mycenaean Palaces II: Revised and Expanded Edition.* Los Angeles: Cotsen Institute of Archaeology, 2007.

Numerous goods were discovered in Cyprus, which seemed to be an intermediary location between Mycenaean Greece, Anatolia, and the Levant.[89] More artifacts were found here than in any other location besides the actual Mycenaean settlements. Trade with inland Bronze Age civilizations, though, appears to have been limited. The Mycenaeans struggled to transport goods across landmasses, meaning groups like the Hittites, who were almost landlocked, were difficult to reach. Some other well-known trade routes were along the coast of the Black Sea, also visible in the map.[90] Goods such as swords have been found as far away as the location of contemporary Georgia. Archaeologists believe such trade was not conducted on land routes, but rather that the Mycenaeans sailed as far as they could, crossed the small land bridge available or found an alternative water route, and then traded.

To the west, archaeologists discovered products like Mycenaean pottery as far as Sicily, southern mainland Italy, and the Aeolian islands. Even more surprising were fragments discovered in southern Spain, indicating the potential for a trade route there as well. To the north of the Mycenaean Greeks, some pottery, amber with Linear B symbols, and even bronze double axes from the 13th century BCE have been discovered in locations like Germany, Ireland, and England.[91] Scholars continue to debate whether the Mycenaeans traded directly with the peoples of Wessex and Cornwall or whether the artifacts traveled there through intermediaries.

While the economy might have been pre-monetary, it is clear that the Mycenaeans still traded extensively with neighboring

---

[89] Thomas F. Tartaron, *Maritime Networks in the Mycenaean World*, Cambridge: Cambridge University Press, 2013, p. 29.

[90] Cline, "Rethinking Mycenaean International Trade with Egypt and the Near East," p. 196.

[91] Budin, *The Ancient Greeks: An Introduction*, p. 53.

Bronze Age civilizations. They imported raw materials and items they couldn't make themselves, such as glass, and in return exported manufactured goods like pottery and bronze weapons. Although much remains to be discovered, the picture painted by unearthed artifacts signifies that the Mycenaean Greeks were powerful, able to hold their own on an international stage, and possessed the technology required to travel across the Mediterranean and safely trade with the neighboring civilizations.

But what of Mycenaean history? Unfortunately, it's easier for scholars to get a better grasp on trade and culture than on actual events for reasons explained in the next chapter.

Chapter 4 – The Shaft Grave Era, c. 1600 – 1450 BCE

Although the Mycenaean Greeks possessed a syllabic script called Linear B, not much is known about events, specific individuals, or even large-scale wars. Documents with writing frequently did not survive the vicissitudes of time, if they were even preserved at all. Most Bronze Age civilizations recorded information on tablets made of wet clay. While some clay documents were preserved by hardening the material over a fire, most were wiped clean and the tablets reused. So, archaeologists, scholars, and historians need to turn to non-textual sources to gather information. For the early Mycenaean Greeks, the best source is graves.

The first known period of the Mycenaean civilization was called the Shaft Grave Era, which lasted from roughly 1600 BCE to 1450 BCE. During its early stages, Mycenaean civilization was heavily influenced by the Minoans, a rival group in the Mediterranean that lived on islands like Crete and Thera. Both the Mycenaeans and the Minoans were cultures that influenced the later ancient Greeks, who would form the basis of what is now known as Greek civilization.

During the 1600s BCE, the Mycenaeans started to develop sophisticated centers of power on the Peloponnese and create a series of settlements that could trade with and defend one another. The Mycenaeans additionally experienced a population boom that allowed for the creation of the Mycenaean warrior elite society for which it became known for.[92] Around this time, the Mycenaeans started to develop structures called *megarons*, rectangular great halls supported by four columns that formed the basis of Mycenaean palaces, as well as fortifications that would evolve into the palaces of later centuries.[93] Defensive walls started to be built around the same time as the *megarons*, indicating the Mycenaean desire to remain separate from the dozens of other groups inhabiting the Greek peninsula.

The Foundation of a *Megaron* Outside of Mycenae
https://commons.wikimedia.org/wiki/File:MiceneMegaron.jpg

Around the Shaft Grave Era, the Mycenaeans slowly met and established trade routes and diplomatic relationships with neighboring civilizations. In particular, they formed long-lasting relationships with the nearby Minoan and Cycladic civilizations. The Mycenaeans did not know the Cycladic people well, but they did have a modicum of trade. The Minoans were the Mycenaeans' primary trading partner. The Mycenaeans even adopted numerous

---

[92] Louise Schofield, *The Mycenaeans*, Los Angeles: J. Paul Getty Museum, 2006.

[93] Richard T. Neer, *Greek Art and Archaeology: A New History, c. 2500–c. 150 BCE*, New York.

Minoan artistic and architectural practices, and they might have even taken and adapted the written language to suit their own needs—this would be the potential transformation from Linear A to Linear B. Evidence for the deep relationship between the Mycenaeans and the Minoans comes from the depiction of Mycenaeans on a Minoan fresco on the island of Akrotiri, as well as the presence of pottery from each civilization found on one another's territory.

Outside of the Cycladic civilization and the Minoans, the Mycenaeans started to export their pottery and other goods across the Mediterranean Sea. Artifacts and remnants of objects like pots and jugs have been found as far as the western coast of Asia Minor, with some key sites including Lebanon, Egypt, Palestine, Troy, Cyprus, and Miletus. Unfortunately, historians are unable to piece together many of the actual events that happened during this period due to the lack of written histories or records.

Since not much history is known, archaeologists and historians instead define this period based on mortuary practices. Contemporary scholars have access to a plethora of graves for which this era earned its name. A shaft grave or shaft tomb is a distinct form of burial structure that is partially submerged in the ground and tends to feature a pebble floor and wooden slat roof, with multiple people being buried in the two or three rooms created. These shaft graves were the most common form of burial for the elites in society and tended to include numerous luxury items and objects that remained preserved for millennia. These items give intricate clues about how the Mycenaeans lived and the development of architecture, art, and society in general. It's unclear what happened to regular Mycenaeans, but they might have been buried in lesser graves that did not survive.

Mycenaean elites were laid to rest in shaft graves with distinctive objects that demonstrated gender roles, the wealth of the civilization, and the general formation of a wealthier noble class. Archaeologists uncovered the bodies of Mycenaean men adorned with gold masks and armor, while women wore gold crowns and clothes with jewelry and ornaments.[94] Royal shaft graves were discovered outside the acropolis of Mycenae, signifying the rise of the Greek-speaking royal dynasty which would permanently shape Mycenaean culture and make it the seafaring economic power it remained until the Late Bronze Age Collapse.[95] The prosperity of the civilization is especially obvious due to the presence of solid gold burial masks. Perhaps the most important archaeological sites for this time period would be Grave Circles A and B, which are those sites outside of Mycenae.

A Gold Funeral Mask
National Archaeological Museum of Athens, CC0, via Wikimedia Commons
https://commons.wikimedia.org/wiki/File:Mycene_gold_mask_1_NAMA_Athens_Greece.jpg

Toward the end of the Shaft Grave Era, circa the 1500s BCE, the Mycenaean elite started to be buried in imposing structures called *tholos*, or beehive tombs. These were larger, made of stone, and had vaulted roofs. The *tholos* represents a conundrum for archaeologists because it's hard to tell whether they belonged solely to the elite with the commoners instead being buried in communal tombs, as there are some tombs that have numerous bodies,

---

[94] Schofield, 2006, pg. 32.

[95] Oliver Dickinson, *The Origins of Mycenaean Civilization*, Götenberg: Paul Aströms Förlag, 1977.

indicating they might have been communal. There is evidence that competing political or military factions attempted to build the grandest tholos in attempts to outdo one another in the game of conspicuous burials. The most famous of these *tholoi* is the Treasury of Atreus, also called the Tomb of Agamemnon after the famous Greek mythical hero. The Treasury of Atreus was perhaps the most impressive Mycenaean gravesite from this time period and demonstrated the prosperity of the civilization toward the end of the Shaft Grave Era. It was not only one of the most massive graves, but it also possessed some of the greatest gold treasures ever recorded in the history of Mycenaean archaeological discovery.

Cross Section of the Treasury of Atreus
https://commons.wikimedia.org/wiki/File:Schatzhaus_des_Atreus,_Querschnitt.jpg

Chapter 5 – The Koine Era, c. 1450 – 1250 BCE

The Koine Era, c. 1450-1250 BCE, was when the Mycenaeans started to gain more power in the Aegean Sea thanks to the eruption of Thera. Thera was a collection of islands inhabited by the Minoans that formed a caldera. When it erupted, the force sent a series of earthquakes and tidal waves across the sea, destroying numerous Minoan settlements c. 1500 BCE, sending the Minoan civilization into decline. This allowed the Mycenaean fleet to gain access to new trade routes and turn its attention to the domination of the Minoans, who possessed valuable resources, ports, and commercial relationships with other civilizations.

Around 1450 BCE, the Mycenaeans wrested control of the Minoan capital on Crete and conquered numerous islands as far as Rhodes.[96] With the Minoans crippled, the Mycenaeans would have become the dominant power in the Aegean Sea propped up by their military and uniform culture on mainland Greece. This would become the Mycenaeans' golden era due to their power and development for the next two centuries. With the control of the

---

[96] Schofield, p. 71-72.

Aegean, the civilization was in an advantageous position to trade with others, especially societies in Asia Minor (the western coast of Anatolia seen below). The location of the Aegean Sea in respect to the Peloponnese and the rest of the Mediterranean is included here, with the sea marked in blue.

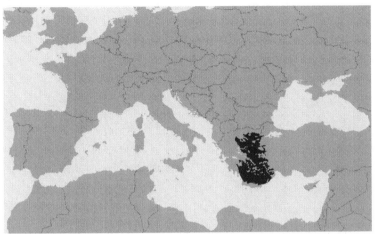

The Territory of the Mycenaeans
https://commons.wikimedia.org/wiki/File:Locatie_Egeische_Zee.PNG

Around the 14th century BCE, the Mycenaeans started to trade with new civilizations by filling in the gaps left behind by the Minoans. Some of the farthest routes went to Apulia in Italy, smaller settlements in Spain, Amman in the Near East, and Cyprus. Some of the palatial states established new cities in these areas, including in Miletus by 1450 BCE. Miletus allowed the Mycenaeans to come into close proximity with the Hittites, with whom the Mycenaeans had a complicated relationship.

Around 1400 BCE, the Mycenaeans started to build their impressive palace structures and *megaron* buildings and fortifications. Cyclopean walls appeared around Mycenae and Tiryns, while the foundations for palaces were erected in Thebes, Athens, Midea, Pylos, and Iolcos in Thessaly. Around this period, the former Minoan capital of Knossos on Crete became a new Mycenaean complex, as the Mycenaeans built a new throne room and changed the architecture. The palatial centers became more complicated and developed into a sophisticated bureaucracy around the same time, while the settlements demonstrated more cultural and societal unity.[97] Special offices were made to oversee industries and trade, and this is also the period of time when the *wanax* appeared as a position in their society.

Involvement with the Hittites

During the Koine Era, the Mycenaeans appeared to have the most contact with the Hittites. The Hittites were another Bronze Age civilization that lived in Anatolia, a region in the Near East. In Hittite records, a group called *Ahhiyawa* (*Ahhiyawa* was a translation of the word Achaeans, which the Mycenaeans sometimes used for themselves) appears between the years 1400 BCE and 1220 BCE. These documents are some of the best sources for Mycenaean involvement in Anatolia and nearby areas because of the sheer abundance of materials. Archaeologists discovered that an entire building of clay tablets—the preferred method of writing—were preserved when the building caught fire. The heat hardened the clay, keeping records intact.

Around the Koine Era, the Mycenaeans had diplomatic relations with the Hittites but also seemed to clash with them on the battlefield. The Mycenaeans repeatedly interfered in the affairs of the Anatolian kingdoms, even supporting anti-Hittite rebellions and uprisings in settlements and vassal states.[98] This often left the Mycenaeans and Hittites at odds, and there appeared to be several conflicts that led to combat.

Hittite records indicate that a Mycenaean *wanax*, written in the Hittite language as Attarsiya, attacked several vassal states in western Anatolia. Some historians believe that Attarsiya was a translation of Atreus, who was a mythological Greek hero and the

---

[97] Kelder, *The Kingdom of Mycenae: A Great Kingdom in the Late Bronze Age Aegean*, p. 11.

[98] Kelder, *The Kingdom of Mycenae: A Great Kingdom in the Late Bronze Age Aegean*, p. 23.

founder of a heroic family. Conflicts between the Hittites and the Mycenaean *wanax* continued to occur with one notable event happening in 1315 BCE when the Mycenaeans backed an uprising in one of the Hittite vassal states. By 1260 BCE, the Mycenaean king was recognized as an equal with the other Bronze Age leaders near the Mediterranean, including the Hittites, the Egyptians, the Babylonians, and the Assyrians.[99] At this period, the Mycenaeans supported yet another vassal state revolt, this time led by a leader called Piyama-Radu. The Mycenaeans appeared to take advantage of unrest wherever it occurred and went on to take the island of Lesbos from Piyama-Radu when he started to lose power.[100]

Historians also believe that conflicts between the Hittites and the Mycenaeans led to the conflict known by the Greeks as the Trojan War.[101] At some point, the Hittites attacked and laid siege to Troy, which was listed under the name *Wilusa* in Hittite records. Unlike the myth, no giant wooden horses are mentioned, and the war came to an end when the kings exchanged correspondences to create a treaty that would end the conflict.

---

[99] Kelder, *The Kingdom of Mycenae*, p. 119–120.

[100] Kelder, *The Kingdom of Mycenae*, p. 27.

[101] Trevor Bryce, *The Kingdom of the Hittites* (New ed.), Oxford: Oxford University Press, 2005, p. 361.

Chapter 6 – The Collapse, c. 1250 – 1100 BCE

Their power could not last, however. Although the Mycenaeans secured themselves a favorable position between 1450 and 1250 BCE, trouble was on the horizon. What loomed was a mysterious force that suddenly and thoroughly decimated many of the Bronze Age civilizations in Europe, Asia, and North Africa. This was the Late Bronze Age Collapse, a disastrous event whose exact causes are unknown. Despite numerous advantages, the Mycenaeans would be unable to maintain their position in the Mediterranean with the arrival of the unknown.

Decline and Revival

The decline of the Mycenaeans can best be understood as occurring in a series of waves that mounted over a century and a half and slowly wreaked destruction. The first wave struck c. 1250 BCE, when a series of mysterious disasters struck influential palatial states. Thebes and Orchomenos burned to the ground, while important Boeotian fortifications like Gla were abandoned and left to stand empty. In Mycenae, the main citadel was sieged and burned, resulting in an expansion of existing stone fortifications. Some states constructed massive subterranean passageways to allow for escape and connections to underground cisterns, indicating some sort of massive attack either occurred or was feared. Centers like Athens, Midea, and Tiryns chose to build even more Cyclopean walls while Mycenae doubled the size of their citadel before it burned down.[102]

After a decade of misfortune, the situation evened out, and the Mycenaeans were able to resume their way of life. Culture flourished, and the people once again turned their attention to harassing the Hittites, who seemed to be the main enemy of the Mycenaeans. Around 1220 BCE, the Mycenaeans once again supported a vassal state rebellion and also lashed out against Assyria through an embargo. However, such actions could have been the result of a serious decline in trade throughout the Mediterranean.[103] States were unable to maintain a solid political background which led to civilian unrest and unruly militaries. Some other civilizations experiencing difficulties were the aforementioned Hittites and Assyrians, as well as the Egyptians and the Babylonians. By 1190 BCE, a powder keg waiting for a single spark ignited and destroyed the vibrant Mediterranean way of life.

The Final Collapse

No one is sure what triggered the second wave of destruction that hit Mycenae in 1190 BCE and sent shockwaves through the rest of the palatial states. All archaeological evidence shows is that the city was mostly destroyed and eventually reoccupied with a fraction of its original population.[104] Something happened that killed off a major portion of the Mycenaeans, resulting in chaos and disorder. In 1180 BCE, Pylos went next, leaving behind a series of hardened clay tablets with inscriptions in Linear B. These tablets include references to hasty defense preparations that ultimately led nowhere. No information is given about who the

---

[102] Castleden, *Mycenaeans,* p. 219.

[103] Tartaron, *Maritime Networks in the Mycenaean World.*

[104] Cline, *1177 B.C. The Year Civilization Collapsed.*

attacking force might have been, and the palace was destroyed in a massive blaze.[105]

Refugees fled from multiple sections of mainland Greece and immigrated to new areas. The hardest hit areas, including Boeotia, experienced dramatic population declines from a combination of high mortality rates and fleeing families. Many Mycenaeans went to Cyprus and the Levantine coast, which appeared to have avoided destruction. Strangely, not all the palatial states were hit by disaster. Some, like Athens, remained untouched and would go on to become one of the most famous Greek city-states in history. Aegean islands also prospered but only for a short period of time before the arrival of the Greek Dark Ages.

What Caused the Collapse?

Although the first instinct of many people is to guess that the Mycenaeans fell prey to the attacks of another civilization or marauding hordes, scholars aren't so sure. Many believe something significant needed to happen to weaken the power of the palatial states before an assault against any of the large settlements would have succeeded. The most likely avenue of decline for the palatial states was through the enfeeblement of the palace system, the administration which kept the world running. This could have happened through either a population movement or some form of internal conflict.

In the first theory, a population movement occurred because the Mycenaeans found themselves threatened by a rival native Greek group called the Dorians. This idea, called the Dorian invasion, is supported by a broad range of archaeological evidence. Toward the end of the Mycenaean time in power (1200-1100 BCE), new types of burials popped up in the civilization's territory, including something called a cist grave. A cist is a type of stone box, similar to a coffin, used to store multiple corpses. They were sealed

---

[105] Freeman, *Egypt, Greece and Rome: Civilizations of the Ancient Mediterranean* (3rd ed.).

and could be above or below ground. Cist graves were not used by the Mycenaeans, which indicates that a new group was encroaching upon the palatial states. At the same time as the new graves appeared, a new Greek dialect, called Doric, started to appear in surviving records, and a ceramic style termed "Barbarian Ware" became mixed with traditional Mycenaean pottery fragments.

According to the Dorian invasion hypothesis, the Dorians were from northern mainland Greece and started to head south. Their migration resulted in the devastation of Mycenaean territorial borders, as the Dorians were not a friendly group.[106] As they traveled, they razed and burned settlements and took over arable farmland and other valuable natural resources. Eventually, they encroached upon the settlements of Mycenae and Pylos, among others.

The Dorian invasion hypothesis is at odds with another prevailing idea, which is that the Mycenaeans were one of the numerous victims of the Sea Peoples. The Sea Peoples are one of the most mysterious forces in ancient history because no one is quite sure who they were. The Sea Peoples came from the Mediterranean Sea and devastated many of the civilizations along its eastern shores, including Egypt. Many peoples in Anatolia and the Levant disappeared, unable to battle the tide of barbarian warriors coming from the water. In Hittite records, the Mycenaeans are often associated with the Sea Peoples, potentially because of ethnic group similarities.[107] According to some scholars, this association means that some of the Sea Peoples were the Dorians seeking to expand their borders. Others believe the Dorians weren't the real problem, and it was the Sea Peoples all along.

---

[106] George Emmanuel Mylonas, *Mycenae and the Mycenaean Age*. Princeton, NJ: Princeton University Press, 1966, p. 231-232.

[107] Robert Drews, *The End of the Bronze Age*, Princeton: Princeton University Press, 1993, p. 49.

Another potential scenario is that the Mycenaeans destroyed themselves through internal warfare and rebellions. If civil unrest was great enough in several palatial states, then the palace administration would no longer be effective. This theory comes in two flavors. In the first, the palatial states warred with one another over territory, resources, and other disputes. In this theory, the onus of destruction is placed on the elite warrior class as they possessed the most power. In the second flavor, a dissatisfied lower free class grew tired of the strict hierarchical system and rebelled against the *wanax* and his administration.[108] In either case, all that remained of the once prosperous Mycenaean Greeks were impoverished settlements that lacked sophisticated trade and culture.

A final theory is that natural factors disrupted agriculture and trade, causing rebellions or making it easy for enemies to invade the palatial states. Some of the most commonly hypothesized events are climate change, droughts destroying crops, and earthquakes from the nearby volcanoes. After all, the Minoans were most likely devastated by the aftershocks of an eruption, so it seems logical for the Mycenaeans to have suffered a similar fate.[109]

Whatever the case may be, by 1100 BCE, Mycenaean Greece was at an end. Although part of the population still existed, the Mycenaean political structure and way of life had given way to poverty, poor trade, little social connection, and the rise of new cultural systems like the Dorian Greeks. But although gone, the Mycenaeans were not forgotten. During the Greek Dark Ages, which took place from c. 1100 – c. 800 BCE, Mycenaean culture continued to exist and be spread in some form. It would take on new ideas and adapt and evolve over the centuries, eventually becoming the dominant culture of one of the most famous civilizations in history—the ancient Greeks.

---

[108] Tartaron, *Maritime Networks in the Mycenaean World*, p. 19.
[109] Ibid.

Chapter 7 – The Precursors of Greek Religion

Religious worship among the Mycenaean Greeks was based on cult centers rather than organized religion. Statuettes that might have been offerings have been unearthed, lending credence to the idea that there might have been developed shrines in Phylakopi, Delphi, Abae, Delos, and other locations. Although multiple deities existed, the Mycenaeans tended to focus on individual gods in different urban and rural centers. Most deities possessed their own religious sites which could be in buildings, palaces, or natural geographic features like caves. Some important cult sites were places like Lerna, which appeared to be a house sanctuary with a temple, an open-air altar, an image of the deity, and some religious artifacts that might have been used in ceremonies and sacrifices. There is also evidence of animals having been sacrificed. Some scholars speculate whether humans might have gone under the knife as well—a common practice among Bronze Age civilizations— but there is not much to support this theory.

Despite archaeologists believing they have evidence for cult worship, identifying religious elements for the Mycenaean Greeks is no easy feat. Because there is no evidence for central organized religion, picking out cult sites and individual deities are difficult.

Since Linear B was used sparingly and the Mycenaean Greeks interacted with other groups such as the Minoans, the Mycenaean religion no doubt infused elements from other practices into their own worship. This makes it hard to determine what ideas were Mycenaean and what came from other cultures. Specific religious practices are also difficult to decipher because there are no records, and all scholars can extrapolate from are a handful of artifacts like statuettes, knives, and pottery.

Another source of controversy is whether or not the Mycenaean Greeks were the originators of the famous ancient Greek religion. Some historians insist that the Mycenaeans developed most of the deities found in the ancient Greek pantheon even if the concepts and relationships changed during the Greek Dark Ages. Others, like Sir Moses I. Finley, insist that the Mycenaeans possessed little to no influence on the ancient Greeks. One of the biggest debates continues to be about the world depicted in the works of the poet Homer. Some believe the epics reflected the Mycenaean culture and their religion as well, while others caution not to put too much meaning into the text. Whatever the case may be, there is evidence that the religion of the Mycenaean Greeks was the genuine origin of the future Greek religion, with numerous deities getting their first appearances between 1600-1100 BCE.

The Mycenaean Deities

The three primary deities who occupied places of privilege in the religion of the Mycenaean Greeks were Poseidon, Demeter, and Persephone. In ancient documents inscribed with text in Linear B, the trio can be found referenced to as the "two queens and a king," or *wa-na-ssoi* and *wa-na-ka-te*.[110] Poseidon, written as *Po-se-da-o*, appeared to have some association with the position of the *wanax*. He is what is known as a chthonic deity, or a god associated with the subterranean world beneath the earth. This term can also be translated as supernatural or related to the

---

[110] Mylonas, *Mycenae and the Mycenaean Age*, p. 159.

underworld. In the case of Poseidon, he appeared to be connected to earthquakes and was referenced using the appellation *E-ne-si-da-o-ne*, or Earth Shaker. He might have also represented the river spirit of the underworld that divided the realms of the living and dead.[111]

Often in association with Poseidon were references to multiple ladies or a single lady or mistress with the title *Po-ti-ni-ja*, which literally translates to "lady." These inscriptions primarily come from tablets discovered in Pylos, and she may or may not have had a significant shrine at the Pakijanes site in the region.[112] Some archaeologists note similarities between *Po-ti-ni-ja* and the Minoan "mistress of the Labyrinth" from Crete. Both women appeared to hold a role of monumental importance in their respective religions, but little information is forthcoming about their identities. Some historians believe the *Po-ti-ni-ja* is Demeter or her daughter Persephone.

Demeter and Persephone are, by all accounts, two of the oldest Greek deities with special initiation rituals held each year called the Eleusinian mysteries. Multiple records indicate the two goddesses were Mycenaean in origin. In Greek culture, they often were called the "two goddesses" or "the mistresses," demonstrating their prominence and recognizable nature. Linear B inscriptions discovered at Pylos refer to two connected goddesses called *Pe-re-swa* and *Si-to-po-ti-ni-ja*.[113] While *Pe-re-swa* is associated with Persephone, *Si-to-po-ti-ni-ja* was an agricultural goddess with a name based on the word *sito*, or wheat. A connection has been made with Demeter, who was the goddess of the harvest with the cult title *Sito*.

---

[111] Nilsson, *Greek Popular Religion.*

[112] Mylonas, *Mycenae and the Mycenaean Age*, p. 159.

[113] John Chadwick, *The Mycenaean World,* Cambridge: Cambridge University Press, 1976, p. 95.

The famous Eleusinian mysteries of ancient Greek culture originated during the Mycenaean period c. 1500 BCE. The rituals appear to have been based on an ancient Greek vegetation cult designed to bring about good harvests and may have stolen some elements from the nearby Minoans. Since the cult started as a private one, meaning there was no palatial state recognition or organization, few records remain about its practices. However, similarities between the establishers of the Eleusinian mysteries and the cult of Despoina can be found. Historians believe the cult of Despoina worshiped an early form of Persephone. Documentation for Despoina comes from Arcadia, a region in the Greek Peloponnese, where there are adequate records of primitive Arcadian myths that support the existence of figures resembling Poseidon, Demeter, and Persephone.

In Arcadian myths, which came before the Mycenean myths, Poseidon was the river spirit of the underworld who pursued Demeter as a horse. Demeter changed into a mare and ultimately bore two children: a male horse called Arion and a daughter named Despoina with either the head or body of a mare. This story gave rise to multiple artistic choices in religious relics and idols, including animal-headed statues of Demeter, Despoina, and other deities throughout Arcadia. Mycenaean frescoes c. 1400 BCE continued this tradition, showing individuals wearing animal masks in some sort of procession or party. Their jewelry also features these animal masks or half-animal humans, as a gold ring discovered in Tiryns shows a procession of demons that are not quite human or animal.[114] Some historians hypothesize that this Mycenaean tradition became transplanted in the world of the ancient Greeks through the myth of the Minotaur, although others argue the Minotaur is more of a Minoan creation. Whatever the case may be, Demeter and Despoina were heavily associated with

---

[114] Martin Persson Nilsson, *Geschichte der Griechischen Religion* (3ᵈ ed.), Munich: C.H. Beck Verlag, 1967, p. 293.

springs, animals, and plant life, while Poseidon was given the subterranean and water. A primitive form of Artemis even appears, going by the title "mistress of the animals." It's generally accepted that she might have been the first nymph, which is a spirit that was bound to a specific tree, plant, or body of water.

Hylas and the Nymphs by John William Waterhouse, 1896.
https://commons.wikimedia.org/wiki/File:Waterhouse_Hylas_and_the_Nymphs_Manche ster_Art_Gallery_1896.15.jpg

In the Arcadian tradition, and still during the time of the Mycenaean Greeks, Artemis was the daughter of Demeter and perhaps the most popular goddess in mainland Greece.[115] Her name was written as either *A-te-mi-to* or *A-ti-mi-te* in Linear B. Some scholars hypothesize she was based on the Minoan Britomartis, who was a goddess represented by two lions on numerous gold artifacts taken from locations like Crete. Around Sparta, archaeologists discovered wooden masks made to resemble human faces that would have been worn during the rituals of the vegetation cult. These masks harken back to the time of the Mycenaeans, indicating Artemis was connected to Demeter even then. Artemis may also have been connected to a Minoan "cult of the tree," famed for its orgies and wild, ecstatic dancing.[116]

---

[115] Pausanias. *Description of Greece*, VIII–37.6.

[116] Nilsson, Martin Persson, *Geschichte der Griechischen Religion*, p. 281.

Some other Mycenaean deities were Paean (*Pa-ja-wo*) and Athena (*A-ta-na*). Paean was the personification of a song that could heal patients afflicted with a variety of maladies and diseases, making him perhaps the first mythical Greek physician. As time went on, Paean started to represent the song of victory as well as magicians in general, and it is thought that he might have ties to Apollo. Athena as a name appears in Linear B inscriptions from Knossos and appears to have been the goddess of the palace as well as the goddess of war. She was depicted carrying a figure-of-eight shield and sometimes had her name written as *A-ta-na po-ti-ni-ja*, or Mistress Athena. Historians have noted the connection between these texts and how Athena is referred to as Mistress Athena in Homeric works.[117]

Meanwhile, archaeologists and historians continue to draw correlations between names and figures found in Linear B tablets and other members of the ancient Greek pantheon. As of the last decade, scholars believe they have found references to Zeus, Hera, Ares, Hermes, Hephaestus, and more minor gods like Erinya and Eileithyia. Hephaestus may be the Mycenaean *A-pa-i-ti-jo*, but his wife, Aphrodite, is absent from texts. Hera's famous epithet, "cow-eyed," appears in documents as *Qo-wi-ja*, which is why historians believe she might also have been among the Mycenaean pantheon.[118] She is often mentioned with her husband, although not in great detail.

---

[117] Chadwick, *The Mycenaean World*. Cambridge: Cambridge University Press, p. 88.

[118] Chadwick, *The Mycenaean World*. Cambridge: Cambridge University Press, p. 95.

Chapter 8 – Art and Architecture

Although many people think of the ancient Greeks or Romans when they imagine stunning architecture or infrastructure, the Mycenaeans were actually one of the first civilizations to develop a comprehensive network of roads and city plumbing. For example, their most famous project was the series of roads that crossed the Peloponnese, making it easier to deploy troops and protect various settlements.[119] A massive defensive wall also protected the Isthmus of Corinth and other weaker areas, indicating that the civilization had not only the technology to defend itself but also a reason to do so.

The Mycenaean Greeks developed their own art and architecture but drew inspiration from the Minoans and other ethnic Greek groups that lived on the mainland. In terms of art, the civilization left behind beautiful examples of metalwork, frescoes, and pottery that provide an insight into the available technologies of the time and what the Mycenaeans viewed as beautiful or worthwhile to paint. Architecture tells similar information but can

---

[119] Kelder, *The Kingdom of Mycenae*, p. 116.

also indicate where centers of power were located and how defensive the Mycenaeans needed to be.

Palaces and Average Dwellings

Palaces were the most significant piece of architecture in the palatial states since they were the home of the administration. The geographical location of the palace tended to vary based on the terrain in each state, but the structure was always built somewhere central but with natural defensive barriers. For example, the palaces of Mycenae, Pylos, and Tiryns, three of the most well-preserved sites, can be found on the summits of hills or rocky outcrops with room to build the rest of the settlement around it.[120] Archaeologists know a wealth of information about the palaces because most of them have been discovered. In Central Greece, the palatial structures of Thebes and Orchomenos are partially uncovered, while the palace built in the Acropolis of Athens has worn away to almost nothing.

Palaces possessed some similar features no matter which state in which they were constructed. The focal point was always the *megaron*, which was used as a throne room. This room possessed a circular hearth surrounded by four columns that held up the heavy ceiling. Thrones were to the right of the entrance, while many of the other walls were covered with rich decorations to demonstrate the wealth of the administration and ruling family. To reach the *megaron*, visitors needed to go through a courtyard which could be reached through a *propylon*, which is essentially an open gated entryway. An example is included below.

---

[120] Fields, *Mycenaean Citadels c. 1350–1200 BC* (3ʳᵈ ed.), p. 19.

Propylon

Throughout the palatial states, the palaces shared numerous painting styles and iconography. Marine images were popular, including depictions of dolphins, octopi, and fish. Around the *megaron* were numerous open courtyards which led to rooms like storerooms, living quarters, and workshops. Some palaces possessed reception or greeting halls as well. There might have been two stories to the palaces, and archaeologists believe the living quarters of the royal family were upstairs and away from the hustle and bustle of life.

Archaeologists and historians know less about the standard domestic settlement than the palaces. However, it's believed such structures were single level buildings made of mudbricks of varying sizes. Roofs were made out of thrushes, hay, and sometimes timber, and animals seem to have been kept in either a closed yard, courtyard, or sometimes even in the house.

Metalwork

Most examples of Mycenaean metalwork come from the burial goods taken from Grave Circles A and B near Mycenae. The Mycenaean Greeks tended to make smaller metal pieces out of precious materials and saved bronze for use in weapons and tools. Some types of metalwork include cups, signet rings, jewelry, brooches, and funerary masks. Famous examples of these items are the Mask of Agamemnon, Nestor's Cup, the Theseus Ring, and the Silver Siege Rhyton. Specialty artisans most likely did smaller pieces of work using precious metals while blacksmiths dedicated their time to weaponry, tools, and horseshoes. Based on the architecture of the palace centers and the goods found there, archaeologists believe that skilled metalsmiths lived near the administration of the palatial states.

Figures and Figurines

Evidence suggests the Mycenaeans did not create large sculptures, but they did make a variety of small statuettes, figures, and figurines, with clay being the most common material. Objects of this variety have so far been discovered in almost every known Mycenaean archaeological site, indicating the practice of making such items was commonplace and perhaps even necessary as part of the culture. Some figurines appear to serve religious purposes while others were more decorative. Statuettes for cult purposes have been found in Tiryns and Agios Konstantinos.

Most Mycenaean Greek figurines are of women, and they tend to be anthropomorphic or zoomorphic, meaning they possess animalistic anatomy or characteristics. Female figurines can be divided into three main categories which experienced surges of popularity during different time periods. The groupings were phi-type, psi-type, and tau-type. A phi-type figurine resembled the Greek letter phi, which means the arms give the body a round shape. The phi-types date back to roughly 1450 BCE. Next came the psi-types, which resembled a woman with raised, outstretched arms. These originated around the 1250s BCE and quickly became popular. The tau-type came last, not appearing until the 1100s BCE. These looked like the Greek letter "tau." Archaeologists guess the figurines possessed multiple purposes. First, they were most likely votives for home altars since they are found frequently in domestic garbage heaps. Second, they were probably children's toys since they are found in the graves of deceased boys and girls, sometimes clutched to the chest.[121]

Greek "Phi"

1234qwer1234qwer4, CC BY-SA 4.0 <https://creativecommons.org/licenses/by-sa/4.0>, via Wikimedia Commons https://commons.wikimedia.org/wiki/File:Greek_letter_phi_on_font_lines.svg

Greek "Psi"

1234qwer1234qwer4, CC BY-SA 4.0 <https://creativecommons.org/licenses/by-sa/4.0>, via Wikimedia Commons https://commons.wikimedia.org/wiki/File:Greek_letter_psi_on_font_lines.svg

---

[121] K.A. and Diana Wardle "The Child's Cache at Assiros, Macedonia," in Sally Crawford and Gillian Shepherd (eds): *Children, Childhood and Society: Institute for Archaeology and Antiquity Interdisciplinary Studies (Volume I)*, Oxford: Archaeopress, 2007.

Greek "Tau"

Frescoes

Like much of their culture, the Mycenaeans were influenced by the Minoans when it came to their frescoes, or elaborate wall paintings. Pieces can be found all over mainland Greece in palaces as well as domestic dwellings, with some of the best examples originating from Pylos, Mycenae, Zygouries, and Tiryns.[122] The Mycenaeans painted their frescoes by applying the paints directly to the stone surface of the wall without an intermediary substance. Brushes appeared to be used, potentially made from horsehair. As with the Minoans, the Mycenaeans depicted men using the color red and women with the color white. Precious metals corresponded with the three primary colors as well: gold was yellow, silver was blue, and bronze was red. Popular scenes and subjects for the frescoes were hunting, religious processions, bull-leaping, famous battles, mythological narratives or events, and general geometric shapes. Archaeologists and art historians have noticed similarities between the themes on frescoes and those on pottery.

---

[122] Sara A. Immerwahr, *Aegean Painting in the Bronze Age*, University Park: Pennsylvania State University Press, 1990.

Fresco of a Mycenaean Woman
https://commons.wikimedia.org/wiki/File:Fresco_of_a_Mycenaean_woman,_circa_1300_BC.jpg

Pottery

Pottery is perhaps one of the greatest assets the contemporary scholarly community possesses when it comes to understanding the Mycenaeans. Not only was pottery ubiquitous, meaning almost every living Mycenaean needed to have a pot to function in society, but so much of it has survived thousands of years of erosion and natural disasters that professionals are able to identify where fragments came from, what style they were, who might have used the completed vessel, and the cultural and economic significance of the object.

The majority of Mycenaean pottery consists of terracotta ceramics that were shaped and fired by hand to create a variety of styles. Completed vessels could have been used for a broad range of reasons, including for the storage of surplus food, the fermentation of wine, the carrying of water, or simple ornamentation and decoration. The study of these objects has a long and complicated history in the field of archaeology due to naming conventions, issues of misidentification, and the failure of developing classification systems during the first half of the twentieth century. Despite these problems, scholars have created a comprehensive system of Mycenaean pottery classification.

To count as Mycenaean pottery, a piece needed to be produced between 1600 and 1000 BCE and be created by recognizable Mycenaean Greek potters. Some pieces found in the region of Mycenaean settlements share some similarities to Mycenaean vessels but were discovered to have been Minoan instead. Work from other civilizations and locations in the Mediterranean, including the Levant, have also been discovered outside places like Mycenae. Meanwhile, Mycenaean pottery has been found in abundance at locales like Italy and Sicily, indicating the potential presence of strong trade routes.[123]

Archaeologists divide Mycenaean pottery into four main phases which possess their own categories and intricacies. These phases are the Early Mycenaean, the Middle Mycenaean, the Palatial Period, and the Post-Palatial Period.[124] Although artisans and individuals manufactured pottery during each period and the pieces needed to be used in daily life, archaeologists believe that the specimens found belonged mainly to the elite and upper classes. Pottery was the work of slaves or lower-class people, but the poor could not afford to bury their dead with these pieces. Instead, the wealthy would often be laid to rest with their most elaborate or beautiful vessels, allowing them to be preserved. Pottery might also have been used during religious ceremonies and as gifts between the Mycenaean rulers; these pieces were typically

---

[123] Evans, A.J. "Knossos: I The Palace (Plates XII and XIII)," *The Annual of the British School at Athens*, 1901, p. 3–69.

[124] Rutter, *The Oxford Handbook of the Bronze Age Aegean*, ed. by Eric H. Cline, Oxford: Oxford University Press, 2012.

selected for preservation as well. Some examples of Mycenaean pottery are seen below, including rhytons, which are cups shaped like animal heads.

A False-Necked Jar
Metropolitan Museum of Art, CC0, via Wikimedia Commons
https://commons.wikimedia.org/wiki/File:Terracotta_stirrup_jar_MET_DP1890.jpg

Bull's Head Rhyton, c. 1300-1200 BCE
https://commons.wikimedia.org/wiki/File:Bull-rhyton_BM_A971.jpg

These pictures demonstrate a range of eras and styles, but there are some similarities between the pieces. Pottery tended to be thick and made of sturdy clay, which was baked and dried before being painted. The Mycenaeans favored geometric patterns, marine life, and flowers. In some pieces, artisans might cover the surface with a scene such as part of a battlefield. Archaeologists believe the examples shown above represent pottery most likely owned by the wealthy, who would have been able to commission painted work. Without such pieces though, contemporary audiences would be unable to understand the function of pottery, its lessons about Mycenaean social class, and what technologies the civilization had access to.

Conclusion

One of the most frequently asked questions about the study of ancient civilizations is one that makes scholars cry but needs to be answered: Why do we, as humans, care about the way people lived thousands of years ago?

In the case of the Mycenaeans, there are numerous reasons for contemporary audiences to be interested. As a people, the Mycenaeans dominated much of the Mediterranean and laid the groundwork for arguably the greatest Western civilization to come to fruition. Human evolution and development do not occur in a vacuum. Instead, it can best be understood as a long chain filled with pits, gaps, enclosed circles, and the all-important connections that bind societies together. The Greeks as modern people know them, and by extension, all of the civilizations and countries influenced by them, would not exist if not for the Mycenaeans.

Outside of these practical reasons for needing to understand ancient civilizations, there is also natural curiosity. How could people live on such harsh terrain as the Peloponnese and still develop a cohesive administration with a powerful army and navy capable of establishing trade routes that would have taken months to travel? How did the humans of thousands of years ago live?

Were they like us?

The Mycenaeans play an important and pivotal role in human development in the Mediterranean region, and they also contributed much-needed innovations in essential technologies like engineering and architecture. Although many modern individuals know little about them, it's safe to say that life wouldn't be the same if this sturdy group of people hadn't decided to build their settlements on the rocky outcrops of Greece almost 4,000 years ago.

So, what did they do? Why should we remember them? The Mycenaeans developed a political structure and religion that continue to be one of the most recognizable in history. Their trade routes in the Mediterranean connected disparate societies, and their military advancements would allow for the development of Sparta, perhaps the most legendary fighting culture known to the West. The Mycenaeans also possessed the first instance of written Greek, and many words used in languages like English are actually Mycenaean in origin. In engineering, they launched large-scale projects that would not be rivaled in Europe until the arrival of the Romans and their famous roads. As the precursors and creators of a culture that would be adopted and perfected by one of the most influential peoples in history, it should come as no surprise that many ancient historians consider Mycenaean Greece to be a cradle of civilization.[125]

---

[125] Castleden, *Mycenaeans*, p. 231.

Part 5: The Etruscans

A Captivating Guide to the Etruscan Civilization of Ancient Italy That Preceded the Roman Republic

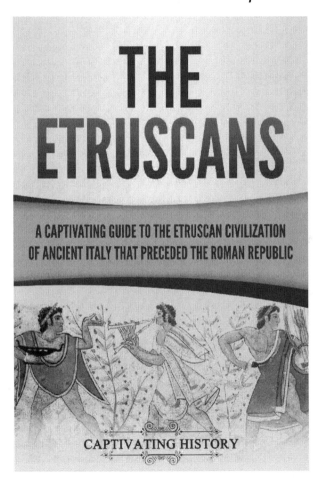

Introduction – Who Were the Etruscans?

Almost everyone has heard of the Romans, but far fewer know of the Etruscans. The Etruscans were one of the most powerful civilizations in ancient Italy before the rise of the Romans. They thrived from 900 BCE until their eventual absorption into Rome around 100 BCE and enjoyed an expansive stretch of territory called Etruria. One could mark their lands as including Tuscany, western Umbria, northern and central Lazio, along with some settlements in nearby Campania, Lombardy, Romagna, Veneto, and the Po Valley. These Etruscans developed their own language, culture, and religion but also demonstrated the multiculturalism and cultural assimilation common among the civilizations around the Mediterranean Sea. They would only crumble when they became involved in the Roman-Etruscan Wars and failed to defeat the massive republic forming at their doorstep.

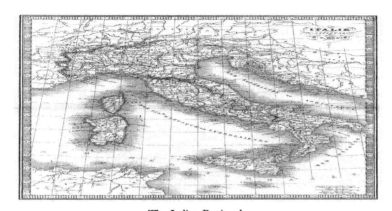

The Italian Peninsula

The predecessors of the Etruscans were the Villanovans, from whom the Etruscans took some elements of culture and language. Due to their position in Italy and ethnic origin, the Etruscans were considered part of the Italics, an Indo-European ethnolinguistic group which originated from Northeast Africa. Archaeologists and anthropologists can trace the Italic migration to Italy as far back as the 2nd millennium BCE. While the Italics settled in Rome, other Indo-European travelers would travel to new locations and become the Spanish, Romanian, French, and Portuguese, among others. When discussing the Etruscans, people need to use years followed by the abbreviation BCE, which stands for Before Common Era. This is referring to the point before year 1 in the modern Gregorian calendar. So, when this volume refers to the Etruscan civilization as beginning around 900 BCE, it means the Etruscans started 900 years before year 1, or 2,919 years before the year 2019.

The Etruscans were an ancient civilization during the Iron Age, the last stage in the three-stage system developed by archaeologists to describe the progress of civilizations based on their available technologies. As members of the Iron Age, the Etruscans possessed the knowledge of ferrous metallurgy or ironworking. They could develop carbon steel to make stronger weapons, armor, and implements like farming tools that would give them an advantage in military affairs and growing crops. The Iron Age succeeds the Bronze Age which was when civilizations learned how to create bronze tools and developed a proto-writing system. The Etruscans already had their own form of writing by the time of their development.

The majority of modern information about the Etruscans does not come from their writings but from the archaeological interpretation of artifacts. For scholars of the Etruscans, these artifacts can be funerary and burial goods, graves, the remnants of buildings, jewelry, paintings, frescoes, inscriptions, weapons, tools, and other items that still remain after two millennia of environmental hazards, looting, and grave robbing. Some written sources do exist, but they are rare. Information can also be gathered from the writings of nearby civilizations and cultures like the Romans, who wrote extensively about the Etruscans. These sources need to be taken with a grain of salt, though, as ancient historians and philosophers were prone to exaggeration and biases in their interpretations.

The importance of the Etruscans can be traced back to Rome though. The Roman Republic, and later the Roman Empire, was an unusual conqueror because it would absorb and assimilate elements of the cultures it dominated. A standing practice was to allow the defeated to continue practicing their culture and religion so long as they paid their taxes on time. Such a procedure was part of why Christianity would seep into the Roman Empire around the 1st century CE, for example. For the Etruscans, this meant they influenced aspects of Roman civilization, one of the most powerful cultures in the history of the Western world.

The word "Rome" is Etruscan in origin as are the names of its mythological founders "Remus" and "Romulus." Several of the Roman creation myths centered on branches of the Etruscans breaking off to found Rome, and Rome itself used to be a part of Etruscan civilization before it broke away and started to develop its own society. When the Etruscans were absorbed, elements of their culture, language, and religion would seep into Roman practice. Before their assimilation, the Etruscans gifted Rome with much of its political science and technology. Through the Etruscans, the Romans developed monarchy, walls, drainage systems, and the powerful forum.

The Etruscans shouldn't only be studied as the influencer of Rome, but it is the connection through which most individuals have heard of their illustrious civilization. Other interesting developments of the Etruscans were their flamboyant fashion, complex political structure, urban planning, and fatalistic religion. As the reader of this volume, check and see where the Etruscans sound similar to the Romans but also interpret what made the Etruscans unique, what rings of assimilation of other cultures like the Greeks, and determine whether it was possible for the Etruscans to avoid their fate against the Romans during the 1st century BCE.

Chapter 1 – Politics, Government, and Social Structure

To understand Etruscan history and culture, one needs to understand the basic social structure of their civilization first. The organization of the state affected the power of the city-states, how the average individual lived, and the Etruscan response to warring neighbors, foreign influences, and trade. The first place to look is at the political structure and government because the state often exerted control over the lives of the individuals in one form or another. For the first few centuries, the government of the city-states would possess little power beyond collecting taxes and offering some modicum of protection. However, it did not take long for the government to grow and give way to powerful leagues and aristocrats.

Political Structure and Government

Similar to numerous other ancient civilizations, the Etruscans moved away from the chiefdom and tribal forms of governance possessed by their ancestors and developed a centralized state. This state consisted primarily of male nobles who would have been the chiefs or tribal leaders in previous times. While this central state did exist, the Etruscan city-states remained divided and thus not all regions were active participants in this new form of multistate government. The Etruscan use of the centralized state separated them from the nearby Italics, who would become the Romans at a later date. During the Etruscan lifespan, these Italics continued to organize themselves in a series of chiefdoms that made power less organized and concentrated. The Etruscan state, on the other hand, began as a monarchy, but it rapidly switched to an oligarchic democracy wherein elite families possessed power and voted amongst themselves to decide the future of the Etruscan state and its people. This change occurred sometime during the 6th century BCE.

Historians describe the Etruscan political structure as a theocracy, or a government based around a central state religion. The state government possessed the ultimate authority over individual tribal and clan organizations, and it consisted of elites from each one while also ensuring that the adherents to state power shared a common religion and obeyed religious law. A Gorgon can be found in Etruscan decorations, and archaeologists believe the symbol represented the power of the government and its ability to control the life and death of its inhabitants.[126] Beneath the state itself were smaller politically united units called city-states, also called the *methlum* or districts. The general population was called the *mech*, while numerous magisterial positions existed to collect taxes and preserve domestic order, along with a variety of other functions yet unknown to scholars. Some of their titles were the *parnich,* the *purth*, the *camthi,* and the *macstrey,* but the exact translations of these titles are unknown. The ruler of a methlum

---

[126] The Gorgons were three women in Greek mythology who were cursed to have their hair turned into live, writhing, venomous snakes. The most famous is Medusa, but she had two sisters as well who were immortal: Stheno and Euryale. While contemporary scholars often view a Gorgon as a monster, it was a powerful symbol in the Mediterranean that represented tenacity, durability, and power.

was called the *zilach*, while older Etruscan texts also call the position the *lucumo*, or sacred monarch.

The city-states, or methlum, gathered into three confederacies or leagues that needed to consist of twelve methlum each. The names of the leagues are unknown because of how little the Etruscan language has been translated. Scholars believe the requirement of having exactly twelve methlum was related to a religious association with the number. A league was called a *mech rasnal*, and every year, the members of the mech rasnal would meet at a sacred place called a *fanu* and discuss their current affairs and plans for the next year. The meeting also included the election of the *zilath mechl rasnal*, the individual who would head the league for the next year. Women appear to have been barred from these meetings and from holding political or military office altogether.

The Etruscans would continue to use this centralized political structure until war with Rome broke out around the 4th century BCE. According to historical sources, Rome was potentially a member of one of the *mech rasnal*, most likely the Latian or Campanian league. When Rome attacked the Etruscans, they disrupted the original power structure and caused internal dissent that weakened the political states as a whole. Over time, the political hegemony of Rome would overpower the remaining Etruscan outposts, and the Etruscan culture would morph into Roman civilization.

Law and Order

There were multiple social and economic classes in the Etruscan civilization. At the top of society were the wealthy elites who held the majority of the government positions, almost all of the wealth, and controlled many of the trade routes and city affairs. They also were more likely than others to be military commanders. While the elites were always above the other members of Etruscan society, their position became more distinct and pronounced over the centuries until the monarchy could be described as an oligarchy run by the wealthy few. These families were aristocrats and tended to have different rights and legal standards than the other social classes. Most could hold property, pay fines instead of facing prison or other forms of punishment, and had a voice in government.

Below the aristocratic families was a large population of free men and women. In the formative years of the Etruscans, some could be traders, merchants, and craftsmen and craftswomen of great skill. Over time, the focus shifted, and the majority of those illustrious positions belonged to a very small group of families that could be described as the middle class. The middle class did not have extra rights like the aristocracy but did have the money needed to have better living conditions than the poor majority. The rest of the population were poor laborers, farmers, construction workers, and general subsistence workers who needed to stay busy to survive. Men of this class had some legal rights, far more than women, and could possess and inherit property with few restrictions beyond the order of birth and age. They were also free to come and go as they pleased and were the heads of their households, with the power of life and death over their wives and children. This situation existed among the aristocratic families as well.

Although women were barred from public offices, they possessed more rights in Etruscan society than they would under Roman rule. Inscriptions found with frescoes and pottery reveal that respectable married women possessed the right to engage in leisure activities and attend parties with their husbands. They could drink wine in public and appeared capable of property ownership. A woman could even inherit property if there was no surviving male heir in the family line. If a male did live, then the property would automatically be given to him. Otherwise, women held a social and legal position underneath men, who were considered their superiors. This situation only became more exaggerated over time as the Etruscans became less egalitarian and more closely resembled the lifestyle of the Roman Republic.

On the bottom rung of the social ladder was the slave class. Like most ancient cultures, the Etruscans used a significant slave class to bolster public projects and serve the wealthy families that could afford them. Most slaves were possessed by influential nobles who could feed and shelter massive slave populations to work as farmers, quarry workers, miners, potters, soldiers, metalworkers, entertainers, household servants, winemakers, tutors, and other professions responsible for the daily upkeep of the civilization. Most slaves did not belong to one particular race or culture as most were prisoners of war who had been captured from other Etruscan cities or locations outside of Etruria. Others were bought from African and Middle Eastern trading partners that also engaged in the Mediterranean slave trade. Scholars know little about individual servants although their names sometimes appear in frescoes and tomb paintings that include the names of everyone featured.

The Etruscans were accustomed to slave revolts which frequently resulted in armed uprisings. The revolts became more common beginning in the 4th century BCE. Archaeologists and scholars think that regular Etruscan citizens such as laborers often became involved in the uprisings as well due to poor working conditions and the large wealth disparity between the majority poor and the minority rich. Lacking money meant that individuals could not gain opportunities to improve their social position, so most people were trapped as impoverished laborers.

The Importance of the Family in Society

The first hints of the importance of family in Etruria come from the surviving tombs in Etruscan necropoli. The majority of the surviving tombs belong to wealthy aristocrats who interred their relatives in the family crypt over centuries. Archaeologists and historians associate this practice with the rise of the aristocratic family as a fixed institution of Etruscan society. Parallels are drawn between this Etruscan institution and the Romans, who had a group called the *gens*, and some believe the Etruscans were the initial model for the Romans. After all, the Roman *gens* was essentially a fixed familial institution that closely resembled that of the Etruscans. This new aristocratic institution grew as the Etruscans thrived through trade routes around the Mediterranean Sea and acquired wealth, power, and fame. Almost all wealthy cities and the assorted aristocrats were situated on the coast since ports received the majority of the resources acquired through trade.

The Etruscans called the family the *lautn*. At the center of the lautn was a central married couple called the *tusurthir*, which emphasizes the importance of monogamy in their culture. The pairing between one man and one woman was seen as the most significant relationship in the family unit. The images carved upon the lids of sarcophagi tended to be of married couples in their youth, smiling, enjoying one another's company, and reclining beside each other. The best example is the Sarcophagus of the Spouses, pictured below. Sometimes the couple would be interred in the same sarcophagus so they could be together in the afterlife. While most marriages were arranged by a woman's father and the future husband, romantic love appeared to be important.

The Sarcophagus of the Spouses, 519 BCE
Saverio.G, CC BY-SA 4.0 <https://creativecommons.org/licenses/by-sa/4.0>, via Wikimedia Commons https://commons.wikimedia.org/wiki/File:Villa_Giulia_WLM_18_30.jpg

Although the Greeks and Romans believed the Etruscans were a sexually loose society, historians believe such interpretations were misunderstandings about the role of the family and the relative freedom of women in Etruria. Greek and Roman writers frequently wrote of the sexual availability of the Etruscan women, implying that virginity and sexual purity were not valued and that women were free to take multiple partners. In fact, this was not the case. Women possessed more rights in Etruscan society than their counterparts in Greece and Rome and were allowed to socialize with men and leave the house to interact with other parts of society. Despite this freedom, Etruscan social norms still required romantic and sexual faithfulness since the couple was the center of the family unit. The importance of the couple can be seen in funerary inscriptions in tombs since inscriptions list a person's name as well as their father's and mother's names. In many other ancient cultures, only the father's name was typically given.

Continuing with the relevance of the family was the importance of names. There were a few different stages of development when it came to naming conventions, which is understandable considering the Etruscans existed for over 900 years. Historians are unsure whether or not the majority of the population participated in Etruscan naming conventions or whether they were reserved for the aristocrats. Either way, the family and the central couple remained important for free Etruscans. Slaves were most likely not included in such family units due to their low position.

The first part of the Etruscan name was the praenomen, which everyone possessed. Even slaves would have a praenomen. This was the first name and featured gender markers such as *arnth/arntia, aule/aulia,* or *larth/lartha.* Women were not forced to take male names or a derivative of their father's or husband's name. This was unusual, as other Italic peoples like the Romans lacked specific female names. Indeed, many Etruscan names were reserved entirely for women, once again demonstrating the rights and general freedom of Etruscan women in comparison to ladies in other ancient societies.

Men's and women's names differed when it came to patronymics and gamonymics. Men received a patronymic, which typically associated the son with the father or a general clan. So, for example, a man might be named *larth arnthal*, which meant "Larth, son of Arnuth." Women, meanwhile, were identified with a gamonymic. A gamonymic was the husband's name and is sometimes seen as similar to the Western practice of married women taking their husband's surname. When this wasn't the case, Etruscan women sometimes possessed a matronymic that identified them as the daughters of their mothers. In a few cases, archaeologists discovered tombs of men that had matronymics and women with patronymics, hinting at a potential change over time. It's possible that children took the name of whichever parent possessed a better social position. However, in general, Etruscan society tended to be patrilineal and patriarchal, potentially as a holdover from the Villanovans.

Another part of Etruscan naming conventions was the nomen gentile. The nomen gentile was the family name similar to a surname. These seemed to appear during the Etruscan orientation, also called the Orientalizing period. There were male and female forms of the nomen gentile, and it tended to come immediately after the praenomen but before the patronymic or gamonymic. Historians believe the Romans copied Etruscan naming conventions as the same model can be seen in both civilizations. Other classes may have used these naming conventions, but it definitely meant more to the aristocratic class as these conventions were more significant to them as these naming conventions were important for identifying kinship and family connections.

Family connections were solidified through kinship conventions. Kinship is defined as how people describe themselves in relation to others. For example, someone saying "I am the daughter of Marcela" is identifying her kinship to Marcela as well as her role in the family. To support the idea of a patrilineal society, women could describe themselves as the daughter of a father or the wife of a husband, while men would say they were the son of a father but never the husband to a wife, even if she came from a higher position. The Etruscans tracked six generations of vertical kinship or lineage, so most individuals—especially aristocrats—knew the names of their great-great-great-great-grandfather. All people had a *mi* (I), and an *apa* and *ati* (father and mother). Individuals also recognized their *sec* or *clan* (daughter or son) as well as grandsons (*nefts*) and great-grandsons (*prumaths*). The words for granddaughters and great-granddaughters are difficult to determine.

Families and kinship were how the Etruscans described and understood themselves, making it a central aspect of society. A person who lacked such information was most likely a slave and also lacked the social standing of other members of the civilization. Again, much of the information historians possess comes from the study of aristocratic families, which might have been more clear and severe in the delineation of their families due to their wealth, property, and positions of power in society.

Chapter 2 – How an Individual Lived

Underneath the broad political system of the Etruscans were the thousands of people that kept the state and society running efficiently. Even after the division into social classes, people were further divided by their gender, profession, and where they lived. After all, the life of a female potter in a coastal city would be vastly different from that of a male farmer in the interior regions.

When it comes to gender, the Etruscans only believed in two: male and female. Men were considered the superior gender and tended to possess more rights and opportunities than women. Most freemen could inherit property and possessed the right of life and death over the family members under their control. The oldest male tended to be the head of the household and had power over his wife, children, and his mother if she lived in the home. Wealthy men were literate, could hold political and military positions, and were allowed to attend events, parties, and symposiums without chaperones. They could also drink wine in public and possessed more sexual freedom than women since there was no expectation for men to be virgins. Men could pick their wives and would arrange the marriage with the woman's father—she rarely possessed any input.

For the average freeman, literacy and power were out of reach. Most worked as common laborers, farmers, and quarry workers. They labored all day to earn money to buy food and resources but would come home and be in charge of the house. They possessed almost no role in childcare but did make the final decisions regarding how money was spent and what the wife and children were allowed to do.

Although women lacked many of the rights and opportunities of their male counterparts, they possessed more gender equality in Etruscan society than other women in similar ancient civilizations like the Greeks. Well-to-do women of elite families tended to be literate and were allowed to attend social events and symposiums when accompanied by their husbands. If no male heirs could be found, the oldest female heir was capable of inheriting property and wealth. When listed in documents or in the captions for paintings and artwork, women tended to be given several names— their birth name and the surname adopted upon marriage. Their artwork also depicts women participating in athletic activities, parties, and feasts.

Despite these advantages, the lot of the common woman was difficult. Most would never be able to inherit property, were illiterate, and were expected to marry young, manage the household, and raise children. While they could go out in public, wear jewelry, and tended to have clothing that exposed more skin, the average woman's life was hard. Like men, most women worked from dawn to dusk. Many were laborers while the majority prepared the family's food, maintained the house, slaughtered animals, gathered plants, made medicinal treatments, and weaved and made clothes. Unlike men, women were expected to remain virgins until marriage and did not usually pick their own partner.

Housing

There is evidence that the Etruscans engaged in early city planning. The first settlements were built on plateaus and ridges that were easily defended from enemies. Most towns also possessed ditches and sometimes stone walls to reduce vulnerability. One surviving settlement called Marzabotto hails from the 5th century BCE and was oriented along a north-south axis with a grid pattern. This made it easy for individuals to navigate the streets but was also related to superstitious beliefs among the Etruscans. The Etruscans focused on rituals and rites that determined the layout of buildings, and some particular arrangements were deemed auspicious for the inhabitants as well as the town in general. While the full details of the rites are vague, scholars believe they involved the saying of prayers and the reading of omens in the environment.

Etruscan homes were made from easy-to-gather, perishable materials like sun-dried mudbricks, wood, and waddle and daub for the walls. Stone and rock-cut chambers were reserved for tombs and the wealthy, and even then, homes were more likely to be large mudbrick homes. During the 7th and 6th centuries BCE, circular and oval huts appeared to be the most common design. Ruins discovered at Acquarossa demonstrates that the walls once had a plaster coating for extra protection and possibly aesthetic purposes. Wooden poles were used to support woven thatch roofs, and evidence indicates that some houses also had terracotta decorations like lotus motifs and palmettes, while stone would sometimes be used to create sturdy foundations and lower floors. These strengthened levels would prevent the lower sections of the house from collapsing under the weight of the other materials.

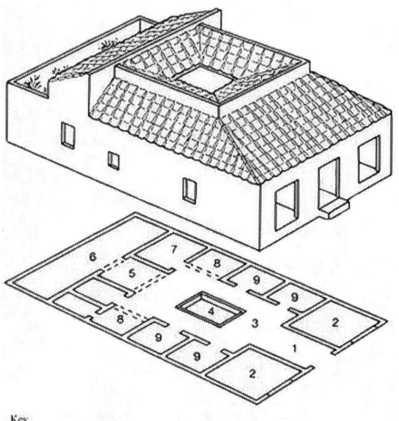

Key
1. *fauces*—entrance passage
2. *tabernae*—shops
3. *atrium*—hall
4. *impluvium*—rainwater basin
5. *tablinum*—passage room
6. *hortus*—garden
7. *triclinium*—dining room
8. *alae*—side-rooms
9. *cubiculum*—bedroom

The Anatomy of an Etruscan Aristocratic House
https://commons.wikimedia.org/wiki/File:Domusitalica.png

The Anatomy of an Etruscan Aristocratic House

Some homes used saddle tiles around the apex or center of the roof. The central tile would have a hole carved in the center through which smoke could escape from fires and light could enter the house. A disc would be kept near the roof to cover the hole when it rained. Around the late 6th and early 5th centuries BCE, these roof tiles would replace thatch in the majority of homes. Beams would be protected by nailing terracotta tiles or plaques to the ends to cover exposed edges. In the early 6th century, houses also evolved to possess a single floor with multiple rooms, a hall, and sometimes a private courtyard where families could greet guests, plant vegetables and herbs, and keep animals like chickens. In other cases, multiple houses would be grouped around a central courtyard that would have rock-cut drainage channels attached to town cisterns.

Archaeologists struggle to distinguish between the house styles of aristocrats and commoners because the houses that remain are the opulent buildings of the nobles. In general, scholars think that poorer folk most likely lived in more ramshackle dwellings that would not have stood the test of time. These were most likely built of mudbrick, wood, and other more destructible materials.

Starting in the mid-6th century BCE, large private buildings started to be built with gabled roofs and columns. Archaeologists specializing in architecture believe these designs came from Phoenicia and Asia Minor, two regions with whom the Etruscans traded. These public edifices included an atrium with a shallow basin that collected rainwater for drinking and cooking. Opposite of the atrium was a room with a cistern, hearth, and servants' quarters.

Diet

The Etruscans did not leave behind any recipes that archaeologists can reconstruct, but archaeological findings have discovered some of the most common foods. The majority of evidence comes from the household items discovered in ancient kitchens as well as the types of meals depicted in paintings and the decorations of ancient necropoli. From this evidence, scholars can determine that the majority of the Etruscan population did not eat meat on a regular basis. If there was a banquet, guests would feast on roasted game, poultry, and pork. Pigs were the most common domesticated animal because they could eat various kinds of food and did not require large grasslands or fields. The terrain and flora of Etruscan territory featured numerous oak trees and forests where pigs were allowed to run free and eat acorns and other goods. At the end of the day, people would find their pigs and bring them back for the night.

An everyday meal for an Etruscan individual most likely consisted of cheese, legumes, porridge, and assorted herbs and vegetables. Garlic and onions were the most common seasonings for meals, and soups could be made in the same pot and consumed by the entire family. Olives were grown in massive groves and used to make olive oil which could be used with food, but it also served a ritual purpose. Olive branches and leaves were a popular symbol in Etruscan frescoes as well. Grapes were raised to make wine for drinking and rituals. Unlike modern wines, ancient wines tended to be watered down so it could be consumed on a regular basis. The fermentation of the grapes was used to prevent the transfer of bacteria that lived in regular freshwater. While the Etruscans did not know about bacteria, they did know that drinking plain water often made people sick. So, they would often combine it with another liquid and then allow it to ferment and create alcohol, which would destroy the effects of sickness.

Other than grapes, olives, onions, and garlic, other popular crops were beans, peas, melons, figs, broad beans, lentils, chickpeas, barley, and millet. Apple trees were sometimes raised in orchards while berries could be gathered from bushes in the countryside. When the Etruscans did eat meat, it was livestock or animals hunted in the nearby forests. Other than pigs, this could have been goats, chickens, ducks, rabbits, boar, and deer. Fishing was done in nearby rivers and seas. To complement their fruits, vegetables, and meats, the Etruscans developed a way to turn grains into an even tastier treat: There is evidence to show the Etruscans made pasta out of dough with fundamental rolling pins.

Cooking food was a time-consuming task that could take all day, and despite the lengthy process to cook food, the Etruscans consumed two meals each day. Most baking and cooking were done over open fires, and the grains for bread needed to be ground before consumption. Women made a wide variety of breads, including flat grape bread, a food still eaten today. Some important utensils they used were saucepans, colanders, graters, and pans.

Clothing

Information about the clothing of the ancient Etruscans comes from artifacts like bronze sculptures, painted figures, carvings in stone reliefs, and the images drawn on funerary urns. The fibers used to make the clothes are unlikely to have survived the rigors of decomposition. Although much of Etruscan culture was absorbed by the Romans, archaeologists and historians are able to distinguish between Etruscan and Roman fashion thanks to preserved images. What was discovered is that the Etruscans favored flamboyant, colorful garments and designs that stood out, especially for the upper classes.

Clothing was created from fabric made by weaving natural fibers. Discoveries of artifacts reveal important tools such as spindles, loom weights, and spools existed long before the Etruscans in the same area, indicating they most likely inherited their knowledge of weaving from their predecessors, the Villanovans. Many Etruscan women were responsible for weaving wool at home to create clothing for the family, but they were not the only ones. Some paraphernalia discovered in tombs indicate that men also wove and might have repaired their own clothes since women had other tasks outside of the home. Over time, the development of agriculture and the rise of metallurgy meant the Etruscans were able to develop a manufacturing class capable of weaving and clothing production on a larger scale. Families no longer had to take care of wool on their own and could buy fabrics and linens from specialized sellers instead. The Etruscans were famed for their linen production and also produced wool, treated animal hides, and cotton for regular use. Most could be dyed to denote status and give the clothing its flamboyant characteristics.

Archaeologists can trace the influence of Ionia and the Near East in Etruscan culture since the people of Etruria favored soft conical hats, decorative and colorful patterns, and pointed footwear dyed with bright colors. Greek influence also occurred, with individuals wearing long dresses held together by brooches, simple white cloaks called a *himation,* and short sleeved tunics called a *chiton.* Greek fashion was most common in the coastal cities where trade occurred and goods and artwork from Greek cities were visible. Greek-styled clothing tended to be made from lightweight linen instead of other materials.

The actual design of everyday clothing is difficult to define, however. Most of the resources archaeologists and historians have come from frescoes and other wall paintings that tend to depict individuals in finery and ceremonial clothes. The costumes of musicians and dancers are not reliable since almost every culture has specific clothing for performances. However, historians believe that, in general, the Etruscans favored lightweight clothing in a variety of colors, cuts, styles, and designs. Patterns were popular, as was flamboyancy and other extravagances, especially upon the aristocracy.

Clothing for women was no exception to the use of color and style. Women typically wore bodices, cloaks, and short jackets in a broad range of colors such as orange, green, royal blue, red, and yellow. Patterns could include vertical and horizontal stripes as well as polka dots. Dresses could be sleeveless or have a variety of sleeve lengths, but there was no distinct cut beyond an arch cut over the feet. Tassels and decorative fringes were popular as well. Female clothing tended to be loose in the skirt itself but a tad tight-fitting around the waist and chest to accentuate curves.

Clothing for men was also flamboyant. They tended to wear short tunics or jerkins that were belted. Long tunics were popular for religious and political offices. Like the articles of clothing for women, colors like blue, green, orange, yellow, and red were often used as dyes. A soft cone-shaped hat was worn and held in place with cloth or leather chin straps. Again, it can be difficult to determine the exact nature of a man's everyday clothing since men were often painted in their finery, military gear, or ceremonial robes rather than the average outfit of an individual.

Etruscan Dancers in the Tomb of the Triclinium, c. 470 BCE
https://commons.wikimedia.org/wiki/File:Etruskischer_Meister_002.jpg

The Etruscans were perhaps the originator of the toga, which was called the *trebenna*. This style of clothing was a long piece of fabric carefully folded and secured in place over an individual's left shoulder. The upper classes wore it to distinguish themselves from others and would often dye such clothing in bright colors like red and blue. Such styles would be adopted by the Romans later who would wear red and purple togas as signs of victory and glory. In most cases, though, the Etruscan trebenna was simple, white, and worn by all freemen.

Unlike the Greeks to whom the Etruscans are often compared, the Etruscans regularly wore shoes. The most common type of footwear appears to have been a pointed shoe that was a cross between a boot and a slipper. These were tied into place and were frequently dyed green or burgundy with deeper, richer colors being common for wealthier individuals. Slaves and poor free men and women typically wore simple sandals that were held onto the foot through the use of cross-straps. These were likely not made of leather but instead cloth and wood. The sandals discovered in tombs tended to have metal studs and thin metal slips around the soles, potentially to improve durability. During periods of cold and wet weather, the Etruscans most likely covered their boots or sandals with thin metal shoes made of sheet bronze.

Chapter 3 – The Origin of the Etruscans

When it comes to their origins, the Etruscans possess a long and complex history. While scientists can do modern genetic studies of skeletons to determine the ethnic origin of the Etruscans as a people, the Romans and Greeks that followed their illustrious civilization developed their own hypotheses. The Romans viewed themselves as separate from the Etruscans despite copying much of their culture and thus needed a way to explain how the Etruscans settled in Italy. They developed one hypothesis to explain the origin of Etruscan civilization in the Early Iron Age, while the Greeks also came up with their own explanations. The following hypotheses were created by several influential historians and political figures of varying cultures throughout the Mediterranean: Roman writer Livy, Roman politician Pliny the Elder, and Greek historians Dionysius of Halicarnassus, Hellanicus of Lesbos, and Herodotus.

Autochthonous (Indigenous) Origin

Dionysius of Halicarnassus stated the first theory about the origin of the Etruscans when he wrote: "Indeed, those probably come nearest to the truth who declare that the nation migrated from nowhere else, but was native to the country, since it is found to be a very ancient nation and to agree with no other either in its language or in its manner of living."[127]

This theory became known as the autochthonous or indigenous theory, which asserted that the Etruscans were original or native inhabitants of the Italian Peninsula. This meant they did not migrate from another location and were also descendants of the Villanovan culture that came before the Etruscans distinguished themselves. Some historians have agreed with this assertion throughout the 20th and 21st centuries, arguing that the Iron Age Villanovans should actually have been called "Proto-Etruscans" since the Etruscan language did not appear in a vacuum.[128] Some move further and describe the Etruscans as an ethnic island community that avoided the barrage of Indo-European language speakers that dominated the rest of the ancient world.

Some historians called out the unusual treatment the Etruscans received in academic circles, arguing that just because the Etruscan civilization no longer existed in its original format did not mean that it was a foreign ethnic group. Italian historian and archaeologist Massimo Pallottino was the biggest proponent of the Etruscans being native to their home in Etruria, stating that "no one would dream of asking where Italians or Frenchmen came from originally; it is the formation of the Italian and French nations that we study."[129]

Allochthonous (Non-Indigenous) Origin

Another idea was that the Etruscans did not originate on the Italian Peninsula at all. This particular theory was pushed by Greek and Roman authors who viewed the Etruscans as a historical

---

[127] Dionysius of Halicarnassus, *Roman Antiquities, Book I Chapters 30*, 1.

[128] Giuliano Bonfante and Larissa Bonfante, *The Etruscan Language, An Introduction (Revised Edition),* Manchester: Manchester University Press, 2002, p. 3.

[129] Eric Pace (1995-02-20). "Massimo Pallottino, 85, Expert on Ancient Etruscans, Is Dead". *The New York Times.* Retrieved 2010-05-02.

problem. This had to do with the idea that the Etruscans were simply too different from the other Italics because of their theology and unusual freedom for women, amongst other traits. When describing where the Etruscans came from, the Romans often harkened back to their own amalgamations of their culture and Greek mythology, claiming the Etruscans were unlike themselves. The Romans believed they were the descendants of the fugitives from Troy following the Greek Trojan War. The Etruscans, meanwhile, were some other outside force.

Herodotus, the Greek writer and historian, claimed that the Lydians believed the Etruscans were actually former Lydians from Asia Minor. He stated that for the Etruscans:

This is their story: [...] their king divided the people into two groups, and made them draw lots, so that the one group should remain and the other leave the country; he himself was to be the head of those who drew the lot to remain there, and his son, whose name was Tyrrhenus, of those who departed. [...] they came to the Ombrici, where they founded cities and have lived ever since. They no longer called themselves Lydians, but Tyrrhenians, after the name of the king's son who had led them there.[130]

Modern authors tend to dispute the claims of the Romans and Greeks, stating that the claims of the Etruscans having originated in another location were spread for a variety of political reasons. For the Romans, they wanted to differentiate themselves from their enemy since the Romans and the Etruscans frequently battled with one another for resources and territory. Meanwhile, the Etruscans themselves might have put forth the idea that they were originally Greek or came from Asia Minor to further their foreign policy and trade routes.

---

[130] *Histories* 1.94.

Sea Peoples Origin

The Sea Peoples were a mysterious force from the Mediterranean Sea during the 14th to 13th centuries BCE that disrupted many of the Bronze Age civilizations and left them to pick up the tattered remnants of society. Whoever this mysterious force was, they were a power to be reckoned with that managed to garner new bases of influence in the western Mediterranean. Some historians, notably Massimo Pallottino, believe that the Etruscans might have been this force. However, the majority of scholars remain unconvinced simply because there is no conclusive evidence to support such a theory.

Pallottino bases his hypothesis on the word *Tyrrhenoi* which appears in Egyptian inscriptions when the Egyptians described the Sea Peoples.[131] This word can be connected to the Etruscans because they were called the Tyrrhenians by some of their neighbors during the 6th and 5th centuries BCE. However, scholars can find no significant linguistic links between the Etruscans, the Sea Peoples, and inscriptions in Lemnos that some claim connects the Etruscans to powerful Mediterranean pirates.

Could the Etruscans have been the Sea People of legend? It's possible but improbable considering the lack of evidence. The contemporary world may never possess a definitive answer, but that doesn't mean a link is not worth investigating.

Modern Genetic Studies

The development of new genetics technology means scientists can test the DNA left behind in ancient Etruscan skeletons as well as modern Tuscan populations to get a better idea of the Etruscan ethnic origin. Humans, despite moving to new locations over time, can be categorized into several prominent groups of DNA that indicate their native homeland. After examining multiple samples of Etruscan skeletons as well as modern Tuscan DNA, scientists

---

[131] Pallottino, *The Etruscans*, 49ff.

determined that there is significant evidence to support the theory that the Etruscans were native to the Italian Peninsula. Meanwhile, the studies also explained that there is not enough evidence that indicates the contemporary populations of Tuscany are the direct descendants of the Etruscans.132 While there has been some debate about the authenticity and accuracy of ancient DNA testing, it's possible to make an educated guess that the Etruscans most likely possess an Autochthonous origin.

The largest mtDNA study was conducted in 2013. Based on maternally-inherited DNA, the Etruscans most likely came from a native population. This study extracted and determined the type of mitochondrial DNA from fourteen individuals from two necropoli. The information from these batches of mtDNA was analyzed alongside other older samples as well as contemporary and medieval DNA from Tuscan populations and an additional 4,910 individuals that live in the Mediterranean. The DNA was run through several million computer simulations to discover similarities and links between the samples. The results indicated that the Etruscans could be considered the forebearers of medieval Tuscans and that the ancient populations could be considered comparable to mtDNA from Anatolia. This supports a theory that the Etruscans might have migrated from Anatolia between 6,000 and 7,000 years ago during the Neolithic Revolution. This means the Etruscans were genetically the closest to Neolithic farmers from central Europe, so their heritage was most likely native European.[133]

Several other mtDNA studies were conducted between 2007 and 2018. In each study, the scientists compared samples of mtDNA and attempted to distinguish similar haplogroups between known ancient populations to see if there was more evidence to

[132] Perkins, Phil (2017). "DNA and Etruscan Identity". In Naso, Alessandro. *Etruscology*. Berlin: De Gruyter. pp. 109–118.

[133] Ghirotto S, Tassi F, Fumagalli E, Colonna V, Sandionigi A, Lari M, et al. (2013). "Origins and Evolution of the Etruscans' mtDNA". PLoS ONE. 8 (2): e55519. doi:10.1371/journal.pone.0055519.

support the idea that the Etruscans either developed from native European populations, came from Anatolia, or perhaps migrated from another origin point in the Middle East or Africa.[134] In each study, the scientists needed to account for potential DNA degradation, which involved stringent testing and working with damaged or contaminated DNA from archaeological finds.[135]

Most of the tests revealed new information that has made it difficult to determine the exact origin of the Etruscans. Some scientists believe there is a Middle Eastern origin such as from Anatolia while others remain convinced the Etruscans came from somewhere in central Europe. British archaeologist Phil Perkins provides a succinct analysis of the DNA studies conducted over the last twenty years in a collective volume entitled *Etruscology*, which was published in 2017. In the book, he writes: "None of the DNA studies to date conclusively prove that Etruscans were an intrusive population in Italy that originated in the Eastern Mediterranean or Anatolia" and "there are indications that the evidence of DNA can support the theory that Etruscan people are autochthonous in central Italy."[136]

---

[134] A haplogroup is a scientific term that refers to a category of haplotypes, or DNA alleles inherited from a single parent.

[135] Mateiu LM, Rannala BH (2008). "Bayesian inference of errors in ancient DNA caused by postmortem degradation". Mol Biol Evol. 25 (7): 1503–1511. doi:10.1093/molbev/msn095.

[136] Perkins, Phil (2017). "DNA and Etruscan Identity". In Naso, Alessandro. *Etruscology*. Berlin: De Gruyter. pp. 109–118.

Chapter 4 – The Etruscan Orientation, c. 600-400 BCE

The Etruscans went through an orientation period where they developed a culture and society distinct from the Villanovans that preceded them. Around 600 BCE, the Etruscans would be the most successful of the Italic peoples because of its stable political situation, military, trade routes with other ethnic groups and civilizations in the Mediterranean region, and thriving culture. Although there are little to no surviving written sources, historians are able to piece together much of the Etruscan history through artwork, archaeological remains, architecture, and documents written by the Romans, who would rise to prominence after a series of wars with the Etruscans. Many scholars view the Etruscan orientation period as one of the most significant moments of time for the Italian Peninsula because it demonstrates not only the numerous paths of development that the Italic groups could take but also why Rome was able to be so successful and overtake the peninsula through its military and ideologies.

Archaeologists and historians frequently divide Etruria between the northern and southern settlements. As one can see by studying the Etruscan leagues, the southern city-states or settlements were the most advanced and developed while the few city-states to the north tended to be weaker. The most prominent of the city-states to emerge during the Etruscan orientation were Tarquinia, Veii, Cerveteri, Vulci, and Orvieto. These settlements possessed the most progressive architecture, including stone temples and terracotta tiles on homes with rock foundations. Cisterns and rock-cut drainage systems were additionally common. Settlements like Tarquinia and Veii possessed satellite communities, indicating significant control over the surrounding terrain and geography.

During the 5th century BCE, the Etruscans developed a political system based on the central city-states. Within the settlements, there existed a hierarchy of noble families who possessed the majority of resources and tended to intermarry with one another. A leader comparable to a king called a *lucumo* led each city-state, but there did not appear to be a royal line of lineage. Instead, the title was given to a chosen man from one of the elite or aristocratic families, usually whichever one possessed the strongest military and most resources upon the death of the last lucumo. The presence of a monarchy was not indicative of stability but rather power centralization based around a group of prominent families. These families most likely fought between one another for control and authority.

However, this lucumo became prominent during the 5th century BCE and appeared to be associated with the meeting of the Etruscan League each year to elect a single representative of the twelve Etruscan settlements that participated. This Etruscan League—the name roughly translated by linguists—was the most powerful of the three leagues the city-states organized themselves into. Debate continues about the extent of the lucumo's practical powers, but it can be inferred that the position was ritualistic and sacerdotal and that the chosen individual possessed significant religious duties that needed to be fulfilled. Meanwhile, legitimate power was divided between other influential individuals and magistrates, similar to the Romans that would come later.

Around the time of political orientation came a period of military development as the Etruscan city-states worked to become more dominant and militaristic to maintain and expand their territory. According to historian Christopher Smith, "the Etruscans were developing a form of warfare similar to Greek warfare."[137] Instead of wearing light, flexible armor and carrying lightweight swords and assorted weaponry associated with the small tribal units of the Bronze Age, soldiers instead started to be decked out in heavy armor and carried multiple implements like round shields, spears, and swords. Some hoplite warfare appeared to be in effect but was the exception rather than the rule. In hoplite warfare, soldiers fought with spears and shields in tightly-knit formations called phalanxes. Soldiers could come from the general population of freemen while commanders were elites.

Much of what is considered Etruscan culture developed during the orientation period throughout the 5th and 4th centuries BCE. Architecture morphed and started to feature large buildings constructed around central public courtyards while streets in cities like Veii show signs of urban planning and development around a distinct linear system with a clear north-south orientation. Another important city is Marzabotto, established around 500 BCE. This city is one of the most organized, built around a square system with neat buildings. Its necropolis, in contrast, is messy and irregular, although no one quite knows why. Artwork additionally reached its peak, and some of the wealthiest burials appeared at this point. The elites developed a culture of consumption and spectacular displays of wealth to cement their position in the burgeoning aristocracy. These would include lavish funerals that lasted a few days as well as rich burial objects.

Trading points also emerged in the settlements of Pyrgi and Gravisca. These city-states were significant regions because they

---

[137] Christopher Smith, *The Etruscans: A Very Short Introduction*, Oxford: Oxford University Press, 2014, p. 65.

provide information about Etruscan trade with civilizations and towns outside of the Italian Peninsula with the other distinct ethnic groups and societies near the Etruscans. These locations allowed for a higher degree of mixing between different peoples as well as the possibility of intermarriage, although this was not common. Historians theorize that the Etruscans used to be more open to other peoples between the 7th and 6th centuries BCE but then became closed off around the 5th century BCE to keep foreign cultures outside of the central urban centers and away from the major ports on the Mediterranean Sea. An influx of Greek culture can be found in Pyrgi and Gravisca, including several deities that would be incorporated into the religions of the Italics. The Etruscans also started to worship and display their deities in distinctly Greek ways, although they used terracotta rather than marble.

While scholars are capable of describing broad trends in the activity of the Etruscans, specific historical events are difficult to determine. Most contemporary students associate history with concrete dates and details, but scholars of the Etruscans do not receive such information. This is because there are no records such as clay or marble tablets that have survived the rigors of environmental degradation and erosion. Instead, historians and archaeologists piece together history by examining burial objects and the age of cities and artifacts found throughout the region. Through these methods, historians can see that the Etruscans became more aggressive during their orientation period, attempting to move both north and south out of their territory and into the territory of the other nearby Italics.

When the Etruscans attempted to move south, they failed drastically, losing significant settlements and territory along with the associated trade routes. This loss was balanced by success in the north where the Etruscans were able to overtake some small, weak towns that were most likely underpopulated at the time. Multiple settlements appeared at this time, including Marzabotto, Spino, and Pisa. According to historians like the aforementioned Christopher Smith, these settlements were crucial to the complicated trade networks of the Etruscans.[138] Individual cities were important to making the system work as those settlements along the coast provided connections to other civilizations like the Greeks. These settlements would then, in turn, pass goods inland while sending Etruscan manufactured goods like pottery outwards.

During the orientation period, the Etruscans displayed some traits of colonization. It is certain they developed settlements outside of their territory which they were protective of and used as trading outposts and footholds in regions beyond the Italian Peninsula. However, historians debate whether the term "colonization" is truly accurate since the Etruscans did not take any drastic steps to make solely Etruscan settlements off of the mainland. Another issue is that the Etruscan civilization was not organized around one single state power but was instead an amalgamation of city-states that were known to exclude one another in political and military ventures. For example, the expansion to the north deliberately excluded many of the southern city-states, potentially because of their failures to further the borders southward.

Eventually, Etruria would develop a relationship with Campania. Campania is a region in southern Italy that was once populated by three groups of ancient Italics who spoke the Oscan language: the Osci, the Aurunci, and the Ausones. Another people called the Samnites would eventually move into the region from central Italy during the 8th century BCE. The extent of the relationship between Etruria and Campania is murky and difficult to understand. There was an obvious cultural connection between the two regions since they shared similar developments and traditions. One example of a city with similarities is Pontecagnano, which shared agriculture, some elements of language, and even

---

[138] Smith, *The Etruscans*, p. 70.

similarities in artwork such as fewer depictions of Greek mythological figures. Interactions between Etruria and Campania increased between the 7th and 6th centuries BCE, as demonstrated by the influx of artifacts found in the region.

However, the extent and power dynamic of the relationship is obscured by time. Some historians look to Rome for an example of what an Etruscan relationship with an Italic society would be like. At first glance, this procedure seems like a sound idea. But there are some major issues. To begin with, early Roman history is an enigma to contemporary historians because the best sources come from historians like Livy who was writing about the 8th century BCE during the mid-1st century BCE under the reign of Augustus during the Roman Empire. Livy, the most prominent Roman historian, himself lamented his lack of sources and believed many were destroyed during fires in the 4th century BCE. His writings are also heavily influenced by Roman mythology and popular culture. For example, the Romans believed they were the descendants of the exiled Trojans from the famous Greek Trojan War outlined by Homer's *Odyssey*. One Roman writer, Virgil, even wrote the *Aeneid* describing the Trojan exile and the foundation of Rome.

Another problem with focusing on the relationship between the Etruscans and the Romans is that Rome was a far more powerful society when compared to the societies of Campania. Unlike Rome, Campania struggled to gain territory and a military foothold in the Italian Peninsula. The Romans, on the other hand, were building a significant cultural and militaristic force and were already pushing at their borders. This means the Etruscans and the Romans operated on a much more even playing field while the Etruscans and the peoples of Campania would have been unequal. It is entirely possible that Etruria dominated Campania and manipulated them for resources, but it is also likely their relationship was cordial and friendly. Unfortunately, no one can tell.

The orientation period was characterized by inner city violence and discord. The development of a strong Etruscan culture was not indicative of peace or harmony between the Italic peoples. Histories recorded by the Romans demonstrate that it was not uncommon for influential leaders to set out and bring their followers with them in the search for power and conquest. These leaders could establish their own settlements with these people and add more complexity to the political landscape of the Italian Peninsula. It's possible such discord allowed the Etruscans to become powerful, but such power could not last. There was simply too much competition in the Mediterranean, not only between the Italic peoples but also with the Greeks, the civilizations of the Levant and Anatolia, and the societies rising in North Africa.

A major blow to the Etruscans came following a war between the Persians and the Phoenician Greeks. When the Persians attacked the Phoenician Greeks and drove them from some of their colonies, the Greeks turned to the Mediterranean to find new locations for settlements. One of the islands they set their eyes upon was Corsica. Corsica was of strategic importance to the Etruscans, and Etruria was not pleased to see the island to the west populated by Greeks. To eliminate the new threat, the Etruscans formed an alliance with the Carthaginians in North Africa to expel the Phoenicians. The Carthaginians were also displeased with the loss of Corsica and were struggling with an increased population of Greek refugees. Together, Etruria and Carthage threw the Greeks out of Corsica around 540 BCE, and Carthage took the island.

The Phoenicians, having been displaced once more, settled in Calabria instead. And despite their victory, the Etruscans suffered greatly. After stoning its Phoenician prisoners to death, Etruria was struck by a calamity: plague. A devout religious society, the Etruscans turned to an oracle to beg for a solution to the problem and were informed that their treatment of the Phoenicians was the cause. To avoid such an incident again, the Etruscans were more lenient in their foreign policy from the late 6th century BCE

---

onwards but continued to aggressively protect their borders and colonies outside of the Italian Peninsula. This allowed them to secure Sardinia, the Lipari Islands, and sections of Corsica.

This jealous defense of its borders resulted in Etruria attacking Cumae, a Greek settlement in Campania. Historians are unsure of the exact reasons why Cumae fell into Etruscan sights, but Etruria moved on the city and attempted to claim it through conquest. Later ancient sources exaggerate the size of the Etruscan army and pose numerous reasons for the potential attack. One was that Etruria simply wanted to expand. Another was that Etruria feared a strong Rome and wanted to snuff out pro-Roman sentiments in Cumae. Neither picture is likely the whole truth, but no matter what happened to cause it, the Etruscan attack upon Cumae failed anyway.

Around 474 BCE, the Etruscans attacked Cumae again, this time bringing with them a contingent of Carthaginians. Unable to withstand both armies, Cumae appealed to the nearby tyrant of Syracuse. This tyrant sent his fleet to help protect the city, resulting in a massive victory for Cumae and an embarrassing defeat for the Etruscans. The Etruscan force that attacked Cumae most likely consisted of southern coastal cities. Although future Greek and Roman writers described the victory as being humiliating and a deathblow for the Etruscans in Campania, this is most likely not the case again. If anything, the failure to take Cumae was probably just one step of many leading to the decline of Etruria's influence in Campania.

The most probable explanation for the decline of Etruscan influence in the region was the arrival of the warlike Oscan-speaking Samnites. This group came down from the central Apennines and were one of the Italic tribes described earlier. They rose to prominence through the 430s and 420s BCE, having dominated Capua and then setting their sights on Cumae. The cities were taken in 423 and 421 BCE, respectively. The Oscan-speaking Samnites brought, along with their armies, waves of settlers whose culture and language became dominant in Campania throughout the 5th century BCE, completely displacing and then annihilating Etruscan culture there. Archaeologists can trace the loss of Etruscan burial practices, political titles, and naming conventions as they became replaced by Oscan traditions. Even the figure of the warrior became more prominent, kicking out the Etruscan scholar and artist as the ideal.

As the 4th century BCE began, the Etruscans were poised to receive another kick to the backside. This time, it was from a boot worn by Gaul invaders. The Gauls were a group of Celtic peoples in west-central Europe during the Iron Age. Many people remember them because of their ongoing conflict with the Romans. Roman historian Livy offers several explanations as to why the Gauls decided to move south, and the Etruscans are blamed in both of them. In the first story, a foolish Etruscan named Arruns of Clusium went north in shame after his young ward raped his wife and exposed her in public. While there, he demonstrated the glory of the plains of Etruria and enticed the Gauls south as settlers and workers. Once they arrived, Arruns was unable to control them.

Livy himself points out several problems with the first story, notably issues with the timeline of events. If the problem had been caused by a man of Clusium, the Gauls would not have crossed the Alps over two hundred years ago since Clusium had no significance until after the Gauls arrived. Instead, Livy finds the second narrative more believable: The Gauls had been enticed to the south by offers to work as mercenaries. Again, this employment was proposed by the Etruscans, who had been successfully managing a functioning relationship with their barbarian neighbors to the north for several hundred years. A problem developed, however, when travel across the Alps, the mountain range in northern Italy, became easier. The Gauls, who believed in the practice of dispersed settlements, crossed the mountains and started to move down into the southern peninsula, raping and pillaging all the way. The Etruscans were naturally affected, and even Rome was sacked in 387 BCE.

The exact ways in which the Etruscans were affected are murky. There is evidence, especially in the rapid construction of rushed battlements around Etruscans city-states, that the Gauls targeted settlements throughout Etruria as well as Rome. The loss of farmland and other arable lands to the Gauls, seen by the presence of "barbarian" artifacts in former Etruscan territories, indicates that the Etruscans were unable to fully suppress the Gauls. Many of the city-states were forced to come together more often and try to cooperate further. Some historians believe the three leagues of the city-states met more frequently and included more important political figures as well.

A Woodcut Depicting the Gauls' Invasion of Italy
https://commons.wikimedia.org/wiki/File:Brennus_and_Camillus.jpg

With the arrival of the Gauls, the Etruscan death knell had been tolled. Already floundering during the 5th century BCE, the situation would only grow worse for the once proud civilization. By

400 BCE, the Etruscans had lost enough power and influence to be threatened by another dominant neighbor: The Romans. Although the Romans had been sacked by the Gauls, they were on the rise and forming a powerful republic that would expand and one day become an even greater empire. As for the Etruscans, they experienced their golden age during their orientation and managed to spread their culture and society across the Italian Peninsula and even into Greece, as well as adopting elements from these other civilizations. Could the Etruscans have been classified as an empire during this time? Perhaps not, since their power was not centralized and did not rely on military dominance. But they were certainly a cultural tour de force that was a power to be reckoned with. Unfortunately, the Romans would soon see to their assimilation.

Chapter 5 – The Roman Conquest, c. 400-20 BCE

The relationship between the Etruscans and Romans was long and complex, and archaeologists and historians sometimes have difficulty distinguishing between events and determining the accuracy of ancient sources. By the start of the 5th century BCE, the rivalry between the two states had grown more serious as they battled for territory and resources. Although the Romans had incorporated numerous aspects of Etruscan culture into their own, there was no love between the two peoples. Livy, the Roman historian, laid out what he viewed as a complete history between the Etruscans and the Romans, starting with the original foundation myth of Rome.

The Early Roman Version of Events

In this myth, King Mezentius led the Etruscans to ally with King Turnus of the Rutili, one of the Italic city-states. Together, they attacked the exiled Trojans and the Latin peoples. Readers of this volume will note that the Etruscans themselves were Italics, so already the history written by Rome possesses some errors since they claimed the Etruscans were an outside force recruited by the Italic Rutili to fight against the Romans. In the ensuing war, the

Latins and Trojans won while Turnus perished in battle. The Etruscans, Trojans, and Latins agreed to a peace and determined that the Tiber River would be the main boundary between the groups.

Around the 8ᵗʰ century BCE, the first king of Rome emerged on the scene. This man, Romulus, was powerful enough to draw the ire and envy of the Etruscans, who viewed Rome as a growing threat in the peninsula. One of the Etruscan city-states, Fidenae, started to decimate Roman territory and the surrounding farmlands which led Romulus to march upon the Etrurian main city of Fidenae and establish a camp roughly a mile from its borders. Romulus ordered part of his troops to set up an ambush in the wilderness outside of the city while he marched up to the gates with the rest. He provoked the Etruscans to exit and ambushed them when they gave chase to the Romans. Romulus then took the town.

At this point, the citizens of the Etruscan city-state of Veii concerned themselves with their consanguine brothers and sisters in Fidenae and decided to launch an incursion into Roman territory. The Veientes were successful in marauding the countryside and brought back their bounty to Veii. Romulus, however, followed the Etruscans with his own army and battled the Veientes outside of the city walls. The Romans won yet again, and the Veientes walled themselves back in Veii. After the Romans destroyed much of the surrounding countryside, Veii sued for peace. They received one hundred years of civil relations but needed to give up a portion of their territory to the Romans in exchange. Fidenae, meanwhile, supposedly became a colony.[139]

In the 7ᵗʰ century BCE, several of the Etruscan city-states and Rome once again went to war. Rome was now on its third king, Tullus Hostilius. Fidenae and Veii broke the treaties they signed with Rome by building military fortifications and encroaching upon Roman territory once more. The Romans defeated the two city-

---

[139] Livy, *Ab urbe condita.*

states once again and took even more territory. Once again, in the 6th century BCE, Rome attacked Veii and the rest of the Etruscan settlements. Livy wrote little of this war except stating that the Roman king at the time, Servius Tullius, routed an impressive Etruscan army that solidified his position as ruler. More peace treaties were developed, and Servius' successor, Tarquinius Superbus, would renew the documents later on.

In 509 BCE, the Roman aristocrats overthrew the Roman monarchy and replaced it with the Roman Republic. The republic elected the first consuls, and the deposed Roman king, Tarquinius, rallied the support of the Etruscan city-states of Veii and Tarquinii. The king, who was himself descended from the Etruscans, led the forces of both settlements into battle. The Etruscans once again lost to Rome at the Battle of Silva Arsia. Later that same year, the new Roman Republic would attack Veii once more in a fresh dispute. The exact reasons for the attack are unknown. This dispute ended several months later, but the unsatisfactory conclusion would spawn further conflicts less than half a year later.

In 508 BCE, yet another conflict emerged, this time between the Etruscan city of Clusium and Rome. The deposed Roman king had gone to Clusium to drum up support, and the people of the city-state agreed to help him. They marched upon Rome as one of the most powerful Etruscan armies to have ever existed. Fearing that the population of Rome would defect and join the enemy, the Roman Senate implemented a number of short-term decrees including giving the lower classes tax-exempt status and vouchers for expensive salt. When the Clusium force attacked Rome, the populace had been turned against the invaders, and Rome was once again victorious. The king of Clusium, Lars Porsena, attempted to establish a blockade and siege the city next. However, the Romans trapped the Clusian forces setting up the blockade's perimeter, thus ending the measure. Despite this, the siege continued as planned. During the ensuing conflict, a young Roman attempted to assassinate Porsena but was captured. According to

Livy, he impressed Porsena by announcing his name and sticking his hand in a fire to prove his loyalty to Rome, and Porsena let him go free for his bravery. At some point, the Romans and Etruscans agreed on a truce.

Around 507 BCE, Porsena sent ambassadors to the Roman Senate to ask for Tarquinius to be restored to the throne. When they refused, Porsena asked Tarquinius to leave Clusium for good. He then returned captured hostages to Rome in exchange for some of the territory that had been taken from the city-state of Veii. The Roman authors who discuss the siege and the war half-believed the events were true but were also convinced that other sections were entirely mythical, especially the story of Porsena and the assassin who stuck his hand in the fire.

The next conflicts between the Etruscans and Rome occurred between 505 and 476 BCE. The primary Etruscan aggressor was the city-state of Veii, one of the most powerful Etruscan settlements. In both cases, the Etruscans allied themselves with several of the Italic peoples who were also attempting to resist Roman expansion. Due to their rapidly advancing military technology, growing population, and aggressive culture, the Romans won both the wars against the Etruscans and Sabines in 505 and 504 BCE as well as the Fabian War between 483 BCE and 476 BCE. According to Livy, the Etruscans joined so many conflicts to try and break Rome's growing power and frequently took advantage of Roman political tension. This resulted in city-states like Veii often joining random groups in the hopes of gaining even a modicum of advantage over their neighbors. Unfortunately, it never panned out.

Between 475 and 474 BCE, Veii participated in the Veii-Sabine Alliance. This was yet another conflict when the Veientes joined together with the Sabines and recommenced hostilities against Rome. Veii lost once again and lost even more territory. The only other actions recorded between the various factions are battles between Rome and the Etruscan city-states of Sutrium, Nepete, and Tarquinii between 389 BCE and 386 BCE.

Etruscan-Roman Relations Between 400 and 360 BCE

In 390 BCE, the Gauls once again attacked the Romans, having first sacked the city of Rome in the 6th century BCE, and managed to defeat them at the Battle of the Allia. The Gauls sacked Rome, razing the city, capturing slaves, and making off with their gold, food, and other resources kept in the local storehouses. In 389 BCE, the Etruscans tried to take advantage of Rome's temporary weakness. Two of their city-states raised armies, and the Etruscans became allied with two peoples called the Volsci and the Aequi. They all marched upon Rome, causing the city to appoint Marcus Furius Camillus dictator. This dictator marched upon the other Italics first before then turning his attention to the Etruscans.

The Etruscans crumbled under the Roman forces despite having managed to conquer the main city of Sutrium, one of Rome's allies. In a series of three separate wars all held back to back, the Etruscans once again lost much of their territory and their foothold in northern Italy. Rome took many of the Etruscans as hostages and auctioned them off as slaves until the Etruscans paid reparations to the Romans for damages done during the war.

In 387 BCE, the Etruscans once again started to gather together military forces to try to stop the Roman expansion. The Romans, catching wind of this information, called upon their allies and rebuffed the Etruscans when they tried to attack several border settlements and forces. A myriad of Etruscan cities did their best, but the losses were too great. Several of the cities in southern Etruria were lost, and Rome gained new garrisons and started to reinforce their borders, preparing for conflict with Tarquinii, one of the last powerful Etruscan cities in the region.

Etruscan-Roman Relations between 360 and 350 BCE

In 358 BCE, Tarquinii sent out a force to raid Roman border settlements and bring back resources such as food, gold, and slaves. A man named Consul Gaius Fabius Ambustus was assigned to handle the situation but was defeated, resulting in the sacrifices of 307 prisoners of war held by the Etruscans. The next year, Rome decided to declare war with another Etruscan city-state, and that settlement allied with Tarquinii to attempt to stop the raiding and pillaging. The war went back and forth for five or six years, resulting in heightened tensions.

In 352 BCE, the Romans believed the Etruscan League, that alliance of twelve major city-states, was plotting severe action against the city of Rome. In response, the Roman Republic decided to appoint a dictator. In Roman political culture, the politicians could choose to elect a ruler who held ultimate power for one year in a time of crisis. Fearing for the safety of their city, the republic nominated Gaius Julius Iulus as a dictator. After two years of battling, the territories of Rome, Tarquinii, and another Etruscan city-state whose name is unknown were completely ravaged. Eventually, the Etruscans asked for a truce. The Romans, also weary of combat, decided to give each of the Etruscan city-states a forty-year period of peace to recover from the damage.

Since many of these events were recorded by Roman historians, modern scholars dispute the authenticity of several facts. First, the Romans frequently write of Etruscan aggression as the cause of the wars, but Rome itself was known for having an aggressive policy of expansion. It is also difficult to determine the accuracy of Roman accounts since their historians frequently twisted facts to make themselves look better, as have most civilizations in history. Some other problems with their explanations also arise, especially related to the casualties from the conflicts. Some Romans claim over 8,000 Etruscans were murdered in a single battle due to their incompetence, but the Etruscan population in the city-states would not have been large enough to support such an army.

Either way, the Etruscan-Roman relationship between 360 BCE and 350 BCE was not good. Frequent warfare was common, and the Etruscans were always on the losing side of these interactions. Much of the Etruscan territory was gone and now in Roman hands, including much of their agricultural land and trade routes. It didn't help that the population was also declining from deaths in battle and starvation.

The Battles of Lake Vadimo

The Battles of Lake Vadimo, located along the Tiber River, were the conflicts that ultimately broke Etruscan resistance against Rome. The first took place in 310 BCE and would be the largest battle in history between the two civilizations. It began when the Etruscans attacked the Roman city of Sutrium and attempted to wreak havoc once more in the surrounding countryside. In response, the Romans met the Etruscan troops and tried to break the siege. Despite some victories, the Romans were initially unsuccessful. A consul named Quintus Fabius Maximus Rullianus then started to raid the Etruscan heartland, causing destruction and devastation. As a result, the Etruscan city-states sued for peace once more.

The three Etruscan city-states of Arretium, Cortona, and Perusa were given a treaty guaranteeing a thirty-year truce, but many of the remaining city-states remained hostile and refused to give in to Roman pressure. They worked together to secure the forces necessary for a massive army and met the Romans at Lake Vadimo. This narrow battlefield made it difficult for the Romans to fight in their usual style of several spaced-out battalions, which gave the Etruscans a brief advantage. Both sides exhausted their resources and forces, sending many soldiers to die. After a long and bloody struggle, the Etruscans were forced to flee from the Roman reserve cavalry. An ensuing campaign by the Romans over the next year resulted in all of the Etruscan cities suing for peace. The Etruscans lost many of their finest troops, territories, and resources in the first Battle of Lake Vadimo, and they would never again return to their previous glory. One could argue their fate against the Romans would be sealed on the exact same battlefield in 283 BCE when the second Battle of Lake Vadimo was fought.

During the second Battle of Lake Vadimo, the Etruscans allied with several Gallic tribes called the Boii and the Senones. They marched against Rome and were met by a massive force headed by Consul Publius Cornelius Dolabella. The Romans won, and the Etruscans were forced to acquiesce many of their lands and resources as punishment. Unfortunately for contemporary students, little information remains about this battle. Livy, who covered so much of Roman history, wrote numerous books, but the books containing the story of the second Battle of Lake Vadimo have not been discovered and are believed to have been destroyed. Historians need to content themselves with a text by Polybius, who leaves out many details and is more inclined to exaggeration and the incorporation of mythology. Polybius' version of events is as follows.

The second Battle of Lake Vadimo started when a group of Gauls besieged the city of Arretium. The Romans sent aid and were defeated, resulting in the death of their leader. This occurred around 283 BCE. When the Romans sent envoys to negotiate the return of hostages from the Gauls, the envoys were summarily slaughtered. In retaliation, the Romans marched on Gaul and were met by a tribe called the Senones. The Senones, who inhabited a section of northern Italy, were vanquished and sent packing which allowed Rome to found the colony of Senigallia.[140]

According to Polybius, "hereupon the Boii, seeing the Senones expelled from their territory, and fearing a like fate for themselves and their own land, implored the aid of the Etruscans and marched out in full force."[141] Together, the Senones and the Etruscans marched upon Rome but were cut down by the Roman army, at which point they sent an embassy to sue for peace. The story is then continued by another historian, the Greek Appian of Alexandria. He possessed Roman citizenship and published

---

[140] Polybius, *The Histories*, 2.19.7-13.

[141] Polybius, *The Histories*, 2.20.1-5.

several volumes about the history of the Romans as well as of several of the civilizations throughout the Mediterranean.

Appian discussed the wars between the Romans and the Gauls in the Italian Peninsula as well as Julius Caesar's conquest of Gallic territory that took place in a series of three wars. Unfortunately, much of Appian's writing only survived in fragments that do not explain much about the series of events between the Romans and the Gauls. In his account of the second Battle of Lake Vadimo in 283 BCE, he reiterates Polybius' account stating the Etruscans and the Gauls allied themselves with one another to attempt to overpower the Romans. While his works do not mention the exact location of the battle or the final outcome, he does state that Roman ambassadors eventually met with the Etruscans for peace. In the accounts of Polybius and Appian, it's clear that the Etruscans failed in their second attempt to halt the expansion of the Romans. Multiple city-states lost their territory and arable farmland as well as independent access to trade routes with other civilizations such as Greece.

After the second Battle of Lake Vadimo, the Etruscan resistance was almost at an end. Most of the city-states were no longer independent and were forced to kowtow to the Romans through the payment of tribute and demilitarization. Eventually, only two cities maintained their independence by the end of the 280s BCE: Vulci and Velusna.

The Conclusion of the Wars

The second to last holdout for the Etruscans was the city-state of Vulci. Vulci was one of the wealthiest settlements and rested in the northern end of Etruria. It was a coastal city with strong trade networks that allowed it to fill its coffers with money, treasures, and artwork from numerous other states, including Greece and Carthage. They were one of the twelve members of the Etruscan League. It would manage to hold out until 280 BCE when it was sieged and taken by Tiberius Coruncanius. The final holdout was

Velusna, a city-state about which little is known. Historians debate its exact position in the peninsula, but most agree it was likely in the region of Umbria. Following centuries of warfare and conquest, the Etruscans finally met their defeat in 264 BCE when the final resistance in Velusna was crushed.

The Etruscans as a people and as a culture were not finished so quickly, but any political autonomy was lost. The Etruscans were now one of many Italic peoples under the dominion of Rome, which was ever expanding its sphere of influence and territory. While under Roman influence, the Etruscans were forced to pay taxes to first the republic and then the empire following the Social War and the fall of the republic. Before these events, some Etruscans managed to obtain Roman citizenship for themselves and even obtained some level of power, but there was little Etruria could do independently. This situation continued in such a matter for centuries until it decided to fight back through the Social War.

The Social War lasted from roughly 91 BCE to 89 BCE and was the rebellion of the various Italic peoples subjugated by the Romans. Historians are baffled about what the goals of the Italics were during the Social War. Some argue that they wanted Roman citizenship which would have entitled their aristocrats to participate in government and the soldiers and others to potentially receive other land grants. Others believed they wanted Rome to stop giving huge swathes of territory to native-born Romans which was depriving the Italics of their own lands and livelihoods. Still others think the Italics wanted full independence, which was not going to happen. Most agree that citizenship was the most likely goal since it would solve the second problem and also ensure the Italics could receive a slice of Roman wealth as the republic continued to expand.[142]

---

[142] Christopher J. Dart, *The Social War, 91 to 88 BCE: A History of the Italian Insurgency against the Roman Republic*, London: Routledge Publishers, Inc., 2014.

While the Social War had some initial successes and sections of the Italics were granted citizenship, the Italics ultimately came out on the wrong side of the conflict. They won roughly fifty years of peace and some modicum of autonomy, but they were constantly pulled into the intricacies of Roman politics. Etruria, despite having some victories, would lose the culture it once possessed as it was assimilated further and further into Rome. Rome, for its part, would preserve some aspects of the Etruscan culture and spread them throughout its territory, but the 1st century BCE was the time that Etruria's final bell tolled.

Chapter 6 – Mythology and Religion

Etruscan religion comprised a conglomeration of the religious practices and beliefs of the preceding Iron Age Villanovan culture and the nearby Greeks and Phoenicians. Etruscan religion would additionally share similarities with Roman mythology which developed concurrently and also heavily borrowed from the ancient Greeks. Over time, as the Etruscans found themselves assimilated into the Roman Republic during the late 4th century BCE, their mythology would become part of classical Roman culture since the Romans tended to absorb the local customs and deities of the peoples they conquered.

The Etruscans possessed a system of belief called immanent polytheism. Polytheism refers to the practice of believing in and worshiping more than one god while the immanent part means that visible phenomena were thought to be the manifestations of divine power. For examples, thunder and lightning was the domain of one god and caused directly by that deity while the growth of crops could be the work of another. The Etruscans further believed their deities could influence human affairs and people and could be persuaded, angered, dissuaded, or pleased by the actions of mortals. This ability to potentially influence the gods explains many of the Etruscan rituals and superstitions, as pleasing the deities to convince them to bestow favor was a central part of their culture. After all, an angered deity could cause war, strife, famine, disease, and death.

As usual, the Romans had something to say about the Etruscan religion. Livy described them as the most religious of men, a culture and society based around steadfast worship and theocratic control with a series of learned priests responsible for the well-being of the populace. Others, such as Seneca the Younger—a Roman Stoic philosopher—wrote at one point that the difference between the Romans and the Etruscans was simple:

Whereas we believe lightning to be released as a result of the collision of clouds, they believe that the clouds collide so as to release lightning: for as they attribute all to deity, they are led to believe not that things have a meaning insofar as they occur, but rather that they occur because they must have a meaning.[143]

Here, Seneca the Younger references a crucial part of Etruscan mythology, which was that everything happened for a reason. Nothing in the natural world was meaningless, and all was the work of the gods. When a storm arrived, it possessed a meaning that needed to be interpreted by the proper authorities. If the crops did not grow, then a deity was displeased and needed to be pacified through rituals. Furthermore, such logic did not extend only to major events but even the minutiae of day-to-day life. The wind blows with a purpose and not just because a light breeze came off of the Mediterranean Sea.

However, Roman interpretations of Etruscan religion need to be swallowed with a grain of salt because the two cultures possessed similar yet disparate systems of worship and overarching tenets and beliefs. According to Roman sources, the Etruscans were plagued by a gloomy and morose fatalism due to their belief in a powerful,

---

[143] Seneca the Younger. "II.32.2". *Naturales Quaestiones.*

unwavering pantheon whose actions could not be stopped. Submission was necessary because the decisions of the deities were irrevocable and irreversible. The problem is that this interpretation does not match with the evidence discovered by archaeological sources which seem to indicate there was less a system of fatalism and more of a realist ideology that understood death was inevitable and focused on one's perceived well-being in the afterlife. This focus often appeared in burial and funerary practices and art.

Deities, Spirits, and Mythological Creatures – Organization

Etruscan art indicates the presence of three separate layers of deities that possessed varying levels of power and importance. The layer of lesser gods was those of indigenous origin that might have been adopted and adapted from the Villanovans and other preceding Italics. Others were most likely divinities related to small settlements and ancestral lines that were incorporated into larger Etruscan society. Some of the known deities in this layer were Catha and Usil, the two sun gods; Tiyr, the moon; Selvans, some sort of god related to civil affairs; Turan, the goddess of love; Laran, the god of war; Leinth, the goddess of death; and the unidentified Maris, Thalna, Turms, and Fufluns. Fufluns bears some unknown connection to the city of Populonia and the Roman population, but historians have been unable to identify specific linguistic characteristics that would provide more information. Some of the many deities were believed to be essential to the divination of signs or responsible for controlling specific regions of the sky. The sky itself was divided into sixteen separate sections each controlled by a separate god or goddess.[144]

The next layer consisted of higher deities that scholars believe were adopted from the major gods of the Indo-European cultural system. These deities can be found in multiple societies with an Indo-European cultural base with some slight name changes due to linguistics. Some examples of other subscribers to this Indo-

---

[144] Macnamara, *Everyday Life of the Etruscans*, p. 154.

European mythology were the Hittites, Greeks, Slavics, Baltics, and Celtics. Peoples like the Romans are considered proto Indo-European, part of the societies and cultures that adopted and then changed traditional Indo-European mythology.

As adherents to some elements of Indo-European mythology, the Etruscans possessed a layer of deities that consisted of the standard pantheon. Among the deities in this group are Tin or Tinia, the sky; Uni or Juno, the wife of the sky and mother goddess; and Cel, the earth goddess. These were the heavenly deities and the founders of the known universe and humankind. The chief god was always the god of the sky while the goddess of dawn was typically his wife with some variation. The role of the earth goddess varied based on culture, but she usually was either the mother or wife of the sky. In some cases, she was his child. The Etruscans did not adhere to Indo-European mythology as closely as some others. To them, Tinia was the god of lightning associated with the sky. Students of classical Greek and Roman mythology might draw some comparisons to Zeus here.

Finally, the Etruscans adopted several of the Greek gods during the Etruscan orientation period discussed earlier. Such gods were shuffled into each of the Etruscan religious layers, but the most important wound up in the third. Among these were Aritimi (Artemis or Diana), Menrva (Minerva or Athena), and Pacha (Bacchus or Dionysius). Over the centuries, the Etruscans would begin to mix the three distinct layers of deities, resulting in the all-powerful trinity of Tinia, Uni, and Menrva. These chief gods were the subjects of much religious art, especially terracotta forms and paintings.

In the Etruscan language, a god or goddess was called an *ais*, which would later morph into *eis*. The plural form was *aisar*. Each domain or home of a deity was known as a *fanu* or *luth*, a sacred place with religious meaning. Many of the abodes of the deities were actually graves or temples where the faithful could go to worship. At these abodes, the faithful were required to make a *fler*, or multiple *flerchva*, offerings. Offerings tended to be consumable goods such as roasted meat, the sacrifice of an animal, wine, or sometimes olive oil. Specific offerings could be given for favors or requests, and some rituals were conducted at specific times of the year to guarantee certain events like a successful harvest or safe passage for a ship.

The early Etruscans did not assign physical forms to their deities and avoided anthropomorphizing their existence. The gods and goddesses did not seem to exist in any human form but were rather natural phenomena such as bolts of lightning and the sound of thunder in the sky. The complex relationships and emotions many polytheistic civilizations associated with their deities did not seem to develop until much later, potentially during the Etruscan orientation. Archaeologists and historians believe the Greeks had a heavy hand in instigating such changes. From the Greeks, the Etruscans took the practices of anthropomorphism as well as sacrificial paraphernalia and artistic representation, resulting in more distinct, relatable deities and a greater cult of sacrifice at religious sites.[145]

There was a category of spirits that the average Etruscan would be familiar with. These were the *man* or *mani*, the souls of deceased ancestors that remained around their *mun* or *muni*, the tombs in which they were buried. Contemporary audiences might consider them similar to ghosts that haunt their place of rest. Around the 5th century BCE, iconography in tombs and necropoli began to show the souls of the deceased making their way to the underworld somewhere underneath the world that living humans inhabited.[146] The best example in Etruscan art can be found in the Francois Tomb in Vulci. These spirits are referred to as *hinthial*, or the "one who is underneath."

---

[145] Smith, *The Etruscans*, p. 88.

[146] Krauskopf, I. 2006. "The Grave and Beyond." *The Religion of the Etruscans*. edited by N. de Grummond and E. Simon. Austin: University of Texas Press. p. 73-75.

Divination

The Etruscans stood out amongst their neighbors due to their emphasis on divination, the practice of reading signs from the gods to understand the past, present, and future. Divination could be carried out on multiple scales, with some skilled figures being able to divine the will of the deities for the future of a city-state while others stuck more to the personal matters of individuals. In Etruscan religion, there were two famous seers who had shown them their religion and the practice of divination. These were Tages, a young, childlike figure who had sprung up from a tilled field with prescience, and Vegoia, a woman of whom little is known.[147]

Tages was a sage who took the form of a young boy that appeared in a freshly plowed field. He taught the Etruscans about the art of divination, and some Etruscan sources state he might have been the grandson of Jupiter. Cicero describes the myth of his appearance thusly:

They tell us that one day as the land was being ploughed in the territory of Tarquinii, and a deeper furrow than usual was made, suddenly Tages sprang out of it and addressed the ploughman. Tages, as it is recorded in the works of the Etrurians (Libri Etruscorum), possessed the visage of a child, but the prudence of a sage. When the ploughman was surprised at seeing him, and in his astonishment made a great outcry, a number of people assembled around him, and before long all the Etrurians came together at the spot. Tages then discoursed in the presence of an immense crowd, who noted his speech and committed it to writing. The information they derived from this Tages was the foundation of the science of the soothsayers (haruspicinae disciplina), and was subsequently improved by the accession of many new facts, all of which confirmed the same principles. We received this record from them. This record is preserved in their sacred books, and from it

---

[147] Macnamara, *Everyday Life of the Etruscans*, p. 153.

the augurial discipline is deduced.[148]

This version of the legend of Tages' appearance seems to have been based upon Etruscan folktales and religious documents, lending it some credibility. Over time, the supposed teachings of Tages would become one of the most significant elements of Etruscan society, controlling every action that individuals performed.

Divination, after all, was an essential part of daily life. The Etruscan society was built on a foundation of religious beliefs with the deities and their portents revealing proper action in the present and potential outcomes for the future. No major decision was taken without the appropriate authority figures consulting a seer or someone capable of divining the will of the gods. This led to a powerful class of priests and other religious servants.

There appears to have been some form of religious scripture, but the exact rhetoric is unknown. Roman writers such as Valerius Maximus and Marcus Tullius Cicero refer to a corpus called the *Etrusca Disciplina*, a supposed scripture that revealed the burning questions of Etruscan religion. According to sources, the corpus did not focus on prophecies or the traditional stories and lessons one might associate with scripture. Instead, it concentrated on determining the will of the gods and one major question: If the gods created the universe and humanity and had a plan for their creation, why was there not a clear system of communication to ensure that plan was carried out correctly? The Etruscans accepted their deities' inscrutable motives and wills and did not attempt to form doctrines to explain the intention of the gods. Instead, they developed their elaborate system of interpretation. To ignore the signs was to embrace heresy and death, and it was important to interpret the will of the gods even if the portents were unpleasant. There exists some speculation that the Etruscans stopped fighting Rome because the portents revealed they were going to be

---

[148] Marcus Tullius Cicero, "II.50-51," *On Divination.*

assimilated anyways, but the sources for this idea are Roman and contain inherent bias.

Some remnants of this system have been found and adapted into the summaries of Massimo Pallottino, who committed to text a short version of multiple scriptures related to divination. The first was the *Libri Haruspicini* which explained the theories and rules behind divination from animal entrails. The next was the *Libri Fulgurales*, which described how to divine lightning strikes in the many domains of the sky. Third was the *Libri Rituales*, a document of which little seems to have survived. Next came the *Libri Fatales*, a document that detailed the correct method of founding and building cities and shrines, draining fields for cultivation, developing laws and ordinances within Etruscan territory, and the proper way to measure space and divide time into understandable units.[149] The fifth text was the *Libri Acherontici* or the text explaining the afterlife and the proper form of burials. Finally, there was the *Libri Ostentaria* which explained how to interpret prodigies. The revelations of Tages can be found in the *Libri Tagetici* as well as the *Libri Haruspicini* and the *Acherontici*. The revelations of the prophetess Vegoia exist in the *Libri Vegoici*, the *Libri Fulgurales*, and the *Libri Rituales*.[150]

A major corpus for the Etruscans was the *Etrusca Disciplina* which was a set of rules that explained the proper conduct for all forms of divination. This broad set of guidelines has been called a religious and political constitution for the Etruscans. While it does not dictate laws or ethics, it does tell the proper way for humans to ask questions and receive answers for the deities above.

Although some neighbors of the Etruscans respected them for

---

[149] This might sound extreme, but remember that numerous civilizations throughout time looked to religion to create an understandable calendar, and that the modern Gregorian calendar used throughout the Western world is based in the Christian religion with the first year being the year after Christ's crucifixion.

[150] Pallottino, M. (1975). Ridgway, David, ed. *The Etruscans*. Translated by Cremina, J (Revised and Enlarged ed.). Bloomington & London: Indiana University Press, p. 154.

their devotion, others mocked their faith and almost crippling reliance on divination. The Romans, in particular, seemed especially scornful as their religious structure was more practical and political in nature, as one could see with their process of deifying emperors in later centuries. One particular mockery came from the famous Cicero who wrote:

For a hasty acceptance of an erroneous opinion is discreditable in any case, and especially so in an inquiry as to how much weight should be given to auspices, to sacred rites, and to religious observances; for we run the risk of committing a crime against the gods if we disregard them, or of becoming involved in old women's superstition if we approve them.

He then quipped, regarding divination from the singing of frogs: "Who could suppose that frogs had this foresight? And yet they do have by nature some faculty of premonition, clear enough of itself, but too dark for human comprehension."[151]

The Priesthood

Members of the priesthood were responsible for all divinatory inquiries as well as many of the rituals and rites related to temples. The Romans possessed multiple words for such figures, including the haruspices or sacerdotes. The Etruscans used several different terms in various descriptions, including *capen, maru, eisnev,* and *hatrencu,* which all are terms for a priestess. There was also a separate category of religious art associated with the haruspices called haruspicy. Most modern sources use the Roman term to be concise. The great city of Tarquinii was rumored to have had a college of no less than sixty haruspices, both men and women.[152] In later centuries, women would be pushed out of religious roles as their status in Etruscan society grew inferior to their male counterparts. Members of the priesthood were almost always elites

---

[151] De Divinatione, section 4.

[152] Pallottino, *The Etruscans*, p. 154.

who had been trained in the art of divination from a young age.

Despite the existence of a specific priest class, every individual in society was expected to possess certain religious responsibilities as expressed in an *alumnathe* or *slecaches,* meaning sacred society. All public events needed to be conducted with a *netsyis* or *nethsra,* a male or female individual responsible for reading the bumps on the liver of a sacrificed sheep. A magistrate called the *cechase* would also be chosen to care for sacred objects. Among the Etruscans, the liver was the most significant internal organ, a trait similar to the Babylonians, another culture of Indo-European mythology. One of the most puzzling artifacts of Etruscan heritage is a bronze model of a liver. Because scholars cannot read what is written upon it, no one knows the true purpose of the artifact. Some speculate that it is a medical model, while others think that the Etruscans, like the Babylonians, might have considered the liver the center of the body and assigned it more significance than the other organs.

The Liver of Piacenza
Piacenza_Bronzeleber.jpg: Lokilech, CC BY-SA 2.5

The Afterlife and Burial Traditions

The afterlife was central to Etruscan belief and was a conglomeration of numerous influences from the surrounding area. There were several broadly Mediterranean beliefs, including the idea that a soul's prosperity in the afterlife was heavily related to the treatment of a deceased individual's remains. Etruscan tombs were similar to domestic structures but were made from more durable materials such as stone or were cut into sturdy rock faces. Such tombs tended to be spacious and could hold multiple burials but were often reserved for the elites and their families who could afford such treatment. Paintings were added to the walls and often depicted lavish scenes and potentially the loved one in question. Grave furniture and other funerary goods were added to the tombs, and the Etruscans seemed to believe that the deceased were able to take their possessions with them into the afterlife. For the wealthy, the actual sarcophagus of an individual was designed to look like the deceased in the prime of their life and might also bear the image of their spouse. In other cases, the deceased might be placed on a stone bench that bore a headrest related to their gender. Not everyone could afford a sarcophagus, and many poor individuals were sent to the afterlife through a mixture of inhumation and cremation. These ashes and bones were placed in an urn that represented the deceased, and the urn was often buried or kept in a communal tomb for safekeeping.

Cut Stone Etruscan Tomb

The early Etruscans practiced cremation more than inhumation, but inhumation itself became popular during the Etruscan orientation. Many burial practices were also based on local practices and the environment. The northern territories, for example, favored cremation long after the south embraced inhumation. Ashes and bones were stored in handmade pottery urns and sometimes metal for wealthier individuals. Depending on a person's status, they might also have a carved or alabaster urn such as the king found in Volterra to the north. For the elite, it was not uncommon for ashes and bones to be placed in a full-sized sarcophagus. All deceased individuals were put in tombs, and none were buried or left exposed as this could mean difficulty in reaching the afterlife.

Etruscan Burial Urns Shaped Like Huts
https://commons.wikimedia.org/wiki/File:Maquettes_of_houses_from_c_1000_BC.jpg

While the early Etruscans believed that the spirits of the deceased remained around their tombs, the religion developed so that it was believed there was a transmigration to a world beyond for the soul. The afterlife was modeled after Hades, the Greek afterlife rather than the deity of the underworld. The Etruscan underworld was controlled by the goddess of death, Aita. Charun guided the dead to the afterlife and was a strange blue figure who wielded a hammer and was imposing to all who saw him. The Etruscans populated their afterlife with famous Greek heroes, implying some kinship with the civilization.

The interior of tombs resembled a household which provides information about what domestic architecture might have looked like. Tombs tended to have gabled roofs to distinguish them from other buildings and possessed many rooms connected by doorframes and windows. There were no actual doors in the tombs, at least based on surviving evidence. There were porches and columns, separate dining rooms and bedrooms off of the burial chamber to replicate a house, and even carvings designed to look like kitchen implements and household tools. The entire effect was decidedly domestic. The heads of carved stone beds, along with some of the sarcophagi that featured heads, were shaped like semi-circles for men and triangles for women.

Chapter 7 – Art and Music

Artifacts that qualify as Etruscan were made between the 9th and 2nd centuries BCE. Around 600 BCE, Greek techniques and motifs began to influence the work of Etruscan painters, potters, and metalsmiths. Despite the influx of new methods, the Etruscans maintained several characteristics distinct to the society's artistic sensibilities. For example, instead of marble, Etruscan artists preferred to develop figurative sculptures of terracotta, a more accessible substance for statues and sarcophagi. Wall paintings and the creation of frescoes also continued to be popular, and most metalworking was done in bronze and could include engraved gems. Bronze jewelry was often embedded with semiprecious stones and jewels in an example of fine metalwork.[153]

Records indicate that Etruscan bronze sculptures were one of the civilization's most popular exports, with samples crossing the Mediterranean Sea to reach the Middle East and North Africa. Unfortunately, few large samples remain since bronze was a valuable material. Future generations would melt down the statues to recycle the metal for different purposes. Any surviving bronze works tend to come from tombs which were full of grave goods.

---

[153] Boardman, John ed., *The Oxford History of Classical Art*, 1993, OUP, p. 350-351.

Otherwise, sculpture was done from terracotta. Despite possessing large marble quarries, including some with elegant Carrara marble, its development and export would not be done until the time of the Romans. Tombs also held numerous frescoes that depicted feasts, parties, and mythological scenes. Unlike tombs, temples featured many of their decorations on the outside, including painted terracotta antefixes.

The other common form of Etruscan artwork were pieces of bucchero. Bucchero was a form of fine pottery crafted by reducing the amount of oxygen in a kiln while the pottery was fired. Etruscan pottery also distinguishes itself through fine paintings which were adopted from Greek methods. Evidence demonstrates that the Etruscans actually imported more Greek vases than any other group in the Mediterranean. Many vases depicted religious scenes of significance since religion was such a central part of their culture.

A Bucchero Vase
https://commons.wikimedia.org/wiki/File:Bucchero_oinochoe_Terme.jpg

Classification and History

Etruscan artwork and techniques are best understood when classified by time period. This is because the civilization lasted for several centuries and experienced changes over time rather than all at once. The earliest period began when the Etruscans were just starting to differentiate themselves from the Villanovans. Over time, other periods would emerge due to the influence of other ancient cultures like the Greeks, Phoenicians, Assyrians, and even

Egyptians. While the Etruscans adopted certain trends and technologies, they still remained consistent and unique.

The periods of Etruscan art are as follows:

900 – 675 BCE – Early Villanovan: The best examples of Early Villanovan art come from grave goods and funerary art such as urns shaped like homes and huts. Also popular was impasto pottery covered with geometric decorations, some of the easier shapes for the burgeoning potters to create on the surface of wet clay. Impasto pottery itself was rough and not as refined as it would be in future centuries, and many pieces contained chips of mica or stone that were not removed before firing. Bronze metalworking also emerged but was done in small pieces and decorated through molding or adding incised lines in the metal before it hardened. Statuettes could be created but were typically handles or other fittings for larger pieces.

675 – 575 BCE – Oriental or Orientalizing: The Etruscans experienced large-scale foreign trade throughout the Mediterranean during this period. Numerous civilizations such as the Greeks were interested in precious metal ores available in Etruria, and the Etruscans traded away such resources in exchange for unique pieces of foreign art. The Greeks were the most influential trading partner, and the Etruscans experienced an influx of goods as well as the immigration of some artists who remained and produced pieces. Greek-styled painted vases appeared, and lions entered the scene as well and can be found in paintings despite most of the Etruscans never having seen one. Styles from the Egyptians and the Near East developed with the popularity of palmettes and other motifs. Bucchero pottery emerged, and so did the potter's wheel, making production easier and more skilled.

575 – 480 BCE – Archaic: After the Orientalizing period, Greek influence continued to grow since the Etruscans and Greeks attempted to expand their territory into the same regions. The Etruscans prospered, and their economic and cultural successes extended to their artwork. Temples appeared with bright terracotta decorations covered with elaborate designs and paintings. Figurative art also emerged, depicting humans and narratives. Although these also appeared during previous periods, they were basic and not well-formed. Painters created frescoes in tombs, and the stories from Greek mythology were popular subjects. The Etruscans also received the bonus of having numerous Greek refugees thanks to the Persian conquest of Ionia around 546 BCE. This brought many artists and a period of decadence, development, and refinement in art.

480 – 300 BCE – Classical: In many ways, the Classical period was one of decline. The Etruscans reached their peak during the Archaic period, and the volume of art produced was reduced during the 5th century BCE as prosperity shifted to the interior and the society focused more on battling with their enemies such as Rome. Previous trends continued in new pieces without new innovations or technologies. Stone sculpture became more popular than terracotta, while a new style of vase painting called red figure emerged. This particular pottery type focused almost entirely on painting using red pigments, hence the name. Around the same time that red figure emerged, the Etruscans also started to boost their trade with other cultures, although it didn't last long thanks to war and strife. Bronze was exported, and major cities were lost to the Romans, including the powerful Veii.

Red Figure Vase c. 330 BCE

300 –50 BCE – Hellenistic: The Hellenistic period was the downfall of Etruscan civilization and thus of their artwork since the major city-states were absorbed by the Romans during their expansion. Around this time, archaeologists and art historians struggle to distinguish between Etruscan and Roman pieces since the Romans started to imitate Etruscan styles. Most forms of Etruscan object-based art disappeared, although there are some painted vases and tombs emerging during the 2nd century BCE. The Greek influence here is extensive with some sculptures exclusively designing life-sized bronze statues of Greek models.

Throughout each time period, the most ubiquitous forms of artwork were sculpture and pottery with terracotta being the standard medium. Terracotta is a form of earthenware developed by sculpting wet clay and then baking it to harden the material. Vessels and statues would both be made from terracotta, and the pieces would sometimes be large, though most were small enough to fit in tombs with the sarcophagi and funerary furniture. Some examples of terracotta statuary can be seen below in the images of two young men, one with a helmet and one without. The one on the right, although it is difficult to see, is wearing a helmet over his curly hair that ends where his neck would meet the shoulders. These were made between the 3rd and 2nd centuries BCE and show distinct Greek influences.

Metalwork
Metropolitan Museum of Art, CC0, via Wikimedia Commons
https://commons.wikimedia.org/wiki/File:Terracotta_head_of_a_youth_MET_DP119670.jpg

Metalwork
Metropolitan Museum of Art, CC0, via Wikimedia Commons
https://commons.wikimedia.org/wiki/File:Terracotta_head_of_a_youth_MET_DP254648.jpg

While the Etruscans did not work with many metals in art, they were masters of bronze and built or sculpted numerous statues and statuettes throughout the centuries. Many such pieces grace museums throughout Europe and bear distinct resemblances to Greek works. The Romans were especially fond of Etruscan metalwork and both traded for pieces and looted them, sending them back to their home during the Roman-Etruscan Wars. According to Pliny, over 2,000 bronze statues were stolen from the city of Volsinii alone once it was captured and razed.[154] The best surviving example of Etruscan bronze work is the large and complex Monteleone chariot made in roughly 530 BCE.

The Monteleone possesses a strange and vague history rife with controversy. Historians struggle to determine how it finally came to rest in the Metropolitan Museum of Art in New York City; the administrative district of Monteleone attempted to have it returned to Italy but failed. Instead, they received a full-scale replica. The Monteleone chariot is most likely based off of a standard riding model and demonstrates Etruscan building techniques and designs. The original frame is made of wood and covered in hammered bronze sheets for protection. There are inlaid amber and ivory for extra decoration, a depiction of Achilles receiving his armor from

---

[154] Pliny: Historia Naturalis xxxiv.16.

his mother Thetis, and even nine spokes on the wheels. The number of spokes stands out because the Greeks only used four, while other civilizations in the Mediterranean used six or eight. It is clear the Etruscans managed to distinguish themselves from the other cultures around them while also incorporating some techniques, especially when it came to bronze.

The Monteleone Chariot
Metropolitan Museum of Art, CC0, via Wikimedia Commons
https://commons.wikimedia.org/wiki/File:Bronze_chariot_inlaid_with_ivory_MET_DP13 7936.jpg

Besides statues, the Etruscans made a variety of other bronze objects, including casings for mirrors and the settings of jewelry and other adornments. A particular technique was to engrave lines into pieces and to then fill them with a liquid white material that would harden and highlight the design and its complexity. Unfortunately, many pieces that would have once included the white substance are missing it, and this can ruin the effect of the works in contemporary settings since the linear designs are more difficult to identify.

Other than bronze, the Etruscans worked a small amount with silver and gold which were far rarer metals and reserved primarily for jewelry for the wealthy elites. Such jewelry could be rings, necklaces, bracelets, brooches, and breast ornaments such as the one below.

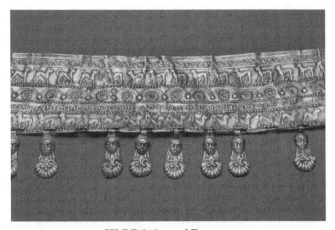

Wall-Painting and Frescoes
https://commons.wikimedia.org/wiki/File:Etruscan_-_Breast_Ornament_(%3F)_-_Walters_57707_-_Detail.jpg

Most surviving Etruscan paintings come from the wall frescoes in tombs. These frescoes, while exposed to the elements like air and dampness, avoided the perils of sunlight, rain, and other harsh environmental factors. The most common source of tomb paintings is Tarquinia which features pieces from 670 BCE to 200 BCE. The majority of the survivors were painted between 520 and 440 BCE. This form of Etruscan artwork possesses a significant importance to scholars of the ancient world. It is known that the Etruscans were heavily influenced by the Greeks at the time in which the paintings were done. Unfortunately, the tradition of Greek wall painting had been almost entirely decimated by time, meaning there are few remnants left. By examining the work of the Etruscans, scholars believe they can learn about the Greek equivalents by identifying elements that seem out of place or inspired by Greek mythology.[155]

Etruscan frescoes were made by plastering a wall and then applying fresh paint on top. The plaster and paint were allowed to

---

[155] Steingräber, Stephan, *Abundance of Life: Etruscan Wall Painting*, 2006, J. Paul Getty Museum, Getty Publications, p. 9.

dry together so the paint became a part of the plaster and was less likely to chip away. Colors could be made by grinding up minerals to create different colors that would then be added to a basic liquid paint mixture. Brushes were made out of wood and animal hair and sometimes stone. Animal hair would always be used as the bristles since it was the most abundant soft material available. Around the mid-4th century BCE, the Etruscans learned the practice of chiaroscuro modeling, which is the use of strong contrasts between light and dark to give better definition to figures. They were able to portray depth and volume better, adding much-needed definition to their pieces. Mythological scenes were depicted more than instances of everyday life, and proportion tended to be absent in artwork. This means that the mythological scenes often possessed figures of irregular sizes that were too big for their surrounding environments.

Some of the best examples of Etruscan frescoes are the Tomb of the Leopards and the Tomb of the Dancers, also called the Tomb of the Dancing Women. Both are from burial chambers and seem to date from the 5th century BCE, although the dating is difficult for the Tomb of the Dancing Women. In these same tombs, archaeologists found beautiful examples of ceramic pottery which was a common funerary good.

A Ceramic Boar Vessel, c. 600-500 BCE
Daderot, CC0, via Wikimedia Commons
https://commons.wikimedia.org/wiki/File:Boar_Vessel,_600-500_BC,_Etruscan,_ceramic_-_Cleveland_Museum_of_Art_-_DSC08263.JPG

Music

Historians, archaeologists, and other scholars cannot reconstruct the lyrical strains of Etruscan music from artifacts, tomb illustrations, or inscriptions, but they can interpret lines left in Roman sources, decipher sounds based on the shapes of instruments, and reconstruct a close imitation of Etruscan music. Unfortunately, the information posited by scholars is highly theoretical and must be taken with a grain of salt. This issue is not unique to the Etruscans as scholars possess similar problems when trying to reconstruct the music of other ancient civilizations such as the Greeks and Egyptians.

In general, the Etruscans possessed an oral musical tradition which meant musical education and songs were most likely passed down between individuals by demonstration and audible teaching rather than through written notes. This is the most likely scenario but also one based on circumstantial evidence since there are few surviving musical pieces or records. Those that do exist tend to be carved into funerary art or steles.

Music would accompany work, leisure, and even warfare. Professional musicians and dancers were not accorded much respect but were seen as significant and important parts of Etruscan culture. Solemn and ceremonial events such as games, festivals, funerals, and celebrations like the *Fanum Voltumnae* were often accompanied by music and dancers. Military drills possessed musical cues and pieces, as did sporting competitions, hunts, and—of course—banquets, parties, and other festivities. While there were professional dancers, the common Etruscan populace was additionally fond of dancing, and it might have featured in some rituals. The Etruscans played music not only during the meal portion of a banquet but also while the food was being prepared and afterward when individuals would gather during convivial drinking sessions after consuming the meal.

Historians believe the Etruscans assigned religious and spiritual significance to music as the Etruscans appear to have believed that certain songs, lyrics, and notes possessed magical powers. Some sacred books feature repetitive rhythmic phrases that might have been crucial during the funerary process. Elaborate events such as funerals might have had written scores to ensure everyone remained in time and tune, but none survived, making this theory another instance of educated speculation.

Etruscan Musician with Barbiton, Tomb of the Triclinium
https://commons.wikimedia.org/wiki/File:Etruskischer_Meister_001.jpg

During the funeral ceremony, the sweet, inviting sound of the auleta (flute) and lyre would lighten the atmosphere of the banquet, persuading participants to dance. There is little known of the original Etruscan names of their musical instruments, and therefore, historians and scholars use the Latin or Greek names instead. We can classify them into three categories: percussion, string, and wind instruments.

Percussion instruments such as bells, campanella (tintinnabulum) and crotalus (castanets) have been found. These instruments could have been easily carried by young dancers.

From Pliny the Elder's description of the tomb of Lars Porsena, we can draw some interesting conclusions. As with many other objects with Apotropaic function, bells were mounted on the tomb with the objective of producing sounds when they were moved by the wind, thus repelling evil presences. Apotropaic function means the instrument was thought to ward off evil spirits through its sounds. A modern example of something having an apotropaic function would be wind chimes, which some spiritual individuals think can protect homes from evil thoughts and spirits.

String and Wind Instruments

The most common Etruscan string instruments were the lyre and barbitone, also called a kithara. A lyre consisted of seven strings strung along a sound box. This sound box would be made from the shell of a turtle or wood depending on where it was crafted and the materials available. The barbitone was similar but larger.

The Etruscans possessed numerous wind instruments to create their music. The primary five were the Aulos, the Cornu, the tuba, the Lituus, and the Tibia. The Aulos was a form of double flute with a double mouthpiece. Musicians used a Capistrum to keep it in place, which was a strap that wrapped around the head. This double flute is considered the mascot of Etruscan instruments because of its popularity in the culture. Apparently, Etruscan flutists were legendary throughout the Mediterranean with the Greeks and Romans both writing of and praising the musicians' skill. Some legends state that the flutists were capable of luring wild boar out of the forests with their pleasing melodies during hunts.

The Cornu was a coiled brass instrument with a massive diameter for loudness. It was most likely worn coiled around the shoulders and probably possessed practical benefits for hunting and even warfare. Over time, its versatility made it popular for ceremonial events. The Lituus, meanwhile, was an L-shaped wind instrument made of bronze. Excavated pieces measure up to 160 centimeters (roughly 63 inches) long. The exact purpose and sound of the Lituus are ambiguous, but it did not appear to be as popular as other instruments, especially the tuba.

The Etruscan tuba was different from the modern brass instrument. It resembled a straight trumpet and would be made of copper or iron. The long tube ended on one side in a bell shape while the other held the mouthpiece. This tuba was not designed to create a pleasing sound but rather to be as loud as possible because the tuba was used during battles and athletic games. Intimidation through sound was a popular tactic, and the tuba would continue to be used by the Romans later on to signal for movements during battles as well as at funerals and during sacrifices. The Tibia was different as it was a type of flute played during religious ceremonies as well as sad events. The notes were much more nuanced and pleasing, and sources mention that the Tibia was played to chase out a plague in Rome during the 4th century BCE.

Chapter 8 – The Etruscan Language and Writing

The Etruscan possessed their own written and spoken language that existed throughout Etruria and its colonies. Linguists believe the Etruscan language influenced the development of Latin and was based in the Indo-European language group alongside other important languages such as Spanish, Romanian, and French. It's difficult to determine what Etruscan might have sounded like when spoken since it is essentially a dead language. This problem is compounded by the fact that scholars struggle to decipher what little remaining text exists. There are roughly 13,000 surviving inscriptions written in Etruscan. Most are short but are written in bilingual and sometimes trilingual texts with the sentence written first in Etruscan and then again in Latin, Greek, or Phoenician.

Bilingual texts allow scholars to decipher some difficult words since they can pair the Etruscan word with its equivalent in a more well-known language. There are several dozen loanwords from other languages, but Etruscan still remains unique and distinct. The study of Etruscan as a language is a source of numerous conundrums. Some scholars believe Etruscan was an isolate, or a language that developed on its own and was not related to others. Others think it was one of the Tyrsenian languages, a hypothetical extinct language that developed independently of other Mediterranean languages. Without more information, the Etruscan language might remain a mystery for many years to come.

There are some known traits. The Etruscan language is agglutinating which means the nouns and verbs have inflectional endings that affect how they are spoken. Nouns also have separate masculine and feminine forms based on who they are related to, and there are singular and plural numbers or forms for nouns and verbs. This means there are separate nouns for a single man, a single woman, multiple men, and multiple women. Linguists have been able to identify changes in the language over time, especially when it comes to the alphabet.

The Etruscan language possessed its own alphabet that was derived from the Greek alphabet, and Etruscan would go on to be the source of the Latin alphabet in later centuries. Historians even think that the Etruscan language traveled north and became the Elder Futhark alphabet which consists of the oldest runes in the Germanic region. Some further think that Etruscan influenced significant words in western European culture, including "person" and "military." These words possess no Indo-European roots, which is where scholars infer the connection. The Etruscan system of writing is divided into two historical phases: the Archaic from the 7th to 5th centuries BCE and the Later from the 4th to 1st centuries BCE. The first phase used the early Greek alphabet while the second phase started to ignore or modify the letters to create a more distinct writing system.

Literacy

When discussing literacy in ancient civilizations, it's important to remember that the majority of the population would have been illiterate. The average individual had no reason to know how to read or write and would have lacked educational opportunities. Instead, literacy was reserved for aristocrats and merchants who needed to keep track of records and could enjoy the history and stories developed by the elite. Religious officials such as priests were also literate since they needed to read the books on divination and rituals for different festivals and celebrations. Later on, the only literate people in the Etruscan language were some wealthy Romans who taught themselves the language because of an interest in history or other antiquarian subjects.

Historians can tell that fundamental literacy was common throughout the Mediterranean, especially in port cities. This fundamental literacy means that people could usually identify words based on their spellings but not actually read. Some individuals would also be able to recognize their names but not actually write. This phenomenon is like a modern person knowing that the letters "cow" refers to a cow but not actually being able to read the letters. The word is known on sight without further knowledge and becomes more of a symbol than a legitimate written word.

The Etruscans left numerous inscriptions on monuments and in tombs, and the differences between the writing styles indicate multiple scribes. Most inscriptions are from 700 BCE, so even the first Etruscans possessed some form of more advanced literacy, although it was not common. At the same time, there is evidence that the Etruscans possessed a rich literary culture in which many could not participate. Romans like Livy and Cicero often referred to several codified books about Etruscan religious rites, including the aforementioned *Etrusca Disciplina*, the *Libri Haruspicini*, the *Libri Rituales*, and the *Libri Fulgurales*. At the same time, there was an unidentified fourth set of Etruscan books that discussed animal gods. The only fully surviving book is the *Liber Linteus Zagrabiensis* which survived thanks to somebody using its linen as mummy wrappings in Ptolemaic Egypt.

The Romans appeared to be able to read Etruscan for a few centuries after the Etruscan culture started to be assimilated into Rome. Over time, only a few dedicated scholars with an interest in history could read Etruscan. The last known individual who possessed a knowledge of the written language was Emperor Claudius, who lived from 10 BCE to 54 CE. He wrote a twenty-volume treatise on the Etruscans as well as a dictionary, both of which have been lost to time. This is a shame since he compiled the dictionary by interviewing the last few surviving elders who spoke Etruscan natively.

Besides the few fluent Romans, there were also many regular individuals who unwittingly spoke Etruscan terms that had been absorbed into the standard Roman vocabulary. These were such words as *columna* (column), *populus* (people), and *tuba* (trumpet). Perhaps the most unusual one is one that is used in modern English and possesses a far different context—*vagina*, which originally meant sheath and now refers to female genitalia.

Outside of Italy, Etruscan literacy died out fast following 300 BCE. Because the Etruscans lost their colonies and Mediterranean settlements rapidly during their decline in the 5th and 4th centuries BCE, it is no surprise that Etruscan was replaced by other languages such as Greek and Latin. So, while inscriptions have been found in regions such as the Black Sea, the Balkans, Corsica, Elba, and Greece, the language itself would not have been spoken much past 300 BCE.

Writing

Scholars of ancient languages believe that the Latin written script is derived from the Etruscan alphabet. This alphabet uses an Euboean variant of the Greek alphabet that uses the letter digamma, which is absent from some other versions of Greek. The Greek written script most likely arrived in Etruria through Cumae and Pithecusae. These two cities were Greek colonies on the Italian Peninsula near Etruria and disputed territory that the Etruscans and Greeks would battle over. These settlements were Euboean Greek, meaning they were the most likely point of transfer for the Greek alphabet to the Etruscans.

The Etruscan alphabet possessed twenty-six letters and would be adapted into Latin later on. The entire alphabet is present on a bucchero terracotta vase currently held by the Metropolitan Museum of Art in New York City. It was constructed between 650 and 600 BCE, meaning the alphabet developed early in the history of Etruria. Some examples are also on the Liver of Piacenza seen below. Despite the alphabet having twenty-six letters, the Etruscans actually did not use four of them since they had no syllabic sound for *b, d, g,* or *o.* Writing was done from right to left, which is backward for most people literate in European languages. Some regions of Etruria, though, appeared to write from left to right. Early writing did not space words but did put a dot or a colon between individual nouns and verbs. This means that *sentences.would.look.like.this.* All writing was done phonetically, and there was no standardized spelling, which means city-states most likely had different pronunciations for the same words. This is understandable since it is known there are regional dialects.

The Text on the Liver of Piacenza
https://commons.wikimedia.org/wiki/File:Haruspex.png

The written Etruscan speech gives further hints about how the language sounded when spoken. Written speech placed heavy emphasis on the first syllable but then ignored many of the remaining consonants and vowels, which would have made the words sound like they trailed off. Examples can be seen in writing that show this practice, one such example being the writing of the name Herakles, the Greek mythological hero. Most people might recognize his name as the Roman Hercules. In Etruscan, Herakles is written as *Hercle*, which ignores the syllables after the first one and erases most of the spoken vowels. In other cases, writers would double up on vowels and add the first vowel at the end of the other syllables. So, instead of *Hercle*, a scribe might write *Herecele*. They are recycling the "e" to create a phenomenon called "vowel harmony" but historians still struggle to interpret Etruscan texts because of a lack of knowledge of word spellings and meanings.[156]

[156] Pallottino, Massimo (1955). The Etruscans. Penguin Books. Translated from the Italian by J. Cremona, p. 261.

Chapter 9 – Architecture

Archaeologists discovered numerous examples of Etruscan architecture built between 700 BCE and 200 BCE. These ruins record the history of the Etruscan culture as it slowly separated from the Villanovans, rose to its golden age, and then declined before being assimilated by the power of Rome. Based on the evidence available, scholars can infer that the Etruscans preferred to build important buildings from hewn stone and wood while more temporary structures were constructed from mudbrick and other easier to make materials. Terracotta tiles were staples for temples, palaces, and aristocratic homes, and as technology progressed, they could even be found on regular houses.

Archaeologists who specialize in buildings have been able to determine that there were several periods of significant artistic influence over the centuries. For example, the Etruscans adored Greek architecture beginning in the late 7th century BCE and began to incorporate elements such as columns in their buildings. As mentioned previously, the Greeks were one of the Etruscans' greatest trading partners, so it was only natural that such cultural and artistic elements would be shared. Etruscan architecture would then go on to influence the Romans which could be considered a copy of the Etruscans for centuries until the Romans managed to develop their own design.

The greatest source of information about Etruscan architecture comes from tombs, which have been discussed already in some detail. These tombs existed in massive necropoli outside of the Etruscan cities. Necropoli were gargantuan graveyards in which the Etruscans buried their loved ones to preserve their bodies and souls but also prevent the rot of decomposing corpses from affecting the cities. Some other surviving sources of architecture are temples, houses, city walls, and even roads carved in stone. Not everything was preserved in good condition, but careful, educated guesses can fill in many of the gaps.

Temples

Temples, as modern audiences understand them, did not exist for the first few centuries of the Etruscan civilization. Instead, the Etruscans worshiped in open-air enclosures until roughly 600 BCE. At that point, the Etruscans started to mimic the Greeks and built impressive edifices and monuments. Archaeologists debate whether the temples were essentially glorified houses built along the same designs as the standard noble abode or if they were actually unique in their own right.[157]

In these temples, the base platform or the podium where the priest stood would be made of stone. The rest of the temple could be made of mudbrick, wood, and other more perishable materials. These materials could not stand the test of time and reduced what archaeologists could discover. It is possible that there were Greek-inspired portico columns made of stone in some of the larger structures, but these disappeared. However, evidence remains at Veii of Greek-inspired architecture, and Roman writers such as Vitruvius often mention Greek elements in Etruscan temples that no longer survive.

---

[157] Vedia, Izzet, *The Archaeology of Etruscan Society*, 2007, Cambridge University Press, 19-21.

Vitruvius, a Roman author who died in 15 BCE, wrote about how the Roman temples were sometimes built in the Etruscan style, but it's unclear when Vitruvius would have actually seen an Etruscan temple or if he was trying to make educated guesses. On the one hand, the descriptions offered by Vitruvius match the sketches developed by archaeologists in some respects. On the other hand, there are also numerous differences. At the end of the day, archaeologists content themselves by rationalizing that the temples no doubt possessed numerous forms since there was a 400-year period in which they were built. Attempting to fit them into one mold would be like trying to make all French Catholic churches built between 1400 CE and 1800 CE look the same.

Based on ruins and Vitruvius' descriptions, Etruscan temples featured three doors and three cellae for each of the main deities. Cellae is the plural of cella, which is a hidden area inside Greek and Roman temples where the cult image of a deity was kept. A cult image is a human-made object often worshiped in homage to the deity it represents, similar to an idol. Temple orientations might have been decided by the movement of birds, which were believed to be an omen from the gods, and terracotta decorations were common. Temples were even more colorful among the Etruscans than among the Greeks and Romans, who were pretty flamboyant in their work. Painted terracotta was popular for roof tiles and the base of columns, while even more painted pieces would be used to form statues of gods and mythological heroes.

The Etruscans influenced the Romans in the general structure of temples. Archaeologists know both cultures focused on the front of the edifice while neglecting the sides and the back. So, the front was typically raised, the temple could only be entered from the front, and there were often columns supporting the roof along the portico, which is the small section of the roof supported by columns and open on three sides. In Etruscan temples, the portico was far deeper than in the Roman equivalents. In later years, the Etruscans started to model their structures on the Greek Aeolic,

Ionic, and Corinthian styles. Doric was also sometimes used, and fluted columns became popular around the 5th century BCE. Later on, the Etruscans would also mimic the Egyptians by incorporating cavetto moldings and palmettes. It is possible that traders might have brought these styles back with them after having stopped in Egyptian ports.

A Palmette
https://commons.wikimedia.org/wiki/File:Palmette.jpg

Temple of Jupiter Optimus Maximus

Some individuals reading this volume might have heard of the Temple of Jupiter Optimus Maximus, which was the oldest temple in Rome of its prodigious size. The temple was dedicated to Jupiter, Juno, and Minerva, and historians and archaeologists believe it was dedicated around 509 BCE. However, a fire destroyed the structure in 83 BCE, resulting in it being rebuilt in the Greek tradition in 69 BCE. It would go on to be ruined and rebuilt two more times before its modern form appeared. When the Temple of Jupiter Optimus Maximus was originally built, Etruscan specialists were brought to Rome to provide information about the techniques required to build such a large temple. They left their fingerprints upon the original design, which included developing and painting unique terracotta features such as antefixes.

In the story of the Temple of Jupiter Optimus Maximus can be seen the significance of the Etruscans upon the Romans. Their designs and skills were so great that they were called to Rome to assist the builders there. Descriptions of the original temple are also important for helping contemporary specialists figure out some of the intricacies of Etruscan temple designs. They know that the original temple had an area of 200 feet by 200 feet and that the edifice was so well-constructed that it survived 400 years of daily use by the population of Rome. The presence of the painted terracotta is ubiquitous as well, a favorite choice for art and architecture alike. Some other features were wide eaves, broad colonnades, and a highly decorated roofline that would have drawn the attention of passersby.[158]

Roads and Transportation Networks

Etruscan roads are difficult to study. Several significant Roman roads, including the Via Cassia, were built over Etruscan predecessors, resulting in the loss of valuable information about Etruscan road technology. Other sites were neglected enough to provide a rudimentary image of what roads might have looked like. The majority were packed earth, but some also had gravel and tufo (tuff) edging blocks. The tufo blocks are intriguing because they were constructed of solidified volcanic ash and appear to have been transported over long distances to construct the roads. Larger, more often traveled upon roads also had central drainage channels to prevent flooding. While Etruscan roads did run between major settlements, they were also built into the countryside where fields and orchards might have been so produce could be brought to the cities easier. Some of the largest roads were 34 feet wide and 7.4 miles long.

Archaeologists discovered another form of road in the Vie Cave. Here can be seen narrow passageways cut into the sides of hills that have changed little over thousands of years. Historians

---

[158] Denarius of 78 BC.

believe the iron-rimmed wheels of the Etruscans cut into the soft bedrock of the hills, leaving ruts that needed to be smoothed over. This process eventually created the roads. Like other forms of architecture and urban planning, Etruscan road building evolved over time. During the 7th and 6th centuries, most roads were basic affairs designed for pedestrians and some animals like mules. As time passed, the city-states made a concerted effort to develop engineered roads that could handle the wheels of carts laden with people, crops, and goods for trade. Most bridges were made of long wooden beams of timber, although there is evidence stone was used underneath the wood for extra support.

Walls and Fortifications

The Etruscans tended to develop their cities in locations that required few walls and fortifications, so many early settlements lacked such accoutrements until the 8th century BCE. Around this time, mudbrick walls started to appear. They would soon be replaced with rough stones. The Italian Peninsula was the frequent subject of wars and external attacks so it was only natural that the Etruscans would start to protect their territory. Most walls possessed a rampart for easy access as well as a ditch dug in front of them. Gates were built into the wall so travelers and farmers could enter the town. Wealthier settlements designed the gates with arches while poorer areas made do with rough squares. The best surviving Etruscan wall is the Porta Marzia at Perugia which was built shortly before Rome took the territory. Most settlements only had one surviving wall, but Volterra proved to be different. Volterra is unique among archaeological finds because the settlement has two surviving walls instead of one.[159] Over time, walls and fortifications advanced in design. While the first walls were rough and haphazard, following models exhibited stonework of fine quality. Many were made using rectangles of ashlar while

---

[159] Axel Boëthius, Roger Ling, Tom Rasmussen, *Etruscan and Early Roman Architecture*, Yale University Press Pelican history of art, 1978, Yale University Press, p. 66-68.

others were distinctly cyclopean.

The Porta Marzia

Physical Tombs

Many of the characteristics of tomb architecture have already been covered, but those of the wealthy possessed some distinct differences in their location and types of grave goods. Wealthy Etruscans built their tombs far from the cities, usually in the heart of large necropoli. Ceramics were the most popular grave good as were luxury items that the rest of the population could not afford, such as jewelry and items made from precious metals and studded with colorful stones and gems. Multiple generations of the same family were buried in these tombs, which were often cut into large rock faces. Others were built of cut, shaped stone.

Above-ground tombs were constructed in rows that resembled modern tenement houses. Others were tumuli (the plural of tumulus, which is an ancient burial mound typically made of packed earth) with entrances leading to chambers below. Almost all tombs resembled houses inside with numerous hallways, bedrooms, and large entry chambers filled with burial furniture. Columns were popular for the wealthy, and architects would even design unnecessary stone beams above to mimic multiple floors or a roof. Most tombs possessed fresco paintings as decoration.

Chapter 10 – Surviving Text and Literature

While few and far between, some Etruscan texts survived the ravages of time and reveal information about this culture that spanned seven centuries.[160] These texts use a form of the Greek alphabet because of the close contact between the Greeks and Etruscans over geographical space for colonies as well as through general trade and cultural exchange. Other texts feature the Etruscan alphabet that is more related to the Euboean Greek alphabet and tend to be the tomb inscriptions discovered in the mainland of the Italian Peninsula.[161] Of the texts that remain, many are religious and funerary texts that were inscribed in stone, and most are from roughly the 4th century BCE. Besides legitimate original documents and texts, there are also surviving quotations and allusions written by classical authors from other cultures, including the oft-mentioned Romans.

---

[160] While the Etruscans were around for roughly nine centuries, their culture was only prominent for about seven.

[161] Bonfante, Giuliano and Bonfante Larissa. *The Etruscan Language: An Introduction.* Manchester: Manchester University Press, 2002.

Some of the quotations and references include notes by Diodorus Siculus in the 1ˢᵗ century BCE who described the Etruscans as possessing a truly astounding literary culture that stood out as one of the culture's chief achievements. Despite being a shining accomplishment, historians and scholars know little about the written language because all that is left of funerary texts is the repetition of the same phrases found in inscriptions on sarcophagi. Even these were understood only because some enterprising soul decided to repeat the same phrases in Punic and Latin as well, creating a trilingual epitaph. Others can be found from famous individuals like Livy, who wrote extensively during the 1ˢᵗ century BCE about the early relationship between the Etruscans and Romans.

When not looking at funerary texts, scholars can study inscriptions left on monuments. The Italian government has strict laws about the preservation of such monuments and artifacts and ensures they are not tampered with by vandals and environmental hazards. However, the government stepped in too late as many monuments and walls were taken down, destroyed, or repurposed for building materials over the last two millennia. What remains is in the process of being cataloged but reveals essential insight into what the Etruscans deemed important and noteworthy.

Funerary texts and monuments are important, but another source of information is inscriptions made upon portable objects that were often left in tombs. These can be coins, cistae, rings and their gemstones, and artifacts called specula. Coins are a personal favorite of historians because of their abundance and ability to survive the elements. After all, almost all ancient peoples protected coins and other forms of currency. All of the Etruscan-minted coins discovered come from between the 5ᵗʰ and 3ʳᵈ centuries, which can indicate that the use of metal coinage that was unique to the Etruscan civilization developed around the midpoint of their civilization. These coins were made of gold, silver, and bronze and typically featured a denomination, whoever the minting authority was, and a cameo. Scholars can learn about Etruscan writing by seeing the full and abbreviated city names visible upon the coinage, which is useful for figuring out the alphabet. Naturally, there is significant cultural information embedded in the coins as well since mythological images and beasts often appear. These could be the hippocamp, the sphinx, Apollo, Zeus, and gorgons.

Cistae, meanwhile, were bronze containers in which women would store sundries, makeup, perfumes, and other small possessions. Some historians compare them to modern makeup or jewelry boxes. These tended to be in a variety of geometric shapes, particularly circles and rectangles. They had feet and lids, attached figurines, carvings, and often painted scenes from Greek and Etruscan mythology. They are important for the comprehension of language and written text because many bear inscriptions about the manufacturer, the owner, and some descriptions about the images and figurines. Imagine possessing a jewelry or toiletry box with a scene from a favorite movie or play—the writing would be explaining that scene. Over 118 cistae were discovered in a single location, providing a wealth of information.

An Etruscan Cista, c. 600-500 BCE

Rings and their gemstones are an unusual source of Etruscan texts. These were some of the most plunderable goods uncovered in tombs throughout Etruria. Many were patterned gold and had materials like agate, carnelian, and even sard embedded in the rings. However, some were plain with hollow and engraved settings depicting scarabs and scenes from Greek mythology. Occasionally, such pieces of jewelry would have writing, which sometimes included the names of mythical heroes.

Finally, there were the specula. The singular of specula is speculum and referred to a circular or oval hand mirror. They were manufactured between 530 and 100 BCE, and they were used almost exclusively by women and were called the *malena* or *malstria* in Etruscan. There are a known 2,300 of these mirrors around the world, and many more are suspected of having been looted and kept in private collections. These mirrors tended to have handles of bone, ivory, and wood as well as a brass back for the mirror. Many have intricate carvings and cameo scenes from mythology that once again have inscriptions explaining what is happening in the images. A committee created by historian Massimo Pallottino resolved to publish the inscriptions and pictures of every known *malstria* in 1979. However, the endeavor did not reach fruition, and no official document was created.

The Liber Linteus Zagrabiensis

When not looking at snippets of writing, historians of the Etruscans possess only two longer, defined sources: The *Liber Linteus Zagrabiensis* and the *Corpus Inscriptionum Etruscarum*. The *Liber Linteus Zagrabiensis*, which is Latin for the "Linen Book of Zagreb," is the only existing linen book of Etruscan writing and can be dated to around 300 BCE. It remains almost entirely untranslated because of the lack of knowledge about the written and spoken Etruscan language. That which is known has pointed toward the Linen Book of Zagreb as being some sort of ritual calendar to be used for religious purposes. In a strange turn of events, the linen from the book was preserved in Ptolemaic Egypt when someone decided to use the fabric as mummy wrappings. The linens and text are now kept in Zagreb, Croatia, hence the name.

The *Liber Linteus Zagrabiensis* was written around 250 BCE. The mention of local gods leads paleographic specialists to think the text was produced somewhere in southeast Tuscany near four major Etruscan cities called Arezzo, Chiusi, Cortona, and Perugia. When opened, the text is arranged in twelve columns that need to be read from right to left, and each of these columns represents a page. The first three are in ruins, and no one has yet been able to determine how the text might have once begun. The Etruscans wrote the book using black ink for the text and red ink for lines and diacritics. The text would have been folded similar to an accordion so that the pages sat atop one another like a codex. In total, there are roughly 230 lines and 1,200 legible words.

After careful study, scholars believe this text is a religious document or calendar because it mentions dates alongside the names of influential deities. There are also dates for processions and ceremonies as well as crucial repeated phrases that sound like liturgies. The word for "priesthood" and those for "sacred fraternity" also appear.

The Corpus Inscriptionum Etruscarum

The other existing text for the Etruscans is not, in fact, something compiled by the Etruscans by themselves. The *Corpus Inscriptionum Etruscarum* (Body of Etruscan inscriptions) is a corpus created by Karl Pauli and his followers and eventually donated to the Uppsala University Library in 1933. This text can be used as a reference index because of its organization through a simple number system, and it contains numerous texts obtained from tablets and other relevant sources. The *Liber Linteus Zagrabiensis* is one such document considered part of this collection. Other important texts are:

The *Tabula Capuana* (The Inscribed Tile from Capua) from the 5th century BCE

The lead foils of Punta della Vipera from 500 BCE

The Cippus Perusinus, a stone tablet of 46 lines in the Etruscan language

The Piacenza Liver (mentioned earlier)

The Tabula Cortonensis, a bronze tablet from Cortona

A stele, from a Sanctuary at Poggio Colla, potentially about the goddess Uni

This work allows scholars to understand more about the Etruscans than can be gleaned from the available material resources. However, historians need to remember that many citizens of Etruria were illiterate and uneducated, and most would not be able to record their thoughts and ideas. Despite such a setback, and although there are not many sources, text and literature can provide valuable information about what the Etruscans deemed important enough to record. They also ensure that the Etruscans did not die when their civilization was assimilated by the Romans.

Conclusion – The Absorption of Etruria

As always, when discussing an ancient civilization, there arises a question that stabs every historian, archaeologist, anthropologist, and other aficionados of the old in the heart. Why does anybody care, and what is the value in knowing about a culture like the Etruscans and their home of Etruria? To understand the significance of the Etruscans, it's important to think of history not as a line of development but as a series of circles with numerous connections and loops upon itself.

In the grand scheme of the world, the Etruscans form one of these circles. The Greeks form another, and the Romans still another. Together, these three civilizations and numerous others in the Mediterranean overlap to create a thick mesh of history, culture, and language that affected the development of a myriad of civilizations in every continent on the planet—yes, this includes Antarctica. Without one circle, the others do not fit together correctly. Without the Etruscans, Rome wouldn't have been the same, and every culture touched and affected by Rome would have turned out differently. This is the ripple effect. One action has thousands of consequences that spread out around it like a drop hitting the water.

Even if someone doesn't find Rome and the Etruscans significant in contemporary society, it doesn't mean they should be ignored and the civilizations banished to oblivion. Cultures like the Etruscans tell modern individuals how ancient people used to live. What made them tick? What made them happy? Sad? Where did they work? How did their families live? Answering such questions can develop concepts within the individual such as empathy. It allows people to imagine themselves thousands of years ago and understand that humans that walked the earth were just that: human. They possessed every drop of cognizance present in the humans today and had their own hopes and dreams.

Looking back upon the Etruscans, their daily lives, and how their civilization grew and declined, imagine the same happening today.

How does it make you feel?

Here's another book by Captivating History that you might like

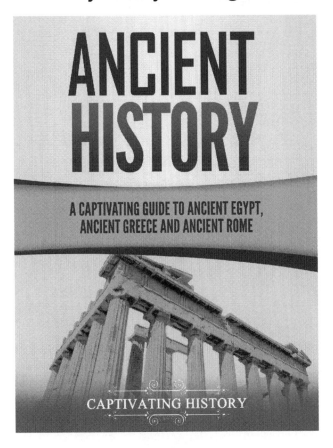

Free Bonus from Captivating History (Available for a Limited time)

Hi History Lovers!

Now you have a chance to join our exclusive history list so you can get your first history ebook for free as well as discounts and a potential to get more history books for free! Simply visit the link below to join.

Captivatinghistory.com/ebook

Also, make sure to follow us on Facebook, Twitter and Youtube by searching for

Bibliography

A. E. Astin, F. W. Walbank, M. W. Frederiksen And R. M. Ogilvie, *The Cambridge Ancient History: Volume VIII - Rome And the Mediterranean to 133 B.C., Cambridge*, Cambridge University Press, 1989.

A. Salimbeti And R. D'amato, *The Carthaginians 6th–2nd Century BC*, New York, Osprey Publishing, 2014.

Alfred J. Church, *Carthage or the Empire of Africa*, London, T. Fisher Unwin, 1889.

Amy McKenna, *The History of Northern Africa*, New York, Britannica Educational Publishing, 2010.

B. H. Warmington, *Carthage*, London, Trinity Press, 1960.

C. Lopez-Ruiz and B. R. Doak, *The Oxford Handbook of the Phoenician and Punic Mediterranean*, Oxford, Oxford University Press, 2019.

Christa Steinby, *Rome versus Carthage: The War at Sea*, Barnsley, Pen and Sword Maritime, 2014.

Cottrell Leonard, *Hannibal: Enemy of Rome. New York,* Da Capo Press, 1992.

Dexter Hoyos, *Hannibal's Dynasty Power and Politics in the Western Mediterranean, 247-183 BC,* London, Routledge, 2003.

Dexter Hoyos, *Mastering the West: Rome and Carthage at War*, Oxford, Oxford University Press, 2015.

Dexter Hoyos, *The Carthaginians*, London, Routledge, 2010.

Fernand Braduel, *Memory and the Mediterranean*, New York, Alfred A. Knopf, 2001.

J. D. Fage, *The Cambridge History of Africa Volume I*, Cambridge, Cambridge University Press, 1978.

J. Desmond Clark, *The Cambridge History of Africa Volume II*, Cambridge, Cambridge University Press, 1982.

Josephine Crawley Quinn, *In Search of The Phoenicians*, Princeton, Princeton University Press, 2018.

Phillip C. Naylor, *North Africa: A History from Antiquity to the Present*, Austin, University of Texas Press, 2009.

R. Bosworth Smith, *Carthage and the Carthaginians*, London, Longmans, Green and Co., 1913.

R. Docter, R. Boussoffara and P. ter Keurs, *Carthage: Fact and Myth*, Leiden, Sidestone Press, 2015.

Richard Miles, *Carthage Must Be Destroyed: Rise and Fall of an Ancient Civilization*, New York, Viking Penguin, 2010.

Serge Lancel, *Carthage: A History*, New Jersey, Wiley-Blackwell, 1995.

Adams, Ellen. *Cultural Identity in Minoan Crete: Social Dynamics in the Neopalatial Period.* New York: Cambridge University Press, 2017.

Betancourt, Philip B. *The History of Minoan Pottery.* Princeton: Princeton University Press, 1985.

Bourbon, F. *Lost Civilizations.* Barnes and Noble, Inc. New York, 1998.

Bouwman A. and Rühli, F. "Archaeogenetics in Evolutionary Medicine." *Journal of Molecular Medicine* 94 (2016): pgs. 971-977. 10.1007/s00109-016-1438-8

Cameron, M.A.S.; Jones R. E. and Philippakis, S.E. "Scientific Analyses of Minoan Fresco Samples from Knossos." *The Annual of the British School at Athens* 72 (1977): pgs. 121-184.

Carr, H. Graham. "Some Dental Characteristics of the Minoans." *Royal Anthropological Institute of Great Britain and Ireland* 60 (August 1960): pg. 119-122. https://www.jstor.org/stable/2797174.

Castleden, Rodney. *Minoans: Life in Bronze Age Crete.* New York: Routledge, 1993.

Cole, Sara. "The Wall Paintings of Tell el-Dab'a: Potential Aegean Connections." Pursuit - *The Journal of Undergraduate Research at the University of Tennessee* 1, no. 1 (2010).

D'Agata, Anna Lucia. "The Many Lives of a Ruin: History and Metahistory of the Palace of Minos at Knossos." *British School at Athens Studies* 18 (2010).

Gillis, Carole and Nosch, Marie-Louise B. *Ancient Textiles: Production, Crafts and Society.* Oxford: Oxbow Books, 2007.

Ghose, Tia. "Mysterious Minoans Were European, DNA Finds." *LiveScience.* 2013.

Higgins, Reynold. *Minoan and Mycenaean Art.* London: Thames and Hudson, 1997.

Higgins, R. *The Aegina Treasure - An Archaeological Mystery.* London: 1979.

Hood, Sinclair. *The Minoans: Crete in the Bronze Age.* London: Thames & Hudson, 1971.

Hughey, Jeffrey. "A European Population in Minoan Bronze Age Crete." *Nature Communications* 4 (2013): pg. 1861. 10.1038/ncomms2871.

J.S. "Saffron and the Minoans." *Pharmacy in History* 47, no. 1 (2005): pg. 28-31. https://www.jstor.org/stable/41112251.

Jones, Bernice R. "Revealing Minoan Fashions." *Archaeology* 53, no. 3 (May/June 2000): pg. 36-41. https://www.jstor.org/stable/41779314.

Katz, Brigit. "DNA Analysis Sheds Light on the Mysterious Origins of the Ancient Greeks." *Smithsonian.*

Lobell, Jarrett A. "The Minoans of Crete." *Archaeology* 68, no. 3 (May/June 2015): pg. 28-35. https://www.jstor.org/stable/24364735.

Manning, Sturt W.; Ramsey, Christopher Bronk; Kutschera, Walter; Higham, Thomas; Kromer, Bernd; Steier, Peter; and Wild, Eva M. "Chronology for the Aegean Late Bronze Age 1700-1400 B.C." *Science* 28, no. 312 (2006): pg. 565-569. 10.1126/science.1125682.

Marinatos, Nanno. "Minoan Religion." Columbia: University of South Carolina.

Marinatos, Spyridon. *Some Words about the Legend at Atlantis* (2nd ed.). Athens: C. Papachrysanthou, 1972.

McCoy, Floyd W. and Heiken, Grant. "Tsunami Generated by the Late Bronze Age Eruption of Thera (Santorini), Greece." *Pure and Applied Geophysics* 157, no 157 (2000).

McEnro, John C. *Architecture of Minoan Crete: Constructing Identity in the Aegean Bronze Age.* University of Texas Press, 2010.

Molloy, Barry P.C. "Martial Minoans? War as Social Process, Practice and Event in Bronze Age Crete." *The Annual of the British School at Athens* 107 (2012): pg. 87-142. https://www.jstor.org/stable/41721880.

Noble, J.V. "The Wax of the Lost Wax Process". *American Journal of Archaeology.* 79, no. 4 (1975).

Pendlebury J.D.S. and Evans, Arthur. *Handbook to the Palace of Minos and Knossos with Its Dependencies.* Kessinger Publishing, 2003.

Phillips, Jacke. "Egyptian Amethyst in the Bronze Age Aegean." *Journal of Ancient Egypt Interconnections* 1, no. 2 (2009). DOI:10.2458/azu_jaei_v01i2_phillips.

Preziosi, Donald & Hitchcock, Louise A. *Aegean Art and Architecture.* Oxford History of Art series, Oxford University Press, 1999.

Pulak, Cemal and Bass, George F. "Bronze Age Shipwreck Excavation at Uluburun." Institute of Nautical Archaeology.

Rose J.B. and Angelakis, A.N. *Evolution of Sanitation and Wastewater Technologies through the Centuries.* London: IWA Publishing, 2014.

Schofield, Louise. *The Mycenaeans.* J. Paul Getty Museum, 2007.

Sigurdsson H, Carey, S, Alexandri M, Vougioukalakis G, Croff K, Roman C, Sakellariou D, Anagnostou C, Rousakis G, Ioakim C, Gogou A, Ballas D, Misaridis T, & Nomikou P. "Marine Investigations of Greece's Santorini Volcanic Field." *Eos* 87, no. 3 (2010).

Thompson, James G. "Clues to the Location of Bull Jumping at Zakros." *Journal of Sport History* 19, no. 2 (1992): pg. 163-168. https://www.jstor.org/stable/43610538.

Tite, M.S.; Y. Maniatis; D. Kavoussanaki; M. Panagiotakic; J. Shortland; S.F. Kirk. "Colour in Minoan faience." *Journal of Archaeological Science* 36, no. 2 (2009): pgs. 370-378.

Warren, Peter. "Knossos: New Excavations and Discoveries." *Archaeology* (July /August 1984): p. 48-55.

Weiner, Malcolm. "Realities of Power: The Minoan Thalassocracy in Historical Perspective." *AMILLA: The Quest for Excellence*, 2013. doi: http://www.academia.edu/30141237/ Realities of Power The Minoan Thalassocracy in Historical Perspective AMILLA The Quest for Ex cellence. Studies Presented to Guenter Kopcke in Celebration of H is 75th Birthday 2013 pp. 149 173

Barnett, Richard D. "Phoenicia and the Ivory Trade." *Archaeology* 9, no. 2 (1956): 87-97.

Bikai, Patricia M. "The Phoenicians: A Bibliography." *Bulletin of the American Schools of Oriental Research*, no. 279 (1990): 65-66.

Chaney, William R. and Basbous, Malek. "The Cedars of Lebanon: Witnesses of History." *Economic Botany* 32, no. 2 (1978): 118-123.

Elayi, Josette. *A monetary and political history of the Phoenician city of Byblos in the fifth and fourth centuries BCE.* Winona Lake: Eisenbrauns, 2014.

Elayi, Josette. *The History of Phoenicia.* Lockwood Press, 2018.

Ercolani, Andrea and Xella, Paolo. *Encyclopedic Dictionary of Phoenician culture.* Peeters Publishing, 2018.

Martin, Rebecca S. *The art of contact: comparative approaches to Greek and Phoenician art.* Philadelphia: University of Pennsylvania Press, 2017.

Moreno Garcia, Juan Carlos. *Dynamics of production in the Ancient Near East: 1300-500 BC.* Philadelphia: Oxbow Books, 2016.

Peckham, J. Brian. *Phoenicia: Episodes and Anecdotes from the Ancient Mediterranean.* Eisenbrauns Publishing, 2014.

Sherratt, Susan. "Greeks and Phoenicians: Perception of Trade and Traders in the Early First Millennium BC." In *Social Archaeologies of Trade and Exchange: Exploring Relationships Among People, Places, and Things* by Alexander A. Bauer, Anna S. Agbe-Davies, and Robert W. Preucel, p. 119-142. Walnut Creek: Left Coast Press, 2010.

Woolmer, Mark. *A Short History of the Phoenicians*. New York: I. B. Tauris, 2017.

Woolmer, Mark. *Ancient Phoenicia: An Introduction*. London: Bristol Classic Press, 2011.

Bryce, Trevor. *The Kingdom of the Hittites*. Oxford: Oxford University Press, 2005.

Budin, Stephanie Lynn. *The Ancient Greeks: An Introduction*. New York: Oxford University Press, 2009.

Castleden, Rodney. *The Mycenaeans*. New York: Routledge, 2005.

Chadwick, John. *The Mycenaean World*. Cambridge: Cambridge University Press, 1976

Cline, Eric H. *1177 B.C. The Year Civilization Collapsed*. Princeton: Princeton University Press, 2014.

Cline, Eric H. "Rethinking Mycenaean International Trade with Egypt and the Near East." In Galaty, M.; Parkinson, W. *Rethinking Mycenaean Palaces II: Revised and Expanded Edition*. Los Angeles: Cotsen Institute of Archaeology, 2007.

Cline, Eric H. *The Oxford Handbook of the Bronze Age Aegean*. Oxford: Oxford University Press, 2012.

Sigrid Deger-Jalkotzy and Irene S. Lemos, eds. *Ancient Greece: From the Mycenaean Palaces to the Age of Homer*. Edinburgh: University of Edinburgh Press, 2006.

Dickinson, Oliver. *The Origins of Mycenaean Civilization*. Götenberg: Paul Aströms Förlag, 1977.

Drews, Robert. *The End of the Bronze Age*. Princeton: Princeton University Press, 1993.

Evans, A.J. "Knossos: I The Palace (Plates XII and XIII)." *The Annual of the British School at Athens*, 1901.

Fields, Nic. *Bronze Age War Chariots*. Oxford: Osprey Publishing Company, 2006.

Fields, Nic. *Mycenaean Citadels c. 1350–1200 BC* 3rd ed. Oxford: Osprey Publishing Company, 2004.

Freeman, Charles. *Egypt, Greece and Rome: Civilizations of the Ancient Mediterranean* 3rd ed. Oxford: Oxford University Press, 2014.

Gilstrap, William; Day, Peter; Kaza, Konstantina; Kardamaki, Elina. "Pottery Production at the Late Mycenaean Site of Alimos, Attica." *Materials and Industries in the Mycenaean World: Current Approaches to the Study of Materials and Industries in Prehistoric Greece.* University of Nottingham, 9–10 May 2013. Nottingham, UK. pp. 13–14.

Horrocks, Geoffrey. *Greek: A History of the Language and Its Speakers* 2nd ed. Oxford: Wiley-Blackwell, 2010.

Immerwahr, Sara A. *Aegean Painting in the Bronze Age.* University Park: Pennsylvania State University Press, 1990.

K.A. and Diana Wardle. "The Child's Cache at Assiros, Macedonia." In Sally Crawford and Gillian Shepherd (eds.): *Children, Childhood and Society: Institute for Archaeology and Antiquity Interdisciplinary Studies (Volume I).* Oxford: Archaeopress, 2007.

Donald Kagan and Gregory F. Viggiano, eds. *Men of Bronze: Hoplite Warfare in Ancient Greece.* Princeton: Princeton University Press, 2013.

Kelder, Jorrit M. *The Kingdom of Mycenae: A Great Kingdom in the Late Bronze Age Aegean.* Bethesda: CDL Press, 2010.

Mylonas, George Emmanuel. *Mycenae and the Mycenaean Age.* Princeton: Princeton University Press, 1966.

Neer, T. Richard. *Greek Art and Archaeology: A New History, c. 2500–c. 150 BCE.* New York: Thames and Hudson, 2012.

Nilsson, Martin Persson. *Geschichte der Griechischen Religion* (3rd ed.). Munich: C.H. Beck Verlag, 1967.

Nilsson, Martin Persson. *Greek Popular Religion.* New York: Columbia University Press, 1940.

Pausanias. *Description of Greece*, VIII–37.6.

Schepartz, Lynne E., Sharon R. Stocker, Jack L. Davis, Anastasia Papathanasiou, Sari Miller-Antonio, Joanne M. A. Murphy, Michael Richards, and Evangelia Malapani. "Mycenaean Hierarchy and Gender Roles: Diet and Health Inequalities in Late Bronze Age Pylos, Greece." In *Bones of Complexity: Bioarchaeological Case Studies of Social Organization and Skeletal Biology.* Edited by Haagen D. Klaus, Amanda R. Harvey, and Mark N. Cohen. Gainesville: University of Florida Press, 2017.

Schofield, Louise. *The Mycenaeans*. Los Angeles: J. Paul Getty Museum, 2006.

Tartaron, Thomas F. *Maritime Networks in the Mycenaean World*. Cambridge: Cambridge University Press, 2013.

Barker, Graeme and Rasmussen, Tom. *The Etruscans*. Oxford: Blackwell Publishers Inc., 1998.

Bell, Sinclair and Carpino, Alexandra A. *A Companion to the Etruscans*. Hoboken: John Wiley & Sons, Incorporated, 2015.

Boëthius, Axel; Roger Ling; Tom Rasmussen. *Etruscan and Early Roman Architecture*. Yale University Press, 1994.

Bonfante, Giuliano and Bonfante Larissa. *The Etruscan Language: An Introduction*. Manchester: Manchester University Press, 2002.

Bonfante, Larissa. *Etruscan Myths*. London: British Museum Press, 2006.

C. Vernesi e Altri. "The Etruscans: A Population-Genetic Study." *American Journal of Human Genetics*, March 2004.

Cunningham, Reich. *Cultures and Values: A Survey of the Humanities*. 2006.

De Grummond, Nancy Thomson and Simon, Erika. *Religion of the Etruscans*. Austin: University of Texas Press, 2014.

De Grummond Nancy Thomson. *Etruscan Mythology, Sacred History and Legend: An Introduction*. University of Pennsylvania Museum of Archaeology, 2006.

Dupuy, Trevor. *The Harper Encyclopedia of Military History*. Rizzoli Harper Collins Publisher, 1992.

Helmut Rix. "Etruscan." In Roger D. Woodard. *The Ancient Languages of Europe*. Cambridge University Press, 2008. p. 141–64.

Hughes, Robert. *Rome: A Cultural, Visual, and Personal History*. 2012.

Izzet, Vedia. *The Archaeology of Etruscan Society*. New York: Cambridge University Press, 2007.

Leland, Charles Godfrey. *Etruscan Magic and Occult Remedies*. New Hyde Park: University Books Inc., 1963.

Macnamara, Ellen. *Everyday Life of the Etruscans*. New York: Dorset Press, 1973.

Marcus Tullius Cicero. "II.50-51." *On Divination.*

Perkins, Phil. "Chapter 8: DNA and Etruscan Identity." In Naso, Alessandro. *Etruscology.* Berlin: De Gruyter, 2017. p. 109–18.

Perkins, Phil. "DNA and Etruscan Identity." In Perkins, Phil; Swaddling, Judith. *Etruscan by Definition: Papers in Honour of Sybille Haynes.* London: The British Museum Research Publications, 2009. p. 95–111.

Smith, Christopher. *The Etruscans: A Very Short Introduction.* Oxford: Oxford University Press, 2014.

Spivey, Nigel. *Etruscan Art.* New York: Thames and Hudson, 1997.

Tacitus, Cornelius. *The Annals & The Histories.* Trans. Alfred Church and William Brodribb. New York, 2003.